Fratelli Tutti

†

STUDIES IN WORLD CATHOLICISM

Michael L. Budde and William T. Cavanaugh, Series Editors
Karen M. Kraft, Managing Editor

Studies in World Catholicism offers scholarly, pastoral, and general readers alike the best of interdisciplinary research about and from the multifaceted worlds of Catholicism, which has seen its center of gravity shift from the so-called global North to Africa, Asia, and Latin America. In this series, authors from around the globe engage with both large-gauge theoretical questions and the particularities of specific communities and contexts, crossing disciplinary boundaries between theology, social ethics, history, cultural studies, political science and more.

This series is a project of the Center for World Catholicism and Intercultural Theology (CWCIT) at DePaul University in Chicago, one of the leading scholarly institutes focusing on Christianity as a transnational reality. More information on the Center and its work is available at http://cwcit.depaul.edu. Proposals for the series may be sent to series editors William T. Cavanaugh at wcavana1@depaul.edu or Michael L. Budde at mbudde@depaul.edu.

Recent Titles in This Series

Daughters of Wisdom: Women and Leadership in the Global Church. Vol. 12, 2023.

African Ecological Ethics and Spirituality for Cosmic Flourishing: An African Commentary on Laudato Sí. Vol. 11, 2022.

For God and My Country: Catholic Leadership in Modern Uganda. Vol. 10, 2020.

Gathered in My Name: Ecumenism in the World Church. Vol. 9, 2020.

Pentecostalism, Catholicism, and the Spirit in the World. Vol. 8, 2019.

The Church and Indigenous Peoples in the Americas: In Between Reconciliation and Decolonization. Vol. 7, 2019.

For the complete list and ordering information, please visit www.wipfandstock.com/series and click on "Studies in World Catholicism."

Fratelli Tutti

A Global Commentary

EDITED BY
William T. Cavanaugh, Carlos Mendoza-Álvarez, OP, Ikenna Ugochukwu Okafor, and Daniel Franklin E. Pilario, CM

FOREWORD BY
Cardinal Michael Czerny, SJ

CONTRIBUTORS

Kochurani Abraham
Albert E. Alejo, SJ
Kurt Appel
Francisco de Aquino-Júnior
Frederick Christian Bauerschmidt
Sharon A. Bong
Cleusa Caldeira
Charles B. Chilufya, SJ
Neomi De Anda
Ma. Marilou S. Ibita
Stan Chu Ilo
Daniel Izuzquiza, SJ
Kelly S. Johnson
John Bosco Kamoga, CSSp
Mumbi Kigutha, CPPS
Cesar Kuzma
Albertus Bagus Laksana, SJ

Ernestina López-Bac
Toussaint Kafarhire Murhula, SJ
Norah K. Nonterah
Ikenna Ugochukwu Okafor
Idara Otu, MSP
Daniel Franklin E. Pilario, CM
Carolina Robledo Silvestre
Anna Rowlands
Carmenmargarita Sánchez de León
Manuel Victor J. Sapitula, CM
Roberto Tomichá-Charupá, OFMConv
Stephan van Erp
Soledad del Villar Tagle
Jamie L. Waters
Felix Wilfred
Raúl Zibechi

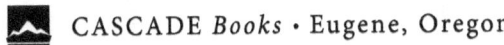
CASCADE Books · Eugene, Oregon

FRATELLI TUTTI
A Global Commentary

Studies in World Catholicism 13

Copyright © 2024 Wipf and Stock Publishers. All rights reserved. Except for brief quotations in critical publications or reviews, no part of this book may be reproduced in any manner without prior written permission from the publisher. Write: Permissions, Wipf and Stock Publishers, 199 W. 8th Ave., Suite 3, Eugene, OR 97401.

Cascade Books
An Imprint of Wipf and Stock Publishers
199 W. 8th Ave., Suite 3
Eugene, OR 97401

www.wipfandstock.com

PAPERBACK ISBN: 978-1-6667-1997-0
HARDCOVER ISBN: 978-1-6667-1998-7
EBOOK ISBN: 978-1-6667-1999-4

Cataloguing-in-Publication data:

Names: Cavanaugh, William T., editor. | Mendoza-Álvarez, Carlos, editor. | Okafor, Ikenna Ugochukwu, editor. | Pilario, Daniel Franklin E., editor. | Czerny, Cardinal Michael, foreword.

Title: Fratelli tutti : a global commentary / edited by William T. Cavanaugh, Carlos Mendoza-Álvarez, OP, Ikenna Ugochukwu Okafor, and Daniel Franklin E. Pilario, CM; with a foreword by Cardinal Michael Czerny.

Description: Eugene, OR : Cascade Books, 2024 | Series: Studies in World Catholicism 13 | Includes bibliographical references and index.

Identifiers: ISBN 978-1-6667-1997-0 (paperback) | ISBN 978-1-6667-1998-7 (hardcover) | ISBN 978-1-6667-1999-4 (ebook)

Subjects: LCSH: Catholic Church. Pope (2013- : Francis). Fratelli tutti. | Social justice. | Reconciliation. | Globalization. | Church and the world. | Christian life.

Classification: BV4647.B7 F7195 2024 (print) | BV4647.B7 F7195 (ebook)

01/11/24

Cardinal Michael Czerny's "A Seamless Ethic for Siblings All: The Hope of *Fratelli Tutti*" © 2022 by *Thinking Faith*. Used with permission.

English translation of Carmenmargarita Sánchez de León's "To the Whole Inhabited Earth" © 2022 by Karen M. Kraft. Used with permission.

English translation of Carolina Robledo Silvestre's "'Searching, We Find Ourselves': Indignation and Radical Empathy in a Suffering Mexico" © 2022 by Karen M. Kraft. Used with permission.

English translation of Cesar Kuzma's "Building Hope from a Fallen Humanity: A Latin American Theological Perspective" © 2021 by Cristina Silva. Used with permission.

English translation of Cleusa Caldeira's "On the Way to Pluriversal" © 2021 by Cristina Silva. Used with permission.

English translation of Francisco de Aquino-Júnior's "An Unhealthy Society" © 2021 by Cristina Silva. Used with permission.

English translation of Raúl Zibechi's "Peoples on the Move: Francis's Political Utopia" © 2022 by Karen M. Kraft. Used with permission.

English translation of Roberto Tomichá-Charupá, OFMConv, and Ernestina López-Bac's "Dreaming a New Humanity: Human-Cosmic Synodality from the Perspective of the Foreigner and the Hidden Exile" © 2022 by Karen M. Kraft. Used with permission.

English translation of Soledad del Villar Tagle's "Paths of Re-Encounter: Forgiveness, Liberation, and Nonviolence in Times of Transitional Justice" © 2022 by Karen M. Kraft. Used with permission.

Scripture texts marked (NAB) are taken from the New American Bible, revised edition © 2010, 1991, 1986, 1970 Confraternity of Christian Doctrine, Washington, DC, and are used by permission of the copyright owner. All Rights Reserved. No part of the New American Bible may be reproduced in any form without permission in writing from the copyright owner.

Scripture texts, prefaces, introductions, footnotes, and cross references marked (NABRE) are taken from the New American Bible, revised edition © 2010, 1991, 1986, 1970 Confraternity of Christian Doctrine, Inc., Washington, DC. All Rights Reserved. No part of this work may be reproduced or transmitted in any form or by any means, electronic or mechanical, including photocopying, recording, or by any information storage and retrieval system, without permission in writing from the copyright owner.

Scripture quotations marked (NIV) are from the Holy Bible, New International Version®, NIV®. Copyright © 1973, 1978, 1984, 2011 by Biblica, Inc.™ Used by permission of Zondervan. All rights reserved worldwide. www.zondervan.com The "NIV" and "New International Version" are trademarks registered in the United States Patent and Trademark Office by Biblica, Inc.™

Scripture quotations marked (NRSV) are from the New Revised Standard Version Bible, copyright ©1989 the Division of Christian Education of the National Council of the Churches of Christ in the United States of America. Used by permission. All rights reserved.

Scripture passages marked (PDT) are taken from the Holy Bible Easy to Read Version (ERV). Used by permission of Bible League International © 2014.

Contents

Contributors | xi

Foreword by Cardinal Michael Czerny, SJ | xv

Introduction by William T. Cavanaugh, Carlos Mendoza-Álvarez, OP, Ikenna Ugochukwu Okafor, and Daniel Franklin E. Pilario, CM | 1

Part One: Dark Clouds Over a Closed World

1: The Real Divides in Africa | 9
NORA K. NONTERAH

2: Where Are We Going? A Reality Check | 17
MANUEL VICTOR J. SAPITULA, CM

3: An Unhealthy Society | 27
FRANCISCO DE AQUINO-JÚNIOR

4: In Praise of Complaint | 36
FREDERICK CHRISTIAN BAUERSCHMIDT

Part Two: A Stranger on the Road

5: The Good Samaritan as a Model of Fraternal Solidarity | 47
STAN CHU ILO

6: The Use of Luke 10:25–37 in *Fratelli Tutti* | 56
MA. MARILOU S. IBITA

7: Building Hope from a Fallen Humanity: A Latin American Theological Perspective | 65
CESAR KUZMA

8: A Biblical Model of Love | 73
JAIME L. WATERS

Part Three: Envisaging and Engendering an Open World

9: The Existential Imperative of Openness to the Other in Africa | 83
JOHN BOSCO KAMOGA, CSSP

10: Radicalizing Love: A Gendered Critique of Malaysia's Management of Migrants and Refugees in the Time of COVID-19 | 92
SHARON A. BONG

11: Dreaming a New Humanity: Human-Cosmic Synodality from the Perspective of the Foreigner and the Hidden Exile | 101
ROBERTO TOMICHÁ-CHARUPÁ, OFMCONV, AND ERNESTINA LÓPEZ-BAC

12: A Call for Openness | 111
KURT APPEL

Part Four: A Heart Open to the Whole World

13: Four Marks of an Ecclesiology of Migration | 121
IDARA OTU, MSP

14: The Challenges of Migration in Asia | 131
KOCHURANI ABRAHAM

15: On the Way to Pluriversal | 140
CLEUSA CALDEIRA

16: Living with the Grace of Neighbors: The Promise of Universal Fraternity for Europe | 149
STEPHAN VAN ERP

Part Five: A Better Kind of Politics

17: Reinventing Political Arrangements: A New Starting Point | 161
TOUSSAINT KAFARHIRE MURHULA, SJ

18: Political Love: Beyond the Good Samaritan Charity | 170
ALBERT E. ALEJO, SJ

19: Peoples on the Move: Francis's Political Utopia | 180
RAÚL ZIBECHI

20: *Fratelli Tutti*: A New Political Imagination? | 189
ANNA ROWLANDS

Part Six: Dialogue and Friendship in Society

21: Dialogue and Encounter for Global Poverty
Eradication: Global Justice Perspectives | 199
CHARLES B. CHILUFYA, SJ

22: The Path of Dialogue, Solitude, and Hope: Voices from Asia | 208
ALBERTUS BAGUS LAKSANA, SJ

23: "Searching, We Find Ourselves": Indignation and
Radical Empathy in a Suffering Mexico | 217
CAROLINA ROBLEDO SILVESTRE

24: Why Not "Amiability and a Culture of Encounter"
as the Title of Chapter 6? | 226
NEOMI DE ANDA

Part Seven: Paths of Renewed Encounter

25: Truth, Mercy, Justice, and Peace Meet | 237
MUMBI KIGUTHA, CPPS

26: Conflict, Violence, and Reconciliation | 245
DANIEL FRANKLIN E. PILARIO, CM

27: Paths of Re-Encounter: Forgiveness, Liberation, and
Nonviolence in Times of Transitional Justice | 257
SOLEDAD DEL VILLAR TAGLE

28: "There Is No Life on This Side of the Fire": Conflict and
Penitential Memory on the Path of Encounter | 264
KELLY S. JOHNSON

Part Eight: Religions at the Service of Fraternity in Our World

29: An Affirmation of God's Universal Paternity and a
Repudiation of Religious Persecutions | 275
IKENNA UGOCHUKWU OKAFOR

30: Pope Francis and Interreligious Dialogue:
Reading Chapter 8 of *Fratelli Tutti* | 284
FELIX WILFRED

31: To the Whole Inhabited Earth | 294
CARMENMARGARITA SÁNCHEZ DE LEÓN

32: Religions Serving Fraternity: Roots, Trunk, Fruits | 303
DANIEL IZUZQUIZA, SJ

Index | 311

Contributors

From Africa

Charles B. Chilufya, SJ, Director of the Jesuit Justice and Ecology Network Africa (JENA)—Nairobi

Stan Chu Ilo, Professor of Catholic Studies and Research Professor at the Center for World Catholicism and Intercultural Theology (CWCIT), DePaul University—Chicago, IL, USA

John Bosco Kamoga, CSSp, Superior of the Ugandan Spiritans Group—Kampala

Mumbi Kigutha, CPPS, Organizing Secretary of the Pan-African Catholic Theology and Pastoral Network—Chicago, Illinois, USA

Toussaint Kafarhire Murhula, SJ, Professor of Political Science at Université Loyola du Congo—Kinshasa

Norah K. Nonterah, Professor of Religious Studies at Kwame Nkrumah University of Science and Technology—Kumasi, Ghana

Ikenna Ugochukwu Okafor, Adjunct Professor of Intercultural Theology at the University of Vienna—Vienna

Idara Otu, MSP, Lecturer in Dogmatic Theology at the National Missionary Seminary of St. Paul—Abuja, Nigeria

From Asia

Kochurani Abraham, Vice President of the Indian Theological Association—Kottayam, Kerala, India

Albert E. Alejo, SJ, Lecturer in Sociology and Anthropology at Ateneo de Manila University—Quezon City, Philippines

Sharon A. Bong, Professor of Gender and Religious Studies at Monash University Malaysia—Selangor, Malaysia

Ma. Marilou S. Ibita, Associate Professor of Theology and Religious Education at De La Salle University—Manila

Albertus Bagus Laksana, SJ, Faculty in the Department of Theology at Sanata Dharma University—Yogyakarta, Indonesia

Daniel Franklin E. Pilario, CM, Dean and Professor at the St. Vincent School of Theology, Adamson University—Quezon City, Philippines

Manuel Victor J. Sapitula, CM, Faculty at the St. Vincent School of Theology, Adamson University—Quezon City, Philippines

Felix Wilfred, Emeritus Professor at the State University of Madras—Chennai, India

From Latin America

Francisco de Aquino-Júnior, Professor of Theology at the Catholic University of Forteleza (Fortaleza, Brazil) and the Catholic University of Pernambuco—Recife, Brazil

Cleusa Caldeira, Postdoctoral Researcher at the Jesuit Faculty of Philosophy and Theology (FAJE)—Belo Horizonte, Brazil

Cesar Kuzma, Professor of Systematic Theology at the Pontifical Catholic University of Rio de Janeiro—Rio de Janeiro

Ernestina López-Bac, Member of the Latin American Ecumenical Network for Indigenous Pastoral Ministry—Guatemala

Carlos Mendoza-Álvarez, OP, Tenured Professor in the Department of Theology at Boston College—Boston, Massachusetts, USA

Carolina Robledo Silvestre, CONACYT Chair at the Center for Research and Advanced Studies in Social Anthropology (CIESAS)—Mexico City

Carmenmargarita Sánchez de León, Faculty at the Theological Community of Mexico (CTM)—Mexico City

Roberto Tomichá-Charupá, OFMConv, Director of the Latin American Institute of Missiology at the Catholic University of Bolivia—Cochabamba, Bolivia

Soledad del Villar Tagle, Doctoral Candidate in Systematic Theology at Boston College—Boston, Massachusetts, USA

Raúl Zibechi, Columnist/Analyst for *La Jornada* (Mexico) and *Brecha* (Uruguay)—Montevideo

From North America and Europe

Kurt Appel, Professor and Director of the Research Center on Religion and Transformation at the University of Vienna—Vienna

Frederick Christian Bauerschmidt, Professor of Theology at Loyola University Maryland—Baltimore, Maryland, USA

William T. Cavanaugh, Director of the Center for World Catholicism and Intercultural Theology and Professor of Catholic Studies at DePaul University—Chicago, Illinois, USA

Cardinal Michael Czerny, SJ, Prefect of the Vatican Dicastery for Promoting Integral Human Development—Rome

Neomi De Anda, Associate Professor of Religious Studies at the University of Dayton—Dayton, Ohio, USA

Daniel Izuzquiza, SJ, Coordinator with the Jesuit Migrant Service—Almería, Spain

Kelly S. Johnson, Associate Professor and Fr. Ferree Chair of Social Justice at the University of Dayton—Dayton, Ohio, USA

Anna Rowlands, St. Hilda Associate Professor of Catholic Social Thought and Practice at Durham University—Durham, England

Stephan van Erp, Associate Professor and Coordinator of the Research Unit on Systematic Theology and the Study of Religions at KU Leuven—Leuven, Belgium

Jamie L. Waters, Associate Professor of Old Testament at Boston College School of Theology and Ministry—Boston, Massachusetts, USA

Foreword

A Seamless Ethic for Siblings All: The Hope of *Fratelli Tutti*

CARDINAL MICHAEL CZERNY, SJ
*Prefect of the Vatican Dicastery for
Promoting Integral Human Development*

I AM DELIGHTED TO contribute to this first global commentary on a papal encyclical. *Fratelli Tutti* has put forth a powerful vision of worldwide sisterhood and brotherhood, and I am so glad to see the truly global discussion taking place in these pages, provoked by the vision of Pope Francis.

Catholic social doctrine, Cardinal Joseph Bernardin wrote, is based on two inseparable truths about the human person:

> Human life is both sacred and social. Because we esteem human life as sacred, we have a duty to protect and foster it at all stages of development, from conception to death, and in all circumstances. Because we acknowledge that human life is also social, we must develop the kind of societal environment that protects and fosters its development.[1]

Appreciating the wisdom and relevance of this teaching, we continue his legacy. His second successor as archbishop of Chicago, Cardinal Blase Cupich, has enriched Bernardin's ethical teaching with this explicit emphasis:

> The Church is calling for a consistent ethic of solidarity that aims at making sure no one, from the first moment of life to

---

1. Bernardin, "Address for the National Consultation," 29.

natural death, from the wealthiest community to our poorest neighbourhoods, is excluded from the table of life.[2]

"I came so that they might have life," declared Jesus, "and have it more abundantly" (John 10:10, NABRE). Pope St. Paul VI used the expression "integral human development" to convey the idea of life in abundance, life to the full, the flourishing of human life in salvation history.[3] "Integral" because the sacred and the social imply each other, and because the human and creation are completely interconnected (as *Laudato Si'* spelled out). So, ours is a multifaceted mission on earth: to care for one another, for we are all sibling offspring of God, and to care for our common home. "Integral Human Development" is the name of the Vatican's dicastery where I serve.

Please note: there are several related and even synonymous terms at work here—sacred, seamless, social, solidarity, consistent, inclusive, integral. Let them help us to pay closer attention, open our minds and hearts, broaden our horizons, and move us toward various relevant frontiers. In the background, I make use of the "see-judge-act" methodology that has become widespread in Catholic social analysis. First, understand the issues in their multifaceted complexity; next, affirm a resolution consistent with one's values and principles; and then identify concrete paths forward to commit to.

Fratelli Tutti is our primary text of reference,[4] seeking to render our church's pastoral mission, solidarity, and ethics as inclusive as creation and redemption.

Common Origin / Common Dignity / Siblings All

"The Book of Job sees our origin in the one Creator as the basis of certain common rights: 'Did not He who made me in the womb also make him [the slave]? And did not the same One fashion us [both] in the womb?'"[5]

St. John reflected: "See what love the Father has bestowed on us that we may be called the children of God. Yet so we are" (1 John 3:1, NABRE).

From the Gospels, from the apostles, from the early writings of the church fathers to today's encyclicals and exhortations, the church's moral and social doctrine develops to protect human dignity and promote a more adequate understanding of the human person. It begins with fully

---

2. Winters, "Cupich." Cf. Winters, "Cardinal Cupich Points."
3. Paul VI, *Populorum Progressio*, 14–17.
4. Cf. Czerny and Barone, *Siblings All*.
5. Francis, *Fratelli Tutti*, 58 (hereafter cited in text as *FT*), quoting Job 31:15; Job bases a slave's claim to justice on creation common to both freeman and slave.

acknowledging that we are created by God, are children of God, and are made in the image and likeness of God.

In the Gospels, when he gives us the Lord's Prayer, Christ instructs us to address God with the familial word *abba*—a name even more intimate and informal than our word "father." The Sermon on the Mount encourages us to regard each other as "children of God." The Acts of the Apostles depicts the community of first Christians as sibling believers in a family wherein all was shared according to need. St. Paul's Epistle to the Ephesians continues in this vein, describing us as siblings in the family of God, united as a mystical body.

The recent *Document on Human Fraternity* opens with: "In the name of God, who has created all human beings equal in rights, duties and dignity, and who has called them to live together as brothers and sisters, to fill the earth and make known the values of goodness, love and peace . . . ."[6] So we are born not in isolation but as siblings in God's family, not self-sufficient but with gifts and obligations, called to care and share but free to sin, members of one human family and indeed one mystical body.

A Flawed and Deteriorating Anthropology

But over and over humans have acted as if to deny our common origin, dignity, and siblinghood, and continue to do so. Tragically, unjustly, and acting contrary to life, the momentum of our age frustrates integral human development and neglects the divinely appointed role to care for our common home. We act against the sacredness of human life, and against solidarity with one another and with creation.

At its core, many of the contradictions that our present age poses for integral human development turn on erroneous understandings of the human person: flawed anthropology. For one hundred and thirty years, Catholic social teaching has been trying to correct this flawed and corrupted anthropology.

Let's go back to the first social encyclical. In *Rerum Novarum*, written in 1891, Pope Leo XIII referred to the various classes of society, foreseeing their being "united in the bonds of friendship, but also in those of sibling love" in an anticipation of *Fratelli Tutti*:

> They will understand and feel that all men are children of the same common Father, who is God; that all have alike the same last end, which is God Himself, who alone can make either men or angels absolutely and perfectly happy; that each and all are

---

6. Francis and Al-Tayyeb, "Document on Human Fraternity." Cf. Francis, *Fratelli Tutti*, 285.

redeemed and made sons of God, by Jesus Christ, "the first-born among many brethren" (Rom 8:17); that the blessings of nature and the gifts of grace belong to the whole human race in common, and that from none except the unworthy is withheld the inheritance of the kingdom of Heaven.[7]

In 1931, in his encyclical *Quadragesimo Anno*, Pope Pius XI called this corrupted understanding of the human person a "poisoned spring."[8] He meant the idea—associated with libertarians at that time and with today's neoliberals—that the right ordering of economic life should be left to free market competition. For Pius, this represented an "evil individualistic spirit."

In 1967, Pope St. Paul VI similarly addressed the problem in his encyclical, *Populorum Progressio*, and even more directly in his 1971 apostolic letter, *Octogesima Adveniens* in which he recalled that "at the very root of philosophical liberalism is an erroneous affirmation of the autonomy of the individual in his activity, his motivation and the exercise of his liberty."[9] While exalting economic efficiency to the point of dominating all other values, individual autonomy was attractive as a defense against totalitarian tendencies.

Pope St. John Paul II made the crucial point that, while private property is legitimate and valid, the right to it must always be subordinated to the universal destination of goods, the notion that the goods of the earth are given by God to all persons. Pope St. John Paul refers to this as a "social mortgage":

> It is necessary to state once more the characteristic principle of Christian social doctrine: the goods of this world are originally meant for all. The right to private property is valid and necessary, but it does not nullify the value of this principle. Private property, in fact, is under a "social mortgage," which means that it has an intrinsically social function, based upon and justified precisely by the principle of the universal destination of goods.[10]

And indeed, in *Fratelli Tutti*, Pope Francis returns to this theme, arguing that the right to private property should be considered a secondary natural right, subordinated to the universal destination of goods.

Pope Emeritus Benedict XVI also contributed to our understanding of Catholic social doctrine. He worried about the effects of globalization

---

7. Leo XIII, *Rerum Novarum*, 25.
8. Piux XI, *Quadragesimo Anno*, 88.
9. Paul VI, *Octogesima Adveniens*, 35.
10. John Paul II, *Sollicitudo Rei Socialis*, 42.

on human bonds: "As society becomes ever more globalised, it makes us neighbours but does not make us siblings,"[11] he noted. He goes on to list some of the concrete problems of globalization:

> The global market has stimulated first and foremost, on the part of rich countries, a search for areas in which to outsource production at low cost with a view to reducing the prices of many goods, increasing purchasing power and thus accelerating the rate of development in terms of greater availability of consumer goods for the domestic market. Consequently, the market has prompted new forms of competition between States as they seek to attract foreign businesses to set up production centres, by means of a variety of instruments, including favourable fiscal regimes and deregulation of the labour market. These processes have led to a downsizing of social security systems as the price to be paid for seeking greater competitive advantage in the global market, with consequent grave danger for the rights of workers, for fundamental human rights and for the solidarity associated with the traditional forms of the social State.[12]

Over time, as church, we grow into understanding human nature, leaving behind flawed anthropologies that were used to justify slavery, the oppression of women, etc. Catholic social teaching at its best is an honest effort to keep on improving our appreciation of our nature, setting misrecognitions aside. We seek to accompany society and its evolving political cultures in the same task: holding up a mirror, examining in the light of scriptures, calling to repentance, and trying again. It is therefore with considerable humility that we claim the church as an expert in humanity.[13]

Good Anthropology Comes First

This same concern with addressing flawed anthropology infuses *Fratelli Tutti*. The title of chapter 3, "Envisaging and Engendering an Open World," expresses the goal of the encyclical's thinking. The starting point is this anthropological affirmation that quotes *Gaudium et Spes*: "Human beings are so made that they cannot live, develop and find fulfilment except 'in the sincere gift of self to others'" (FT 87).[14]

---

11. Benedict XVI, *Caritas in Veritate*, 19.
12. Benedict XVI, *Caritas in Veritate*, 25.
13. Paul VI, *Populorum Progressio*, 13—"esperta in umanità," but the official English translation says, "The Church, which has long experience in human affairs...."
14. See also *FT* 111: "The human person, with his or her inalienable rights, is by

These words from *Gaudium et Spes*, comments John Paul II,

> can be said to sum up the whole of Christian anthropology: that theory and practice, based on the Gospel, in which man discovers himself as belonging to Christ and discovers that in Christ he is raised to the status of a child of God, and so understands better his own dignity as man, precisely because he is the subject of God's approach and presence, the subject of the divine condescension, which contains the prospect and the very root of definitive glorification.[15]

Fratelli Tutti goes on to explicate how the "gift of self" is the path to fullness:

> Nor can they fully know themselves apart from an encounter with other persons: "I communicate effectively with myself only insofar as I communicate with others." No one can experience the true beauty of life without relating to others, without having real faces to love. This is part of the mystery of authentic human existence. "Life exists where there is bonding, communion, fraternity; and life is stronger than death when it is built on true relationships and bonds of fidelity. On the contrary, there is no life when we claim to be self-sufficient and live as islands: in these attitudes, death prevails." (*FT* 87)[16]

"Authentic human development concerns the whole of the person in every single dimension," including the transcendent dimension, and the person cannot be sacrificed for the sake of attaining a particular good, whether this be economic or social, individual or collective.[17]

For Francis, self-giving, the continuous giving of self, is what grounds and orients integral human development. When does a person fully experience his or her dignity as a creature loved by God and acknowledged by humankind? This happens when a person reaches the existential point of freely and consciously opting for the gift of self to others and for others.[18] This depends not only upon "external" conditions (the right to food, housing,

---

nature open to relationship. Implanted deep within us is the call to transcend ourselves through an encounter with others."

15. John Paul II, *Dominum et Vivificantem*, 59.

16. In *FT* 87, Francis is quoting Gabriel Marcel, *Du refus à l'invocation*; see also Francis, "Angelus."

17. Benedict XVI, "Educating Young People," 3.

18. Similar points are emerging in Black theologies of struggle: dignity is not found in a static sense as apprehension but rather experienced and understood in the act of struggling against indignities others suffer and in the gift of self in solidarity. Cf. Lloyd, *Black Dignity*.

work, healthcare, education, social services, etc.) but also inner ones (personal maturity always seeking to get beyond narcissistic self-centeredness).

Because our present age militates against this Christian understanding of the human person, it therefore fails to promote authentic integral human development and instead pushes so many fake models, so many deformations, so much pessimism and "why bother?" Pope Francis takes sharp aim at the ideology in which self-interest and indifference are not only tolerated but justified and indeed imposed, solidarity is sidelined as optional, the common good reduced to an abstraction, and people deprived of their proper hope. To counter these tendencies, it is urgent for the church to proclaim to each one of us, that it is in making a gift of myself to others that the meaning of all that I am is at stake and becomes real.

"It Is Irksome When the Question of Ethics Is Raised" (*Evangelii Gaudium*, 203)

In 2009, in his encyclical *Caritas in Veritate*, Pope Benedict correctly interpreted the global financial crisis (we're still living with the fallout) as a crisis of ethics. Four years later, a few months after becoming pope, in *Evangelii Gaudium*, Francis robustly rejected the neoliberal claim that the free market alone can foster human flourishing:

> In this context, some people continue to defend trickle-down theories which assume that economic growth, encouraged by a free market, will inevitably succeed in bringing about greater justice and inclusiveness in the world. This opinion, which has never been confirmed by the facts, expresses a crude and naïve trust in the goodness of those wielding economic power and in the sacralized workings of the prevailing economic system. Meanwhile, the excluded are still waiting. To sustain a lifestyle which excludes others, or to sustain enthusiasm for that selfish ideal, a globalization of indifference has developed. Almost without being aware of it, we end up being incapable of feeling compassion at the outcry of the poor, weeping for other people's pain, and feeling a need to help them, as though all this were someone else's responsibility and not our own. The culture of prosperity deadens us; we are thrilled if the market offers us something new to purchase. In the meantime, all those lives stunted for lack of opportunity seem a mere spectacle; they fail to move us.[19]

19. Francis, *Evangelii Gaudium*, 54.

In *Laudato Si'*, Pope Francis condemns a culture of relativism, which "drives one person to take advantage of another, to treat others as mere objects."[20] He is deeply concerned with what he calls integral ecology, the idea that how we treat nature and our fellow human beings are interconnected.

Soon after, in possibly some of his strongest remarks delivered on the global economy, in a speech to popular movements in Bolivia in 2015, Pope Francis denounced the current economic system: "The first task is to put the economy at the service of peoples," he says. "Human beings and nature must not be at the service of money. Let us say NO to an economy of exclusion and inequality, where money rules, rather than service. That economy kills. That economy excludes. That economy destroys Mother Earth."[21]

This is a strong indictment. And once again, this exclusionary stance comes from a flawed anthropology. In *Fratelli Tutti*, Pope Francis criticizes this disordered anthropology of individualism, which leads to a distortion of the idea of liberty. To quote the Holy Father: "Liberty becomes nothing more than a condition for living as we will, completely free to choose to whom or what we will belong, or simply to possess or exploit. This shallow understanding has little to do with the richness of a liberty directed above all to love" (*FT* 103). Moreover, "individualism does not make us more free, more equal, more fraternal. The mere sum of individual interests is not capable of generating a better world for the whole human family" (*FT* 105).

Taking direct aim at the neoliberal ideology, Francis declares:

> The marketplace, by itself, cannot resolve every problem, however much we are asked to believe this dogma of neoliberal faith. Whatever the challenge, this impoverished and repetitive school of thought always offers the same recipes. Neoliberalism simply reproduces itself by resorting to the magic theories of "spillover" or "trickle"—without using the name—as the only solution to societal problems. There is little appreciation of the fact that the alleged "spillover" does not resolve the inequality that gives rise to new forms of violence threatening the fabric of society. (*FT* 168)

Succinctly bringing together all the dimensions:

> The right of some to free enterprise or market freedom cannot supersede the rights of peoples and the dignity of the poor, or, for that matter, respect for the natural environment, for "if we

---

20. Francis, *Laudato Si'*, 123.
21. Francis, "Address to Second World Meeting."

make something our own, it is only to administer it for the good of all." (*FT* 122)[22]

Illustrating a Consistent Ethic for Tomorrow

The tunic or undergarment that Jesus wore on his way to Calvary was woven in one piece from top to bottom (John 19:23). This image was first used as a moral ideal by the Catholic pacifist Eileen Egan in 1971, and nearly forty years ago,[23] Cardinal Bernardin began making the expression and related idea of a consistent life ethic more widely known and accepted. I would like to draw out this theme to elaborate further the church's teaching on economics. In so doing, I hope to give support to Bernardin's profound insight that the church's teachings on human life and social life find their coherent expression in the Christian mission of promoting integral human development.

Since *Rerum Novarum* of 1891, for over one hundred and thirty years, the church has expressed support for the market economy on two conditions: that it be properly regulated and that its protagonists be guided by appropriate virtues. The church teaches that a market economy requires participants who have been formed in virtue. In addition, the church teaches that markets need to be directed by legitimate authority toward universal public goods and toward the common good of all. As noted earlier, it cannot be left to the free competition of forces. It cannot be dominated by the flawed anthropology of libertarianism and neoliberalism.

Especially in response to the 2008 financial crisis, the church has observed that markets lack intrinsic means to modulate their operation for public goods such as care for the environment, public health, or preferencing distributive justice for those in poverty. Nor are economic markets able in themselves to respect principles of morality. If suppliers are willing to sell and consumers are willing to buy, then anything can be traded—human trafficking is a horrible example. So, the church consistently and repeatedly denounces market economies when their excesses result in neglecting the needs and diminishing the lives of significant majorities, leaving them vulnerable, marginalized, and impoverished.

As Pope Benedict XVI explained in *Caritas in Veritate*:

> Economic activity cannot solve all social problems through the simple application of commercial logic. This needs to be

22. Here, Francis is quoting *Laudato Si'*, 95.
23. At a lecture at Fordham University on December 6, 1983.

directed towards the pursuit of the common good, for which the political community in particular must also take responsibility. Therefore, it must be borne in mind that grave imbalances are produced when economic action, conceived merely as an engine for wealth creation, is detached from political action, conceived as a means for pursuing justice through redistribution.[24]

Theoretically, the global market economy should be a coming together of sellers and buyers in which production provides goods and services to be purchased by individualized consumers for their needs and wants. Free market advocates insist that if the market is truly free, then by the logic of competition, it yields the most efficient outcome, the highest quality, and the greatest satisfaction of consumer demand.

Of course, no perfectly free market has ever existed. Producers and sellers organize in monopolies or international conglomerates to manipulate supply and prices. The state and other outside powers intervene for reasons both noble and self-interested. Indeed, the market is always subject to the rules laid down by society and politics—whether we are talking about libertarianism, with its emphasis on property rights, or social democracy, which elevates economic rights. There is always a directing principle.

Regardless of their degree of freedom, however, economic markets powerfully shape the choices and the character of those who participate in their operation. In fact, market operations can create conditions of moral relativism. As I already noted, Pope Francis raises the specter of the "culture of relativism" when, in *Laudato Si'*, he sees it as "the same disorder which drives one person to take advantage of another, to treat others as mere objects, imposing forced labour on them or enslaving them to pay their debts." It is furthermore,

> the mindset of those who say: "Let us allow the invisible forces of the market to regulate the economy and consider their impact on society and nature as collateral damage." In the absence of objective truths or sound principles other than the satisfaction of our own desires and immediate needs, what limits can be placed on human trafficking, organized crime, the drug trade, commerce in blood diamonds and the fur of endangered species?[25]

The market mindset shapes how human beings understand themselves, their perception of values, their worldview. And it does so facelessly and automatically.

---

24. Benedict XVI, *Caritas in Veritate*, 36.
25. Francis, *Laudato Si'*, 123.

A favorite example of mine is bottled water. Years ago, an expert in this field showed me how problematic bottled water is. Bottled water puts a price on what should be readily available. In many parts of the world, beer is cheaper and cleaner than water; this can have a social cost because of domestic violence and other complications. Discarded plastic bottles are a significant source of environmental degradation. Bottled water also de-incentivizes governments from providing clean drinking water, for municipally provided water from a tap, defined as a public service, needs to meet higher standards of purity than water sold as a food item. How can the majority of us be manipulated into spending money on an item sold in an environmentally damaging container, when what's delivered to our homes is purer and much cheaper? It's nothing short of astonishing.

Challenges on a Global Scale

Let us now briefly examine how our global economy promotes the viruses of materialism and consumerism on the world stage. Because its invisible hands inexorably promote what sells over anything that does not sell, the global economy often makes it difficult even for well-meaning participants to choose what might be better for the common good, better for the impoverished among us, better to care for the environment—in other words, morally better.

The anthropology promoted in the economic sphere is that of *homo economicus*. It conceives of the human person as individualized and competitively driven to maximize material self-interest and to look at the world simply as a mere collection of objects to be bought and sold. Even other human beings can be objectified for self-interest or else viewed merely as competitors to be overcome. Seen in this guise, the human being becomes not a beloved creation of God, but simply another tool or resource in the market economy.

The false anthropology of *homo economicus* can be opposed and overcome by an economics infused by the principles of Catholic social teaching.[26] And let's be clear that Catholic social teaching is primarily concerned, not with dos and don'ts, but with bringing the good news into the public sphere and directing practical responses to real problems posed by current events, including economic injustices, in the light of the Gospel and Catholic tradition.[27]

---

26. Annett, *Cathonomics*.
27. Rowlands, *Towards a Politics of Communion*.

Fratelli Tutti warns that the enormous power of our global economy works to separate us from solidarity with others. Pope Francis writes that the economy "unifies the world, but divides persons and nations . . . . We are more alone than ever in an increasingly massified world that promotes individual interests and weakens the communitarian dimension of life. Indeed, there are markets where individuals become mere consumers or bystanders" (*FT* 12).

In light of the enormities of the global economy and driven by that economy to focus on material self-interest and to see others as competitors, the human person feels isolated and vulnerable. Alone against the vast forces of the global economy, we feel weak and at risk. Indeed, we can experience this as a profound alienation and fear for ourselves. And of course, the poor, those whom the economy fails, are seen as "lazy" and "losers," further adding to their isolation and sense of defeat.

Alienation and fear unleash a downward spiral that some might seek to resolve by seeing the world as a confrontation of us-versus-them. In the words of Pope Francis:

> Ancient conflicts thought long buried are breaking out anew, while instances of a myopic, extremist, resentful, and aggressive nationalism are on the rise. In some countries, a concept of popular and national unity influenced by various ideologies is creating new forms of selfishness and a loss of the social sense under the guise of defending national interests. (*FT* 11)

As we know from past centuries and the current one, many can be led to resolve their alienation and fear via submission to leaders who feed on resentment or promise retribution.

Why does it seem more and more difficult for our church to teach effectively about the human person? Why does a flawed conception seem to entrench itself deeper and deeper in the structures of modern life? And where else do we see it manifest besides flawed economics? A longer discussion could certainly examine the technocratic paradigm, which Francis castigates in *Laudato Si'* for its distortion of the essential human character and perhaps also the perverse dynamics of mass society spawned by aberrations of mass social media.

The Consistent Ethics of Life and Solidarity

To sum up so far: the functioning of the global market economy tends more and more to objectify the human person, isolate the human person in fragile and fearful individualism, and prioritize self-interests over the common good. All of this is fundamentally at odds with the sanctity and dignity of human life.

Some seem to connect the idea of a consistent ethic of life and solidarity exclusively with biological life from conception to natural death. But to limit our understanding of the consistent ethic of life to mere bodily human life is a worrisome reduction of the full richness of the church's teaching on the sanctity and dignity of human life. Consider, for example, how the global economy results in sweeping inequalities for life and for opportunities to live with dignity. Do not the shorter life spans and higher infant mortalities of those in poverty cry to heaven for justice and mercy in the same way that deaths of the unborn do? Are not the indignities and mistreatment of the lives of those marginalized and oppressed by the invisible hands of the market also contrary to what we should perceive as the consistent ethic of life?

Fratelli Tutti speaks of the unregulated market's anti-life attitude as "throwing away" or "discarding" others:

> This way of discarding others can take a variety of forms, such as an obsession with reducing labour costs with no concern for its grave consequences, since the unemployment that it directly generates leads to the expansion of poverty. In addition, a readiness to discard others finds expression in vicious attitudes that we thought long past, such as racism, which retreats underground only to keep re-emerging. (*FT* 20)

Nor can mere toleration ever be enough, leading as it inevitably does to a pernicious relativism:

> Under the guise of tolerance, relativism ultimately leaves the interpretation of moral values to those in power, to be defined as they see fit. "In the absence of objective truths or sound principles other than the satisfaction of our own desires and immediate needs . . . we should not think that political efforts or the force of law will be sufficient. . . . When the culture itself is corrupt, and objective truth and universally valid principles are no longer upheld, then laws can only be seen as arbitrary impositions or obstacles to be avoided." (*FT* 206)

A larger picture of what it means to be pro-life, of what we should understand to be the consistent ethic of life, begins to become clearer. It is certainly not enough to simply oppose abortion and euthanasia. Nor is it enough to recognize and tolerate the dignity of all lives, even with special tolerance for those who, unlike us, are marginalized or poor.

No, Christ's garment is truly seamless and whole. To be genuinely pro-life also requires accompanying, welcoming, and joining together with others as sibling children of God—especially those who, because of their difference, are hardest for us to love. A consistent ethic of life is also a consistent ethic of solidarity.

Fratelli Tutti and Conclusion

The contemporary world is at odds with the ethic of solidarity that is so essential in the Christian conception of the human person. In militating against solidarity, moreover, the processes of the contemporary world also militate against the ethic of life. Our age's dynamics seen in the global economy promote a radical but also a fragile and fearful individualism that impels us to look upon others not as our siblings under God but as others whose differences must be spurned, as competitors to be dominated, as objects for our use, and as potential threats to be feared.

> If we accept the great principle that there are rights born of our inalienable human dignity, we can rise to the challenge of envisaging a new humanity. We can aspire to a world that provides land, housing and work [*tierra, techo, trabajo*] for all. This is the true path of peace, not the senseless and myopic strategy of sowing fear and mistrust in the face of outside threats. For a real and lasting peace will only be possible "on the basis of a global ethic of solidarity and cooperation in the service of a future shaped by interdependence and shared responsibility in the whole human family." (*FT* 127)[28]

Pope Francis builds toward this global ethic from the most local level: the Good Samaritan encounter that answers the question, "who is my neighbor?" The Samaritan not only sets aside his personal priorities; he even helps someone whom his community sees as an enemy. This is the summit of solidarity, of treating the other as *thou*. The parable reminds us, says Francis, of "an essential and often forgotten aspect of our common humanity: we were created for a fulfilment that can only be found in love. . . . We . . . cannot allow anyone to go through life as an outcast" (*FT* 68). Recognizing each other as the sibling offspring of God that we are, let us come together in solidarity and social friendship to rebuild this broken world, our only home, this human race, our one and only family under God.

---

28. Here, Francis is quoting his "Address on Nuclear Weapons," given at the Atomic Bomb Hypocenter Park in Nagasaki, Japan, on November 24, 2019.

Bibliography

Annett, Anthony M. *Cathonomics: How Catholic Tradition Can Create a More Just Economy.* Washington, DC: Georgetown University Press, 2022.

Benedict XVI, Pope. *Caritas in Veritate: On Integral Human Development in Charity and Truth.* Vatican City: Libreria Editrice Vaticana, 2009. https://www.vatican.va/content/benedict-xvi/en/encyclicals/documents/hf_ben-xvi_enc_20090629_caritas-in-veritate.html.

———. "Educating Young People in Justice and Peace." Message given from the Vatican in Rome, December 8, 2011. https://www.vatican.va/content/benedict-xvi/en/messages/peace/documents/hf_ben-xvi_mes_20111208_xlv-world-day-peace.html.

Bernardin, Cardinal Joseph. "Address for the National Consultation on Obscenity, Pornography, and Indecency." In *Consistent Ethic of Life: Joseph Cardinal Bernardin*, edited by Thomas G. Feuchtmann, 27–35. Kansas City, MO: Sheed and Ward, 1988.

Czerny, Cardinal Michael, and Christian Barone. *Siblings All, Sign of the Times: The Social Teaching of Pope Francis.* Maryknoll, NY: Orbis, 2022.

Francis, Pope. "Address on Nuclear Weapons." Address given at the Atomic Bomb Hypocenter Park in Nagasaki, Japan, November 24, 2019. https://www.vatican.va/content/francesco/en/speeches/2019/november/documents/papa-francesco_20191124_messaggio-arminucleari-nagasaki.html.

———. "Address to Second World Meeting of Popular Movements." Address given at Expo Feria Exhibition Centre in Santa Cruz de la Sierra, Bolivia, July 9, 2015. https://www.vatican.va/content/francesco/en/speeches/2015/july/documents/papa-francesco_20150709_bolivia-movimenti-popolari.html.

———. "Angelus." Homily given at St. Peter's Square in Vatican City, November 10, 2019. https://www.vatican.va/content/francesco/en/angelus/2019/documents/papa-francesco_angelus_20191110.html.

———. *Evangelii Gaudium: On the Proclamation of the Gospel in Today's World.* Vatican City: Libreria Editrice Vaticana, 2013. https://www.vatican.va/content/francesco/en/apost_exhortations/documents/papa-francesco_esortazione-ap_20131124_evangelii-gaudium.html.

———. *Fratelli Tutti: On Fraternity and Social Friendship.* Vatican City: Libreria Editrice Vaticana, 2020. https://www.vatican.va/content/francesco/en/encyclicals/documents/papa-francesco_20201003_enciclica-fratelli-tutti.html.

———. *Laudato Si': On Care for Our Common Home.* Vatican City: Libreria Editrice Vaticana, 2015. https://www.vatican.va/content/francesco/en/encyclicals/documents/papa-francesco_20150524_enciclica-laudato-si.html.

Francis, Pope, and Grand Imam Ahmad Al-Tayyeb. "A Document on Human Fraternity for World Peace and Living Together." Abu Dhabi, February 4, 2019. https://www.vatican.va/content/francesco/en/travels/2019/outside/documents/papa-francesco_20190204_documento-fratellanza-umana.html.

John Paul II, Pope. *Dominum et Vivificantem: On the Holy Spirit in the Life of the Church and the World.* Vatican City: Libreria Editrice Vaticana, 1986. https://www.vatican.va/content/john-paul-ii/en/encyclicals/documents/hf_jp-ii_enc_18051986_dominum-et-vivificantem.html.

---. *Sollicitudo Rei Socialis: For the Twentieth Anniversary of Populorum Progressio.* Vatican City: Libreria Editrice Vaticana, 1987. https://www.vatican.va/content/john-paul-ii/en/encyclicals/documents/hf_jp-ii_enc_30121987_sollicitudo-rei-socialis.html.

Leo XIII, Pope. *Rerum Novarum: On Capital and Labor.* Vatican City: Libreria Editrice Vaticana, 1891.

Lloyd, Vincent W. *Black Dignity: The Struggle against Domination.* New Haven: Yale University Press, 2022.

Paul VI, Pope. *Octogesima Adveniens: On the Occasion of the Eightieth Anniversary of the Encyclical* Rerum Novarum. Vatican City: Libreria Editrice Vaticana, 1971. https://www.vatican.va/content/paul-vi/en/apost_letters/documents/hf_p-vi_apl_19710514_octogesima-adveniens.html.

---. *Populorum Progressio: On the Development of Peoples.* Vatican City: Libreria Editrice Vaticana, 1967. https://www.vatican.va/content/paul-vi/en/encyclicals/documents/hf_p-vi_enc_26031967_populorum.html.

Pius XI, Pope. *Quadragesimo Anno: On Reconstruction of the Social Order.* Vatican City: Libreria Editrice Vaticana, 1931. https://www.vatican.va/content/pius-xi/en/encyclicals/documents/hf_p-xi_enc_19310515_quadragesimo-anno.html.

Rowlands, Anna. *Towards a Politics of Communion: Catholic Social Teaching in Dark Times.* New York: Bloomsbury, 2021.

Winters, Michael Sean. "Cardinal Cupich Points to a New Consistent Ethic of Solidarity." *National Catholic Reporter*, May 31, 2017. https://www.ncronline.org/blogs/distinctly-catholic/cardinal-cupich-points-new-consistent-ethic-solidarity.

---. "Cupich: 'A Consistent Ethic of Solidarity.'" *National Catholic Reporter*, September 18, 2015. https://www.ncronline.org/blogs/distinctly-catholic/cupich-consistent-ethic-solidarity.

Introduction

William T. Cavanaugh, Carlos Mendoza-Álvarez, OP, Ikenna Ugochukwu Okafor, and Daniel Franklin E. Pilario, CM

THE FIRST SECTION HEADING in Pope Francis's encyclical *Fratelli Tutti* is "Without Borders," and it is in that spirit that we present this volume, which we believe is the first global commentary on a papal encyclical. Pope Francis published *Fratelli Tutti* in October 2020 in the midst of interrelated global crises: climate catastrophe, ongoing racial injustice, a widening gap between the rich and the desperately poor, battles over human migration, the rise of authoritarian politics and the erosion of democracy, all exacerbated by the COVID-19 pandemic. The encyclical provided a sobering assessment of the devastation but also a hopeful vision of solidarity and healing. The responses in this book not only reflect on *Fratelli Tutti* from a great diversity of locations and perspectives but also attempt to model Francis's call to fraternity and sorority within this volume. In these pages, scholars from around the world create a conversation meant to embody one of the virtues that Francis elicits in the encyclical: creative openness to the reciprocal gifts of others.

As editors who come from different parts of the world—one each from Africa, Asia, Latin America, and North America—we share some of the same concerns and experiences. Authoritarian politics and political division seem to be on the rise everywhere, for example, and the pandemic has left no corner of the world untouched. Certainly, climate change is of concern for every living thing on the planet. Often, however, our experiences of even those shared concerns vary. The impact of climate change is different in different parts of the world, and those differences depend too often on the wealth or poverty of those impacted. The wealthier countries produce the most greenhouse gases, while the poorer countries suffer the worst consequences of global warming. As the essays in this volume make clear, where our concerns and experiences overlap, it is often because of fraught histories of exploitation. Racial injustice and the oppression of indigenous peoples are legacies of European and North American colonialism in other parts of the world. Ethnic conflict in Africa is often an inheritance from different tribal groups being played off one another by colonial powers. Poverty and the experience of people discarded by what Pope Francis calls "throwaway culture" is an effect of wide disparities in a capitalist economy from which only a select few benefit. Nationalist and populist movements in Europe and the US cannot be understood without understanding the volatility of the Middle East, Africa, Central America, and Asia, which in turn cannot be understood apart from military and economic interventions in those places from Europe, the US, and China.

To point to the interrelated nature of our problems, as the essays in this volume do, is also to point to the interrelated nature of any possible solution. We must encounter one another—across geographical, cultural, racial, gender, and ethnic differences—as sisters and brothers. This is the profound insight at the core of Pope Francis's reflection on fraternity. The longing for universal brotherhood and sisterhood is the leitmotif that has inspired religions, arts, and sciences at every stage of history. This longing is a universal dream that, in monotheistic religions, goes back to the call that Abraham and Sarah heard in Ur of the Chaldeans more than four thousand years ago, according to the biblical narrative, since then opening the way to the three wisdom traditions of Judaism, Christianity, and Islam. It was expressed as a social utopia in the anthropocentric revolution of modern thought—as in the French Revolution's call to *Liberté, Egalité,* and *Fraternité*—often justifying the socioeconomic and political programs of modern states. In recent times, fraternity has been translated as resistance to the planetary predation of hegemonic patriarchal capitalism, by social and popular movements interweaving alternate worlds from below and from the reverse of history. The preeminence of fraternity has inevitably moved the virtue to the center of theological discourse, so much so that it can be said to have initiated a major academic and pastoral shift in contemporary theology. A French theologian, Marie-Jo Thiel, observes that "we do not choose our siblings, but we welcome fraternity by rechoosing our brothers and sisters because there is a fundamental human duty that one imposes on oneself as a requirement of humanity. Biological relations are neither everything nor nothing, they are a first layer of proximity in the service of learning about otherness and the beneficiaries of this opening to the world."[1]

In an address to the Pontifical Academy of Social Sciences on May 3, 2017, Pope Francis confessed his fondness for the virtue of fraternal solidarity, saying: "From the beginning of my pontificate, I wanted to point out that 'our brothers and sisters are the prolongation of the Incarnation for each of us' (cf. *Evangelii Gaudium*, 179). Indeed, the protocol by which we will be judged is based on brotherhood: 'As you did it to one of these, the least of my brethren, you did it to me' (Mt, 25:40)." Noting then that fraternity is always complementary to solidarity, he said that "while solidarity is the principle of social planning that allows the unequal to become equal, fraternity is what allows the equal to be different people. Fraternity allows people who are equal in their essence, dignity, freedom, and their fundamental rights to participate differently in the common good according to their abilities, their life plans, their vocations, their work, or their charisms of service."[2] Hence, its ability to harmonize diversity in unity makes fraternity the most unique and important virtue in a postmodern context of cultural and religious pluralism—the virtue upon which genuine dialogue can thrive and bear fruit.

Theology, which has too often confined God and the people of God into hegemonic discourses, has a role to play in building communities of fraternal solidarity. Pope Francis has clearly learned much from Latin American liberation theology, but *Fratelli Tutti* expands the emphasis from a hermeneutic of liberation to one of fraternal solidarity, from the narrative of Exodus to that of Deuteronomy in Old Testament biblical history. These two are not opposed: Deuteronomy's theology of fraternal solidarity is intrinsically connected to YHWH's act of liberation in Exodus and its ethics of brotherhood (Deut 15:1–18). The Deuteronomic precepts of the Old Testament are being reenacted today in the rediscovery of the theological and social significance of fraternity. The compass with which the Old Testament community navigates the sociopolitical landscape is what Pope Francis presents to the world today as fraternity and social friendship. Jesus affirms the importance of this "compass" in the New Testament with the parables of the Good Samaritan and the Last Judgment, and thus authenticates fraternity as a pillar of the spirituality of the kingdom.

The way that Pope Francis highlights the parable of the Good Samaritan resonates with the importance that Ivan Illich gave to that parable a few decades ago to justify his theological criticism of modernity. Illich thought that the point of the parable was not that the neighbor was *everybody*, but

1. Thiel and Feix, *Le défi de la fraternité*, 23.
2. Francis, "Message from the Holy Father," §1.

rather that the neighbor was *anybody*, that is, any wounded body that contingency or providence put in one's path. The Incarnation revealed the divinity in the flesh of the other, a spontaneous calling of flesh to flesh for the mutual healing of wounds. The church and the state had corrupted this impulse to mutual care and love of neighbor by institutionalizing and bureaucratizing and disincarnating it. Pope Francis reads the parable as a social poetics of mutual recognition rooted in the incarnation of God in Jesus of Nazareth as the criterion of universal redemption.

The essays in this volume taken together constitute an attempt to perform this social poetics of mutual recognition. From many different locations across the globe, and from many different disciplines, the authors in this volume share critiques of the forces that smother this mutual recognition: colonialism, neoliberalism, patriarchy, among others. The essays in this volume attempt to recover the voices of those without voice—or even better, silenced voices, especially the voices of the poor, women, indigenous peoples, and even the earth, for too long treated like an inanimate source of raw material rather than a living organism pulsing with the creative grace of God. We are under no illusion, however, that such a social poetics will be easy and conflict-free. Many of the essays from Africa and Latin America, for example, recognize the ideal of *Ubuntu* or the Latin American dream of *Buen Vivir* (Good Living) and recognize the way that the ideal can obscure power dynamics and failures to put the ideal into practice. The authors of this book do not present an idealized portrait of Christian practice but rather investigate the flashes of redemption, brotherhood/sisterhood, justice and memory with truth, forgiveness and reconciliation that occur in the fragmented history of humanity precisely in the fissures, cracks, and interstices of the hegemonic world. This book opens a conversation that is an invitation to continue talking, always in a climate of both confidence and audacity, with founding texts such as that of Pope Francis to find new meanings, questions, and intuitions to think, understand, and promote social friendship between people, peoples, and cultures. In the midst of exclusion, it is worth highlighting the role of women who, despite often being those who suffer extreme violence, continue to weave networks of peace in the midst of wars, opening windows where there are walls of division and hatred.

Fratelli Tutti draws our attention to the deficiency that lies at the root of social injustice—a moral deficiency that is rooted in an aberrant perception which human beings on opposing sides of economic, social, sexual, religious, and racial divides often have of each other. We are confronted with an exhortation to recognize the essential vocation of living together in the world as a call to reach out and grasp the *Kairos* presented by the Gospel of Christ. The kairotic nature of salvation history obliges men and women of today to see in the ethnic, cultural, gender, and religious diversity of our world an invaluable treasure. For diversity is an opportunity that compels us to be willing to perceive, embrace, and cherish one another as true brothers and sisters, and thus cooperate in building a civilization of love.

Bibliography

Francis, Pope. *Fratelli Tutti: On Fraternity and Social Friendship.* Vatican City: Libreria Editrice Vaticana, 2020. https://www.vatican.va/content/francesco/en/encyclicals/documents/papa-francesco_20201003_enciclica-fratelli-tutti.html.

———. "Message from the Holy Father to the Participants in the Plenary Session of the Pontifical Academy of Social Sciences (28 April–2 May 2017)." Holy See Press Office Summary of Bulletin, April 28, 2017. https://press.vatican.va/content/salastampa/en/bollettino/pubblico/2017/04/28/170428h.html.

Thiel, Marie-Jo, and Marc Feix, eds. *Le défi de la fraternité.* Vienna: Lit Verlag, 2018.

PART ONE

Dark Clouds Over a Closed World

I

The Real Divides in Africa

NORA K. NONTERAH

Introduction

THE ENCYCLICAL *FRATELLI TUTTI* calls for human solidarity and friendship, an exhortation that resonates with the mission of the church as outlined in *Lumen Gentium*, which describes the church as a sacrament of communion with God and of unity among all humans.[1] One hears the echo of Jesus's prayer to the Father, "that they may all be one" (John 17:21, NABRE). The encyclical thus focuses on what Pope Francis calls universal fraternity, and the first chapter deals with certain trends that serve as threats to the unity of humankind, threats described by the pope with the imagery of "dark clouds" and "a closed world."

With this intentional choice of words, Pope Francis tries to provoke thought and draw attention to what is happening in the world. He presents two strong dynamics at the core of human solidarity, namely, *hope* and *despair*. Speaking of "Dark Clouds over a Closed World" he points to the key issues that divide and threaten humankind today and argues that human solidarity is imperative. The African continent is more than ever in need of this solidarity. The ideas of communality, human relationality, and solidarity, expressed in concepts like "Ubuntu" and "Ujama," demonstrate Africa's

---

1. *Lumen Gentium* sees the church as a sacrament—a sign and instrument of communion with God and of unity among all humans. Second Vatican Council, *Lumen Gentium*, 1.

desire for human unity. However, the ideals expressed in these concepts have remained yet unrealized on a continent that is ravaged by conflicts and wars, political instability, poverty, and underdevelopment.

In this chapter I seek firstly to appraise the work of Pope Francis from the point of view of how it addresses the real problems facing Africa. Secondly, I seek to raise critical questions relevant for an assessment of the threats to and strengths of human solidarity according to the spirit of the encyclical. I will do this by first giving a summary of the first chapter of the encyclical and then use the points raised therein in evaluating the situation in African society.

Despair: A Cloud of Gloom in a Closed World

Pope Francis's perception of the world as "closed" suggests a lack of sensitivity to the needs of "the other," which logically leads one to expect that the human race would seek and provide avenues for the opening up of the world. This expected opening does not seem to be happening. Hence, Pope Francis presents this chapter as an intentional and stark exposition of the challenges that confront human togetherness—challenges that he metaphorically sees as "dark clouds." He does this by revealing how the opportunities available to humankind are being misdirected toward destruction. For instance, unity and solidarity have been turned into "populist and ultra-nationalist" ideologies (*FT* 11) that sabotage humanity's ability to make progress toward integration. This is a regression of some sort, which as it is, further strengthens disregard for the common good in a world that advances ideas and practices that would have a global economy unify the world (*FT* 12). What is at stake is the loss of a historical consciousness, which leads to promotion of individualism and creation of a culture of manipulation of concepts to serve as tools for domination and injustice. This serves just a few while leaving many with "shattered dreams" (*FT* 10–14).

World leaders, the pope further contends, lack a plan that is inclusive of everyone (*FT* 15–28). In place of healthy political debates to plan for the improvement of lives are cacophonous arguments that create enmity and polarize society (*FT* 15). Manipulation is ever-present, and the extremes of those who live in luxury and those with denied rights and dignity persist (*FT* 22).

Acknowledging the positive advances of science and technology, the pope cautions that there are concerns about how innovations and developmental agendas are sometimes advanced without due consideration for the situations of, and possible repercussions on, others (*FT* 29). Thus, there is "globalization and progress without a shared roadmap" (*FT* 29–31), in which poverty, hunger, and preventable deaths appear to have become an accepted reality. "Pandemics and other calamities in history" (*FT* 32–36) should teach humankind that "no one is saved alone" and that we need to create a society of people who feel a belonging to each other (*FT* 32). It is Pope Francis's regret, however, that the current COVID-19 pandemic might just come and go, as another of the tragedies in human history, without humans learning from it.

Additionally, "creative openness to others" (*FT* 41), which is pivotal for the flourishing of people, is being threatened by the fear of otherness as seen in the migration crisis in the world. Forced by wars, persecutions, the desire for better living conditions, and natural catastrophes, many people emigrate to other countries, usually to the West, where they are routinely met with xenophobic sentiments. The world is experiencing an "absence of human dignity on the borders" (*FT* 37–41) in the face of the migration crisis. There is also "the illusion of communication" (*FT* 42–50) by which information media are abused as tools for promoting hatred, falsehood, and fear. All of these adversely affect the nature of the relationships between humans. The pope also condemns "forms of subjection and of self-contempt" (*FT* 51–53) engaged in by poor countries imitating the cultures and economies of more prosperous countries, even though these cultures and economies do not respect the values of the poor countries. The failure of developing countries to be innovative, creative, and when the occasion requires, proactive in growing in their own way, upholding, confronting, engaging, purifying, and making use of their own cultural values (*FT* 51), leads to a domination that destroys their self-esteem, which is an important determinant for self-development.

Pope Francis concludes the chapter with a call for "a new style of life" that is anchored in our interdependence as a people (*FT* 35). What is evident in Pope Francis's concern is that human interdependence has been ignored and sometimes denied in ways that create camps of the "we" and the "them." These camps, which are supported by ideologies of self-centeredness, individualism, nationalism, and rejection of historical consciousness, are what I shall look at in evaluating the reality of human interdependence in Africa.

The Real Divides in Africa: Mechanism at Play

The real divides in Africa can be described as a sharp contrast of two worlds. By this I mean a divide between people of different classes, whose situations are sharply and noticeably unequal.

Ethnocentrism and Politics

This sharp contrast of the two worlds is made visible in Africa by the presence of ethnocentrism, which has not only fueled division and the polarization of society but also has had a devastating influence on politics on the continent. In most African countries, ethnicity has determined the choice of political leaders more than the candidate's leadership qualities. Emmanuel Katongole puts it well when he says that what we usually refer to as ethnic conflicts in Africa are "often nothing more than a struggle for political power by Africa's ruling elites, in which the masses are recruited through an appeal to 'ethnicity.'"[2] Such conflicts arise only when the people are mobilized along ethnic lines for the achievement of elite goals. This is possible because negative ethnic and parochial loyalties, which are as dangerous as racism, simply deny humanity to anyone outside the particular camp,[3] thereby equating the meaning of human dignity and value with the interests of a particular group of people—the "we." Overemphasis on the particular group with an inability to move beyond it is dangerous precisely because it leaves room for people to be easily mobilized along kinship lines for the advancement of a few elites' ambitions for political power.

The political divisions then degenerate into parochialism both inside and outside the ethnic groups, leading to the creation of even smaller camps aimed at domination in various local contexts, which the politicians acquiesce to. Against this backdrop, the same politicians are heard daily criticizing these parochial leanings and then begin to appeal to grand concepts like "democracy, freedom, justice or unity" (*FT* 14). Laws and policies then become tools for manipulation and domination and "as meaningless tags that can be used to justify any action" (*FT* 14). The result is that new forms of closed loyalties are created for those who are alike—the rich are friends, the elite understand each other, the poor share a lot in common, the urban folks endorse policies (like centralization or a false decentralization), and the rural folks are left behind. Certainly, the leaders are "lacking a plan for everyone" (*FT* 51). National plans and policies that protect the rich and continue to improve the urban experience receive approval by those who have been chosen to lead but who are incidentally of the same class. There is a fierce resistance to proper decentralization backed by spurious logic. All of the important projects that support growth, ranging from access to basic sources of livelihood, education, healthcare, and transportation are lobbied for by and provided in the cities.

---

2. Katongole, "African Theological Reimagination," 46.
3. Wa Wamwere, *Negative Ethnicity*, 35–37.

Consequences of the Sharp Contrast of Two Worlds

Three consequences of this sharp contrast can be identified:

1. A desperate search for survival
2. The church modeling itself along the lines of the real divides
3. Following the expression of John Samuel Mbiti, "breaking the pot that once held us together"

With respect to the first consequence, the gap between the rich and the poor, the urban and the rural, continues to widen in ways that are not acceptable to those disadvantaged by such a system. Young men and women from many rural parts of Africa feel compelled to move away from the continent to places where they perceive the resources are coming from—the West. And there, they are not "entitled like others to participate in the life of the society, and it is forgotten that they possess the same intrinsic dignity as any person" (*FT* 39).

With respect to the second consequence, ethnocentrism has, sadly, been noted within the church. There have been several instances of strong opposition to the appointment of a bishop to a particular diocese on the basis of ethnocentric biases. A cursory look at parishes in the cities and those in the rural communities also presents a sharp contrast. The outstanding concerns then are, Is the church striving to serve as an example following the model presented in *Ecclesia in Africa*—the church-family of God?[4] Why is parochialism still flourishing and creating patterns of leadership that divide people? Why are members of the same church-family living in sharply contrasting worlds?

Finally, concerning the third consequence, the rich African worldview of human relationality originating from the family and extending to the larger community is regrettably being manipulated as a tool used by politicians to dominate and cause despair. Thus, parochialism serves the ruling and elite class as a mechanism to create despair among the populace. As Pope Francis notes, "The best way to dominate and gain control over people is to spread despair and discouragement, even under the guise of defending certain values" (*FT* 51). Emmanuel Katongole unmasks this dynamic in the contemporary African sociopolitical context, noting how chaos, confusion, and conflicts have become the modalities by which the continent's institutions work.[5]

---

4. In *Ecclesia in Africa*, John Paul II proposed the African understanding of family as a model for the Christian community. See John Paul II, *Ecclesia in Africa*, 43.

5. Katongole, "African Theological Reimagination," 47.

The "intrinsic human value" that is central to Christian teaching and not novel to the African worldview is in crisis. Hence, *Fratelli Tutti* should be understood as speaking about "the dark cloud" over Africa and Africans when it says that "one effective way to weaken historical consciousness, critical thinking, the struggle for justice, and the processes of integration is to empty great words of their meaning or to manipulate them" (*FT* 14). Pope Francis asks: "Nowadays, what do certain words like democracy, freedom, justice or unity really mean?" (*FT* 14). This question is significant for an Africa that is often democratic and yet suffering the adverse consequences of divisions, as exemplified in the persistence of inequities of all forms that threaten "our common being as brothers and sisters" who share a common home.

A "Rethink" Is Possible: Beyond Despair in Africa

Having recognized the real divides in African societies, we must acknowledge that the increased means of improving the lives of everybody—that is, the innovations and inventions in technology and the progress in medicine and science—are not reflected in the lives of all of the world's people. This is because those things, which are made for the improvement of lives, are not only being used inequitably, but are actually sometimes abused to the disadvantage of a portion of the population. As a result, Africa suffers high rates of illiteracy and poverty and a general lack of access to facilities and amenities as compared to the Western world. This is so much so that whereas in the Western world people can still achieve reasonable comfort in their lives without being dependent on the central government, in Africa the situation is the contrary.

Pope Francis's advice not to ignore historical consciousness and not to reject the experiences of those who came before us is an invitation to enter into dialogue with the wisdom that is found in the rich cultural heritage of Africa. Katongole talks about this in very pragmatic terms; namely, as a need "to 'reinvent' African institutions (in the style of Thomas Sankara), by inscribing them with a new imagination."[6] This is because there is need for our political leaders to be deliberately equitable in the distribution of the resources and the benefits that accrue from the exploitation of innovations, with a view to improving the lives of the people. It must involve moral imagination. And by moral imagination, I mean the "capacity to imagine something rooted in the challenges of the real world yet capable of giving birth to that which does not yet exist."[7] In other words, contem-

6. Katongole, "African Theological Reimagination," 47.
7. Lederach, *Moral Imagination*, ix.

porary Africans need to envision the desired future while learning from the experiences of the past and confronting the present disparities on the continent. This moral imagination demands a radically constructive change in mindset and deeds on two levels: the level of the political leadership and that of the general populace.

The call for the recovery of the African as a "being with" according to the understanding of life as Ubuntu will be a call for Africans to "never break the pot that keeps . . . [them] together."[8] This communal life is incompatible with the ethic of individualism. In Ubuntu the "emphasis is put on care and a sense of concern for the wellbeing of others as the main ideal which should guide human economic relations."[9] I remember, vividly, some three decades ago, growing up among my people, the Kasena of Ghana, that every adult female in the village was *nma* (mama) and every adult male was *dekwo* (dad), every older female and every older male was the *zembaro* (big sister and big brother) and they all wielded the authority that goes with their titles. As a result of this, one could be making noise in your house and your parents would admonish you to stop the noise, not really because of the need for there to be silence in your house, but because of the needs of a sick person in the next house. I fondly reminisce about those earlier days of my life when everybody's welfare was everybody's concern, children's upbringing was a responsibility of all, and children ran errands for all, and there was nothing untoward about it. Everyone was part of the one organic entity.

That communal life, in which everybody's welfare was everybody's concern, had a direct effect on the socioeconomic needs of everyone in the community. When somebody came into prosperity, it was shared. Essentially, therefore, what the pope is saying to Africans of today is that they should return to the pristine values of Ubuntu. To return to those basic values of our community life means, "I am for the other person and that person is for me." It also means being responsible for what we become. It is for us to affirm as a people that it is possible for the political arrangements to become more sensitive to the needs of the less privileged, so that the provision of infrastructure that brings about the betterment of the life of the average person is achievable, and so that providing basic amenities like water, electricity, healthcare, and education is considered an imperative.

---

8. John Samuel Mbiti uses this expression to admonish Africans to revisit, valorize, and cherish the communal spirit that was once used to create harmony and peace in society. See Mbiti, "Never Break the Pot," 4.

9. Murovo, "Ubuntu," 45.

Conclusion

In Africa, the real divides that threaten our common being as brothers and sisters manifest in conflicts, hunger, and other situations of despair that are deeply rooted in extreme parochialism. This breeds a denial and a rejection of the values that once made us more united, thereby promoting a pseudo-solidarity that is dangerous to humankind, in which "fraternity" exists only among equals; that is, among the haves and the have-nots.

To begin to break the walls of society, Africans need to use a new imagination that I would call "the moral imagination." This demands affirmative actions that confront the real divides in Africa in pragmatic ways. These affirmative actions can rely on the ethic of communal life expressed as Ubuntu. With COVID-19 as an example, we realize that if one person is vulnerable, the whole population is vulnerable. In the same vein, it must occur to us that if one person dies of hunger, then we have all failed. For nobody's life should be so miserable when we are Africans with Ubuntu.

Bibliography

Francis, Pope. *Fratelli Tutti: On Fraternity and Social Friendship*. Vatican City: Libreria Editrice Vaticana, October 3, 2020. http://www.vatican.va/content/francesco/en/encyclicals/documents/papa-francesco_20201003_enciclica-fratelli-tutti.html.

John Paul II, Pope. *Ecclesia in Africa*. Vatican City: Libreria Editrice Vaticana, September 14, 1995. https://www.vatican.va/content/john-paul-ii/en/apost_exhortations/documents/hf_jp-ii_exh_14091995_ecclesia-in-africa.html.

Katongole, Emmanuel. "African Theological Reimagination Through Stories: How My Mind Has (Not) Changed." In *Faith in Action*. Vol. 3, *Reimagining the Mission of the Church in Education, Politics, and Servant Leadership in Africa*, edited by Stan Chu Ilo et al., 39–60. Eugene, OR: Pickwick, 2020.

Lederach, John Paul. *The Moral Imagination: The Art and Soul of Peace*. New York: Oxford University Press, 2005.

Mbiti, John S. "'Never Break the Pot That Keeps You Together': Peace and Reconciliation in African Religion." *Dialogue and Alliance* 24:1 (2010) 4–21.

Murovo, Felix Munyaradzi. "Ubuntu." *Diogenes* 59:3–4 (2014) 36–47.

Second Vatican Council. *Lumen Gentium: Dogmatic Constitution on the Church*. Vatican City: Libreria Editrice Vaticana, November 21, 1964. https://www.vatican.va/archive/hist_councils/ii_vatican_council/documents/vat-ii_const_19641121_lumen-gentium_en.html.

Wa Wamwere, Koigi. *Negative Ethnicity: From Bias to Genocide*. South Yarra, Australia: Palgrave Macmillan, 2003.

2

Where Are We Going? A Reality Check

MANUEL VICTOR J. SAPITULA, CM

POPE FRANCIS'S ENCYCLICAL *FRATELLI Tutti* initiates a wide-ranging discussion of the values of fraternity and social friendship in the modern world. The first chapter is an extended reading of the "signs of the times," providing the broader context within which the encyclical's appeal to friendship and solidarity becomes an imperative. It describes various aspects of contemporary life that Pope Francis deems problematic, both at the interpersonal and institutional levels.

FT is properly situated within Catholic social teaching—many of the issues it raises align with the reflections of previous popes regarding the "social question" and how the church's faith finds concrete expression in economic, social, and political life. In the first chapter, Pope Francis revisits criticisms of the current global order as found in recent Catholic social teaching. He cites Pope Saint Paul VI's notion of integral human development[1] and Pope Benedict XVI's observations about the rise of new forms of poverty.[2]

Pope Francis likewise invokes his memorable encounter with Grand Imam Ahmad Al-Tayyeb of Egypt. His apostolic journey to Egypt in 2017 is quite notable as an experience of crossing over into a different sociocultural and religious terrain.[3] On several occasions in the encyclical, the pontiff

1. Paul VI, *Populorum Progressio*, 87.
2. Benedict XVI, *Caritas in Veritate*, 21.
3. O'Connell, "Pope Francis's Friendship."

goes back to this experience with the Grand Imam of Al-Azhar to exemplify a commitment to authentic dialogue. He speaks of his shared conviction with the Grand Imam that a "moral deterioration" pervades the modern world. That this common witness to the need for a new animating principle in today's world was announced in Egypt is quite significant: it was made at the threshold of the nations that comprise the "global North."[4] The shared reflection of Pope Francis and the Grand Imam is an attempt to forge a common witness at the margins, and its prospects for grounding an alternative reading of the current state of affairs cannot be ignored.

The malaise in today's world, the pontiff observes, is caused by a globalized indifference (*FT* 30). This indifference is reinforced by an observable decline of historical consciousness and of a sense of connection to one's heritage (*FT* 13), as well as by cultural colonization (*FT* 14). These two tendencies result in the human person being uprooted from her world. Pope Francis expressed particular concern about this disconnection from one's roots. Such an uprooted existence produces various forms of alienation and isolation, and renders everyone, but especially young people, defenseless against the enticements of both unbridled consumerism and extremist ideologies.

The pontiff, in discussing "insufficiently universal human rights," highlights the ongoing scourges of patriarchy, the subjugation of women, and human trafficking as a new form of slavery (*FT* 22–24). What ties these social problems together is the significant disparity between the ideal as expressed in norms (e.g., the Universal Declaration of Human Rights and UN instruments on gender equality) and state treaties (many of which aim at ending all forms of slavery) and the realities on the "rough grounds,"[5] where systematic inequality, gender-based discrimination, and criminal networks practicing human trafficking are still widely tolerated, if not openly promoted.

Besides the inability of existing global structures to address persistent social inequality, the pontiff also refers to growing individual and interpersonal indifference, manifested in extreme forms of individualism and xenophobia. A new global dynamic characterized by shrinking circles of friends and circles of interests (*FT* 97) is pushing its way through neighborhoods,

---

4. Heath, "North-South." This report by the Independent Commission on International Development Issues (or "the Brandt Commission") pointed out that prosperous countries tended to be in the northern hemisphere (Europe and North America except Mexico), while developing countries are generally in the southern hemisphere, with the exception of Australia and New Zealand (which are aligned with the global North in terms of their level of economic development). An imaginary line called the "Brandt Line" separates the global North from the global South.

5. This phrase is a nod to the book, *Back to the Rough Grounds of Praxis* by Daniel Franklin E. Pilario, CM.

communities, and the virtual spaces of social media. This is significant because, apart from the problem of unfulfilled promises and unresponsive institutions, there is a worrying shift at the level of consciousness away from universal love and toward self-preservation. This shift has caused the deployment of an "us v. them" mentality that inflames racist conflicts, marginalizes migrants, and rejects those who are different (*FT* 27).

The COVID-19 pandemic is one of the highlights of the encyclical's first chapter. The world has grappled, and continues to grapple, with the socioeconomic, political, and psychological maelstrom caused by the coronavirus. Despite these problems, however, Pope Francis believes that the current pandemic has the potential to provoke a rethinking and recalibration of humanity's goals and of the motivations animating those goals. It is hoped that the space afforded by the COVID-19 pandemic for a deeper look into existing lifestyles will yield alternative imaginaries of a secure future that hinges not on the metrics of economic success, but on a sense of authentic community and interdependence (*FT* 35).

One of the fresh perspectives offered by the encyclical is in reference to social media, which receives ample attention (a total of nine paragraphs) (*FT* 42–50). The focus on the use of social media demonstrates Pope Francis's broader concern to build communities based on mutual acceptance and support. His observations occasion a closer look at virtual space as a platform to build enduring ties. The picture depicted in the encyclical is not promising: it warns of the superficiality of online relationships (*FT* 47–50) and real instances of social aggression and verbal violence directed against interlocutors (*FT* 44–45). The pontiff also remarked that the frenzy of texting, while fostering a sense of connection with others, cannot be a replacement for careful listening to the other and contemplative silence (*FT* 49).

Contending with the Unevenness of Globalization

Chapter 1 offers an extensive, exhaustive listing of social problems besetting the modern world. In grounding his reflections on fraternity and social friendship, the pontiff clearly steers away from utopian thinking. He indicts the misalignments and failures in today's world, but he also accepts whatever may be considered as good and beneficial, highlighting, among other things, economic progress, advances in technology, and human rights (see, e.g., *FT* 29). Perhaps because the pontiff does not intend to offer a systematic social analysis in the encyclical, the text does not suggest an integrated approach to the problems it identifies, nor is there a framework by which we can link issues together.

Pope Francis is aware that we live in a "global village":[6] the interconnection, exchange, and cross-border flows seen today are quite unprecedented in the history of human civilization. Globalization is a widespread and universal phenomenon that lies the root of the issues and problems that the pontiff addresses in *FT*. Social theorists like Immanuel Wallerstein have conceived of the transformation of global society into a single world system, and Wallerstein argues that this global system reorganizes the relationships between nations at the "core" and at the "periphery" along exploitative lines through an unequal exchange of resources.[7] The state, acting through political leaders and institutions, has a key role to play in asserting and reasserting a nation's position in the world system. This role does not preclude the role played by transnational social classes in maintaining positions of power in the global economy, thus leading to the oppression of marginalized groups across different contexts and localities.

The pontiff is quite forceful in calling attention to the fact that, in today's globalized world, not everyone is able to access the benefits of our increasing capability of harnessing resources that foster human flourishing. In addition, a deeper look at the gains afforded by globalization shows that a comfortable life does not always mean a better life. The main issue is not lack of resources or an inability to achieve progress, but rather, the *unevenness* of progress because of the systemic exclusion of certain sectors from participation and decision-making. The inconsistency that is inherent in cultural and economic globalization is *inclusion without inclusivity*.

The pontiff's remarks on the active co-optation of the call to "open up to the world" so that oppressive market arrangements that further marginalize the already-marginalized nations can be imposed (*FT* 12) resonates with Wallerstein's analysis of the inequalities of globalization.[8] In the liberal capitalist order, the poorer nations of the global South have little leverage against the influential countries of the global North. For instance, the integration of a number of Asian countries into the global chain of production places them in a marginalized position vis-à-vis their counterparts in Europe and North America. Asian countries like the Philippines, India, Bangladesh, Indonesia, and Thailand, among others, have historically been exporters of skilled and semiskilled labor for the benefit of richer countries.[9] While this outbound migration has brought in much-needed revenue to keep these

---

6. McLuhan and Fiore, *Medium Is the Massage*, 63. For the implications of the "global village" concept in religious discourse and institutions, see Sapitula, "Doing Research," 10–11.

7. Wallerstein, *World-Systems Analysis*, 28–29.

8. Wallerstein, *World-Systems Analysis*, 86.

9. Tyner, "Global Cities," 65.

countries economically afloat, it often comes with a high social cost; for example, left-behind children who pay the price of distant and absentee parenting. This is compounded by instances of abuse and marginalization experienced by migrants in host countries.

Globalization—the integration of nations into a single cultural and economic world system—does not make life better for everyone. On the contrary, it has caused an observable decline in an inclusive solidarity, as narrower forms of intragroup associations are weaponized by various groups to monopolize control over resources. The decline of inclusive solidarity has been attributed to the rise of "violent nationalism," wherein nationalistic ideology and symbols are deployed in a perceived "crisis mode" to evoke fear of the other; populism, an anti-institutional ideology that seeks to represent the "will of the people" over established values; and authoritarianism or ultra right-wing politics, which combines autocratic rule and moralistic conservatism.[10]

The recent rise of authoritarian politics has been well-documented. The clearest example is the antimigrant and protectionist rhetoric of the former Trump administration in the US. In South Asia, India's prime minister Shri Narendra Modi displays populist and authoritarian tendencies, although the country formally remains a democracy. In Southeast Asia, a number of countries have seen the rise of authoritarian leaders, either through electoral victory or the seizing of power from democratically elected governments. The rise of Rodrigo Duterte in the Philippines was premised on his populist platform that often disregards human rights, especially in the execution of his administration's War on Drugs, which has seen the death of thousands of suspected drug addicts. His despotic and violent rhetoric has encouraged police brutality and the state-sanctioned silencing of dissent through attacks on government critics and activists. In Myanmar, military forces staged a coup in February 2021 that ousted the duly-elected civilian government. Military and police forces have retaliated violently against those who clamor for a return to democracy and the rule of law, which has resulted in the death of a number of civilian protesters.

Intimations of a Post-Pandemic World

Pope Francis mentioned near the beginning of *FT* that the COVID-19 pandemic unexpectedly erupted as he was writing the encyclical (*FT* 7). He used the opportunity provided by the pandemic to reflect upon the relevance of the issues he was concerned with in light of the challenges it posed. There

---

10. Bieber, "Is Nationalism on the Rise?" 522–23.

is some mention of the tragedy of the pandemic throughout the encyclical, with the most elaborated discussion occurring in the first chapter. The topic is revisited again in passing in chapter 5, where the pontiff outlines the need for a better kind of politics.

The virus that causes the disease known as COVID-19 is a novel form of coronavirus named SARS-CoV-2, first detected in Wuhan in the People's Republic of China in December 2019. From this place of origin, it spread quickly to the rest of the world through person-to-person contact. Severe cases of infection by the virus require medical attention in Intensive Care Units (ICUs) in hospitals. As of April 4, 2021, 2.8 million people had died from the COVID-19 virus worldwide.[11]

In the early stages of the pandemic, a number of governments placed entire countries on lockdown. These measures, while slowing the spread of the virus, led to major problems pertaining to employment and social support for vulnerable sectors of the population. Large numbers of businesses closed down during the pandemic, resulting in layoffs and joblessness. The huge number of cases also strained healthcare systems and exposed healthcare professionals to the virus. The standstill in activity and the isolation caused by lockdowns have strained relationships at many levels, exposing a sizeable portion of the population worldwide to a loneliness and silent suffering that, for the most part, has gone unnoticed.

On the whole, the encyclical does not address the pandemic as substantively as it does other issues. The pontiff's reflections about it are necessarily preliminary since it erupted while he was in the process of writing *FT*.[12] The pope has made very clear that his original inspiration in writing the encyclical was to further reflect on the issues raised by the Document on Human Fraternity for World Peace and Living Together (also known as the Abu Dhabi Declaration), which he coauthored with Sheikh Ahmad Al-Tayyeb, the Grand Imam of Al-Azhar, on February 4, 2019 (*FT* 5). As the pandemic raged throughout the world, however, before the final promulgation of *FT*, the pontiff saw an occasion to encourage a greater awareness of the need for more interdependence in today's world. Pope Francis says that the pandemic "momentarily revived the sense that we are a global community" (*FT* 32). Despite the many problems that the pandemic has brought us, the pontiff believes that it has the potential to contribute to a change in the world's trajectory from extreme forms of individualism and marginalization

---

11. World Health Organization, "Weekly Epidemiological Update": " The tally for April 6, 2021 is 130,459,184 confirmed cases and 2,842,325 deaths (2.2 percent)."

12. "In the Midst of Covid."

of the poor toward the creation of societies that are characterized by inclusivity, coresponsibility, and sharing.

The pontiff indicated one type of potential response to the COVID-19 pandemic; the situation on the ground, however, is much more diverse and uneven. In the early phase of the pandemic, the only universal responses taken by the authorities were a forced reduction in people's mobility and social distancing policies. Other than this, responses to the pandemic varied from country to country, depending on each country's domestic political situation, the availability of resources, and the level of coordinated response to the social problems brought about by the pandemic.[13] The roles of planning and decision-making at the level of governance (national, regional, and local) are especially important in assessing a country's success in handling the pandemic; that is, in limiting the spread of COVID-19 among its population.

India and Indonesia have by far the highest number of cumulative cases in Asia (12,485,509 and 1,527,524 cases, respectively) and also the highest cumulative deaths per 1,000 people (11.9 and 15.1, respectively), as of April 4, 2021. The Philippines ranks third, with 784,023 cumulative cases and 12.2 cumulative deaths per 1,000 people. On the other end of the spectrum are countries like Vietnam, Cambodia, and Mongolia, which each has fewer than 5,000 cumulative cases and lower than 1.0 cumulative death per 1,000 people. In between are countries like Malaysia (349,610 cases and 4.0 cumulative deaths per 1,000), Singapore (60,468 cases and 0.5 cumulative deaths per 1,000), and South Korea (105,279 cases and 3.4 cumulative deaths per 1,000) which, although having high number of cases, have a low number of cumulative deaths.[14] These latter countries took effective measures to contain the spread of the virus and provide assistance and treatment to people who became infected.

Countries like the Philippines have had difficulty containing the spread of the virus for a number of reasons. There is ample evidence to conclude that the country adopted a *security* rather a *public health* approach to the pandemic. While lockdowns have shown success in momentarily slowing the spread of the SARS-CoV-2 virus, COVID-19-related rules and regulations were deployed by security forces (police and military) to "discipline" a population that was perceived to be unruly and noncompliant.[15] There were also instances when lockdown regulations were applied to quell dissent and

---

13. Milani, "COVID-19 Outbreak," 247–48.
14. World Health Organization, "Weekly Epidemiological Update."
15. Sajor, "State Repression."

silence mounting criticism of government inadequacies in dealing with the social problems caused by the pandemic.[16]

Any assessment of the COVID-19 pandemic in light of Pope Francis's desire that it be used as a tool to create a renewed commitment to human solidarity must acknowledge that, while advocating for the reform of existing institutions to address the vulnerabilities that emerged from the pandemic is one course of action, it is not entirely impossible that these same vulnerabilities will be used to further entrench the power of ruling elites. In fact, eighty countries experienced a weakening of democracy and respect for human rights during the pandemic.[17] Thus, the possibility that the chance to initiate meaningful reforms toward greater cooperation and inclusivity will be missed is real. While *FT* unequivocally stood for these values, a more coordinated plan to create a world based on fraternity and social friendship needs to be implemented by key stakeholders worldwide.

A Bridge to the Rest of the Encyclical

The social analysis provided by Pope Francis in the first chapter sets the tone for a fuller discussion of the issues in succeeding chapters. The question of insufficiently universal human rights is dealt with exhaustively in the discussion of universal love in chapter 3. Globalization is a recurring theme throughout the encyclical, taken up in the discussion of openness in chapter 3, the dynamics of locality and universality in chapter 4, and political love in chapter 5. The COVID-19 pandemic is once again referred to in the discussion of market relationships in chapter 5. A more extended discussion of the plight of migrants is found in the section about borders in chapter 4. And finally, issues surrounding communication and internet technologies are revisited in the discussion of social dialogue in chapter 5.

At the end of the first chapter, Pope Francis calls everyone to a "renewed hope." Echoing the message he delivered to young people in Cuba in 2015, the pontiff views hope as "deeply rooted in every human heart, independently of our circumstances and historical conditioning" (*FT* 55). Thus, hope is here presented as a double-edged reality: it is influenced by the contingencies of the human condition, and yet points to aspirations that transcend these same contingencies. The implication of this hope is profound for the encyclical's message of friendship and solidarity to the modern world.

---

16. Dodds et al., "COVID-19 Pandemic," 295.
17. Repucci and Slipowitz, "Democracy under Lockdown."

Hope refers to a virtue planted in the human heart by God (in the pope's words, "deeply rooted in every human heart") that leads back to God. It necessarily has God as its object and is referred to as a "theological virtue."[18] This is the transcendent dimension of hope. As *social hope*, however, aspirations to authentic Christian life in today's world are crafted within the rough grounds of personal circumstance and historical conditioning. This involves, among other things, a critique of existing social structures that inhibit human flourishing and conscientious action to challenge and change these structures. What Pope Francis accomplishes in the first chapter is to provide a critical assessment of powerful forces and tendencies that shape today's globalized world. The attention he accords to marginalized peoples is an important dimension of hope. By pointing out the "dark clouds" that hover over the world's poor, imagining an alternative, inclusive world becomes not only possible, but also an *imperative*. Here, Pope Francis again alludes to the window of opportunity opened by the COVID-19 pandemic—with the current crisis, crafting a more just and inclusive world becomes a more pressing responsibility than ever.

Perhaps Pope Francis's passing reference to hope toward the end of *FT*'s first chapter does not do justice to its importance. He returns to the subject of hope infrequently throughout *FT*, for instance, in his discussion about politics (*FT* 196), peacebuilding (*FT* 228), and religious freedom (*FT* 274). These references, however, always refer back to the double-edged nature of hope that the pontiff outlines in the introduction: hope is a critique of the present and an aspiration for a better and more inclusive future (*FT* 54–55). Together with an invitation to "political love" (*FT* 187–92), an invitation to social hope is one of the highlights of Pope Francis's prophetic message to the world today.

Bibliography

Aquinas, Thomas. *Summa Theologica*. Translated by the Fathers of the English Dominican Province. 22 vols. London: R. and T. Washbourne, 1911.
Benedict XVI, Pope. *Caritas in Veritate*. Vatican City: Libreria Editrice Vaticana, 2009. https://www.vatican.va/content/benedict- xvi/en/encyclicals/documents/hf_ben-xvi_enc_20090629_caritas-in-veritate.html.
Bieber, Florian. "Is Nationalism on the Rise? Assessing Global Trends." *Ethnopolitics* 17:5 (2018) 519–40.
Dodds, Klaus, et al. "The COVID-19 Pandemic: Territorial, Political, and Governance Dimensions of the Crisis." *Territory, Politics, Governance* 8:3 (2020) 289–98.

18. Aquinas, *Summa Theologica*, II–II, q. 17, art. 5.

Francis, Pope. *Fratelli Tutti: On Fraternity and Social Friendship.* Vatican City: Libreria Editrice Vaticana, 2020. http://www.vatican.va/content/francesco/en/encyclicals/documents/papa-francesco_20201003_enciclica-fratelli-tutti.html.

Heath, Edward. "North-South: A Programme for Survival." *The Geographical Journal* 147:3 (1981) 298–306.

"In the Midst of Covid, 'Fratelli Tutti' Asks: Will We Learn Our Lesson?" *Union of Catholic Asian News*, October 8, 2020. https://www.ucanews.com/news/in-the-midst-of-covid-fratelli-tutti-asks-will-we-learn-our-lesson/89803#.

McLuhan, Marshall, and Quentin Fiore. *The Medium Is the Massage: An Inventory of Effects.* New York: Random House, 1967.

Milani, Fabio. "COVID-19 Outbreak, Social Response, and Early Economic Effects: A Global VAR Analysis of Cross-Country Interdependencies." *Journal of Population Economics* 34:1 (2021) 223–52.

O'Connell, Gerard. "Pope Francis's Friendship with the Grand Imam of Al Azhar Inspired the New International Day of Human Fraternity." *America: The Jesuit Review*, December 22, 2020. https://www.americamagazine.org/politics-society/2020/12/22/international-day-human-fraternity-pope-francis-239578.

Paul VI, Pope. *Populorum Progressio.* Vatican City: Libreria Editrice Vaticana, 1967. http://www.vatican.va/content/paul-vi/en/encyclicals/documents/hf_p-vi_enc_26031967_populorum.html.

Pilario, Daniel Franklin E., CM. *Back to the Rough Grounds of Praxis: Exploring Theological Method with Pierre Bourdieu.* Leuven, Belgium: Peeters, 2005.

Repucci, Sarah, and Amy Slipowitz. "Democracy under Lockdown: The Impact of COVID-19 on the Global Struggle for Freedom." *Freedom House*, 2020. https://freedomhouse.org/report/special-report/2020/democracy-under-lockdown.

Sajor, Leanne. "State Repression in the Philippines During COVID-19 and Beyond." *openDemocracy*, July 7, 2020. https://www.opendemocracy.net/en/state-repression-philippines-during-covid-19-and-beyond/.

Sapitula, Manuel Victor J. "Doing Research in the Global Village: Assessing Present Realities and Future Trajectories." *Hapag: A Journal of Interdisciplinary Theological Research* 17:1 (2015) 9–24.

Tyner, James A. "Global Cities and Circuits of Global Labor: The Case of Manila, Philippines." *The Professional Geographer* 52:1 (2000) 61–74. https://www.tandfonline.com/doi/pdf/10.1111/0033-124.00205.

Wallerstein, Immanuel. *World-Systems Analysis: An Introduction.* A John Hope Franklin Center Book 40. Durham: Duke University Press, 2004.

World Health Organization. "Weekly Epidemiological Update on COVID-19—6 April 2021." April 6, 2021. https://www.who.int/publications/m/item/weekly-epidemiological-update-on-covid-19---6-april-2021.

3

An Unhealthy Society

FRANCISCO DE AQUINO-JÚNIOR[1]

Introduction

POPE FRANCIS'S FUNDAMENTAL PURPOSE in his encyclical *Fratelli Tutti* is to propose "a way of life marked by the flavour of the Gospel" (*FT* 1). It is "a modest contribution to continued reflection, in the hope that in the face of present-day attempts to eliminate or ignore others, we may prove capable of responding with a new vision of fraternity and social friendship that will not remain at the level of words" (*FT* 6). *Fraternity and social friendship* are at stake (the goals/objectives) in the current world (the context/reality). For this reason, the encyclical's starting point can only be a consideration of the "present-day attempts to eliminate or ignore others" and of the "many new paths of hope" available in our world (*FT* 54).

Fratelli Tutti is the most recent addition to the tradition of the church's social teaching (the social encyclicals), which is engaged in discerning the "signs of the times." The Second Vatican Council's pastoral constitution *Gaudium et Spes* on the church in today's world affirmed that at all times "the church has always had the duty of scrutinizing the signs of the times and of interpreting them in the light of the Gospel" and that, for this to happen, "we need to recognize and understand the world in which we live, its explanations, its longings, and its often-dramatic characteristics."[2] It is a

---

1. Translated by Cristina Silva.
2. Second Vatican Council, *Gaudium et Spes*, 4.

matter of laboring "to decipher authentic signs of God's presence and purpose in the happenings, needs and desires in which [the people of God] has a part along with other men of our age."[3] It is interesting to note how the expression "signs of the times" refers as much to *current events* as to God's presence and purposes in these events. This apparent conceptual ambiguity is, deep down, an indication of the historicity of salvation (it happens in history and in a historical way) and/or of the theological character of historical events (expression/mediation of or a denial of/obstacle to salvation). This explains the importance and centrality that Francis gives to consideration of our present-day reality in *Fratelli Tutti*.

The pope is not discussing a "cool and detached description of today's problems" (*FT* 56), nor a simple appropriation of the "flood of information" about them (*FT* 50), but rather an authentic "wisdom" that is the result of meeting, listening, and dialogue (*FT* 47–50) that enables us to address the "dark clouds" by finding "new paths of hope" (*FT* 54) in our world and to react with a "new vision of fraternity and social friendship" (*FT* 6). In other words, the pope's consideration of reality takes place in the broader context of the exercise of the church's mission in the world, which is to propose "a way of life marked by the flavour of the Gospel" (*FT* 1).

Our reflection is centered on the first chapter of the encyclical, which deals with the "dark clouds over a closed world" and draws attention to "certain trends in our world that hinder the development of universal fraternity" (*FT* 9). We will begin with a brief review of present-day trends presented by Francis and we will then analyze them, highlighting the root or fundamental problem that causes and expresses itself in these trends.

Current World Trends

Pope Francis's intention in the first chapter is neither "to carry out an exhaustive analysis [n]or to study every aspect of our present-day experience," but simply to draw attention to "certain trends in our world that hinder the development of universal fraternity" (*FT* 9). It will be useful to set forth these trends so that we can understand the dimension and complexity of the problem.

The starting point is the observation that the integration efforts developed in recent decades in several regions of the world seem to now be "Shattered Dreams" (the heading for *FT* 10–14). An example of this is that "ancient conflicts thought long buried are breaking out anew, while instances of a myopic, extremist, resentful, and aggressive nationalism are on

---

3. Second Vatican Council, *Gaudium et Spes*, 11.

the rise" (*FT* 11). Another is that "opening up to the world" has become increasingly synonymous with "openness to foreign interests or to the freedom of economic powers to invest without obstacles or complications in all countries," creating a culture that "unifies the world, but divides persons and nations" and in which "political life becomes increasingly fragile in the face of transnational economic powers" (*FT* 12). This also favors "a growing loss of the sense of history, which leads to even further breakup," (*FT* 13), which leads to the creation of fertile ground for "new forms of cultural colonization" in which peoples lose "not only their spiritual identity but also their moral consistency and, in the end, their ideological, economic and political independence" (*FT* 14).

The fact is that we are "Lacking a Plan for Everyone" (the heading for *FT* 15–28): the strategy of economic globalism is to "spread despair and discouragement," using "hyperbole, extremism, and polarization" as political tools, and to cause politics to no longer involve "healthy debates about long-term plans to improve people's lives and to advance the common good, but only ... slick marketing techniques primarily aimed at discrediting others" (*FT* 15). Going hand in hand with this is that "some parts of our human family ... can be readily sacrificed for the sake of others considered worthy of a carefree existence" (*FT* 18). In addition, "human rights are not equal for all," and there are "many forms of injustice" (*FT* 22); "women ... suffer situations of exclusion, mistreatment and violence" (*FT* 23); some persons "live in conditions akin to slavery" (*FT* 24); there are many wars, terrorist attacks, and persecutions, what Francis calls "a real third world fought piecemeal" (*FT* 25); and "the loneliness, fear and insecurity experienced by those who feel abandoned by the system creates a fertile terrain for various 'mafias'" (*FT* 28).

Our time involves a great paradox: "Globalization and Progress without a Shared Roadmap" (the heading for *FT* 29–31). Certainly, there are "positive advances ... in the areas of science, technology, medicine, industry and welfare, above all in developed countries" (*FT* 29). But there is also "a moral deterioration that influences international action and a weakening of spiritual values and responsibility," as well as "major political crises, situations of injustice and the lack of an equitable distribution of natural resources" (*FT* 29). With this, "the sense of belonging to a single human family is fading," "the dream of working together for justice and peace together seem like an outdated utopia. What reigns instead is a cool, comfortable and globalized indifference" that makes us forget that "we are all in the same boat" (*FT* 30). We live together but are not close: "How wonderful it would be, even as we discover faraway planets, to rediscover the needs of the brothers and sisters who orbit around us" (*FT* 31).

To all this can be added (as a consequence and/or aggravating factor) "Pandemics and Other Calamities in History" (the heading for *FT* 32–36). What could be a chance to change course often becomes an occasion for the radicalization of selfishness and social exclusion. A "worldwide tragedy" like the COVID-19 pandemic "momentarily revived the sense that we are a global community, all in the same boat, where one person's problems are the problems of all" (*FT* 32). And "if everything is interconnected, it is hard to imagine that this global disaster is unrelated to our way of approaching reality. . . . The world itself is crying out in rebellion" (*FT* 34). The pope continues: "All too quickly, however, we forget the lessons of history, 'the teacher of life.' After this health crisis passes, our worst response would be to plunge even more deeply into feverish consumerism and new forms of egotistic self-preservation" (*FT* 35). It should not be ignored that "the notion of 'every man for himself' will rapidly degenerate into a free-for-all that would prove worse than any pandemic" (*FT* 36).

Particularly dramatic is the situation of those who face "An Absence of Human Dignity on the Borders" (the heading of *FT* 37–41). It is sad to see how, both in the propaganda of populist regimes as well as in certain liberal economic approaches, it is argued that "an influx of migrants is to be prevented at all costs," as well as that it is proper to limit "aid to poor countries so that they can hit 'rock bottom' and find themselves forced to take austerity measures," forgetting that "behind such statements, abstract and hard to support, great numbers of lives are at stake" (*FT* 37), including people who "have fled from war, persecution and natural catastrophes" or who are merely "seeking opportunities for themselves and their families" (*FT* 37); who become victims of "unscrupulous traffickers, often linked to drug cartels and arms cartels" (*FT* 38) or of a xenophobic mentality and in the countries of arrival, "often fomented and exploited for political purposes." What is more serious is that sometimes "Christians" do not treat migrants as fully equal human beings, prioritizing "political preferences" over the "deep convictions of our faith" (*FT* 39).

A decisive factor in all of these processes is the "Illusion of Digital Communication" (the heading of *FT* 42–50). The pope states that "oddly enough, while closed and intolerant attitudes towards others are on the rise, distances are otherwise shrinking or disappearing to the point that the right to privacy scarcely exists" (*FT* 42). He further maintains that "digital movements of hate and destruction . . . are not . . . a positive form of mutual help, but simply an association of individuals united against a perceived common enemy" and that with digital communications there is a "risk of addiction, isolation and gradual loss of contact with concrete reality" (*FT* 43); he continues by warning that "social aggression has found unparalleled room for expansion through computers and mobile devices" (*FT* 44). Francis notes that we cannot forget that "there are huge economic interests operating in the digital world, capable of exercising forms of control as subtle as they are invasive, creating mechanisms for the manipulation of consciences and of the democratic process" (*FT* 45). True wisdom presupposes "an encounter with reality" (*FT* 47) and "the ability to sit down to listen to others" (*FT* 48).

All of this produces or triggers "Forms of Subjection and of Self-Contempt" (the heading of *FT* 51–53). Faced with the temptation to take "economically prosperous countries" as "cultural models for less developed countries," Francis warns that "this shallow and pathetic desire to imitate others leads to copying and consuming in place of creating, and fosters low national self-esteem" (*FT* 51). It should never be forgotten that "destroying self-esteem is an easy way to dominate others"; that "behind these trends that tend to level our world, there emerge power interests that take advantage of such low self-esteem, while attempting . . . to create a new culture in the service of the elite"; that "ignoring the culture of their people has led to an inability of many political leaders to devise an effective development plan that could be freely accepted and sustained over time" (*FT* 52); and, finally, that "there is no worse form of alienation than to feel uprooted, belonging to no one" (*FT* 53).

Francis concludes the chapter by warning that, "despite these dark clouds," there are in the world "many new paths of hope," because "God continues to sow abundant seeds of goodness in our human family" (*FT* 54). This will be covered in the following chapters.

An Unhealthy Society (*FT* 65)

Throughout *Fratelli Tutti*, these "trends in our world that hinder the development of universal fraternity" (*FT* 9) are taken up again and again and made concrete in different contexts and in reference to different problems and challenges. But the indications offered in the first chapter are enough for us to realize that these are not easy matters to understand and even less to solve. At issue is a way of conceiving and configuring human life in all its dimensions that is dynamized by the logic of the market: profit, competition, consumption, success, and merit. Let us not delude ourselves or simplify the issue—the problem is the model and pattern of civilization and society that has imposed itself on the world: "a profit-based *economic* model that does not hesitate to exploit, discard and even kill human beings" (*FT* 22); a "*political life*" that is "increasingly fragile before transnational economic powers" (*FT* 12); a *culture*, in which "the sense of belonging to a single human family is fading" and in which "there is a cool, comfortable and globalized indifference" (*FT* 30). All this leads to a *world* in which "some parts of our human family . . . can be readily sacrificed for the sake of others considered worthy of a carefree existence" (*FT* 18). It is this way and model of life that destroys fraternity, reduces nature to a mere economic resource, subordinates the common good to the interests of money, makes people cold and insensitive to the suffering of others, produces victims and discards the poor, the Black, the migrant, women, the elderly, and others.

Three often-recurring blocks of expressions are very important for describing this way of life: *liberal/liberalism/neoliberalism* (*FT* 37, 155, 163, 167, 168), *market/commodity/trade* (*FT* 12, 33, 109, 122, 138, 140, 168, 189, 248), and *individualism/selfishness* (*FT* 11, 13, 43, 89, 105, 113, 166, 170, 209, 222, 275). These expressions form a semantic constellation that are present in all of the church's social encyclicals when they discuss liberalism/capitalism, and they are also key to the social teachings of Pope Francis, specifically as contained in *Fratelli Tutti*.

His critique of liberal/neoliberal logic is clear and radical and can be summarized in the following points: (1) "The marketplace, by itself, cannot resolve every problem, however much we are asked to believe this dogma of neoliberal faith" (*FT* 168); (2) "neoliberalism . . . reproduces itself by resorting to the magical theories of 'spillover' or 'trickle'—without using the name—as the only solution to societal problems," without accounting for the fact that "the alleged 'spillover' does not resolve the inequality that gives rise to new forms of violence threatening the fabric of society" (*FT* 168); and (3) "radical individualism is a virus that is extremely difficult to eliminate," making us believe that "everything consists in giving free rein to our own ambitions, as if by pursuing ever greater ambitions and creating safety nets, we would somehow be serving the common good" (*FT* 105).

The reasons for this radical criticism are also very clear: "This culture unifies the world, but divides persons and nations . . . it makes us neighbours, but does not make us brothers" (*FT* 12); "wealth has increased, but together with inequality" (*FT* 21); "the notion of 'every man for himself' will rapidly degenerate into a free-for-all that would prove worse than any pandemic" (*FT* 36); "if a society is governed primarily by the criteria of market freedom and efficiency, there is no place for [people with disabilities] and fraternity will remain just another vague ideal" (*FT* 109); "development must not aim at the amassing of wealth by a few, but must ensure 'human rights—personal and social, economic and political, including the rights of nations and of peoples'" (*FT* 122); "the right of some to free enterprise or market freedom cannot supersede the rights of peoples and the dignity of the poor, or, for that matter, respect for the natural environment" (*FT* 122); and "the right to private property is always accompanied by the primary and prior principle of the subordination of all private property to the universal destination of the earth's goods and thus the right of all to their use" (*FT* 123).

At stake here, therefore, is the civilizing pattern or the model of society, as dynamized by the logic of the market in its global phase, which has imposed itself on the world in recent decades. This is not a criticism of the market per se as a mechanism of exchange—it is fundamental in complex societies and economies like ours—but of its absolutization or its transformation into an absolute criterion and measure of economics, politics, culture, and even of interpersonal relationships and religions: "There were those who would have had us believe that freedom of the market was sufficient to keep everything secure" (*FT* 33); and "the marketplace, by itself, cannot resolve every problem, however much we are asked to believe this dogma of neoliberal faith" (*FT* 168).

In fact, this way of conceiving, dynamizing, and organizing life, as indicated in the first chapter of the encyclical, in addition to transforming post–World War II efforts toward pacification, integration, and economic-social development into "shattered dreams" (*FT* 10–14), created a world "lacking a plan for everyone" (*FT* 15–28), was responsible for "globalization and progress without a shared roadmap" (*FT* 29–31), produced the "illusion of communication" (*FT* 42–49), generated "subjection and self-contempt" (*FT* 51–53), and left many people "with an absence of human dignity on the borders" (*FT* 37–41). This is its ethical-theological and humanitarian failure.

And this became even more visible and serious in the context of the COVID-19 pandemic, which exposed "our false securities," our "inability to act together," and "a fragmentation that made it more difficult to resolve problems that affect us all" (*FT* 7). The pandemic "momentarily revived the sense that we are a global community, all in the same boat, where one person's problems are the problems of all" (FT 32); further, "the brutal and unforeseen blow of this uncontrolled pandemic forced us to recover our concern for human beings, for everyone, rather than for the benefit of a few" (*FT* 33). The pope also stated about the pandemic that "if everything is interconnected, it is hard to imagine that this global disaster is unrelated to our way of approaching reality.... The world itself is crying out in rebellion" (*FT* 34); it "enabled us to recognize and appreciate once more all those around us who, in the midst of fear, responded by putting their lives on the line. We began to realize that our lives are interwoven with and sustained by ordinary people" (*FT* 54); and it "demonstrated that not everything can be resolved by market freedom. It has also shown that, in addition to recovering a sound political life that is not subject to the dictates of finance, 'we must put human dignity back at the centre'" (*FT* 168).

In the catechesis cycle during the pandemic, throughout the months of August and September 2020, which was entitled "To Heal the World" (now available in book form), Francis strongly insisted on the link between the COVID-19 pandemic and the pandemic of the dominant system. This new pandemic "has highlighted how vulnerable and interconnected everyone is," "shed light on broader social ills" that view people as "objects, to be used and discarded,"[4] and social inequality that is "the fruit of unequal economic growth";[5] it "exposed the plight of the poor and the great inequality that reigns in the world";[6] helped us understand that "these injustices are neither natural nor inevitable" and that "to come out of the pandemic, we must find the cure not only for the *coronavirus* . . . but also for the great human and socioeconomic *viruses*."[7] Francis's insistence on the close link between the "small but terrible virus" and the "larger virus"[8] of social injustice helps us understand the scale of the problem and the challenges that lie ahead. In *Fratelli Tutti*, Francis states that we live in an "unhealthy society" (*FT* 65). Richard Horton, borrowing the expression from epidemiologist Merrill Singer, warned that COVID-19 is more than a "pandemic"; it is a "syndemic," in which biological, social, economic, political, and cultural factors play and interact.[9] Santiago Alba Rico insists that the underlying problem is the capitalist system.[10] A way of life dominated by *market logic* is at issue. Building a way of life driven by *the logic of fraternity* is the big challenge.

Bibliography

Alba Rico, Santiago. "Capitalismo pandémico." *ctxt*, January 4, 2021. https://ctxt.es/es/20210101/Firmas/34633/Santiago-Alba-Rico-capitalismo-pandemico-sindemia-virus-desigualdad.htm.

Francis, Pope. *Fratelli Tutti: On Fraternity and Social Friendship*. Vatican City: Libreria Editrice Vaticana, 2020. http://www.vatican.va/content/francesco/en/encyclicals/documents/papa-francesco_20201003_enciclica-fratelli-tutti.html.

———. *To Heal the World: Catechesis on the Pandemic*. Vatican City: Libreria Editrice Vaticana, 2020.

Horton, Richard. "COVID-19 is Not a Pandemic." *The Lancet* 396 (2020) 874. https://www.thelancet.com/journals/lancet/article/PIIS0140-6736(20)32000-6/fulltext.

4. Francis, *To Heal the World*, 27.
5. Francis, *To Heal the World*, 43.
6. Francis, *To Heal the World*, 35.
7. Francis, *To Heal the World*, 91; emphasis original.
8. Francis, *To Heal the World*, 35.
9. Horton, "COVID-19 Is Not a Pandemic," 874.
10. Alba Rico, "Capitalismo pandémico."

Second Vatican Council. *Gaudium et Spes: Pastoral Constitution on the Church in the Modern World.* Vatican City: Libreria Editrice Vaticana, 1965. https://www.vatican.va/archive/hist_councils/ii_vatican_council/documents/vat-ii_const_19651207_gaudium-et-spes_en.html.

4

In Praise of Complaint

FREDERICK CHRISTIAN BAUERSCHMIDT

A Litany of Complaints?

POPE FRANCIS BEGINS *FRATELLI Tutti* with a litany of complaints. He complains that the post–World War II dreams of growing global unity have been shattered by nationalism and "new forms of selfishness" (*FT* 11) and "coopted by the economic and financial sector" (*FT* 12). He complains about the "loss of a sense of history" that leaves young people "shallow, uprooted and distrustful" (*FT* 13) and subject to "new forms of cultural colonization" that exploit their rootlessness as a tool for domination (*FT* 14). He complains about a public discourse built on "hyperbole, extremism and polarization" (*FT* 15); about a "throwaway culture" that fosters indifference to the unborn and the elderly (*FT* 18, cf. FT 30); about persistent injustice fed by "reductive anthropological visions and by a profit-based economic model that does not hesitate to exploit, discard and even kill human beings" (*FT* 22); about the "culture of walls" that grows from fear of the unknown (*FT* 27) and "a xenophobic mentality" toward migrants (*FT* 39); about "digital campaigns of hatred and destruction" that grow from a "loss of contact with concrete reality" (*FT* 43); about "a frenzy of texting" that leads to an emerging new lifestyle in which we "exclude all that we cannot control or know instantly or superficially" (*FT* 49); and about the way that prosperous countries set themselves up as the cultural norm, leading those in less prosperous countries "to look town on one's own cultural identity" (*FT* 51). And this account of "dark clouds over a closed world" is really just an overture to the complaints that persist throughout the encyclical. Complaints about the "trends in our world that hinder the development of universal fraternity" (*FT* 9) recur in almost every chapter of *Fratelli Tutti*, forming the warp through which the weft of Francis's positive suggestions are woven.

Is there any reason to think that all this complaining is not simply the grousing typical of elderly persons who are forced to live in a world that is increasingly alien to them? Is the opening chapter of *Fratelli Tutti* anything more than the papal equivalent of an old man yelling at kids to get off his lawn? This ill accords, of course, with the popular image of Pope Francis as the progressive pope, the jovial pope, the cool-in-a-grandfatherly-way pope. But no one who has actually observed with any care the words and actions of Francis gives much credence to this popular image. One need only read any of his annual Christmas addresses to the members of the Roman Curia—especially the 2014 address in which he outlined fifteen "spiritual ills" in the course of excoriating his listeners—to know that Francis can often act as a holy scold.[1] So should he follow the advice of two psychologists from the Cleveland Clinic to step back, look within, make a game of it, choose the right channel (e.g., don't complain on Facebook), air valid concerns, find the positives, and practice gratitude?[2]

While I certainly hope that Pope Francis does all of these things, I also hope he does not stop complaining. For complaining has a vital role in the life of the church. Yes, complaining can become the unproductive outward sign of an inward brooding over the world's griefs and anxieties in a way that overlooks the world's joys and hopes. Complaint can tear down the social friendship Francis seeks. But it can also build it up, and this in three ways: as fraternal correction, as penitential confession, and as lament.

Universal Fraternity and Fraternal Correction

What is traditionally called "fraternal correction" (*correctione fraterna*), rooted in Jesus's counsel in Matthew 18, is the Christian practice of holding one another accountable for sin. To complain in this sense is not merely to carp but to confront—to lodge a "complaint" as in a legal process, making an accusation and requesting judgment. This is complaint that has as its goal the remedy of some wrong. Thomas Aquinas notes that in seeking the correction of a wrongdoer we can distinguish between viewing an action as harmful to others and viewing that action as harmful to the doer of the

1. Francis, "Presentation."
2. "How to Stop Complaining."

action. Correction in the former sense is an exercise of the virtue of justice and is carried out by one who has public authority to employ coercive power. Correction in the latter sense, however, is an exercise of the virtue of charity, and it is this sort of correction that is involved in fraternal correction.[3] Charity's complaint against wrongdoing is the first step in the process of fraternal correction, a process that seeks the restoration of the wrongdoer, and not just the rectification of the wrong done. As Francis notes toward the end of the encyclical, "true love for an oppressor means seeking way to make him cease his oppression" (FT 241).

In Aquinas's estimation, a prelate has an obligation to engage in both that correction aimed at justice, which is his particular purview, and that correction that grows from charity, which is commanded of all Christians. He writes,

> Even in fraternal correction, which is pertains to all, prelates have a more weighty responsibility, as Augustine says in book one of *The City of God* (ch. 9). For just as someone ought to bestow worldly benefits especially on those over whom one has worldly care, even more so one ought to confer spiritual benefits, such as correction, teaching, and other such things, on those who are entrusted to one's spiritual care.[4]

In his role as prelate, Pope Francis has an obligation in justice to correct Catholics, who are under his jurisdiction, but also has an obligation in charity, which he shares with every Christian, to call to account all who fall into error, regardless of their ecclesiastical allegiance, since charity knows no bounds. If one takes the title of the encyclical—*Fratelli Tutti*—seriously, then fraternal love's "the universal scope . . . [and] openness to every man and woman" (FT 6), which Francis identifies as the focus of the encyclical, has as a correlate the universal scope of fraternal correction. It is for this reason that Francis does not restrict himself to "religious" complaints but addresses the failings of the human family as a whole. He writes, "while respecting the autonomy of political life, [the Church] does not restrict her mission to the private sphere" (FT 276). Charity ought to lead to a kind of catholicity of complaint that grows out of the universal love of God.

---

3. Aquinas, *Summa Theologiae* II–II q. 33 a. 1.
4. Aquinas, *Summa Theologiae* II–II q. 33 a. 3 *ad* 1.

Penitence and Self-Complaint

If complaint is simply a matter of fraternal correction and not penitential confession, then it degenerates into an exercise in finger-pointing. Indeed, Jesus suggests that confession—which we might think of as complaining about oneself—must be prior to correction of others: "You hypocrite, first take the log out of your own eye, and then you will see clearly to take the speck out of your brother's eye" (Matthew 7:5 NRSV; cf. Luke 6:42). But Christian self-complaint seems largely absent from the litany of complaint that constitutes chapter 1 of *Fratelli Tutti*, appearing only briefly in reference to attitudes toward migrants (*FT* 39) and the susceptibility of Catholic media to "destructive forms of fanaticism" that can lead to the abandonment of "all ethical standards and respect for the good name of others" (*FT* 47). One might be tempted to think that this essential prelude to fraternal correction has been skipped over by Francis due to the universal audience of the encyclical.

This is not, however, entirely the case. Though largely absent from the opening chapter, Christian penitential self-complaint does appear in other places. Francis says explicitly, "Let us stop feeling sorry for ourselves and acknowledge our crimes, our apathy, our lies" (*FT* 78). This acknowledgement shows itself in Francis's discussion of the parable of the Good Samaritan that constitutes the encyclical's second chapter. Noting the religious offices held by those who passed by the man beaten on the road, Francis observes:

> [B]elief in God and the worship of God are not enough to ensure that we are actually living in a way pleasing to God. A believer may be untrue to everything that his faith demands of him, and yet think he is close to God and better than others.... Paradoxically, those who claim to be unbelievers can sometimes put God's will into practice better than believers. (*FT* 74)

This acknowledgment also shows itself in Francis's complaint that disunity among Christians makes the church an uncertain sign of the hoped-for unity of the human race: "we recognize with sorrow that the process of globalization still lacks the prophetic and spiritual contribution of unity among Christians" (*FT* 280). It shows itself also in Francis's reference to the *Shoah* where he quotes a prayer he prayed at the Yad Vashem memorial in Jerusalem: "Grant us the grace to be ashamed of what we men have done, to be ashamed of this massive idolatry" (*FT* 247).

One must, of course, note those things that go unconfessed. The fifth chapter mentions in passing "the sexual exploitation of boys and girls" (*FT* 188) but makes no mention of the church's ongoing sexual abuse catastrophe. The sixth chapter denounces "intolerance and lack of respect for indigenous popular cultures" but makes no mention of the role of Catholics in colonial and neocolonial enterprises, such as the "Indian Schools" of Canada, that sought to destroy those cultures. Even in the penitential prayer at Yad Vashem, it is the crimes of humanity as a whole that are confessed, not the specific role played by Christians in fostering anti-Semitism. While one cannot expect every encyclical to say everything, it might not be too much to ask of the litany of complaint with which *Fratelli Tutti* begins to incorporate more Christian self-complaint. Though addressed to the world at large, and not simply to the church, a more clear and consistent admission of the failures of Christians that have led to the presence of "dark clouds over a closed world" might have made the fraternal correction offered to the modern world more effective and more credible.

Lamentation from Within the Painful Gap

Christians ought not complain just about themselves and their brothers and sisters; they ought also to complain about God—or at least complain *to* God. That is to say, they ought to lament, not simply to give voice to sorrow, but to lodge a word of protest with God. As Rebekah Eklund puts it:

> As a protest, lament points to the painful gap between the way things should be and the way they are. As a prayer directed to God, it calls on God to account for the brokenness of the world, and it demands that God listen and respond—set right what is wrong, mend what is broken, bring light to the darkness—just as it is God's essential character to do so.[5]

It is from within the space of this "painful gap" that Christians lament. They lament because of the gap between two convictions: they believe that the world is manifestly not in accord with God's ultimate intentions for creatures and they believe that it is within God's power to remedy this situation. Were one to see the world askew but not believe in God's power to set it right, what would be the point of complaining to God? But because we believe, we complain. We complain because we believe that something is so wrong with the world that only God can set it right, and our holy impatience at God's seeming inaction is an expression of that faith.

This third sort of complaining is even more muted in *Fratelli Tutti* than the complaint of penitence. But this is not because Francis sees no place for lament. In a 2013 homily he remarks, "To lament before God is not a sin."

---

5. Eklund, *Practicing Lament*, 62–63.

Commenting on the stories of Tobit and Sarah in the book of Tobit, he continues, "They are people in extreme situations and they seek a way out. . . . They complain, but they do not blaspheme."[6] Yet we hear little of lament in this encyclical. Perhaps the one moment when Francis seems on the edge of lament is when he expresses puzzlement at the acceptance by Christians, throughout so much of history, of various forms of dehumanizing violence: "I sometimes wonder why, in light of this, it took so long for the Church unequivocally to condemn slavery and various forms of violence" (*FT* 86). Here Francis briefly speaks from within the painful gap between what grace makes possible and what Christians actually have accomplished, asking why God would tolerate God's people being so unfaithful. But he does not remain long within this space of puzzlement; rather he concludes, "Today, with our developed spirituality and theology, we have no excuses" (*FT* 86). This apparent recourse to the notion that Christians of past ages were simply "undeveloped" in their spirituality and theology undercuts the notion that there is something deeply perplexing about Christian complicity in slavery and violence, something that only God could remedy.

The general tendency of the encyclical is not to see the "dark clouds" catalogued in the first chapter as lamentable in the strict sense of that word—i.e., things for which we hold God in some sense responsible, and that we must call upon God to remedy. The overall thrust of the encyclical seems to be that those things that undermine human fraternity are human creations that can be overcome through human effort: "Through sacrifice and patience, [political leaders] can help to create a beautiful polyhedral reality in which everyone has a place" (*FT* 190). Later Francis notes that, for unbelievers, reflection, experience, and dialogue "could prove sufficient to confer a solid and stable universal validity on basic and non-negotiable ethical principles that could serve to prevent further catastrophes." He does immediately add, "As believers, we are convinced that human nature, as the source of ethical principles, was created by God, and that ultimately it is he who gives those principles their solid foundation" (*FT* 214), rooting our natural capacities in the divine creation, but the further comment—"as Christians, we also believe that God grants us his grace to enable us to act as brothers and sisters"—is relegated to a footnote. That for which lament cries out—the gracious coming of God as rescuer—makes an appearance only between the lines of the encyclical.

Again, in part what we see here is the effect of writing an encyclical addressed not just to the faithful, but to all people of good will. It is possible that lament is something so tradition-specific that it really has no place in

---

6. "Pope Says Lamenting."

a document such as *Fratelli Tutti*. After all, as we have seen, Francis rightly sees lament as an expression of faith in God's capacity to heed voices arising from the painful gap between what is and what could and should be, and perhaps absent such faith lament is simply disempowering complaint. Francis writes, "The complaint that 'everything is broken' is answered by the claim that 'it can't be fixed,' or 'what can I do?' This feeds into disillusionment and despair, and hardly encourages a spirit of solidarity and generosity" (*FT* 75). In the context of the encyclical, the voice of lament is muted almost to the point of silence, so as not to engender a sense of hopelessness.

But as Rebekah Eklund notes, "Lament is an instinctive act, a deeply human one."[7] Perhaps even unbelievers lament, though they may be unable or unwilling to name the one to whom they cry out. Perhaps there is a place even in an encyclical addressed to believer and unbeliever alike to give voice to lament, to acknowledge the intractability of those dark clouds that hinder universal fraternity. Just as fraternal correction without penitence can degenerate into finger pointing, so too penitence without lament can degenerate into either performative breast-beating or a secular asceticism of self-repair. Perhaps the task of the church is not only "to accompany life, to sustain hope, to be the sign of unity . . . to build bridges, to break down walls, to sow seeds of reconciliation" (*FT* 276), as Francis rightly says that it is, but also to lament on behalf of the world from within the painful gap between present reality and hopes not yet fulfilled.

The Full Scope of Complaining

The opening chapter of *Fratelli Tutti* paints a dark picture of our world. But it does not do so without purpose. As I said at the outset, the complaints are the warp through which positive recommendations are woven. They are offered not simply as complaints, but as a structure into which solutions can be fit. My lingering question, however, is whether Francis makes adequate use of the full range of complaint.

The vast majority of the complaints fall into the category of fraternal correction: it is part of Francis's debt of charity to his brothers and sisters that he point out their failings and call them to account. More muted, but still present, is the self-complaint of penitence, particularly in those places where Francis acknowledges the failings of religious believers. Nearly absent, however, is the holy complaining of lament, which highlights the incapacity of human beings to address sufficiently all of the dark clouds over our closed world. I have suggested that part of the reason Francis does

---

7. Eklund, *Practicing Lament*, xv.

this is out of a desire that people—particularly those who are not believers—not simply throw up their hands and surrender to the dark clouds. But I have also suggested that lament might be part of what the church owes to the world. To put it slightly differently, only the full scope of complaining can form a warp adequate to bear the weft of what is needed to attain the fraternity and social friendship that the encyclical seeks. Only a voice that laments as well as corrects and repents can speak a word of hope sufficient to the task before us.

Bibliography

Aquinas, Thomas. *Summa Theologiae*. Translated by Thomas Gilby. Torino, Italy: Marietti, 1948.

Eklund, Rebekah. *Practicing Lament*. Eugene, OR: Cascade, 2021.

Francis, Pope. *Fratelli Tutti: On Fraternity and Social Friendship*. Vatican City: Libreria Editrice Vaticana, 2020. http://www.vatican.va/content/francesco/en/encyclicals/documents/papa-francesco_20201003_enciclica-fratelli-tutti.html.

———. "Presentation of the Christmas Greetings to the Roman Curia." Address given in Clementine Hall, Vatican City, December 22, 2014. https://www.vatican.va/content/francesco/en/speeches/2014/december/documents/papa-francesco_20141222_curia-romana.html.

"How to Stop Complaining: Seven Secrets to Being Happier." Cleveland Clinic Health Essentials, August 30, 2018. https://health.clevelandclinic.org/how-to-stop-complaining-7-secrets-to-being-happier/.

"Pope Says Lamenting Suffering Is Form of Prayer." *Catholic News Agency*, June 5, 2013. https://www.catholicnewsagency.com/news/27372/pope-says-lamenting-suffering-is-form-of-prayer.

PART TWO

A Stranger on the Road

5

The Good Samaritan as a Model of Fraternal Solidarity

Stan Chu Ilo

Introduction

IN HIS NOW FAMOUS interview with *La Civiltà Cattolica* in 2013, Pope Francis describes the church as a field hospital where wounds must be treated before anything else can follow.[1] Chapter 2 of *Fratelli Tutti* provides the praxis for how the church can become a field hospital, and the model for the kinds of ethical and practical commitments that Christians and all men and women of good will can embrace in order to heal a wounded and broken world. It is a chapter that offers us a road map of how we can "go and do likewise" (Luke 10:37, NIV) in imitation of the Good Samaritan. In this chapter, Pope Francis also offers some pointers about how we can develop a theological and ethical foundation for social and fraternal solidarity by deconstructing the forms of social hierarchies and exclusionary practices that have led to so much suffering, injustice, poverty, inequity, and indifference in our world today.

In the chapter, Pope Francis shatters the weak narratives of us vs. them, the binaries of in and out groups, and makes a strong affirmation that we all are our brothers' and sisters' keepers: we all belong, we are all related. God, therefore, "encourages us to create a different culture, in which we resolve our conflicts and care for one another" (*FT* 57). Fraternal solidarity

---

1. See Spadaro, "Big Heart," for Pope Francis's full interview, reprinted in English.

is what he consistently describes as social friendship; that is, a love—which he also refers to as social love or universal openness to all—that is capable of transcending borders in every village, hamlet, city, and nation.

I hope in this commentary to provide a brief summary of the teaching of Pope Francis in chapter 2 and conclude with some socioethical principles for how the faithful can live as healers of wounds in the world today; that is, how the mission of the church as a field hospital, particularly in Africa, can be realized following the example of the Good Samaritan.

The Good Samaritan

The Good Samaritan is presented as one who gave his time to the wounded man. He stopped, he approached the man, and he cared for him. When confronted with a man who was suffering and injured, he saw in this man a family member "deserving of his time and attention" (*FT* 63). This basic decision of the Good Samaritan is presented by Pope Francis as the only condition for rebuilding our wounded world (*FT* 67), for restoring broken social bonds in the world, in our nations and across nations, and shows us that "we are all connected; life is a time for interactions" (*FT* 66). The Good Samaritan goes beyond dry-as-dust abstract moralizing (*FT* 68) to embrace a socioethical praxis that is crystallized by love, because, as Pope Francis points out, embracing love leads us to see clearly the road to our common humanity and to discover our shared bonds. The Good Samaritan thus teaches us that "we cannot be indifferent to suffering; we cannot allow anyone to go through life as an outcast. Instead, we should feel indignant, challenged to emerge from our comfortable isolation and to be changed by our contact with human suffering" (*FT* 68).

The fundamental question that strikes me in Francis's rereading of the response of the Good Samaritan is: *What did the Good Samaritan see in this man that the other characters in the story did not see?* This is a key to capturing something that is often lost in our world today: the capacity to see by coming into contact with the reality of others, to step into the other's shoes so as to become his or her traveling companion. Indeed, the inability to see and the insensitivity in the world today to human suffering is similar to the blindness that the Lord condemned in some of his listeners who failed to perceive, to hear, and to be touched (Mark 8:18; Isa 6:9–10). Pope Francis makes a distinction between those who "care for someone who is hurting and those who pass by; those who bend down to help and those who look the other way and hurry off" (*FT* 70).

The Good Samaritan is a model of social friendship, that is, a kind of love that is capable of transcending borders by seeing in the face of a person who is suffering my own face and the face of Jesus. He is someone who transgresses boundaries of otherness and strangeness to bend down, touch the wound of another, and help another not to die. Love without borders, love until it hurts, love that is selfless and sacrificial, is capable of "restoring dignity to the suffering" and of building a new society where there are no more outcasts, invisibles, or rejected. It is only by this display of sacrificial and risky love that we can heal the world and restore dignity to those who are abandoned by the roadside of history, the many who are condemned to die because they are unwanted, unloved, neglected, dehumanized, oppressed, and abused (*FT* 71).

The starting point then for embracing the spirit of the Good Samaritan is to see in the other what God sees in them, or as Pope Francis writes of the Good Samaritan, "to take a closer look" (*FT* 73). This is key in Pope Francis's many writings. He invites us to a new kind of gaze because the inner Word that is incarnate in history can only be encountered when one is able to see the face of God in the wounded face of another. The poor, the wounded, the marginalized, and the vulnerable are the icons of Christ. This "seeing eye" that sees as God sees is the gift of the Spirit. Pope Francis speaks of the Spirit's gift of unity in his homily for Pentecost in 2020. The Spirit helps us to see our commonality rather than our differences:

> Our principle of unity is the Holy Spirit. He reminds us that first of all we are *God's beloved children*; all equal, in this respect, and all different. The Spirit comes to us, in our differences and difficulties, to tell us that we have one Lord—Jesus—and one Father, and that for this reason we are brothers and sisters! . . . The world sees us only as on the right or left, with one ideology or the other; the Spirit sees us as sons and daughters of the Father and brothers and sisters of Jesus. The world sees conservatives and progressives; the Spirit sees children of God. A worldly gaze sees structures to be made more efficient; a spiritual gaze sees brothers and sisters pleading for mercy. The Spirit loves us and knows everyone's place in the grand scheme of things: for him, we are not bits of confetti blown about by the wind, rather we are irreplaceable fragments in his mosaic.[2]

The greatest pain that many people carry today in the world is their nonrecognition. Racism, for instance, wishes to make people of African descent invisible, to deny our humanity, to distort our narratives and exoticize

---

2. Francis, "Homily"; emphasis in original.

our black bodies, and to nail these bodies to the cross. The pope wonders why it took the church so long to denounce slavery (FT 86), but he fails to denounce its continuing impact in this pandemic of racism, which is a cankerworm that continues to eat at the heart of the church and against people of African descent.

For many Black people throughout the world, whether in the *favelas* of Rio de Janeiro or in East London, whether in the slums of Ajegunle in Lagos, Nigeria, or the slums of Kibera, Nairobi, the world and African societies and governments continue to treat them as the underclass, the ones whose shanty houses are often mowed down by developers and whose high deprivation index and other social determinants that affect their health and quality of life are ignored. How many times in major cities in Africa do Christian worshipers pass by the beggars at the entrances of churches on Sunday? In many big Nigerian cities, the main entrances to churches on Sundays are filled with beggars, who might receive some alms from worshipers, but who are also often removed from the scene. They are seen as a nuisance by some, condemned as misfits by others, and judged as "useless" by a few.

The question emerges strongly: What do you see when you pass by these beggars on your way to worship God like the priest and the Levite (FT 74)? It is obvious that religious faith and external displays of religiosity and generous donation cannot be separated by our failing to see in these brothers and sisters the face of Christ. We must strongly denounce the lack of prophetic confrontation of issues of social justice on our continent of Africa today by the church that has been complicit in genocides, and by church leaders who fail to transcend boundaries of ethnicity and clannish interests in the exercise of their authority. Because the churches in Africa neglect to speak for the poor, and to embody and mediate their narratives through the entire gamut of the church's life, teaching, and institutional culture, they are failing to heal the wounds in the body of Christ, some of which we have brought on people through our rigid pastoral policies and the plague of clerical sexual abuse. The church in Africa cannot accept donations from wealthy church members and government officials who are ignoring the suffering and pains of God's people. In many cases, many of our church members in big cities in Africa have maids and domestic servants who come to live with them from the rural areas but who are not given fair wages, who are treated as slaves, and whose food and general well-being are different from that of the children of their masters and mistresses. In some instances, these mainly female domestic servants (or maids) are also sexually abused.

Through the parable of the Good Samaritan, Jesus calls forth the best of our humanity and encourages us, as Pope Francis teaches, to persevere in love, to go the extra mile for the sake of those who are abandoned by the roadside of life, and to help give dignity to those who are suffering and thus build a better society. The mission of fraternal solidarity begins with each and every one of us, beginning from where you are and paying attention to particular cases and expanding from your own local setting to reaching out to others (*FT* 78). Indeed, each of us is truly a person when we are fully accepted and supported by our communities, especially in those moments when we are down and out. Indeed, for the poor and the wounded of this world, the love of good and committed people and the solidarity we show them are the means through which God comes to them. The only way we can preach God's love to the poor of this world is to make God's love concrete in their lives and social context through solidarity, charity, and fighting for a more just and equitable world.

The future of humanity lies in global solidarity and social friendship. We are all tied together in a common destiny. If the devastating impact of climate change has not succeeded in teaching humanity this lesson that we have a common home and a common destiny, COVID hopefully will make it clearer to us that we are all in this together. Sickness and viruses respect no border lines, nor do they accommodate themselves to our racial, gender, religious, and national biases. In a shared world where we have been given a common home by God, the Good Samaritan teaches us the lesson of transnational identity, which transcends all prejudices (*FT* 85). It invites a shift of our center of meaning, a change in worldview from seeing our diversity as a deficit, to seeing that in this common journey that we make, we are all carrying wounds. Sometimes we are the ones who need a neighbor because we are injured; sometimes we are the one to whom a wounded person is crying out for help on the roadside of life.

The social praxis of the Good Samaritan ideal can only be understood and articulated as an interruptive theology of reversal (*FT* 101), a critical theology that interrogates social practices and disrupts the weak and shifting social norms and cultural habits of ingrained implicit biases and structural violence. These are some of the social evils that prevent a deep and closer encounter with the other at the deepest levels of our humanity, where we experience vulnerability and hunger for the kinds of relationships that can restore our humanity, bandage our wounds, and give us hope. The pope invites us through his teaching in this chapter to develop the praxis of Christian humanism—healing wounds in the spirit of care and closeness like the Good Samaritan (*FT* 79)—in which our faith moves us to embrace the truth that in Christ, we all have become members of the family of God (*FT* 85–86).

We all need to commit ourselves to bending down and touching the wounds of others and doing all that we can to create a healthier and more prosperous and equitable world for everyone. When any woman's rights are violated anywhere in the world, my own humanity is violated; when poverty interferes with the possibility that every little child in the world will live beyond five years, my own life is diminished. Human security, global health, food security, international security and global peace, and the prosperity and protection of our common home should become the responsibility of everyone. Every local problem should become a global problem, and every global problem has ramifications for every part of the world.

Traveling Together in Solidarity With One Another

Pope Francis is proposing that the beginning of mission is truly an encounter with a person, in this case the Lord Jesus, who is also encountered in the poor and the wounded (*FT* 85). A missionary church is more credible when she speaks more of Christ than of herself, when she preaches from the margins and peripheries rather than from the center of power and privilege. So, mission is presented in *Fratelli Tutti* as becoming a Good Samaritan because this way of discipleship challenges us to "expand our frontiers" and "gives a universal dimension to our call to love" (*FT* 84). It invites the faithful to "identify with others without worrying about where they were born or come from." It brings the love of Jesus to all ends of the earth and also brings the faithful into contact with Jesus in our solidarity with our brothers and sisters, especially those who are excluded and abandoned and those who are starving from lack of love and desire to meet Jesus in the faithful.

We can translate the parable of the Good Samaritan into a missional praxis. First, by seeing in each person the face of Christ; second, by designing this mission praxis through daily practices that translate every aspect of the church's mission and every act of Christian witnessing into practical choices for "universal love"; and third, by developing the practices and priorities that bring us closer to the concrete experiences of people's daily lives so that the church and Christians can become the hands that heal the wounds of people and of the world.

In order for this missional praxis to be realized, it is important that the church moves away from fixed notions of history and eschatology and how we fit others into this plan, vision, structure, etc. Mission opens our human gaze wider so that we can witness to God's universal love (*FT* 68, 85) and to the truth of the Gospel that we are created for a fulfillment that can only be found in love. This is important for rethinking humanitarian intervention and the work of Christian charity. The fixed notions and plans of international development agencies and Christian NGOs have failed Africans because they are often built on fixed notions of history and fixed models of development designed elsewhere and rigidly applied to Africa.

Given the asymmetries of power, these imposed structures and plans end up hurting Africans who accept them in an unquestioning way because of this power differential. The mission of global solidarity must be built on the assets of the people, including the poor, who are the best experts on how to become agents of their own destiny. It must begin by seeing beyond the random and disrespectful display of images of African children, refugees, and the suffering poor on the global screen to the assets of local churches and rural women waiting to be discovered, developed, and applied in the construction of a new future for Africa.

Finally, mission brings transformation, healing, new life, new hope, and a new experience of God's love in all those whom we encounter on this journey. It is to find a home in the home of others and to indwell with one another and in the world, making possible human and cosmic flourishing and the irruption of the signs of the reign of God. The images of the inn (the church as a place of healing), the animal (the means through which the Good Samaritan brought the wounded man to the inn), the interruption of the journey, and stepping down to be with the man are all examples of the attitudes required for a renewal of the church's mission and of Christian witnessing to the poor of this world.

Some people might falsely think that helping people requires having so much or doing so much, but it only requires beginning where you are and using the gifts and resources available to you. Sometimes what people who are suffering need from us is to be present to them: to listen to them, to be with them, and to accompany them. This is exactly what the Good Samaritan did. But he even did more—he did not "cut and run." In many instances, we give people alms, and that assuages our consciences because we think that we have helped them, but there is no follow-up. Many international Christian charities begin projects that are often abandoned halfway through. Fraternal solidarity calls on us to stay the course with the poor, to return again and again to them to make sure that we are not simply interventionists, but partners and cotravelers with the poor, who walk with them until they are able to stand on their own and assume full agency for their lives.

Conclusion

The Good Samaritan is employed by Pope Francis in *Fratelli Tutti* to provide a powerful symbol for a structural analysis of structural violence and a sociopraxis for implementing a theory of change that reverses the globalization of indifference through a globalization of solidarity. In Pope Francis's ecclesiology, the emphasis is to reflect on where the church is, rather than who she is. It is in the location of the church and her members—where two or more are gathered in the name of the Lord and doing what Jesus spent his time on earth doing—that we can find the church's true identity. Interestingly, it is in such obscure locations and field hospitals in the face of the COVID pandemic that the light of Christ shines the brightest in the midst of human suffering today (*FT* 56).

The message of the Good Samaritan speaks to the world, but for us Africans its imagery cannot be starker in opening our eyes to the many brothers and sisters in Africa who are wounded and who have been abandoned and condemned to die. Is it enough to bandage their wounds? Is it enough to apply band-aids to help the suffering, the starving, and the millions of our African brothers and sisters whose hopes and dreams are being dashed everyday by global injustice, racism, neoliberal capitalism, and failed and failing African leadership in both church and state? How can theology and the church help to protect and prevent Blacks from being wounded rather than coming in to stop the bleeding and failing many others whose wounds become fatal? How can the church be an agent of justice in the world rather than a provider of temporary solutions through Christian charities? How can we evolve from providing food banks in parishes and writing nice pastoral or anti-racism statements in reaction to occasional racial flare-ups to actually exercising courage to deal with some of the issues pointed out in this chapter? It is important to challenge the systems, structures, and institutions that bring so much suffering to people and to balance our commitment to charity and healing of the wounded with a prophetic engagement on social justice issues, policy intervention, and systemic changes, both in church teaching and in our politics and leadership. It is important to identify who are the robbers whose racist actions and violence have robbed us of our dignity, and whose are the invisible hands who run this racist system locally and globally that has kept Blacks permanently in the choke hold of history.

Ultimately, Pope Francis is calling for a conversion so that we can see that the person who is sometimes regarded as an outsider (the Samaritan), or a misfit, or a person who does not belong may be the one whom God is sending to help us. Every human suffering that we face today in the world stems from the exercise of power by some to benefit a few and hurt others. Power is always tied to the protection and preservation of interests, but in that fight for power it pays to think of those who suffer and what happens to those who are wounded and damaged in the unending fight for power and for the interests of certain groups and individuals that have created an unjust and broken world.

Bibliography

Francis, Pope. *Fratelli Tutti: On Fraternity and Social Friendship.* Vatican City: Libreria Editrice Vaticana, 2020. https://www.vatican.va/content/francesco/en/encyclicals/documents/papa-francesco_20201003_enciclica-fratelli-tutti.html.

———. "Homily of Holiness Pope Francis—Solemnity of Pentecost." Homily delivered at the Vatican Basilica, Rome, May 31, 2020. http://www.vatican.va/content/francesco/en/homilies/2020/documents/papa-francesco_20200531_omelia-pentecoste.html.

Spadaro, Antonio. "A Big Heart Open to God: An Interview with Pope Francis." *America*, September 30, 2013. https://www.americamagazine.org/faith/2013/09/30/big-heart-open-god-interview-pope-francis.

6

The Use of Luke 10:25–37 in *Fratelli Tutti*

MA. MARILOU S. IBITA

LUKE 10:25–37, COMMONLY REFERRED to as the Parable of the Good Samaritan, is central to Pope Francis's encyclical *Fratelli Tutti*. It dominates chapter 2, entitled "A Stranger on the Road." This chapter is an important biblical grounding for the discussion of what the pope calls "fraternity and social friendship." He has set the stage for the need to reflect on this parable in the present global context. The encyclical's introduction offers a glimpse and overview of an ideal world without borders and lived in fraternity, as suggested by the words and experience of Saint Francis of Assisi and by Pope Francis's own reflections and conversations with various individuals and groups globally (*FT* 3–6). The backdrop for the encyclical's reflection on Luke 10:25–37 is chapter 1, entitled "Dark Clouds Over a Closed World," which analyzes the problems of the present world, made worse in the COVID-19 era (*FT* 9–55). Pope Francis cites several biblical passages in support of the need for fraternity and social friendship but focuses especially on the uniquely Lukan and well-known parable at Luke 10:25–37. The ten comments below offer some initial observations about its use in *FT*, how it relates to recent biblical scholarship, and some critical comments for further study, reflection, action, and prayer. I posit that the use and interpretation of this popular story, populated in Jesus's storytelling by male actors with predominantly male interpretative perspectives, needs to include a gender lens so as to truly foster the aims of the encyclical in global contexts, particularly in Asia and the Philippines.

1. *Translation: Content or Process?* The English translation of *FT* cites the New Revised Standard Version of Luke 10:25–37 (*FT* 56), which renders Jesus's questions to the lawyer as, "What is written in the law? *What* do you read there?" This translation yields to an interpretation of 10:26b (πῶς ἀναγινώσκεις) that is focused on the content of the Law. The same is true in the German and the Spanish versions of *FT*. Other translations, however, including the NIV and the NABRE, highlight the interpretative process with the translation "*How* do you read it?" This translation is found in the French, Italian, Dutch, Polish, and Portuguese versions of *FT*. This point is important in view of the richer and more proactive impact of maintaining a process orientation in promoting fraternity and social friendship. I will return to this point at the end of this reflection.

2. *The Larger Literary Context of the Bible and of Luke.* To contextualize the parable, the Pope speaks of an "age-old problem" (*FT* 57) going back to Gen 4:1–16; in particular, the question, "Am I my brother's keeper?" *FT* sets forth the conversation between Jesus and the lawyer but does not discuss the immediate and larger literary context of Luke, which would have emphasized *FT*'s objective of treating strangers on the road properly. Jesus speaks of the peril on the road and how to respond to it while he himself is traveling to Jerusalem. Luke's longer journey narrative (9:51—19:28), as compared to Mark's narrative (10:1—11:1) and Matthew's (19:1—21:1), emphasizes the significance of this parable and the call for the reader to identify with the characters in deciding how to be a neighbor on the road and on the move.[1]

3. *Supporting Biblical Citations.* As a preliminary discussion about dealing with foreigners, *FT* citations to the Torah on the basic understanding that "neighbor" in the command to "love your neighbor as yourself" referred to one's fellow citizen, not to foreigners (Lev 19:18; *FT* 59), and to the core story of the Israelites being foreigners who were later enslaved in Egypt (Exod 22:21; 23:9; Lev 19:33–34; Deut 24:21–22; *FT* 61). *FT* also discusses the broader perspective of a common humanity, noting the experiences of the Israelites as exiled people (Job 31:15 in *FT* 58; Tob 4:15 and Sir 18:13 in *FT* 59). The New Testament citations in *FT* 61 also lay down the basis for a common humanity, the call for "fraternal love" (Gal 5:14; 1 John 2:10–11; 1 John 3:14; 1 John 4:20), and the broader understanding found in 1 Thess 3:12 and 3 John 5. As in other ecclesial documents, these citations serve as warrants of

---

1. See Barreto, "Gospel on the Move."

the claims being made, almost as proof texts. The longer treatment of Luke 10:25–37 is unique, resulting in a deeper characterization of the actors and a stronger impact on today's readers.

4. *Methods of Biblical Interpretation. Laudato Si'* was written in the spirit of ecumenical dialogue with Patriarch Bartholomew (*FT* 5). *FT* was written in the context of interreligious dialogue with the Grand Imam Ahmad Al-Tayyeb (*FT* 5, 29, 136, 192, 285). The interreligious dialogical process is also found in the encyclical's biblical reflections themselves through the inclusion of historical insights from Rabbi Hillel's commentary on Jewish tradition (*FT* 59, 60). This process echoes the encouragement to refer to the Jewish tradition found in the 1993 Pontifical Biblical Commission document, "Interpretation of the Bible in the Church."[2] Amy-Jill Levine's explanation of the parable from a Jewish perspective, highlighting how the enmity between the Jews and Samaritans impacts the story because it relates to accepting help from an enemy, will help present-day readers understand it better (see also *FT* 80–83).[3]

In *FT*, the most prominent method of interpreting the parable is narrative criticism[4] by means of characterizing the actors, seen in *FT* 56–82. *FT* also makes intertextual linkages to the story of the Samaritan woman in John 4 (*FT* 82), and to Matt 25; Rom 12:15; and Isa 58:7 on the plea of the stranger (*FT* 84–86). This method is appropriate for Asia and the Philippines since storytelling and characterization are not alien in our context.[5]

The Samaritan characterization and the exhortation to be in solidarity with the assaulted man exemplify a contextual liberationist approach.[6] The whole of *FT* 70 brings a crucial "moment of truth" in front of suffering: "Will we bend down to touch and heal the wounds of others? Will we bend down and help another to get up? This is today's challenge, and we should not be afraid to face it" (*FT* 70). Thus, despite the heavy burden of the liberationist interpretation, the parable provides no alternative for someone wanting to follow Jesus (*FT*

---

2. Pontifical Biblical Commission, "Interpretation," section I.C.2.

3. Levine, *Short Stories*, 77–115.

4. For a description of narrative criticism, see Pontifical Biblical Commission, "Interpretation," section I.B.2.

5. See, generally, John Paul II, *Ecclesia in Asia*; and Ibita, "Fostering Narrative."

6. For a description of this approach, see Pontifical Biblical Commission, "Interpretation," section E.1.

71). It is, however, crucial to ensure that liberationist interpretations do not foster anti-Judaism or anti-Jewish caricatures and hatred.[7]

5. *Characterization and Character Identification in Luke 10:25–37.* Characterization focuses on what the main actors themselves say and do as well as what the narrator and other actors say or do to, for, or against them in the story.[8] This parable, in the words related by the Samaritan, is action-packed. The overview of the story, beginning with *FT* 63 and continuing with the section subtitled "The Characters of the Story" before *FT* 72 clearly indicate the pope's characterization of the actors. Characterization confronts readers with the extent to which they identify with each of the actors. This is clearly the pope's intention in *FT* 64 as he asks his readers directly: "Which of these persons do you identify with? This question, blunt as it is, is direct and incisive. Which of these characters do you resemble?" Pope Francis's characterization of the actors in the narrative moves immediately to his readers' actions and reactions.

6. *The "Good" Samaritan.* *FT* 63 summarizes the story, but the pope immediately begins focusing on the Samaritan's actions, particularly on the *time and attention* given to the victim. In *FT* 67 he writes, "The parable eloquently presents the basic decision we need to make to rebuild our wounded world. In the face of so much pain and suffering, our only course is to imitate the Good Samaritan," and of the need to "identify with the vulnerable." He asks that we not "be indifferent to suffering" (*FT* 68), and in the same paragraph he exhorts us to "feel indignant, challenged to emerge from our comfortable isolation and to be changed by our contact with human suffering." This response is not in Luke's parable, but it is a necessary critical answer to violence in a world beset by apathy (*FT* 14, 78, 237). In *FT* 79 he states the need to be responsible for the wounded and for the needs of "every man and woman, young and old" with the fraternal spirit of the Samaritan.

The pope speaks of the "Good Samaritan" for the first time in *FT* 62 and then uses this appellation many other times (*FT* 66, 67, 69, 71, 77, 79, and 80; outside chapter 2, *FT* 101 and 165). It is important to note that the Gospel speaks only of a "Samaritan." The description "good" summarizes his actions but is not found in the text. The epithet "Good Samaritan" has, of course, become well-known outside the Lukan and biblical contexts; it has been used in the names of hospitals and in other contexts, including in the name of a law protecting those

---

7. See Levine, *Short Stories*, 109–11.
8. See Rhoads, "Narrative Criticism," 417.

who help people who have been in accidents from legal liability.[9] However, interpretations sensitive to issues of race and ethnicity raise the problem of how the "Good" Samaritan extols him to the exclusion of other Samaritans and as a perpetuation of the Judeans' assertion of their own identity against the Samaritan "other."[10] As Rindge warns: "To call the Samaritan in the story 'good' (a word never used in the text) is to participate in a racist assumption that being 'good' is an unusual and noteworthy achievement for Samaritans."[11] Thus, while the pope deals with the ethnic conflict between the biblical Jews and the Samaritans (*FT* 80–83), it is important to be aware of this possible consequence of his use of the word. In the context of Asia, the othering of peoples like the Rohingya reminds us of the need to be critical of the way we identify people without consideration of their right to self-determination, self-identification, and safety.[12] Racially related hate crimes present a global challenge, one that Asians and people of mixed Asian descent experience in the West but have also suffered at the hands of fellow Asians within Asia and elsewhere.

7. *The Bystanders.* Not surprisingly, these characters receive most of the pope's critique. In *FT* 65, the pope discusses how both those who do harm and the bystanders turn their backs on suffering. For him, this situation makes the parable an ever-new summons to pursue the common good (*FT* 66). In *FT* 69, the pope writes that the "decision to include or exclude those lying wounded along the roadside can serve as a criterion for judging every economic, political, social, and religious project. Each day we have to decide whether to be Good Samaritans or indifferent bystanders." The strongest critique of these characters is at *FT* 73–74, where the pope recognizes their possible excuses, but, in *FT* 74, underscores that "the guarantee of an authentic openness to God . . . is a way of practicing the faith that helps open our hearts to our brothers and sisters," and is more than just being "religious."

8. *The Robbers.* In *FT* 72 Pope Francis notes that "Jesus chose to start when the robbery has already taken place, lest we dwell on the crime itself or the thieves who committed it. . . . The real question is this: will we abandon the injured man and run to take refuge from the violence, or will we pursue the thieves?" Chapter 1 is a critique of a world that gives rise to assaults on human person, and the rest of *FT* responds to

---

9. Levine, *Short Stories*, 78, 104.
10. On this, see Keddie, "Who Is My Neighbor?"
11. Rindge, "Good Samaritan."
12. See, generally, Sarmin, "Ongoing Persecution."

the needs he identifies, particularly where he observes critically that human rights are insufficiently universal (*FT* 22–24, 111). In the context of Asia, neglecting to pursue the robbers and not getting to the bottom of *why there are robbers and the nature of the system that produced and condones the robbers*, will result in more assaults. This is part of the reason why this story of assault is "constantly retold" (see subtitle before *FT* 69). We cannot just keep tending to the assaulted—we need to stop the assaults and the system that pushes people to commit them (see *FT* 75). Biblical and theological interpretation in Asia and the Philippines needs to also include the developments of postcolonial and empire studies to explore how the early Jesus followers navigated the ethic of critical distancing and resistance against the dire effects of Roman colonization that contributed to violence.[13] This challenge and the call for restorative justice is prevalent in Asia and in the Philippines, where populist forms of government are on the rise.

9. *The Assaulted.* In *FT* 63 and 65, Pope Francis describes the story told by Jesus as being about an "assaulted" man. He is the last to be described in the story as the pope relates it in *FT* even if the story revolves around him. In *FT* 76, the pope connects him to the readers of *FT* who identify with him for one reason or another, whether because of institutional neglect, a lack of resources, the consequences of globalization, the visual domestication of their plight on TV, and the use of language that talks about them with "euphemisms and with apparent tolerance." *FT* 84–85 brings into the discussion a related passage on being strangers within the ambit of God's mercy because Jesus identifies with them, as seen in Matt 25:35, 40, and 45. Levine raises a challenging question from the assaulted man's viewpoint, both for biblical times and today: Can we accept help from an enemy?[14] A multifocal perspective that includes both the victim and the Samaritan is needed in interpreting the text.[15]

10. *Obscured Characters.* Pope Francis intended that *FT* would be inclusive. He writes at *FT* 5 that "I have also incorporated, along with my own thoughts, a number of letters, documents and considerations that I have received from many individuals and groups throughout the world." In *FT* 61, he subscribes "to dialogue among all people of good will." Yet for an encyclical that has as its aim the fostering of

---

13. See, for example, Sugirtharajah, *Postcolonial Biblical Reader*; Melanchton, "Toward Mapping"; Ibita, "Ama Namin."

14. See Levine, *Short Stories*, 114–15.

15. See, generally, Moe, "Cross-Cultural and Liberative Hermeneutics."

"fraternity" (even this word reflects male bias) and social friendship, it is stark that the whole of *FT*, including chapter 2, has an almost totally male voice and male perspective. No female voice is explicitly heard in *FT* 286 when the pope says that he found inspiration from "others of our brothers *and sisters* who are not Catholics: Martin Luther King, Desmond Tutu, Mahatma Gandhi, and many more . . . [and also] Blessed Charles de Foucauld" (emphasis added). Moreover, not a single footnote refers to a woman or group of women or their works or writings. The male perspective also predominates in the parable of the Good Samaritan, in which not one character is a woman unless one includes the possibility that the innkeeper (*FT* 56, 78) is a woman or that a male innkeeper employs/asks a female member of the inn to take care of the assaulted man.[16]

Out of the more than 42,900 words (including footnotes) in the English translation of *FT*, women are linguistically present only seventy-five times. This observation obscures women and the impact of real women in Asia, along with the people who are LGBTQI+, who often suffer violence in Asia. I want to highlight the linguistic presence of women in this encyclical since they are not always explicitly mentioned in church documents. Pope Francis wrote that the purpose of the encyclical is to consider the "universal scope" of fraternal love and "its openness to every man and woman" (*FT* 6), to care for "the needs of every man and woman" (*FT* 79), and to make us aware that "God loves every man and woman with infinite love," thereby conferring "infinite dignity upon all humanity" (*FT* 85; cf. *FT* 277). The linguistic presence of women is also found in:

a. the use of the plural "men and women" having a "universal aspiration to fraternity" (*FT* 8);
b. warning about criminality against young men and women (*FT* 24);
c. "men and women working to provide essential services and public safety" (*FT* 54);
d. the role of "men and women" in rebuilding communities (*FT* 67);
e. the need to go beyond the abstract "all men and women are equal" (*FT* 104);
f. "to help ensure a dignified life for all the men and women of East and West" (*FT* 136);

---

16. See Rosenfeld, "Innkeeping," 138–39, 143–45.

g. the recognition of the shared goals of men and women that transcend their differences (*FT* 157);
h. the recognition of men and women politicians, especially the courageous ones (*FT* 193, 194);
i. a call for men and women to exhibit dialogic realism (*FT* 221) and to be peacekeepers (*FT* 225);
j. a warning concerning how they can both lose their way (*FT* 274);
k. their presence in other religions (*FT* 277); and
l. how they can both be manipulated toward violence (*FT* 285).

The pope also uses "his or her" as a pronoun (*FT* 8, 22, 24, 111, 118, 121, 123, 125, 143, 152, 162, 186, 187, 191, 193, 201, and 221). "Brother[s] and sister[s]" is used in *FT* 2, 3, 5, 8, 11, 31, 40, 61, 62, 69, 74, 85, 86, 96, 97, 125, 128, 165, 180, 189, 194, 233, 235, 243, 254, 274, 278, 279, 285, 286, and 287 in the main text and 203 in the footnote. In chapter 2, the Samaritan woman's voice is heard incompletely (*FT* 83; John 4:9) and her witness is silenced at the end of the story (John 4:1–42). A feminine presence is recognized in references to the church using female pronouns (*FT* 276, 278) and finally, another female presence is supplied by Mary (*FT* 278).

Nevertheless, the binary gendering of language cannot fully represent people of goodwill with other genders. This observation shows the need for representation that is vital in fostering human kinship (instead of "fraternity") and social friendship. Violence among and between peoples, particularly directed at the marginalized genders of women and LGBTQI+ happens, especially in Asia and in the Philippines, when they are diminished by not being acknowledged in real life and obscured in language (as in Matt 14:21). Thus, the question of HOW one *reads* and HOW one *writes* (see comment 1 above) and, therefore, HOW one *relates* to and *responds* to the needs of those who are acknowledged or not is vital in achieving the goals of the encyclical. It will do well for the church and Pope Francis himself to heed his point in *FT* 23.

In general, Pope Francis recognizes that in our own personal, communal, and global histories, all possible characters are within us at some point in time (*FT* 69). Yet the need to recognize the marginalized and victimized must be at the forefront of theology and spirituality, as his words in *FT* 86 articulate: "I sometimes wonder why, in light of this, it took so long for the Church unequivocally to condemn slavery and various forms of violence. Today, with our developed spirituality and theology, we have no excuses" (*FT* 86). Following from this, I think that a developed spirituality and theology need to work on what must be changed in politics, the economy, and even in the Christian and Catholic churches, for these are venues where the teachings of Jesus need to be embodied, too, especially in and beyond the COVID-19 era.

Bibliography

Barreto, Eric D. "A Gospel on the Move: Practice, Proclamation, and Place in Luke-Acts." *Interpretation* 72:2 (2018) 175–87.

Francis, Pope. *Fratelli Tutti: On Fraternity and Social Friendship*. Vatican City: Libreria Editrice Vaticana, 2020. http://www.vatican.va/content/francesco/en/encyclicals/documents/papa-francesco_20201003_enciclica-fratelli-tutti.html.

Ibita, Ma. Marilou S. "'Ama Namin (Our Father) . . .': The Ritual, Power, and Politics of a Prayer in the Contemporary Philippine Setting." In *The Critic in the World: Biblical Criticism and Global Realities: Essays in Honor of Fernando F. Segovia*, edited by Amy Lindemann Allen, et al. Atlanta: Society of Biblical Literature, forthcoming.

———. "Fostering Narrative Approaches to Scripture in Asia: The Primary Task of Explicit Recognition." *East Asia Pastoral Review* 46 (2009) 124–41.

John Paul II, Pope Saint. *Ecclesia in Asia*. Vatican City: Libreria Editrice Vaticana, 1999. http://www.vatican.va/content/john-paul-ii/en/apost_exhortations/documents/hf_jp- ii_exh_06111999_ecclesia-in-asia.html.

Keddie, G. Anthony. "'Who Is My Neighbor?' Ethnic Boundaries and the Samaritan Other in Luke 10:25–37." *Biblical Interpretation* 28:2 (2020) 246–71.

Levine, Amy-Jill. *Short Stories by Jesus: The Enigmatic Parables of a Controversial Rabbi*. New York: HarperOne, 2014.

Melanchton, Monica Jyotsna. "Toward Mapping Feminist Biblical Interpretations in Asia." In *Feminist Biblical Studies in the Twentieth Century: Scholarship and Movement*, edited by Elisabeth Schüssler Fiorenza, 105–19. The Bible and Women 9.1. Atlanta: Society of Biblical Literature, 2014.

Moe, David Thang. "A Cross-Cultural and Liberative Hermeneutics of Luke 10:25–37 in Asian and Asian-American Perspective: Reading One Text through the Two Lenses." *Expository Times* 130:10 (2019) 439–49.

Pontifical Biblical Commission. "The Interpretation of the Bible in the Church." *Origins* 23:29 (1994) 497–524.

Rhoads, David. "Narrative Criticism and the Gospel of Mark." *Journal of the American Academy of Religion* 50:3 (1982) 411–34.

Rindge, Matthew S. "The Good Samaritan (Luke 10:25-37)." Bible Odyssey, n.d. https://www.bibleodyssey.org/passages/main-articles/the-good-samaritan-luke-1025-37/.

Rosenfeld, Ben-Zion. "Innkeeping in Jewish Society in Roman Palestine." *Journal of the Economic and Social History of the Orient* 41:2 (1998) 133–58.

Sarmin, Arifa. "Ongoing Persecution of the Rohingya: A History of Periodic Ethnic Cleansings and Genocides." *Intellectual Discourse* 28:2 (2020) 675–96.

Sugirtharajah, R. S., ed. *The Postcolonial Biblical Reader*. Malden, MA: Blackwell, 2006.

7

Building Hope from a Fallen Humanity: A Latin American Theological Perspective

Cesar Kuzma[1]

Introduction

THE SECOND CHAPTER OF Pope Francis's encyclical *Fratelli Tutti* draws our attention to a stranger who has fallen along the way. Its proposal invites us to fraternity and social friendship, which, in the midst of the COVID-19 crisis, makes us understand other realities and other pandemics; this, in turn, demands an awareness of history and a better perception of our context. The text of this second chapter forces us to look at those around us, many of whom are victims of the social system and social structure who are thrown to the outskirts, the margins.

Thus, spurred by this chapter of the encyclical, we intend to propose a critical-dialectical reflection, dividing our text into two parts: initially, we will provide a contextualization of the chapter, seeking to describe the specificity of its approach. Then, we will point out how the issues identified in the encyclical play out in our society, especially in Latin America, with the intention of looking at these problems as challenges, as observed and analyzed from a Latin American theological perspective, with an emphasis on liberation. Our goal is to critically receive the content of the text of *Fratelli Tutti* with the awareness that many aspects of the problems raised are found in our surroundings and the understanding that these problems challenge

1. Translated by Cristina Silva.

us in the search for new paths and directions at the theological, social, and ecclesial levels.

Contextualization and Approaching this Chapter

The reflections presented in the second chapter of *Fratelli Tutti* cannot be seen in isolation. These reflections relate to the themes of the first chapter, which deals with the realities of our society, the many existing challenges, and the various situations that have become even more serious due to COVID-19. The pandemic "exposed our vulnerability and uncovered those false and superfluous certainties around which we constructed our daily schedules, our projects, our habits and priorities" (*FT* 32). In the face of this fact, the text of the encyclical draws attention to our role and responsibility and invites us to walk in hope (*FT* 55), in a sensitive and solidary way toward all those who suffer, especially the poor, so that we can be a support of hope for them, since many of them no longer live in sustainable conditions and cannot wait any longer. It is from this context that Francis leads us to look at the stranger who has fallen, helping us perceive so many others who have fallen around us and who need our care. The text of this second chapter demands an attitude from us that lead to actions allowing us to see the faces of the ones who suffer, draw close to them, recognize their disfigured humanity, and call them to a new life.

This second chapter, written and presented in a profound way and with an engaging mystique, is based on the parable of the Good Samaritan (Luke 10:25–37). The chapter serves as a theological foundation for the later chapters, which contain an invitation to openness and the development of new attitudes, which, attentive to people's many weaknesses, makes the people of God willing to build a new world, a new society in fraternal spaces. The text's intention is not simply to adopt an attitude that does good deeds, as if caring for those who have fallen were merely a social, moral, and/or religious obligation. Of course, this is important action and because it is urgent in our context, it must be done. The proposal narrated in the parable and the presentation of the parable in *Fratelli Tutti* point to something greater, however, which is the cause of the kingdom of God: a kingdom that makes itself happen in the practice of justice, love, and the exercise of gratuitousness, in the zeal for life and in developing a new space for relationships, a space for everyone, a common home. This is a kingdom that is not given to us ready made but to which we are invited and called to build.

By choosing the narrative of the parable of the Good Samaritan, the pope brings to the discussion a reality from Jesus's time that can be inserted into present-day history because the perspective of the parable, the content that is expressed in this type of discourse, allows him to do this. The story was narrated by Jesus in order to confront a reality of his time that related to exclusivist social and religious practices. (Jesus addresses the same issue in other parables.) The story is disconcerting because what is normal and usual makes room for what is unusual, something that deconstructs and tramples on our expectations and plans,[2] offering another path, another point of view. Jesus describes a Samaritan who pities the man by the side of the road and has compassion and thus approaches and attends to him, while the religious men (a priest and a Levite) choose to avoid this path. "The parable eloquently presents the basic decision we need to make in order to rebuild our wounded world" (FT 67). We can say that this narrative challenges us ecclesially and theologically, but it also leads us to assume an ethical stance in front of the world. As we have already pointed out above, this involves not only fulfilling a moral and social requirement by maintaining a good attitude, but, rather, an action that results from an exercise of love, in gratuitousness and mercy, an action that leads us to the horizon of the kingdom, in which the world will, in fact, become new. This parable allows us to put ourselves in the shoes of each of its characters: "All of us have inside of ourselves something of the wounded man, something of the robber, something of the passers-by, and something of the Good Samaritan" (FT 69). There are many situations that produce victims, as well as many that cause us to look away from those who are suffering. These situations are constantly repeated in history (FT 71) says Francis, and the call to act like the Samaritan is a challenge that confronts our humanity—those who have fallen victim to social and political indifference are like us; they are our brothers and sisters and our humanity calls us to leave our social structures and our comfortable spaces to go and meet those who are fragile and perishing at the side of the road. The Samaritan gave the fallen man his time; he left everything to attend to a stranger, a human being, who had fallen. He humbled himself, approached, felt compassion, and took care of the man. He gave him his time, which saved his life (FT 63).

If Jesus, in confronting this narrative in the context of his time, used it to criticize exclusivist attitudes and structures that were obstacles to the kingdom of God, Francis today presents this parable to us as a way of questioning our context, which is also marked by divisions, exclusions, and a structural logic that does not favor the encounter and attention to weakness. Even though this parable is narrated in the historical context of Jesus, its message is not foreign to our time, but "suggests that what is being related

---

2. Marguerat, "Linguagem das Parábolas," 329.

includes a constitutive *relationship with what is mine today*, here and now."³ The message therefore has an appeal that makes us look beyond the here and now and challenges us in our own reality.

Pope Francis states that the perspective of this parable follows the path of human dramas throughout history. He returns to the question asked of Cain about his being his brother's keeper, and affirms that yes, we are responsible for our brothers and for their blood, for their cries that echo everywhere, that reach God and therefore reach us. We cannot live in indifference. We cannot look away or close in on ourselves (*FT* 57). If this story repeats itself, it is because we have gotten used to other people's pain, which does not touch us anymore. These are symptoms of an unhealthy society (*FT* 65), which needs to find ways to remake itself as a community where men and women take on the fragility of others, where there is no room for exclusion, where together we can learn to be close, to lift and rehabilitate those who have fallen so that good may belong to all in common (*FT* 67). There is always time to start over and we must undertake processes that bring transformation (*FT* 77). It is possible to start from below (*FT* 78), from our struggles and resistances (*FT* 79), in love and gratuitousness, in a love that is open to everyone (*FT* 82).

For Christians, it is Christ who has fallen, and in him rests all our dignity. "Whatever you did for one of the least of these brothers and sisters of mine, you did for me" (Matt 25:40). Looking attentively at Jesus and his humanity leads us to look more attentively at all those who are beside us, disfigured and weakened by our society, but welcomed by and connected to this greater mystery. As the Gospel tells us: "For I was hungry and you gave me something to eat, I was thirsty, and you gave me something to drink. I was a stranger and you invited me in, I needed clothes and you clothed me, I was sick, and you looked after me, I was in prison, and you came to visit me" (Matt 25:35–36). May we be like the Samaritan, who reveals our humanity to us. A careful look at our frailties leads us to seek paths of brotherhood.

Challenges and Implications from a Latin American Theological Perspective

The text of *Fratelli Tutti* provokes and challenges us theologically. It seeks to relate the fallen man, a stranger, to the many fallen men and women in our society, people who expect us to look at them and pay attention to their survival. Just as happened in Jesus's time, we can say that today, in our time, it is easier to look away and walk in the other direction because what we cannot

---

3. Schillebeeckx, *Jesus*, 152; emphasis mine.

see does not touch us directly and apparently does not bother us. If we do not see it, we do not feel it, and if we do not feel it, we live as if this evil, this problem, does not exist. This complete indifference is a social alienation that blinds us to the many human dramas and produces exclusion, violence, and death. Apparently, it is easier to follow the priest's and the Levite's attitudes, who look only after themselves and stick to a religious and social viewpoint that keeps them in their positions and legitimizes their attitude. Nowadays, we isolate ourselves in our homes, cars, neighborhoods, and life routines, and we create spaces where "strangers" do not show up and interrupt us. Privatized religion has also found space in our society, articulated in terms of its own interests, not always consistent with what is preached or, in the specific case of Christianity, with the cross that is carried and with the One who was crucified.[4] This is a very present reality and can be seen in the sickness of our society.

This society has seen its problems become greater, aggravated by the COVID-19 pandemic, and many have fallen before our very eyes. People have fallen because of the disease, victims of this deadly virus, and others have fallen because of neglect, unemployment, institutionalized violence, and the indifference of those who govern us and of that part of the population that sees itself as privileged in its spaces and resources, who feel that they cannot be touched by the virus and its consequences. If problems could have been ignored before, now they cannot be because the pandemic has made them worse (*FT* 32). This is a drama that affects everyone, and the overcoming of this evil must be collective: "We are either all saved together or no one is saved" (*FT* 137). This forces us to ask: Who are the many who have fallen? What face do they have? What story, what life do they have? What happened and how did our society allow it to happen? How did we allow these problems to get so much worse? Who are these many who are fallen and begging for our attention, victims of a political and social structure that creates death and inequality?

The text of *Fratelli Tutti* is quite emphatic in saying that there is a stranger on the path, and that if that is so, it is because our society has never allowed itself to see his face, has never bothered to learn about his problems, to have him as a brother who offers us something with his life. If we look at others as strangers, it is as if we do not take part in life with them, so their pain does not touch us; we do not feel that pain ourselves and we do not assume our role and responsibility. For this reason, the text of the parable points at the priest's and the Levite's attitudes as a structural evil, a sin that encourages violence and brings death. The parable forces us to look at the

---

4. Moltmann, *O Deus Crucificado*, 37–45.

stranger and see the humanity in him, just as it has us look at the Samaritan and see in him an example of humanity. The Samaritan helps us know the God who strips himself and comes to meet us, taking on our humanity, making himself fragile and vulnerable, but now no longer a stranger, no longer an "other" but a neighbor. This is the way, and this is the call made to us by faith, because the church (all of us, the people of God) are also called to be a Samaritan and to act with mercy, what Jon Sobrino called the principle of compassion. Reflecting on the same parable, Sobrino insists that, in Latin America, this stranger/wounded person on the road is an entire people who see themselves crucified and the victims of injustices, some historical, others new. Attention to this wounded person decentralizes, because it is the exterior that calls us; the stranger on the path that humanizes the church.[5]

Our weaknesses, which are many, can only be remedied by practicing fraternity, which leads us to believe in humanity again, highlighting that another world is possible. If we are incapable of welcoming the human element and bringing it closer to us, it is because God is also a stranger and our religiosity is of no use. We will always be like the priest and the Levite, looking and walking away from the situation.

Seeing these challenges as Latin America's challenges, it is important to state that they have always been part of the theological discourse of liberation. This estrangement from otherness is caused by a structural evil, a systemic evil, which produces sin, poverty, and death—unjust death. The point of view that makes us strangers and insensitive to others comes from a social structure that does not allow people to be as they are and that causes a large mass of disposable people to emerge, as the pope pointed out in *Evangelii Gaudium*. We live within a globalized world of indifference, and within it the excluded keep on waiting.[6] And if society is not there for them, if they are left for dead along the way, as strangers, who will wait for them? This is a recurring question that we must ask still: Who are those that society transforms into leftovers, into the poor, into people without life and dignity? This same society that advances in technologies and new discoveries does not include everyone. It is for this reason that Gustavo Gutiérrez's question is still relevant and prophetic, as it dares to ask: Where will the poor sleep? Who will wait for them? Who will be there for them?[7] The New Testament tells us that if God is for us, no one will be against us (Rom 8:31); so, if our experience of faith tells us that God is for us, how can we be for them? How can we be the hope of liberation for those who have neither time nor voice?

---

5. Sobrino, *El Principio Misericordia*, 38–41.

6. Francis, *Evangelii Gaudium*, 53–54.

7. Gutiérrez, *Onde Dormirão os Pobres?*

For those who have no life? This is the place where the Christian attitude comes into play.

Poverty questions us; it challenges us in our social position and faith. Within the Latin American theological perspective, the poor are understood as victims of a society of exclusion. These poor have many faces: women, Blacks, young people, drug addicts, the LGBTQI+ community, the homeless, those who do not have access to housing, healthcare, and education. Faced with the many who suffer, Latin American theology, in its liberating character, has always seen the poor as a collective subject. Each face of the poor brings the complaint of structural sin, of systemic evil, of a violence suffered that demands from us a new posture, a confrontation, a questioning of the hope that makes us believe in the Gospel of Jesus. The poor are not strangers on the path, but they are people, they are human, they are our brothers and sisters, and they deserve to be rescued in their humanity because they are hurt in their dignity.

Caring for the poor requires daring, prophecy, and the love and selflessness to be with them, so that together we can be something new. In its fifty years of existence, Latin American theology, focused on liberation, has made the poor a theological place and, by being with them, raised its voice against injustice. This theologizing supported the hope of the poor. Today, the world of the pandemic challenges us, pointing out our wounds and weaknesses. It is necessary to change, it is necessary to advance, it is necessary to go out and open up other paths and processes. The second chapter of *Fratelli Tutti* interrogates us and questions us in our humanity, and our theological practice must follow these questions. This is the novelty and relevance of the encyclical.

Conclusion

In the second chapter of the encyclical *Fratelli Tutti*, Pope Francis reminds us of the parable of the Good Samaritan and makes us see the dramas that are present in our society. He points out to us the condition of many who are fallen and who, as outsiders, are ignored and despised by society. This is the present-day Latin America reality, which has become even more dramatic due to the pandemic. We need to change; we need to take on the dimension of care and start over. Latin American theology has always paid attention to these realities and sought to be an active voice for the many who are excluded from the system, acting as a space of hope for them and with them. Today, this context asks us for closeness with them and a willingness to heal wounds and create fraternity. This is what we welcome from the Samaritan. As Jesus says at the end of the narrative, we must go and do the same.

Bibliography

Francis, Pope. *Evangelii Gaudium: On the Joy of the Gospel.* Vatican City: Libreria Editrice, 2013. https://www.vatican.va/content/francesco/en/apost_exhortations/documents/papa-francesco_esortazione-ap_20131124_evangelii-gaudium.html.
———. *Fratelli Tutti: On Fraternity and Social Friendship.* Vatican City: Libreria Editrice Vaticana, 2020. http://www.vatican.va/content/francesco/en/encyclicals/documents/papa-francesco_20201003_enciclica-fratelli-tutti.html.
Gutiérrez, Gustavo. *Onde Dormirão os Pobres?* São Paulo, Brazil: Paulus, 2003.
Marguerat, Daniel. "A Linguagem das Parábolas." In *Jesus: A Enciclopédia*, edited by Joseph Doré, 325–31. Petrópolis, Brazil: Vozes, 2020.
Moltmann, Jürgen. *O Deus Crucificado: A Cruz de Cristo como Base e Crítica da Teologia Cristã.* Santo André, Brazil: Academia Cristã, 2011.
Schillebeeckx, Edward. *Jesus: A História de um Vivente.* São Paulo, Brazil: Paulus, 2008.
Sobrino, Jon. *El Principio Misericordia: Bajar de la Cruz a los Pueblos Crucificados.* San Salvador: Universidad Centroamericana, 1993.

8

A Biblical Model of Love

JAIME L. WATERS

IN CHAPTER 2 OF *Fratelli Tutti*, "A Stranger on the Road," Pope Francis draws inspiration from the parable of the Good Samaritan to affirm the importance of love of all people as a way to promote the common good. Francis presents a global ideal of love based on the themes and characters that are prominent in the Good Samaritan parable. His treatment is divided into seven short sections that unpack elements of the parable and its implications for readers today. Francis notes that while the text is within Scripture, it includes universal ideas that should influence "all people of good will, regardless of religious convictions" (*FT* 56).

To contextualize his treatment, Francis highlights Old and New Testament texts that reveal the interconnectedness of all people, the shared relationship between creation and creator, attitudes toward neighbors and strangers, and the importance of love. Framing the Good Samaritan parable as a story about how to treat one another, Francis is particularly mindful of the characters' behaviors.

Assessing the Characters

Found only in the Gospel of Luke, Jesus tells the story of the Good Samaritan in response to a lawyer who poses a question about how to inherit eternal life. Rather than directly answer his question, Jesus asks him what the law says on the matter. The lawyer adapts laws from Deut 6:5 (concerning God) and Lev 19:18 (concerning neighbors) saying, "You shall love the Lord your God with all your heart, and with all your soul, and with all your strength, and with all your mind; and your neighbor as yourself" (Luke 10:27, NRSV). When the lawyer presses further on who constitutes a neighbor, Jesus tells the story of the Samaritan. The text itself does not call the Samaritan good, although that is the title often used today based on the person's actions. Influenced by the story, the term Good Samaritan has become a popular way to refer to any person who helps someone, especially a stranger, in need.

In the well-known story, a man traveling on a road is robbed, stripped, and beaten. Three people see the person suffering on the road: a priest, a Levite, and a Samaritan. The priest and Levite pass by, but the Samaritan anoints and bandages the person's wounds, transports him to an inn, and pays the innkeeper two denarii (about two days' wages) to continue to care for him. He offers to repay the innkeeper for any additional expenses when he returns. At the end of the story, Jesus poses the question, "Which of these three, do you think, was a neighbor to the man?" and the lawyer responds, "the one who showed him mercy." Jesus insists, "Go and do likewise" (Luke 10:36–37, NRSV).

Many of Jesus's parables were teaching tools that invited people to compare themselves to characters in the stories. Ancient and modern audiences might expect the priest and Levite to be the model figures, as both were leaders of religious activities in the temple. Yet, both turn away from the person in need, and instead it is the Samaritan who shows mercy. Samaritans were people who traced their ancestry back to the northern kingdom of Israel whose capital city was Samaria. Although Samaritans and Jews had some shared traditions and ancestry, differences in religious practices and beliefs developed. Many first century Jews held negative attitudes toward Samaritans, considering them fringe from Judaism and culturally and ethnically diverse. For Jesus's community, the Samaritan was the unforeseen hero of the story.

Francis highlights the assumptions and expectations that are at the heart of the parable. He recognizes the social distinctions between the three figures, noting that the religious leaders show no regard by overlooking the person in need: "It shows that belief in God and the worship of God are not enough to ensure that we are actually living in a way pleasing to God" (*FT* 74). Likewise, Francis notes that some people who do not belong to a religious tradition can live out the Gospel message of love better than some believers.

The biblical text does not offer a reason for why the priest and Levite ignore the person in need. The most obvious reason is that they did not want to help, consumed with their own lives or matters considered more pressing than a person dying on the road. Another possibility is that they were concerned about becoming ritually unclean, as there were taboos and regulations regarding contact with bodily fluids (cf. Lev 12–15). Another possibility is that the person on the road might have been a Samaritan, so the priest and Levite ignore him because he is an outsider. Luke does not broach the rationale for their disregard because the reason is less important than the inaction. When someone was in need, the religious leaders turned away. The text is intentional in its starkness.

Francis criticizes modern people who, like the priest and Levite, turn away from those who suffer. He posits that many people today are fixated on their own lives, and "the sight of a person who is suffering disturbs us" (*FT* 65). Francis astutely argues that some people only begin to worry about others when situations affect them directly, and he insists that we cannot be indifferent to suffering. In his analysis, Francis minimizes the distinctions between each of the three characters, instead asserting that we are all either the passerby or the one who stops to help. He briefly touches on the idea of each of us possessing aspects of the wounded man, robbers, passers-by, and the Samaritan (*FT* 69). This gloss is notable and could benefit from a more nuanced discussion.

Francis elaborates on the powerful image of the Samaritan helping the stranger in need. The Samaritan's actions exemplify what it means to be a neighbor because he cares for someone without concern for social status, cultural differences, or historical tensions. Any differences are put aside in order to love, revealing the ability of love to transcend barriers and prejudices. This is provocative and is what makes the parable powerful and instructive. Francis affirms that the Good Samaritan parable reminds us that "love does not care if a brother or sister in need comes from one place or another" (*FT* 62).

Common Good and a Call to Action

Francis argues that the actions of the Good Samaritan show a concern for the common good. Elsewhere in *Fratelli Tutti*, Francis elaborates on the common good, perhaps in most detail in chapter 5, but more discussion on this topic in chapter 2 would buttress his important claims. Francis links helping people in need with promoting the common good, using the parable as a paradigm for the power of social bonds: "The parable shows us how a community can be rebuilt by men and women who identify with the vulnerability of others, who reject the creation of a society of exclusion, and act instead as neighbours, lifting up and rehabilitating the fallen for the sake of the common good" (*FT* 67). Francis affirms that everyone has the power and responsibility to create a society that supports the common good for all.

The interest in the common good is important, but the parable also highlights a personal responsibility and interest in individuals based on our shared humanity, a point that could be made more explicitly in the chapter. The Samaritan helps the stranger on the road simply because he is a person in need. Seeing suffering, the Samaritan responds with compassion and care, putting the needs of the distressed person ahead of his need to continue on his way. Such action offers a biblical model for love that all people should emulate. While that attitude is certainly in the interest of the common good, it stems out of a personal encounter and concern for the life of one person, not only for the sake of the common good.

Reading in the United States

Much of Francis's commentary on the Good Samaritan alludes to challenges faced throughout the world, especially in the United States from where my reflection is written. Francis's statements about disinterest and disregard for suffering sadly ring true at this time. He reiterates that the parable teaches that we cannot be indifferent to suffering.

The American backdrop of the encyclical was the convergence of health disparities (exacerbated by the COVID-19 pandemic), racial injustice, police brutality, and political turmoil that have plagued the United States for years and reached a breaking point in 2020. The summer of 2020 was filled with outrage over the murder of George Floyd. Floyd's brutal murder by a police officer was recorded and viewed by millions, and it struck a painful chord that sparked outcry against racial injustice. Many people showed a willingness to help, protect, protest, and support others, inspired and enraged by another instance of a black person dying during an encounter with a white law enforcer.

Francis emphasizes love, restoration, and reconciliation, which enable people to heal a wounded world, build bridges, and create communities that radiate compassion, dignity, and respect. He highlights the principle of subsidiarity as a way to live out the ideals of the parable: "Start at the most concrete and local levels, and then expand to the farthest reaches of our countries and world with the same care and concern that the Samaritan shows" (*FT* 78). In the US, this practice has been visible with many communities rallying together against hatred and division. Unfortunately, those calls for justice and equality were met with resistance, animosity, or disinterest by many people. As some were finally acting like the Samaritan, helping people in need, others continued to look the other way, or worse, actively fight against justice. In the face of many conflicts, Francis emphasizes love that is exemplified by imitating the Good Samaritan.

Shifting the Focus

While Francis's reflection and insistence on love are essential and inspiring, this chapter has some shortcomings. In his commentary, Francis calls on readers to consider who they resemble most in the narrative. Francis focuses his attention on the three people who encounter the person in need. However, far less attention is given to *why* the person is in need or *who* the robbers are. What if a reader most identifies with the suffering person, and what if a reader shares similarities with the robbers?

The emphasis in the parable is on how to respond to suffering, but another important question is *how do we prevent suffering in the first place*? The Lukan Jesus does not raise this concern during this encounter because it is not the primary interest or impetus for the parable. The parable teaches that we are called to respond to the pain of others and that anyone can be a moral example for showing care and mercy. Although the parable does not consider how to prevent suffering, that should not preclude us from addressing this important point. A more proactive statement on preventing suffering is needed, as we should not simply move on to the response to the robbery. We ought to consider who perpetrates crimes and how to stop their actions. The later chapters of *Fratelli Tutti* address this in direct and indirect ways, but examining this point more thoroughly within the context of the Good Samaritan parable would have been valuable.

On the role of the suffering person on the road, Francis notes: "There are times when we feel like him, badly hurt and left on the side of the road. We can also feel helpless because our institutions are neglected and lack resources, or simply serve the interests of a few" (*FT* 76). Some people—especially those who have been historically marginalized because of race, gender, sexual orientation, nationality, and economic status—experience suffering on a regular basis, not only as one unfortunate encounter along the way. For the parable to have a greater impact, the systems and institutions that create and benefit from suffering must be addressed.

In his discussion of the robbers, Francis notes that today's "robbers" are often aided by people who pass by and look the other way. Francis also acknowledges that there are some who use institutions for personal gain and who sow suspicion, distrust, and confusion. In the United States, these individuals unfortunately have held the highest political offices and have been aided by people and media outlets who sow and capitalize on discord. Francis also notes that "robbers" often succeed by people being disillusioned and exasperated by corruption and problems. People who feel a sense of hopelessness in the world may intentionally or unintentionally enable corruption and suffering to persist: "There are many ways to pass by at a safe distance: we can retreat inwards, ignore others, or be indifferent to their plight" (*FT* 73).

Reality Check

At the end of the chapter, Francis ponders why love has not always emanated from the church, especially in light of texts like the Good Samaritan, which clearly affirm its importance. Francis briefly muses why "it took so long for the Church unequivocally to condemn slavery and various forms of violence" (*FT* 86). This wonderment is surprising and out of touch. Unfortunately, the church has not always behaved as the Good Samaritan, sometimes acting like the priest and Levite, or worse, like the robbers. Especially as a Jesuit, Francis should know that "the Society of Jesus relied on enslaved labor globally, almost from their founding. In the United States, the forced labor of enslaved people facilitated the establishment and success of Jesuit missionary efforts and educational institutions until the abolition of slavery in 1865."[1] The church has been silent because it has at times perpetrated evils or benefited from them. Unequivocal condemnation of slavery would require condemnation of the actions of the church, which has not always been of interest to leaders in the church.

Fortunately, there have been efforts to acknowledge the sins of the past, especially regarding slavery, and to take steps toward reparation and reconciliation. In 2015, Georgetown University, the oldest Catholic university in the United States, developed a working group focused on slavery, memory, and reconciliation that has traced the Jesuit institution's historical ties to slavery, connecting with living descendants (GU272 Descendants Association) and committing resources to racial reconciliation projects. In 2021, the Jesuits pledged $100 million as a way to acknowledge and heal some of the damaging effects of the Society's connections to slavery.[2] On a broader scale, in 2016, the Jesuit Conference of Canada and the United States developed the Slavery, History, Memory, and Reconciliation (SHMR) Project in collaboration with Saint Louis University and the St. Louis African-American History and Genealogy Society. The SHMR initiative examines

---

1. Critchely-Menor, "How the Jesuits Are Working," lines 4–8.
2. Georgetown University, "Georgetown Reflects"; Swarns, "Catholic Order."

the history and ramifications of Jesuit involvement in slavery, expressing a commitment to

> a transformative process of truth-telling, reconciliation, and healing that, in conversation with the descendants of people held in bondage, acknowledges historical harms, seeks to repair relationships, and works within our communities to address the legacies of slavery that persist in the form of racial inequities today.[3]

Initiatives like these are essential to promote understanding, reconciliation, and healing. To connect these types of efforts to the Good Samaritan parable, they share parallels with the innkeeper in the story. The innkeeper did not cause the attack on the person, and he does not encounter the suffering person on the road. Yet, he is an integral part of the healing process. Like the Samaritan, the innkeeper rises to the occasion and assists in the recovery, even after the Samaritan leaves.

Despite the problematic musing in paragraph 86, much of the content of chapter 2 of *Fratelli Tutti* is instructive. Francis uses the Good Samaritan parable to articulate a theology of love of all people, condemning beliefs and actions that mistreat and dehumanize and also condemning silence and avoidance of problems. Francis understands the power of the parable to encourage self-reflection. He offers it as a model for articulating the interconnections between all people while advocating for a restorative justice that is grounded on care and mercy. Francis reiterates the necessity of lifting people up who are suffering, calling on everyone to be like the Good Samaritan rather than waiting for others to do what needs to be done. Francis is critical of people who look away out of personal interest instead of promoting the common good. While chapter 2 does not fully address modern-day causes and perpetrators of suffering, the following chapters of the encyclical explore these topics in more detail.

Bibliography

Critchely-Menor, William. "Interview: How the Jesuits are Working to Confront Their History of Slavery." *America: The Jesuit Review*, February 26, 2021. https://www.americamagazine.org/politics-society/2021/02/26/black-history-slavery-jesuits-catholic-reconciliation-240100.

Francis, Pope. *Fratelli Tutti: On Fraternity and Social Friendship*. Vatican City: Libreria Editrice Vaticana, 2020. https://www.vatican.va/content/francesco/en/encyclicals/documents/papa-francesco_20201003_enciclica-fratelli-tutti.html.

---

3. Jesuit Conference of Canada and the United States, "Slavery," lines 1–4.

Georgetown University. "Georgetown Reflects on Slavery, Memory, and Reconciliation." https://www.georgetown.edu/slavery/#_ga=2.127308621.1150609497.1620857490-322427285.1620857490.

Jesuit Conference of Canada and the United States. "Slavery, History, Memory and Reconciliation." https://www.jesuits.org/our-work/shmr.

Swarns, Rachel L. "Catholic Order Pledges $100 Million to Atone for Slave Labor and Sales." *New York Times*, March 15, 2021. https://www.nytimes.com/2021/03/15/us/jesuits-georgetown-reparations-slavery.html.

PART THREE

Envisaging and Engendering an Open World

9

The Existential Imperative of Openness to the Other in Africa

JOHN BOSCO KAMOGA, CSSp

Introduction

THE GOOD IN AFRICA is often obscured by recurrent experiences of civil unrest and violence. The gap between the poor and the rich grows ever wider, and whole sections of the population, including women and minorities, are disenfranchised. More than that, nepotism, exploitation, and abuse of peoples, as well as corruption reign supreme in most African countries. These situations have been highlighted by practices of apartheid in South Africa, genocide in Rwanda, and most recently in the xenophobic violence against migrants in South Africa and against opposition party supporters in Uganda.[1] These and other such experiences that undermine the possibility of living a full and happy life in Africa give urgency and relevance to the pope's invitation to envisage and engender an open world.

Demystifying the Myth that All Is Well in Africa

It has long been assumed that the phrase "communitarian personality" marks and accurately describes the character of the African. However, it is not true that the dictum, "I am because we are, and because we are,

---

1. "Uganda Elections Marred by Violence."

therefore, I am,"² can be fittingly applied to all Africans. Interrogating the question of who is included in the "we" often reveals that the "we" represents only persons belonging to one's group(s) of embeddedness. Consequently, Africans must act resolutely against such exclusivism because all is not well. The pope appears to be talking to Africans directly when he criticizes what he called "closed groups and self-absorbed couples that define themselves in opposition to others" (*FT* 89) that tend to aggressively defend the interests of the in-group and preserve their privileges at all costs, regardless of the cost to others. Africa has suffered from cases of extreme tribalism, the most tragic of which are the 1994 Rwandan genocide and the present troubles in South Sudan fueling the political instability that threatens this nascent nation. In Nigeria, we see how the Muslim north frames its fight in tribal and religious terms against the mainly Christian south by associating the south with Western education. These are not behavior patterns that are unique to these specific communities. They rather represent a trend in the social, political, and economic life of many African communities. Thus, the pope's message in this chapter should be appreciated as an invitation to Africans to cultivate relationships that are open to others for mutual enrichment and to abandon tendencies to think and relate in an exclusive manner.

Thinking in exclusive terms results in what the pope calls "putting love at risk," something that gravely endangers human life (*FT* 92). This is what Mario Aguilar identified as the cause of the Rwandan genocide. There had been a whole history of creating a narrative of opposition between the Hutus and Tutsis. The hatred had been so ingrained that when the genocide was triggered, it was easy for the Hutus to kill the Tutsis, a group that the narrative had long dehumanized and identified as "dangerous cockroaches." The Hutus felt justified to purge the country of the so-called cockroaches.³ That is how tribal and ethnic loyalties can sink human society. Consequently, the pope challenges the African audience to make an honest effort to cultivate and engender loving relationships rooted in self-transcendence. In other words, Africans have to nurture charitable attitudes toward the other. Such a loving disposition toward the other is a vocation rooted in a basic recognition of the inalienable dignity of the other and their right to access the same basic human needs as everyone else (*FT* 93–94).

The assumption that genuine social friendship within a society makes true universal openness possible (*FT* 99) is contestable. On the contrary, relying on friendships, however genuine they may be, can only lead to failure

---

2. For an in-depth discussion of this dictum, see Hord and Lee, "I Am Because We Are."

3. Cf. Aguilar, *Theology, Liberation, and Genocide*, 15–28.

of the effort to engender an open world. People choose their friends and cannot in any way be faulted for not befriending person A or B. No one can rightly claim as a right the friendship of another. A love capable of transcending borders should culminate in what may be called "fraternal solidarity," not social friendship. Pope Francis seems to be aware of the limitations of friendship in his appropriation of the parable of the Good Samaritan (*FT* 101). In Africa, a lot of people have been allowed to waste away simply because they have no recognition, no right connections, no influence or titles, and no resources to make themselves count. They are considered as simply a number in the eyes of others, even of their oppressed fellows. We can think of the many women dying in childbirth in Africa, or the many children subjected to abuses in the mines, in industries, in bars, and on the streets of African towns. People have died in civil wars in northern Cameroon[4] and in South Sudan, and in peaceful protests in countries like Uganda,[5] but such deaths are not accompanied by the same sensationalism as that attached to the death of a political, religious, or cultural leader presiding over the suffering and disenfranchisement of many.

As the pope rightly notes, fraternity, which is an ontological vocation to be lived, calls for something greater that enhances freedom and equality (*FT* 103). According to David Kelsey, this human vocation to self-transcendence is defined by mutual giving and receiving, a relationship that is ontologically ordained.[6] Christians' recognition of the same divine origin of all persons obliges them to recognize, uphold, and defend that fraternity which, unlike friendships freely chosen, is in no way optional. This recognition of the fraternity that defines peoples and guarantees their basic dignity and rights in the commonwealth is fundamental to maintaining harmony and the peaceful coexistence of persons. It is not necessary that people have to be friends—that is a choice. But it is imperative that people live their fraternity and respect it. Doing so means respecting God, who is the principle of unity of persons and the essence of love. Excluding anyone because of the accidents of race, religion, status, or otherwise is an affront to God and is tantamount to blasphemy—it is a choice taken in opposition to God's initiatives and order.

It is deplorable that in many communities in Africa, women, children, the disabled, albinos, the LGBT community, the divorced and remarried, all suffer discrimination. Unfortunately, that discrimination is often justified culturally, religiously, or politically. These people end up forming a

---

4. Karstad, "In Pictures."
5. Daily Monitor, "Bobi Wine Arrested."
6. Kelsey, *Eccentric Existence*, 337.

community of the victims of discrimination, and they are made to play only a marginal or no role at all in defining their positions in society. They are also forced to assert their rights to actively participate in the civil, religious, and social lives of their communities, even when the United Nations charter advocates for them with their governments and religious groups. It is not uncommon to find that when African political and civil institutions are challenged over their failure to act equitably for the socially excluded, invocations of national sovereignty and political independence are offered as a defense. In some cases, even religious leaders have argued against calls to treat other people equitably, hiding behind the so-called cultural heritage of Africa.[7] Hence, Pope Francis laments that excluded persons are effectively rendered existential foreigners (*FT* 97–98). It must be said, however, that it is not an act of benevolence for anyone to guarantee the rights of such persons. It is not a matter of choice but rather a duty and responsibility toward fellow brothers and sisters of the same divine parent.

Africa's Survival Consists in a Willingness to Build a Communion of Communities

In *Fratelli Tutti*, Pope Francis talks about an authentic love that draws people toward universal communion and creates an environment in which no one is isolated or rejected (*FT* 95). Such love overcomes the peripheries, allowing everyone to speak of and identify with a sense of belonging. In Africa, where the gap between peoples is ever-widening, and the ability of some to access opportunities or break certain vicious cycles like poverty and illiteracy is almost impossible, the pope's encyclical must become a Kairos moment. It should serve as a challenge to all, particularly the community's leaders, to probe the factors that create peripheries. African leaders and peoples must resist the tendencies to normalize or accept the existence of peripheries, ghettos, and slums. All must be appalled by existing social inequalities, injustice, and suffering.

For a universal love that promotes all persons (*FT* 106–11) to be nurtured in Africa's fragmented communities, the onus falls on all civic leaders to ensure that an equitable distribution of resources is guaranteed. Moreover, they must preside over the creation of an environment that favors the possibility of all of their constituents having access to a fair share of the available resources. The principle of subsidiarity[8] must be upheld; African governments are not required to give handouts to those in need. Yet,

7. Agbiji and Swart, "Religion and Social Transformation," 6.
8. Pontifical Council for Justice and Peace, *Compendium*, 185–88.

upholding that principle does not lessen the demand on these governments to ensure that there is fair competition for all peoples, which might require that in certain instances particular parts of the country may have to be propped up in order to create an environment of equity and level playing conditions. Recognition needs to be made of historically or naturally disadvantaged communities in Africa. There must be deliberate and targeted development plans to address some of the historical and geographical factors that make certain communities lag behind in development.

Christian discipleship compels the church and other faith groups to be at the forefront of the fight against an unjust status quo. They should proactively engage in the transformation of communities in Africa into equitable loving societies of persons who, although they may differ, are nevertheless united in one common experience of shalom. This means that the church should not be content with a reactionary response to social injustice and oppression. Instead, the church must become proactive by positioning herself constructively through study and anticipation of relevant social, political, and economic trends in the world and in Africa. The church needs to stay ahead of all foreseeable threats and experiences that might harm the human community and harmonious coexistence. This is in line with Vatican II's invitation to the church to read the signs of the times in the modern world and respond to them appropriately.[9] This can only be possible, however, if the church refuses to be compromised by corrupt and unjust persons and systems. To assume a leadership role in the African quest to form a communion of communities bonded by love and respect, the church must in the first place be able to detect those corrupt and unjust systems and persons even when living in a wholly distorted world where the truth about God and the world is no longer obvious.[10]

For this vision to materialize, however, training the church's pastoral agents in a more focused way, by equipping them with theoretical and practical knowledge in the areas of economics, politics, and science and technology, among others, should be the ultimate goal of their formation programs. These pastoral agents should be able to keep abreast of the developments in the world around them. Theological education is no longer enough for an African pastoral agent tasked with the duty of leading the transformation processes of Africa from fragmented communities to a communion of communities. Above all, it means a church that is deeply rooted in her communion with the Lord Jesus her master, through prayer, meditation, and contemplation. It means a church that produces her theologies and initiates

---

9. Second Vatican Council, *Gaudium et Spes*, 3–4.
10. Cf. Kelsey, *Eccentric Existence*, 414–29.

her social engagement on her knees,[11] while also being present to the happenings in society in all the spheres the people of God are defined by. In other words, she must keep the newspaper in one hand and the Bible in the other if she is to authentically discern God's will for Africa today.

Way Forward: Relearning and Living the Dictum, "I Am Because We Are"

Human experience everywhere vindicates Pope Francis's assertion in *Fratelli Tutti* that true beauty of life can only be experienced in human relationships (*FT* 87). Human persons are decidedly connected, and their destinies are shaped by the nature of relationships they choose to build and maintain. This involves creating relationships of fraternity, in which giving and receiving is taken for granted in human communities more as a matter of fact than of choice. The COVID-19 pandemic has exposed how illusory and foolish it is to believe that any person or any people is independent of others. Perhaps globalization, which arguably accounts for the rapid spread of the pandemic, is a gracious opportunity to remind everyone that we belong together. In order to survive as a human family, particularly in Africa, everyone must make it a duty to care for the well-being of the other. Wearing face masks and social distancing are acts of charity toward the uninfected and a protection of oneself. The act of transcending oneself to live and act proactively in favor of the brother or sister next door is invariably a service to oneself and one's own fulfillment.

African societies can emulate their European neighbors, who arguably live the dictum of "I am because we are" more practically. When one considers how contributing to social security funds and a more faithful payment of one's taxes to the country enables Europe to take care of her elderly, disabled, unemployed, and disadvantaged, one realizes that this makes it easier in one's neighborhood to reduce cases of burglary, theft, and murders. It also reduces enormous spending on dependents, thus facilitating the ability to economically climb the social ladder due to increased capacity to save. In other words, one's relatives are not just the business of the immediate family—they are the business of the entire society. The burden of caring for the vulnerable is shared. It is this approach that the pope describes as demonstrating a people's positive growth in moral values (*FT* 113).

The popular colonizer's narrative is that African nation-states were forcibly put together to curb their tribal identities. Some research supports the view that such attempts at combating tribal identities only plunged

11. Prevot, *Thinking Prayer*, 102–3.

the continent further into catastrophe.[12] Somehow the tribal differences became entrenched in the social fabric of many African countries and communities, not because of nature but because of nurture. Therefore, guided by their civic and religious leaders and charismatic persons of good will, African peoples must relearn the basic truths about community building as a vocation of all humans and the only possibility for a truly fulfilling and happy human life. They also have to appreciate anew the values of freedom, mutual respect, and justice right from the beginning of childhood as the only way of restoring to a distorted world the truth about people, creation, and God. This means replacing the mindset of competition with that of cooperation; it means a reformation of the African mind, heart, and psyche. I disagree with the assumption that selfishness does not exist among the poor and suffering, but only among the affluent. Selfishness is not determined by social strata; it is a by-product of human brokenness. The commitment to working for solidarity, equity, and justice that is required to change the status quo in Africa must, therefore, become a spirituality and a way of life.[13] Christ demonstrated this commitment by being in solidarity with the other, particularly the oppressed, even to the extent that he was willing to give up his life for them.

Finally, as the pope indicates, any tangible movement toward engendering a world that is open must be rooted in the human person's reordering of their relationship with the created world (property) and with the power that comes with its acquisition (*FT* 120–27). There is a need to revive and amplify the lessons learned from creation theology that the world's resources should be accessible to all people regardless of where political borders place them. For this reason, we must appreciate the pope's insistence that the immigrant and the refugee must be received with open arms and afforded a charitable welcome rather than be locked out by building walls.[14] Africa has seen many of her children migrate to distant lands, expelled from their homelands by war, hunger, poverty, and lack of opportunities. Although Pope Francis is correct about the right of foreigners to belong wherever they have been forced to migrate, pressure must also be put on the leaders of Africa to address the push factors that lead to so much brain drain from Africa, which involves the loss of a crucial resource needed for nation building: human capital.

Africa will do well if it heeds the pope's call to embrace an alternative way of thinking so as to overthrow the status quo, which is characterized

---

12. Clay, "Nation, Tribe."
13. Rwiza, "Laurenti Magesa," 239–46.
14. O'Connell, "Build Bridges, Not Walls."

by a tiny minority of people owning the greatest percentage of the common good at the expense of the majority. For Africa's only hope of rising up to a social, political, and economic development that ensures equity, charity, and justice lies in proudly and actively admitting that we are our brothers' and sisters' keepers. It lies in the honest and sincere acknowledgment that "I am because we are, and because we are, therefore I am," where our "we" includes all human persons regardless of race, color, religion, status, or nation. This is what true openness to the world should mean to Africa, a continent that must take the pope's invitation as an urgent existential requirement.

Bibliography

Agbiji, Obaji M., and Ignatius Swart. "Religion and Social Transformation in Africa: A Critical and Appreciative Perspective." *Scriptura: International Journal of Bible, Religion, and Theology in Southern Africa* 114:1 (2015) 1–20.

Aguilar Mario. *Theology, Liberation and Genocide: A Theology of the Periphery*. London: SCM, 2009.

Clay, Jason W. "Nation, Tribe and Ethnic Group in Africa." *Cultural Survival Quarterly* 3:9 (1985) 2. https://www.culturalsurvival.org/publications/cultural-survival-quarterly/nation-tribe-and-ethnic-group-africa.

The Daily Monitor. "Bobi Wine Arrested During Protest over Missing Supporters." *The East African*, March 15, 2021. https://www.theeastafrican.co.ke/tea/news/east-africa/bobi-wine-arrested-during-protest-over-missing-supporters-3323590.

Francis, Pope. *Fratelli Tutti: On Fraternity and Social Friendship*. Vatican City: Libreria Editrice Vaticana, October 3, 2020. http://www.vatican.va/content/francesco/en/encyclicals/documents/papa-francesco_20201003_enciclica-fratelli-tutti.html.

Hord, Fred Lee, and Jonathan Scott Lee. "I Am Because We Are: An Introduction to Black Philosophy." In *I Am Because We Are: An Introduction to Africana Philosophy*, edited by Fred Lee Hord and Jonathan Scott Lee, 9–25. Revised edition. Amherst: University of Massachusetts Press, 2016.

Karstad, Ingebjorg. "In Pictures: Untold Stories of Cameroon's War Victims." *Al Jazeera*, April 30, 2020. https://www.aljazeera.com/gallery/2020/4/30/in-pictures-untold-stories-of-cameroons-war-victims.

Kelsey, David H., *Eccentric Existence: A Theological Anthropology*. Vol. 1. Louisville: Westminster John Knox, 2009.

O'Connell, Gerard. "Build Bridges, Not Walls." *America Magazine*, March 31, 2019. https://www.americamagazine.org/faith/2019/03/31/pope-francis-build-bridges-not-walls.

Pontifical Council for Justice and Peace. *The Compendium of the Social Doctrine of the Church*. Washington, DC: United States of Catholic Bishops Conference, 2004.

Prevot, Andrew. *Thinking Prayer: Theology and Spirituality Amid the Crises of Modernity*. Notre Dame, IN: University of Notre Dame Press, 2015.

Rwiza, Richard. "Laurenti Magesa: An African Liberation Theologian." In vol. 2 of *African Theology: The Contribution of the Pioneers*, edited by Bénézet Bujo and Juvénal Ilunga Muya, 231–57. Reprint. Nairobi: Paulines Africa, 2018.

Second Vatican Council. *Gaudium et Spes: Pastoral Constitution on the Church in the Modern World.* Vatican City: Libreria Editrice Vaticana, December 7, 1965. https://www.vatican.va/archive/hist_councils/ii_vatican_council/documents/vat-ii_const_19651207_gaudium-et-spes_en.html.

"Uganda Elections Marred by Violence." Human Rights Watch, January 21, 2021. https://www.hrw.org/news/2021/01/21/uganda-elections-marred-violence#.

10

Radicalizing Love: A Gendered Critique of Malaysia's Management of Migrants and Refugees in the Time of COVID-19

SHARON A. BONG

THIS REFLECTION ON CHAPTER 3 of the pope's most recent encyclical, *Fratelli Tutti*, on fraternity and social friendship, throws into relief Malaysia's management of migrants and refugees, shining an especially bright spotlight on the recent deportation of 1,086 Myanmar nationals. Is the pope's exhortation to "a universal love that promotes persons" (*FT* 106) as the foundational basis of human relationality decidedly naïve in the ways of the world among sovereign nation-states? Or could an ethos of "universal love" for one's neighbor stay the predominantly Malay-Muslim state from exercising the full weight of what Foucault called "biopower,"[1] when the High Court's interim stay order[2] as well as the international law principle of nonrefoulement (i.e., the principle of nonrejection) failed to do so?[3]

To address the radical potentiality of envisaging and engendering an open world (the title of chapter 3 of the encyclical), I begin by interpreting the actions of the Malaysian state taken in the time of coronavirus in terms of the notion of biopower, which characterizes the power of modern states over the life of both their citizenry and strangers. I then move to critiquing

---

1. Foucault, *History of Sexuality*, 140–41, 143–44.
2. Amnesty International Malaysia, "High Court Orders Government."
3. Trevisanut, "Principle of Non-Refoulement," 664.

that exercise of power in light of the encyclical's message. In doing so, I offer a reflection on the potentialities and limits of a faith-based ethos of liberty, equality, and solidarity (fraternity) that complements a secular-based rights framework of international conventions and international relations.

Biopolitics for the Common Good

Existing structures of inequality and inequity have been exacerbated in the time of coronavirus. This phenomenon is exemplified in Malaysia's mismanagement and maltreatment of the migrant (including undocumented) workers, refugees, and asylum seekers referred to in the episode above, culminating in their forced repatriation. Shifts in the state's mindset toward certain outsiders can be detected beginning at the time the first phase of the Movement Control Order (partial lockdown) was executed in March 2020. This institutionalized bias amounts to racial profiling—two million low-skilled migrant workers (largely from Indonesia, Bangladesh, Nepal, and Myanmar),[4] among a labor force of sixteen million, have been targeted instead of white-collar expatriates, mostly belonging to the white race. From an initial assurance[5] that there would be no arrests or deportations of migrant workers (present in the country as the result of both regular and irregular migration), refugees and asylum seekers who came forward to be tested for COVID-19 were, within two months, rounded up and detained following spikes in infections among them.[6] Some empathetic citizens and human rights groups highlighted as the root causes of the outbreaks in these communities the deplorable work conditions in factories and the inhospitable, cramped, and unhygienic dwellings and detention centers they were forced to live in. The corporations running these factories—for instance, the world's top manufacturer of medical gloves (an integral component of Personal Protective Equipment), which had the largest COVID-19 cluster in the country at the end of 2020—were not held accountable for implementing simple practices to reduce the spread of the virus, including social distancing.[7] The divide between citizen and stranger hardened with vitriolic hate speech posted on social media platforms leveled by the former toward the latter, scapegoating them: as vectors of uncleanliness and disease and the embodiment of danger (e.g., crime). This in turn led to more stringent policing of the country's borders and a boat packed with Rohingya refugees

4. International Labor Organization, "TRIANGLE in ASEAN," 2.
5. UNHCR Malaysia, "UNHCR-GoM Joint Action."
6. "Malaysia Rounds Up Migrants."
7. "World's Top Glove Maker."

being turned back,[8] inciting more condemnation of the state by local and international human rights activists and engendering hashtag movements like #Migrantsarehuman.

The state had consistently threatened to deport undocumented migrants, refugees, and asylum seekers as part of its systemic marginalization of these groups, and it followed through on this threat on February 23, 2021, deporting 1,086 of an originally planned 1,200 Myanmar nationals.[9] While documented migrant workers are tolerated because they perform the "three D jobs (dirty, demanding, and dangerous)" that Malaysians refuse to do—but of course with the "three D stigmas (disease, depravity, and drugs)" attached[10]—undocumented migrants, refugees, and asylum seekers, are, in general, simply not tolerated.

The state's initial assurance of goodwill—vowing to eschew arrest and deportation of those who willingly came forward to be tested for COVID-19 for the sake of the common good—earned the commendation and cooperation of the UNHCR Malaysia, the UN's refugee agency in Malaysia. Although the UNHCR Malaysia is not a legally recognized entity in the country, it has registered (after a meticulous process of receiving, documenting, and determining the refugee status of applicants) approximately 180,000 refugees.[11] Among these are 101,000 Rohingyas and 52,000 members of ethnic minority groups, including the Chin and Kachin from Myanmar.[12]

As Malaysia is not a signatory to the 1951 Refugee Convention and its 1967 Protocol, it does not hold itself accountable for setting up formal mechanisms (legislative or administrative) offering adequate protection to refugees and asylum seekers. Amidst the precarity of the state's announced goodwill, which is made concrete only inconsistently given the absence of the legal recognition of refugees, and who are, at best, viewed as "illegal immigrants holding UNHCR cards,"[13] the deportation of the 1,086 Myanmar nationals was necessary from the perspective of the state as being for the sake of the common good—just as previous crackdowns, arrests, and detentions have allegedly been. A day later, the first five hundred thousand doses of the Pfizer vaccine arrived.[14]

---

8. Agence France-Presse News Desk, "Malaysia Turns Back."
9. Amnesty International Malaysia, "High Court Orders Government."
10. Ong, "Translating Gender," 41.
11. UNHCR Malaysia, "UNHCR-GoM Joint Action."
12. Fishbein, "Fear and Uncertainty."
13. Fishbein, "Fear and Uncertainty."
14. Kumar, "Malaysia Starts Covid Vaccines."

Underlying the state's "dangerous deportations,"[15] which have indisputably placed 1,086 individuals at grave risk, particularly as a military-led "COVID coup" had, in the same month, toppled the democratically elected NLD government in Myanmar and resulted in brutal attacks on hundreds of protestors,[16] is the legitimacy of the "biopolitics" that is in the vanguard of modern states. "Biopolitics" as the state exercise of "biopower" was defined by Foucault as a "series of interventions and regulatory controls."[17] This results in the state exercising invasive powers designed to impinge on one's sexual and reproductive health and rights from womb to tomb (i.e., lifelong) in the name of optimizing one's contribution not only to the reproduction of the population or "species body" but also one's production of labor in order to sustain the nation's gross national product.[18] Control of the population and its corollary, the containment of disease, further entail the bracketing off of bodies deemed a threat to the well-being of the primary "species body," which, in the context of modern states that confer (or deny) citizenship status, refers to those with no more than a "UN card." Racism is thus built into the exercise of biopower. The racialization of biopower, when analyzed through a gendered lens, is the basis of sexism; that is, the privileging of men over women, with women's bodies and sexualities made more docile (i.e., regulated). It is also the basis of heterosexism, the privileging of heterosexuality as the norm with nonheteronormative sexualities as aberrant because they are not (re)productive. Where migrant workers (both documented and undocumented), refugees, and asylum seekers, especially women and children, have not only been differently but also disproportionately impacted by extraordinary hardships in the time of coronavirus, the state's deportation of these persons is tantamount to assisted genocide. The state held off with 114 planned deportations due to pressure from local and global human rights organizations, but their fate remains uncertain as the UNHCR has unconscionably been denied access to refugees and asylum seekers since August 2019.[19]

The real-world application of state biopolitics shows that it is deployed in the service of a capitalist, neoliberal (guided) democracy that privileges profit above people. For this reason, biopolitics underscores, naturalizes, and ultimately justifies social inequalities; it does not challenge underlying assumptions—social hierarchization as the natural order, including sexism,

15. Amnesty International Malaysia, "High Court Orders Government."
16. Lee, "COVID Coup."
17. Foucault, *History of Sexuality*, 139.
18. Foucault, *History of Sexuality*, 139.
19. Amnesty International Malaysia, "High Court Orders Government."

racism, and homophobia—nor does it afford concrete solutions for redressing social injustices. This is the way of the world as we know it—the old normal. It is now fitting to turn to the encyclical for an old vision of a new normal in managing human relations, which have become deeply fractured in the time of coronavirus.

A Universal Love for the Common Good

The main takeaway of *Fratelli Tutti* across its eight chapters and 287 paragraphs is not new; it exhorts us to the Christian ethos of loving thy neighbor as thyself, as exemplified in the parable of the Good Samaritan (*FT* 56–86). Like Pope Francis's previous encyclical, *Laudato Si'* (subtitled "On Care for Our Common Home"), *FT* is markedly anthropocentric in foregrounding a human-centered creation within the Christian tradition. Whereas *Laudato Si'* veers toward the danger of repudiating the profound interrelationality of all species, however, *FT* offers a back-to-basics focus on human–human relations; it emphasizes the unsustainability of not recognizing the neighbor in oneself. The irony of a world without borders or at least with porous borders, a reality effected by rapid globalization and unregulated migration, is that humankind, or rather, mankind, has proliferated and hardened divisions among individuals and groups. In the process, the (Westernized) triple goals of "liberty, equality, and fraternity" (*FT* 103–5) of the Enlightenment—the rallying call of the French Revolution—seem further out of reach despite the advancement of the human species in fields like information communication and technology, which is designed to bind together and bond humankind, and despite various indices of universality entailing a global commitment; for example, human rights, international law, and the recently formulated Sustainable Development Goals (SDGs).

In applying concerns raised in *FT*'s chapter 3 to the Malaysian government's perception and treatment of migrant workers, refugees, and asylum seekers, as highlighted above, it becomes apparent that there is a gulf between the vision of "universal love that promotes persons" (*FT* 106–11) and the lived reality of these disenfranchised peoples. Made as we are for love based on "a law of *ekstasis*," we are first called to uphold a "sacred duty of hospitality" that requires us to move beyond ourselves "in openness to others" to attend to their needs, build their capacities, and heal their wounds (*FT* 88–90). The Catholic Bishops' Conference of Malaysia, drawing on *FT*, issued a media statement that opposed the state's deportation of Myanmar refugees: "In a spirit of fraternal love, the church cannot turn a blind eye to those in need and the vulnerable irrespective of who they are and where they come from" and called on "committed Malaysians" to move beyond "individualistic Lenten practices towards cultivating a love and compassion for one another that excludes no one and is open to all . . . where no one is left behind"[20] (echoing the mission of the SDGs). The mobilization of concerned citizens across ethnic and religious lines on social media (as well as the mobilization of protesters in the streets of Yangon) professing their solidarity with these soon-to-be-deported persons and expressing shame at the state's reprehensible actions approximates the gift of hospitality, which is particularly critical in a time of crisis. In doing so, ordinary persons, supported by international allies, promote the moral good and the value of a solidarity which nurtures a "solidity" that is "born of the consciousness that we are responsible for the fragility of others as we strive to build a common future" (*FT* 115). We do these things so as not harden our hearts in front of those who embody vulnerability.

Second, we are called to recognize not only the complementarity of rights-based and faith-based visions but also the greater potentiality of the latter to radicalize the ways in which humans relate to each other. The statement that "every human being has the right to live with dignity and to develop integrally" (*FT* 107) resonates with fundamental principles of human rights and equality that are enshrined in the main UN conventions, most of which have been globally ratified. The cumulative weight of human rights instruments and international law protects refugees' right to migrate, the right to seek and enjoy asylum, the right to be free of torture, and, quite importantly, limits the sovereign rights of states to deny entry to or deport persons who harbor a "well-founded fear of persecution," which is a defining characteristic of the vulnerability of persons fleeing their "home" countries and finding themselves stranded in host countries.[21] The principle of nonrefoulement also entails "positive obligations" that oblige states to "find out about the treatment to which the applicants would be exposed after their return."[22] The Malaysian state's defiance of not only its own High Court's order staying the deportation but also the principle of nonrefoulement that ought to be binding on it (even though it has not ratified the 1951 Refugee Convention and its 1967 Protocol), exposes the limits of the rule of law and secular orders such as protections for human rights. In this regard, *FT* posits the universality of rights, suggesting that they are applicable to all,

20. Catholic Bishops' Conference of Malaysia, "CBCM Media Statement."

21. Trevisanut, "Principle of Non-Refoulement," 665, 667–68. Relevant international law encompasses, among other instruments, the 1948 Universal Declaration of Human Rights, the 1967 Declaration on Territorial Asylum, and the 1984 Convention against Torture and Other Cruel, Inhuman, or Degrading Treatment or Punishment.

22. Trevisanut, "Principle of Non-Refoulement," 669.

at all times and all places. The state's reasoning that it should put its citizens first also makes visible the continuum of violence that sustains state-sponsored and intersecting binaries of men/women, citizen/foreigner, and heteronormative/nonheteronormative (with the first term dominating over the second). These binaries lead to the persecution of "hidden exiles" (*FT* 98) present in a citizenry, including women and the LGBT community,[23] who are treated as lesser citizens and who suffer systemic, often state-sponsored, gender- and sexual-based discrimination and violence.

Third, *FT* offers radical hope in the possibility of engendering a heaven on earth, in the here and now. This is a vision of a socialist utopia that re-envisages the "social role of property" (*FT* 118–20). Property rights have, ironically, been one of the underlying foundations of individual rights; that is, the rights of (white) propertied men. By unlinking the integrity of the person from what they possess (which in some cultures still includes the possession of women, children, and slaves), and deterritorializing national borders, *FT* envisions that "each country also belongs to the foreigner" (*FT* 124)! Adopting this as part of a universal commitment to love would revolutionize the "ethics of international relations" (*FT* 126), which are largely framed by transactional relations, including the exchange of goods, knowledge, and even COVID-19 vaccines; these relations often result in debts that cannot be repaid. Universalizing the ethics of love would upend the state's response to a pandemic like COVID-19, meaning that it would not further torment the least, the last, and the lost but welcome them, literally, into our homes. Universalizing the ethics of love would mean a recognition that "every human being possesses an inalienable dignity" (*FT* 125) and would challenge the paucity of our visions, forcing us to walk the talk; that is, not to bully those fleeing from persecution, not to ravage the weak in their homes, and not to blame minorities for the misfortunes of the majority.

Concluding Remarks

FT challenges us to rise to this "new humanity" (*FT* 127) in which our past, present, and future are inextricably linked. It celebrates humanity's diversity by insisting that our "future is not monochrome" (*FT* 100). It inspires us to dismantle structures of violence that divide, dispossess, and disenfranchise the weak. The subversive potential of *FT*, however, is somewhat muted by its masculinist framework and its use of exclusive language—notably, "fraternity," which elicits homosocial relations that are not inclusive within the Catholic tradition, the generic use of "man," and its saluting only men of

---

23. Pillai, "Blaming LGBT People."

faith who have inspired the pope (the Samaritan woman notwithstanding) (*FT* 286). Illustrative of gender bias that is masked as gender neutrality are the last words of chapter 3 from Pope Francis's address on nuclear weapons delivered at the Atomic Bomb Hypocenter Park in Nagasaki. The pope states that "a real and lasting peace will only be possible on the basis of a global ethic of solidarity and cooperation in the service of a future shaped by interdependence and shared responsibility in the whole human family" (*FT* 127). It is myopic to elide gender differences, among other differences that matter, under the romanticized mantle of "the whole human family." The significance of this commemorative event marks how men (not used generically) used catastrophic violence to end a devastating world war waged on humanity by men. The rapture of a polychromatic, radical love, arguably more than a universal love, can heal ruptured relationships in a deconstructive and reconstructive process that is no more intrinsically peaceful than it is gender-blind or color-blind.

Bibliography

Agence France-Presse News Desk. "Malaysia Turns Back Rohingya Boat Over Virus Fears." *The Jakarta Post*, April 17, 2020. https://www.thejakartapost.com/seasia/2020/04/17/malaysia-turns-back-rohingya-boat-over-virus-fears.html.

Amnesty International Malaysia and Asylum Access Asia. "High Court Orders Government to Halt Deportation of Remaining 114 Myanmar Nationals." February 24, 2021. https://www.amnesty.my/2021/02/24/high-court-orders-government-to-halt-deportation-of-remaining-114-myanmar-nationals/.

Catholic Bishops' Conference of Malaysia. "CBCM Media Statement on Repatriation of Myanmar Nationals Stranded in Malaysia." Archdiocese of Kota Kinabalu, Sabah, Malaysia, February 23, 2021. https://www.catholicadkk.org/2021/02/24/media-statement-repatriation-of-myanmar-nationals-stranded-in-malaysia/.

Fishbein, Emily. "Fear and Uncertainty for Refugees in Malaysia as Xenophobia Escalates." *The New Humanitarian*, May 25, 2020. https://www.thenewhumanitarian.org/news/2020/05/25/Malaysia-coronavirus-refugees-asylum-seekers-xenophobia.

Foucault, Michel. *The History of Sexuality*. Vol. 1. New York: Pantheon, 1978.

Francis, Pope. *Fratelli Tutti: On Fraternity and Social Friendship*. Vatican City: Libreria Editrice Vaticana, 2020. http://www.vatican.va/content/francesco/en/encyclicals/documents/papa-francesco_20201003_enciclica-fratelli-tutti.html.

International Labour Organization (ILO). "TRIANGLE in ASEAN Quarterly Briefing Note, Malaysia." July–December 2020. https://www.ilo.org/wcmsp5/groups/public/---asia/---ro-bangkok/documents/genericdocument/wcms_614381.pdf.

Kumar, P. Prem. "Malaysia Starts Covid Vaccines in Crucial Week for Asian Jabs." *Nikkei Asia*, February 24, 2021. https://asia.nikkei.com/Spotlight/Coronavirus/Malaysia-starts-COVID-vaccines-in-crucial-week-for-Asian-jabs.

Lee, Ronan. "COVID Coup: How Myanmar's Military Used the Pandemic to Justify and Enable Its Power Grab." *The Conversation*, February 17, 2021. https://

theconversation.com/covid-coup-how-myanmars-military-used-the-pandemic-to-justify-and-enable-its-power-grab-155350.

"Malaysia Rounds Up Migrants to Contain Coronavirus, U.N. Warns of Detention Risks." *Reuters*, May 1, 2020. https://www.reuters.com/article/us-health-coronavirus-malaysia-migrants/malaysia-rounds-up-migrants-to-contain-coronavirus-u-n-warns-of-detention-risks-idUSKBN22E04A.

Ong, Aihwa. "Translating Gender Justice in Southeast Asia: Situated Ethics, NGOs, and Bio-Welfare." *Hawwa: Journal of Women of the Middle East and the Islamic World* 9:1–2 (2011) 26–48.

Pillai, Vinodh. "Blaming LGBT People for Covid-19 Is Spreading Fast." *Queer Lapis*, April 5, 2020. https://www.queerlapis.com/blaming-lgbt-people-for-covid19/.

Trevisanut, Seline. "The Principle of Non-Refoulement and the De-Territorialization of Border Control at Sea." *Leiden Journal of International Law* 27:3 (September 2014) 661–75.

UNHCR Malaysia. "UNHCR-GoM Joint Action to Prevent, Manage Covid-19 Infections among Refugees." *UNHCR Malaysia News*, April 13, 2020. https://www.unhcr.org/en-my/news/stories/2020/4/5e94189d4/unhcr-gom-joint-action-to-prevent-manage-covid-19-infections-among-refugees.html.

"World's Top Glove Maker Says Malaysia Worker Died from Covid-19." *Al Jazeera*, December 14, 2020. https://www.aljazeera.com/news/2020/12/14/worlds-top-glove-maker-says-malaysia-worker-died-from-covid-19.

11

Dreaming a New Humanity: Human-Cosmic Synodality from the Perspective of the Foreigner and the Hidden Exile

Roberto Tomichá-Charupá, OFMConv, and
Ernestina López-Bac[1]

Introduction

Throughout the history of Christianity, many believers lived, experienced, and spread—sometimes even by giving their lives—that desire and command of Jesus: "You are my friends, if you do what I command you.... This I command you, that you love one another" (John 15:14–17, NASB). From this existential experience of encounter with Christ as a transformative event, it is possible to understand the words of Pope Francis: "Our relationships, if healthy and authentic, open us to others who expand and enrich us," because "authentic and mature love and true friendship can only take root in hearts open to growth through relationships with others" (*FT* 89). Therefore, "envisaging and engendering an open world" supposes, above all, recognizing and assuming in one's own existence the profound meaning of being human: people who are finite, limited, incomplete.... Hence the urgency to "let oneself be completed" by other creatures, to walk together with them, to engender an open world of brotherhood and sisterhood. It is a challenge, a project, a dream.

1. Translated by Karen M. Kraft.

1. Conviction: Working from Our Differences for an Open and Fraternal World

Saint Francis of Assisi is the "saint of fraternal love, simplicity, and joy ... brother to the sun, the sea, and the wind" and, of course, very united to all humanity, "those of his own flesh" (*FT* 2). And so, in 1219, in the middle of the Fifth Crusade, he visited the sultan of Egypt, al-Malik al-Kamil, in Damietta. Eight hundred years later, Pope Francis wanted to relive this meeting when, in Abu Dhabi, he met with the Grand Imam Ahmad Al-Tayyeb, thus demonstrating what "an open world" means today: "an openness of heart, which [knows] no bounds and transcend[s] differences of origin, nationality, color, or religion" (*FT* 3). It is the commitment to a "culture of encounter" between all human beings—and with all creatures—in order to promote and achieve in every possible instance and with the creative force of the life-giving Spirit—"our inalienable human dignity" (*FT* 127; cf. 30, 232). It means galvanizing a culture of respect, closeness, sensitivity, awe, and continuous learning, which leads us to "acknowledge, appreciate, and love each person" (*FT* 1).

The centrality of the dignity of the human being resonates in a special way in pandemic times, when there is more of a prevailing tendency to discard, persecute, exclude, harass, abuse, and treat with arrogance the weakest peoples. In reality, an open world must welcome everyone; include the least; respect the various nations, peoples, and cultures and preserve "their respective cultural and religious identity," open itself up and value the diverse "in the spirit of human fraternity" (*FT* 129): "to promote that which unites us, and to regard our differences as an opportunity to grow in mutual respect" (*FT* 134). There is openness when there is listening, respect, sensitivity, and welcoming of those who are considered different; when there is an effort to bring together with creativity the global and the local, the internal and the external, the particular and the universal; when, in short, there is a desire to return to that original harmony, beyond the exclusive dialectical dichotomies.

Committing to an open world of brotherhood and sisterhood is a journey of searching, wandering, and even permanent nomadism which knows how to "appreciate[e] the beauty which God bestows beyond [our] borders" (*FT* 142), an incarnate God who becomes earth, air, water, fire by pitching his tent (cf. John 1:14) on the cosmic periphery among the marginalized. Thus, from the periphery and together with diverse creatures, He recreates his own beauty, engenders life, regenerates love, because "[a] living and dynamic people, a people with a future, is one constantly open to a new synthesis through its ability to welcome differences" (*FT* 160). To do this, we must return to the biblical sources and roots: "God is love, and the one who remains in love remains in God" (1 John 4:16; *FT* 4). In the face of struggles for hegemonic power, political and partisan interests, the supremacy of some peoples over others, Pope Francis, following great saints, recalls the path of love as a criterion of virtuous, enterprising, and creative life. Whoever loves considers the beloved "as somehow united to ourselves," "of great value," "dear," precious, and desirable, to such an extent that not only does the beloved become "pleasing (*grata*)" to us but we also give "freely (*gratis*)" to the beloved (*FT* 93).

From the perspective of indigenous spiritualities, all human beings—women and men, the entire creation, our common home, Mother Earth or Mother Water—are the work of the same Creator-Builder God, Heart of Heaven-Heart of Earth. No one is more, and no one is less. There is no inequality but rather reciprocity. Through his Spirit, from the origins of creation, the Builder God has brought forth attitudes, thoughts, and words of wisdom in grandmothers and grandfathers. The Spirit speaks and sings the praises of God, to remind the peoples of their deepest and most profound roots. Ultimately, working for an open world implies experiencing and sharing the overflowing divine gratuity, the abundant gift of God—mercy, which inspires those who feel loved to see and contemplate in the other the God-Mystery in his various names and attributes. Thus, according to the sacred book of the Mayans, the worshipers of the Word do not tire of asking for a new dawn where there is life, peace, and descendants:

> Oh, thou, Tzacol, Bitol! Look at us, hear us! Do not leave us, do not forsake us, oh, God, who art in heaven and on earth, Heart of Heaven, Heart of Earth! Give us our descendants, our succession, as long as the sun shall move and there shall be light. Let it dawn; let the day come! Give us many good roads, flat roads! May the people have peace, much peace, and may they be happy; and give us good life and useful existence![2]

2. Context: Destructive Neocolonialisms and the Recovery of Roots

The commitment to an open world is always historical, contextual, situated; it is pursued in the midst of the vicissitudes, interests, power games, and contradictions of human beings themselves. Pope Francis condemns the ideologies and imaginaries disseminated in various environments and media, which are actually "new forms of cultural colonization" (*FT* 14), of "a kind of 'deconstructionism,' whereby human freedom claims to create

---

2. *Book of the People*, 52.

everything starting from zero" (*FT* 13). Such ideologies "destroy (or deconstruct) all differences so that they can reign unopposed" (*FT* 13). This is the always latent temptation of totalitarianism; of exclusive monoculturalism; of political, cultural and religious fundamentalism—ultimately, of the single, hegemonic, dominant, and colonial thought, which excludes and destroys all diversity, leaving in its wake a great number of martyrs, who defend justice, truth, our common home with their lives. In light of this situation, Francis insists on synodal, brotherly-sisterly witness, promoting prophetic art, self-critical polychromy, and beauty in its various colors, which welcomes differences as creative contributors to the biocosmic symphony.

In the case of Latin America, based on the experience of the Amazonian peoples, the situation is very complicated, because, for example, extractivist neocolonialism advances more and more every day, annihilating the ecosystem and many peoples. In the words of Pope Francis, the "environmental impact of the economic projects of extraction, energy, timber, and other industries . . . destroy and pollute" the common home; the "colonizing interests . . . have expelled or marginalized the indigenous peoples, the river people, and those of African descent."[3] Years earlier, the pontiff had denounced the strong "pressures" on the indigenous people to abandon their lands and thus "make room for agricultural or mining projects that are undertaken without regard for the degradation of nature and culture."[4] In short, the extractive industries of mining, oil, agriculture, logging, or fishing have "been a mechanism of colonial and neocolonial plundering and appropriation," with "different guises over time," and they have "been forged in the exploitation of essential raw materials for the industrial development and prosperity of the global North," with very few benefits for native peoples.[5]

So, how do we envisage and engender an open world? With people committed to taking charge of and caring for their own ancestral intercultural roots, living by the best principles of cultural and Christian memory, thinking-feeling critically, developing consistent prophetic theologies, practicing solidarity with everyone, especially with the weakest (cf. *FT* 13, 115). The alternative is "human impoverishment"[6] and, therefore, self-destruction. Hence, the urgency of the active protagonism of the new generations—adults and young people, in particular—to bring together and harmonize all kinds of differences, starting with the most profound personal contradictions that are present in the heart of every human being and continuing throughout a lifelong journey of reconciliation and integral

---

3. Francis, *Querida Amazonia*, 49 and 9.
4. Francis, *Laudato Si'*, 146.
5. Acosta, "Extractivismo," 2.
6. Francis, *Querida Amazonia*, 33.

healing. There is an urgent need to return to "cultural roots," to community stories and memories, as "points of reference" and guarantees of the identity, wisdom, and "sense of dignity" of the people themselves:[7] "there is no worse form of alienation than to feel uprooted, belonging to no one" (FT 53). That is why Francis insists on inviting young people—though not only them—to "take charge of your roots, because from the roots comes the strength that will make you grow, flourish, and bear fruit."[8] In other words, the "precious personal, family, and collective memories"[9] represent one of the inspiring and predominant resources in the struggles to overcome all kinds of colonialism: social, cultural, religious, epistemic, spiritual.

3. Passion: Feeling-Thinking, Co-Reasoning with the Heart, "Dreaming Together"

Engendering an open world will be possible if comprehensive concern—that is, the passionate and communal commitment to a cosmically human *buen convivir* (living together well)[10]—is combined with deep personal conviction." Francisco de Roma points out the urgent need to "recover the shared passion to create a community of belonging and solidarity worthy of our time, our energy, and our resources" (FT 36). Without a sense of concrete belonging to a single human family, there is no shared solidarity among its members, because there will always be people considered strangers, foreigners, and even enemies, to reject and even destroy. This also happens among people who supposedly know each other, on the sociopolitical as well as the religious-ecclesial level. As a renowned world thinker notes, when reflecting on the coronavirus pandemic a year after its onset: "scientists cooperated globally, whereas politicians tended to feud," and "no serious attempt was made to pool all the available resources, streamline global production, and ensure equitable distribution of supplies."[11] All this to the detriment not only of the people who live in the poorest and most vulnerable countries—already very serious—but even of the very same people who refuse

---

7. Francis, *Querida Amazonia*, 30.
8. Francis, *Querida Amazonia*, 33.
9. Francis, *Querida Amazonia*, 35.
10. Translator's note: See Rodríguez Salazar, "Buen Vivir": *Buen vivir* and *buen convivir* are Spanish translations of "the indigenous words *Sumak Kawsay* (in the Quechua language of Ecuador) and *Suma Qamaña* (in the Aymara language of Bolivia). . . . The richness of the meaning of these ancestral languages is limited to express something that speaks of the Full Life or the fullness of Life as a way of living for people in communities in harmony with nature and in balance in individual and collective relationships."
11. Harari, "Lecciones."

to cooperate, because we are all in the same boat, and "we cannot go on thinking of ourselves, but only together can we do this,"[12] otherwise we will all perish as humanity.

This lack of awareness of feeling *really* human, part of a global family, is also the reflection of a particular individualistic, isolated, closed, and mistaken experience—and understanding—of what we really are. It is a way of life, unquestionably fostered by primarily political-economic power groups . . . a dominant mentality that is expressed in "violent" and "myopic, extremist, resentful, and aggressive nationalism" (*FT* 11, 86, 141). From the southern regions of the world, there still exists an antidote, an urgent alternative: "to learn" from the ancestral wisdoms of various peoples—such as the indigenous—who still preserve a relational, communal life with a more integrated wisdom logic. Incidentally, the Argentine philosopher and theologian Juan Carlos Scannone refers to "popular wisdom," more symbolic than conceptual, and the Colombian sociologist Orlando Fals Borda proposes *sentipensar* (to feel-think) as a method that unites the affective-collaborative with the rational-intellectual, while the Ecuadorian Patricio Guerrero recovers and shares the indigenous experience of *corazonar*[13] as a way of life that seeks to integrate the heart—or the ancestral and insurgent—with reason, or intellectual reflection, of a more properly Western vein. In the same vein, Pope Francis, after having listened attentively to the experience of the Amazonian peoples, incorporates the symbol of the "dream" as a provocative, inspiring, convergent, and articulating axis for responding creatively to the pressing challenges: "How important it is to dream together. . . . Envisaging and pursuing a common project"[14] of justice, peace, and care for the common home. . . . Dreams . . . are built together"; they are true and authentic realities, not "an outdated utopia" (*FT* 8, 150, 30). Every dream, however, requires a keen discernment and a communal

12. Francis, "Extraordinary Moment."

13. Translator's note: See Albarrán González, "Towards a Buen Vivir"—Albarrán González discusses the meaning of *corazonar* in depth, describing it as "decolonial co-design using the heart as guidance" (205) and as "[r[easoning and feeling with the heart, corazón or co-reason. To understand with the heart" (270).

For the relationship of *corazonar* to *sentipensar*, see Cepeda H., "Problem of Being in Latin America," 26—"the nature of sentipensar requires a connection from the heart with nature as a whole; understanding the cosmos with all its meanings and senses implies not a pure and simple reasoning—only reasoning—But a reasoning-with (with-everything-that-is and with-the-heart), that is to say: to co-reason: corazonar. To understand is corazonar."

14. Translator's note: This is the phrase as it appears in the official English translation of *FT*, but in the original Spanish version, the phrase reads "soñar y elaborar un proyecto común," which can also be translated more literally as "dreaming and developing a common project." This more literal translation seems to be more accurate here, and it ties in nicely with the authors' discussion of dreams in Mesoamerican culture.

interpretation, to avoid those false universalistic and neocolonial dreams, sometimes very subtle, that are solely aimed at "levelling, dominating, and plundering" (*FT* 100) all of creation with all of its creatures. Based on the Amerindian experience, the dream is more than a project; it is a symbol of daily life, constant journeying, resistance to domination, cosmic relationship, listening to diversity, and identity in continuous redefinition. For Mesoamericans, the central dream-symbol is the Mayan altar, where each corner or path of the universe is marked by a color that indicates a specific action of God in daily life and converges to strengthen harmony and balance between human beings and with Mother Earth-Water. Francis himself expresses it well: "Let us dream . . . as a single human family, as fellow travelers sharing the same flesh, as children of the same earth which is our common home, each of us bringing the richness of his or her beliefs and convictions, each of us with his or her own voice, brothers and sisters all" (*FT* 8).

4. Synodality: Thinking of Ourselves as "a Single Family Dwelling in a Common Home"

The dream of Pope Francis actualizes the Saint of Assisi's dream of a society built on brotherhood and sisterhood and which should materialize in a church that is *truly* "a home with open doors, because [it] is a mother" (*FT* 4, 276)—that is to say, a church in coexistence, or at least on the synodal journey, where all the baptized can *truly* participate as adults, with a voice and a vote in decision-making. Therefore, it is urgent to work for a synodality *ad intra* and *ad extra*, one that is ecclesial, human, and cosmic, where everything is mutually related and interconnected. Indeed, just as "[u]niversal fraternity and social friendship are . . . two inseparable and equally vital poles in every society" (*FT* 142), so too is brotherhood-sisterhood ecclesial, human, and cosmic, and it places the care of the common home center stage: "we need to think of ourselves more and more as a single family dwelling in a common home. Such care does not interest those economic powers that demand quick profits" (*FT* 17).

The synodal paradigm allows a believing community to maintain an appropriate balance of continual effort and searching to be a true "home," inclusive, hospitable, and a place where all women and men *truly* feel like people. Otherwise, there will be no ecclesial belonging and, much less, an authentic, genuine synodal brotherhood-sisterhood. Furthermore, this "home" is one that is on a self-questioning and prophetic journey, that marches through the desert of life amidst the dominant de facto powers. Hence, rather than a "home" that's materially stable or has a solid structure, it is a precarious, transitory "tent" that quickly relocates to those existential peripheral spaces in order to respond to the cry for life, justice, solidarity. The "tent" is the image of a church on the synodal journey, a church that anticipates and manifests social and cosmic friendship. In practice, however, we must defeat a virus that is in constant mutation: "radical individualism" (*FT* 105).

Ecclesial and human synodality walks hand in hand with cosmic synodality, which involves traveling together, moving forward with people of different cultures, religions, and spiritualities, and sharing the same essential objective, to "care for our common home, our planet.... Those who enjoy a surplus of water yet choose to conserve it for the sake of the greater human family have attained a moral stature that allows them to look beyond themselves and the group to which they belong. How marvelously human!" (*FT* 117).

5. Spirituality: Welcoming "Hidden Exiles" and "Existential Foreigners"

As a means of engendering an open world, a synodality of brotherhood and sisterhood will only be possible based on an authentic spiritual mindset, already present in the lives of our peoples. Recalling the words of Jesus, "you are all brothers and sisters" (Matt 23:8), Pope Francis highlights openness and hospitality as a concrete expression of fraternal love, which is expressed in an "encounter with those outside one's own circle" (*FT* 90): "love calls for growth in openness and the ability to accept others as part of a continuing adventure that makes every periphery converge in a greater sense of mutual belonging (Matt 23:8)" (*FT* 95). The path to a new and inclusive humanity is manifested in knowing how to welcome the other person, receive them, accept them, and value them as such, as someone who belongs to a diverse people, with their own culture and wisdom. Hospitality is the essential condition for a true encounter or—in the words of Boaventura de Sousa Santos—an "ecology of knowledges," which is intercultural and interreligious and which is only possible starting from one's own cultural affirmation.[15] Indeed, when there is awareness and appreciation of one's own cultural and religious identity, it is possible to "find a means of serene, ordered, and peaceful coexistence," which not only accepts, recognizes, and values differences but also lives "rejoicing that, as children of the one God, we are all brothers and sisters" (*FT* 279).

Engendering an open world involves, specifically, welcoming the discarded, excluded, abandoned, and ignored, the "hidden exiles" and

---

15. de Sousa Santos, "Beyond Abyssal Thinking," 45–89.

"existential outsiders" who are often "treated as foreign bodies in society" (*FT* 97, 98), due to various kinds of discrimination: social, cultural, economic, political, ideological, religious, or gender-based. Without the active protagonism of those who are displaced and discriminated against, social friendship will not be possible, much less a diverse brotherhood-sisterhood. Therefore, it's critical that each of us recognize ourselves internally and externally as existential foreigners, travelers, and nomads who, in everyday simplicity and humility, show not only a profound respect for those they meet on the path of life, but who also—learning from Francis of Assisi— even "submit" to them and to each creature, out of love of God.

Hospitality, however, is not only an ethical mindset but also an epistemic posture of feeling-thinking (*sentipensar*) and, therefore, a way to overcome the great destructive "virus" of "radical individualism" (*FT* 105). There is an urgent need to learn from the Amerindian peoples the interrelational logic of *buen convivir* between everything that exists, of knowing that there is a reality that lives and is greater than we are. Therefore, before any activity, we must "ask permission" from the "owner" of each territory or portion of creation, since everything that exists manifests and reveals an ever greater Ultimate Presence. In short, we must recover that spiritual confidence and mystical experience, which is in the heart of hearts of every human being and imparts great resilience and existential consistency. We also must listen to Pope Francis's invitation to "esteem the indigenous mysticism that sees the interconnection and interdependence of the whole of creation, the mysticism of gratuitousness that loves life as a gift, the mysticism of a sacred wonder before nature and all its forms of life."[16]

Therefore, hospitality represents one of the common horizons between the age-old Western Christian tradition and the Amerindian peoples. The Christian East and medieval monasteries "developed a remarkable system of welcoming pilgrims" to such an extent that Saint Benedict himself told the monks following his Rule that "the poor and pilgrims be treated with the utmost care and attention" (*FT* 90). In the case of indigenous peoples, hospitality is generally itinerant, nomadic, and routine in daily life, in the style of Abraham at the Oak of Mambre with the three unexpected strangers (Gen 18:1–16). Indeed, the human being lives and finds fulfillment in dual reciprocity: in the human-relational, which manifests the divine-cosmic, and vice versa. Hence the wise indigenous principle: I am–you are; you look at me–I look at you; you take care of me–I take care of you. . . . We must interweave ourselves and feel-think (*sentipensar*), never ceasing to be ourselves, reinventing languages of life that are ever more inclusive and encompassing,

---

16. Francis, *Querida Amazonia*, 73.

accentuating collaboration in order to remake families and communities and build a family, a society, a more synodal church, overcoming existing neocolonialisms and patriarchies. In essence, it is about strengthening the commitment of Pope Francis: "envisaging a new humanity" (*FT* 127).

Bibliography

Acosta, Alberto. "Extractivismo y Neoextractivismo: Dos Caras de la Misma Maldición." *Cronicón: El Observatorio Latinoamericano*, July 31, 2012. https://cronicon.net/paginas/Documentos/paq2/No.23.pdf.

Albarrán González, Diana. "Towards a Buen Vivir–Centric Design: Decolonising Artisanal Design with Mayan Weavers from the Highlands of Chiapas, Mexico." PhD diss., Auckland University of Technology, 2020. https://openrepository.aut.ac.nz/bitstream/handle/10292/13492/AlbarranGonzalezD2.pdf?sequence=4&isAllowed=y.

Benedict XVI, Pope. *Deus Caritas Est: On Christian Love*. Vatican City: Libreria Editrice Vaticana, 2005. https://www.vatican.va/content/benedict-xvi/en/encyclicals/documents/hf_ben-xvi_enc_20051225_deus-caritas-est.html.

The Book of the People: Popol Vuh. Translated by Delia Goetz and Sylvanus Griswold Morley from Adrián Recinto's translation from Quiché into Spanish. Los Angeles: Plantin, 1954. https://www.latinamericanstudies.org/maya/Popol_Vuh.pdf.

Cepeda H., Juan. "The Problem of Being in Latin America: Approaching the Latin American Ontological *Sentipensar*." *Journal of World Philosophies* 2:1 (2017) 12–27. https://doi.org/10.2979/jourworlphil.2.1.02.

de Sousa Santos, Boaventura. "Beyond Abyssal Thinking: From Global Lines to Ecologies of Knowledges." *Review (Fernand Braudel Center)* 30.1 (2007) 45–89. http://www.jstor.org/stable/40241677.

Francis, Pope. "Extraordinary Moment of Prayer." Prayer given at St. Peter's Basilica, Vatican City, March 27, 2020. https://www.vatican.va/content/francesco/en/homilies/2020/documents/papa-francesco_20200327_omelia-epidemia.html.

———. *Fratelli Tutti: On Fraternity and Social Friendship*. Vatican City: Libreria Editrice Vaticana, 2020. https://www.vatican.va/content/francesco/en/encyclicals/documents/papa-francesco_20201003_enciclica-fratelli-tutti.html.

———. *Laudato Si': On Care for Our Common Home*. Vatican City: Libreria Editrice Vaticana, 2015. https://www.vatican.va/content/francesco/en/encyclicals/documents/papa-francesco_20150524_enciclica-laudato-si.html.

———. *Querida Amazonia: To the People of God and to All Persons of Good Will*. Vatican City: Libreria Editrice Vaticana, 2020. https://www.vatican.va/content/francesco/en/apost_exhortations/documents/papa-francesco_esortazione-ap_20200202_querida-amazonia.html.

Harari, Yuval. "Lecciones de un Año de Covid." *La Vanguardia Internacional*, March 14, 2021. https://www.lavanguardia.com/internacional/20210314/6290059/yuval-harari-lecciones-ano-covid.html.

Rodríguez Salazar, Adriana. "Buen Vivir." Filosofía del Buen Vivir, March 10, 2021. https://filosofiadelbuenvivir.com/buen-vivir-2/.

12

A Call for Openness

Kurt Appel

Prologue

IN MANY PASSAGES, *FRATELLI Tutti* refers to the parable of the Good Samaritan (Luke 10:25–37) and connects mercy with openness to the Other. If, in the first part of the double commandment of love, this love is directed toward the universal God, then the love for one's neighbor cannot be inserted into fixed boundaries. Rather, it accrues from an attitude of mercy in God's name YHWH, which no one can claim as a privilege for themselves and which has to prove itself situationally. The question of the overcoming of limits through this mercy evokes another incident mentioned at the beginning of the Gospel of Mark (Mark 1:21–28[1]), which is also taken up in the Gospel of Luke (Luke 4:31–37). It is Jesus's first symbolic act—the exorcism of an unclean spirit—which is in connection with the special nature of Jesus's teaching. This stands out from the general teachings of scholars of that time (scribes, rabbis, etc.) in Jesus's environment in that it is an act of "authority." One could clarify the meaning of this characterization of Jesus's teachings by adding that it is the authority of God's name YHWH in which Jesus teaches. It bears witness not least to the fact that it has a healing effect (Mark 2:1–11, etc.) and brings about change. In Mark 1:21–28 the oddity is that it is the "unclean spirit" that sees through Jesus. "I know who you are—the Holy One of God" (Mark 1:24, NIV). This statement of the unclean

---

1. For a detailed commentary on this pericope, see Standaerd, *Marco*, 118–28.

spirit goes much deeper than it seems at first sight: First, he recognizes Jesus, which, biblically speaking, means not only an intellectual, but also a deeply emotional and affective knowledge. Second, the Spirit expresses one of the highest confessions of Christ in the entire New Testament: Jesus is called the "Holy One of God," which means nothing less than that Jesus is the concretization of God's Holy Name YHWH, that is, his person and teaching represent the incarnation of the God of Israel and his covenant word.

The question to be raised here, and which may prove significant for a further interpretation of *Fratelli Tutti* (FT) and the Gospel on which it is based, is why it is precisely the demons who recognize Jesus before anyone else and also most profoundly. In Mark, where Jesus's disciples and family "excel" in their lack of understanding of the person of the Holy God, this fact carries particular weight. Could it be that the demons recognize Jesus because they bear a quasi-diabolic resemblance to Jesus, insofar as they express the limitless? After all, the *apeiron*, the boundless, was considered specifically demonic in the ancient world.[2] A closeness of Jesus and the demons was raised as an accusation by Jesus's opponents, but also by his family (Mark 3:20), an accusation that Jesus, however, rejects in the strongest terms (Mark 3:22–30). But if both Jesus and the demons show a transgressive moment, in what ways does their respective boundlessness differ? This question leads to *Fratelli Tutti*, and especially to the third chapter, which deals with the overcoming of borders for the sake of an open world.

A New Narrative of Openness

Fratelli Tutti can be seen as the culmination so far of a project by Pope Francis, namely, to offer a new narrative for global humanity at the beginning of the third millennium.

There is debate among theologians about whether and to what extent the current pope's encyclicals are theologically profound and how they fit into the existing church tradition. In doing so, it is often overlooked that the goal of the central papal letters is not to give doctrinal impetus to theology, but to find a narrative that unites peoples and religions. Therefore, it is hardly a coincidence that, in *Fratelli Tutti*, the film *Pope Francis: A Man of His Word* by director Wim Wenders is quoted, in which the pope's global narrative of universal brotherhood is conveyed cinematically. The pope's homilies, gestures, travels, and official documents are not, as with John Paul II, under the sign of the new evangelization (or re-evangelization)— which, incidentally, failed—of a world that has become secular by a church

---

2. Eco, "Weak Thought," 37–39.

equipped for it. Nor do they continue Benedict XVI's effort to establish a theologically shaped Catholic (separate) world that is supposed to become the spiritual foundation and refuge of those who turn away from a secular modernity that would ultimately have revealed its nihilistic nature. Rather, Francis moves joyfully beyond ecclesiastical institutional boundaries, so to speak. While *Laudato Si'* (*LS*), the first encyclical Francis wrote entirely on his own, owes much to his encounters with Bartholomew, the ecumenical patriarch of Constantinople, *Fratelli Tutti* is even linked to the intellectual exchange with Al-Tayyeb, the most important authority on Sunni Islam.

The programmatic inaugural letter of Francis, *Evangelii Gaudium* (*EG*), draws the outline of a church that stands under the sign of the polyhedron (*EG* 236), that is, it promotes joy in the diversity of ecclesial and ordinary reality of human life. The encyclical *Laudato Si'*, in which a narrative that goes beyond ecclesial boundaries is already emerging (*LS* 3), not only "sings" praise to creation but also connects the wonder of creation with its radical openness, in which God's transcendence reveals itself. The universe, formed of open systems, unfolds itself in this way in its totality, that is, precisely in this openness, in the transcendence of God (cf. *LS* 79). In *Fratelli Tutti*, Francis develops this model further, writing a narrative of openness that is meant to connect not only man and God and man and creation, but all human beings with each other.

Terms such as "openness," "open," and "universal openness," are frequently encountered in *Fratelli Tutti*, as are related phrases, e.g., those that call for "transcending our own limitations" (*FT* 96) and for the "duty of hospitality" (*FT* 90), or passages that oppose "closure" (*FT* 102) and "exclusion" (*FT* 120). If the theme of openness is thus central to the entire encyclical and, so to speak, its substantive core, this is especially true for the third chapter, which calls for "envisaging and engendering an open world."

Envisaging and Engendering an Open World

Openness in Difference

The chapter "Envisaging and Engendering an Open World" clarifies right at the beginning (*FT* 87) that human truth is connected with alterity. The first and radical form of openness happens in the encounter with the Other. Love, transcendence, and alterity are inseparably connected and designate a reality that leads away from the limited world of one's own egocentrism and leads the human being into his true destiny, namely community with the Other and with God, which preserves and does not level the respective differences.

This openness is not only left to personal responsibility but should also determine social existence. Fundamental values such as liberty, equality, and fraternity are owed to such a culture of openness and are also its condition. As already indicated, this is never a matter of duplicating one's sameness but of the opening up of individuals, cultures, and religions—including the church, of course—to their Other.

In addition to the social dimension, Francis also emphasizes a temporal aspect of openness: the Samaritan, he writes first in *FT* 101, was free of "every label and position," that is, free from all the ballast that in church, politics, and society often not only separates people from one another but actually imprisons them in their social status. In this freedom he was able to "change his plans, and unexpectedly come to the aid of an injured person who needed his help" (*FT* 101). The openness to the future is accompanied by a willingness to perceive the Other's wounds and vulnerabilities that are expressions of the openness of creaturely existence. The hearing that opens itself up to the need of the Other corresponds with an interruption of the chronological flow of time that always continues the same. The accompanying directedness of human existence toward the future reminds us of the order of creation (Gen 1:1—2:3), whose innermost moment is the Sabbath as a festive determination and interruption of time, which is opened by the seventh day to its transcendent determination.[3] One could say, then, that the turning to the Other expresses the eschatological dimension of the true Sabbath, which unites people and in which the Other becomes the neighbor.

In these reflections on openness to the unforeseen as the condition of true fraternity, Francis suggests an ecclesiological program: to be church does not mean continuity of the status quo, that is, of a transcendent eternity erected over the uncertainties of temporal existence as a final refuge, but opening toward the Other, which at the same time means opening toward the future and, in the end, the festive arrival of God himself.

The Integrative Power of Openness

The establishment of an open society has its yardstick in its integrative power. This is, again, not about all inhabitants of a territory being subjected to a majority culture and being "integrated" in this melting pot. Rather, it is crucial that people are not excluded on the basis of their otherness. The particular emphasis Pope Francis places on openness is made clear by an uncompromising rejection of all ideologies based on exclusion, be it of a legal, economic, political or social nature. In passing, it should be noted

---

3. See Agamben, *Il tempo che resta*; and Appel, *In Praise of Mortality*.

that the pope also makes a clear statement with regard to the exclusion of women from social participation (*FT* 23). However, especially as far as this issue is concerned, clear concepts of how such exclusion of women, not least from ecclesial decision-making processes, can be changed will be necessary in the immediate future in order to actually be able to credibly invite all to a global narrative of openness.

It is no coincidence that Francis places special emphasis on the openness to people with disabilities, many of whom feel "without belonging and without participating" (*FT* 98). This is not only because many disabled people are at the lowest social rung, but also because they eminently express human vulnerability. Since openness and vulnerability are inseparably linked, these vulnerable groups are primarily the place where not only the open individual and the open community find their measure but ultimately also the transcendence of God, which is inseparably linked to this openness, indicated not least by the open side of the risen Jesus, from which the church springs.

An urgent concern of *Fratelli Tutti* is to "re-envisage the social role of property" (*FT* 118–27), since certain forms of ownership ultimately create insurmountable boundaries between the haves and the have-nots and exclude entire groups of people from a dignified life, making recognition impossible for them. The human being regresses to a consumer or to a supplicant and can thus no longer be recognized in his dignity, which is expressed in self-determination and equal opportunities on the social and political level.

The document shows particular sensitivity and prophetic power in its criticism of the economic liberal idea of achievement. The pope emphasizes that human dignity does not have to be earned but is inherent in the human being (*FT* 107). Above all, according to the pope, achievement is based on a different criterion than in liberalism: it is not measured by one's own advancement, but by one's contribution to an inclusive community and society. The special achievement lies in the establishment of a community based on solidarity, in which everyone has what is necessary for a life of dignity, with recognition being an essential part of this dignity in addition to material security. The creation of such a community includes both the construction of an inclusive civil society and the participation in and promotion of social movements, as well as a state that bears responsibility not only for the citizen but for all those who reside in its territory, thus especially also for the foreigner, because "each country also belongs to the foreigner" (*FT* 124). The vision of an inclusive, fraternal, and—if *Laudato Si'* is taken into account—also ecologically oriented society is completed by the demand for a "new network of international relations" (*FT* 126), which should make it possible that the voices, rights, and needs of peoples who are otherwise powerless pawns of global politics are also heard.

Openness and *Benevolentia*

The basic attitude of openness is also described by Pope Francis with the term *benevolentia*, "[the] attitude that 'wills the good' of others" (*FT* 112). This benevolence as a basic attitude is in radical contradiction to a perverse claim to power—found today, among others, in the once prophetic US Conference of Catholic Bishops[4]—which pretends to be morally superior and from this apparent moral superiority aims at exclusion for the purpose of its own self-assurance and self-legitimization.

In Francis, *benevolentia* becomes a measure of the moral good, which is thus measured by sympathy and compassion with the Other[5] and cannot be reduced to abstract commandments. Perceiving the story of the Other, which is always connected with injuries, thus becomes the basis of this new narrative indicated by *Fratelli Tutti*.

In this context, the question of the addressee of the encyclical arises: in many passages, the primary addressees are the elites of the Western world,[6] to whom an appeal is made to open up to a new community with those on the margins. On this, it should be noted that openness as a basic motif of *Fratelli Tutti* also has to be applied to the narrative of the encyclical itself. It is open to continuations and will require the addition of many stories and voices and, in particular, of those on the peripheries. If the pope, within the framework of his sphere of action, brings the topic of "synodality" to the fore as the next stage, then this synodality will not only have to work through structural questions of the church (including canon law) but will also have to be a place of hospitality for actively raising the voice of the economic and social peripheries. Even if Pope Francis is particularly concerned in this encyclical to make the voiceless heard, the next step will be to make the polyphony of the church and the world yet clearer and to shift the perspective further in the direction of the so-called peripheries.

---

4. One should think of the documents: US Conference of Catholic Bishops, "Challenge of Peace"; and US Conference of Catholic Bishops, "Economic Justice for All." The US Conference of Catholic Bishops, with its attitude of moral self-righteousness, ignoring the suffering of the Other, has now become a symptom of what has gone wrong in the Catholic Church in recent decades.

5. See Godzieba, *Theology of the Presence*.

6. *FT* 19, for example, states: "A decline in the birthrate, which leads to the aging of the population . . ." which can hardly be considered a diagnosis for Africa.

The Guest as a Model of Openness and the Questions of Openness and Boundaries

Overall, *Fratelli Tutti* is a document of universal hospitality. Pope Francis quotes from a wide variety of documents and sources across times, spaces, and religions. In addition, he also speaks of the "sacred duty of hospitality" (*FT* 90) and a welcoming culture that is paradigmatically lived in Benedictine spirituality.

Hospitality and the figure of the guest associated with it go far beyond ethical demands; rather, the figure of the guest implies theological[7] and ontological[8] dimensions. In Matt 25:31–46, Jesus himself identifies with the guest, and Gen 18 links the promise to Abraham with the welcoming of the guest, who thus stands not only at the origin of every human existence—we all began our existence as guests of our mothers—but also at the origin of God's people. YHWH is the guest of his people in the tent of the covenant, and Jesus never appears in the Gospels as the owner of a home of his own but always as a guest. The gift (*Gabe*) that the guest brings symbolizes himself, making him also the host (*Gastgeber*), in whose history and desire the inviter can participate. This is expressed in every Eucharistic celebration when Jesus, as a guest of the community, gives himself and thereby gathers the community, becoming the host (*Gastgeber*) of it. Of particular importance, especially for *Fratelli Tutti*, is the fact that the guest suspends the dichotomy between home and the foreign—and thus also between immanence and transcendence. As the one who does not belong to the home, he is nevertheless at its center, to which a moment of openness is inscribed in the hospitable reception, which constitutes it as a living thing in the first place. In opposition to the Cartesian subject, the guest is never with himself, but is bound in his existence to being received. Being a guest is more fundamental than the self-possession of the subject, and reception and being received establish living existence. The God of the Bible also binds himself to the reception of the faithful (in prayer, discipleship, and proclamation) and reveals himself therein as a living God. The narrative of *Fratelli Tutti* is also on this track: it is perhaps the most hospitable encyclical ever written by a pope, because it springs from the hospitable encounter with the representative of another religion, hospitably welcomes the most diverse documents, and invites to cultivate an ethos and a narrative of hospitality from which no one is excluded on the basis of his religious, ideological, or cultural origin.

---

7. See Theobald, *Le christianisme comme style*.
8. See Bahr, *Die Sprache des Gastes*.

Epilogue

Like the demons encountered in the Gospels, Jesus also permanently crosses boundaries. The way of the demons, however, leads to a completely uniform, entropic boundlessness, to an infinite, from which there can be no exit. The boundlessness of the demonic therefore definitely precludes the possibility of the Other and thus of the hospitable encounter. Jesus, on the other hand, suspends those inhospitable boundaries that make new encounters impossible. He is the living subversion of inhospitable structures, institutions, ideologies, and practices. In this way, he leads to a playful and open approach to boundaries without annihilating the moment of the Other. *Fratelli Tutti*, and in it especially the third chapter, proves to be an opening narrative of the open (this pleonasm may be allowed at this point!) whose ethos will have been measured by the hospitable welcome of the Other and his stories, which are always stories of vulnerable existence as well.

Bibliography

Agamben, Giorgio. *Il tempo che resta: Un commento alla Lettera ai Romani*. Turin: Bollati Boringhieri, 2000.

Appel, Kurt. *In Praise of Mortality: Christianity as a New Humanism*. Leiden: Brill, 2021.

Bahr, Hans-Dieter. *Die Sprache des Gastes: Eine Metaethik*. Leipzig: Reclam, 1994.

Eco, Umberto. "Weak Thought and the Limits of Interpretation." In *Weakening Philosophy: Essays in Honour of Gianni Vattimo*, edited by Santiago Zabala, 37–56. Montreal: McGill-Queen's University Press, 2007.

Francis, Pope. *Evangelii Gaudium: On the Proclamation of the Gospel in Today's World*. Vatican City: Libreria Editrice Vaticana, 2013. https://www.vatican.va/content/francesco/en/apost_exhortations/documents/papa-francesco_esortazione-ap_20131124_evangelii-gaudium.html.

———. *Fratelli Tutti: On Fraternity and Social Friendship*. Vatican City: Libreria Editrice Vaticana, 2020. https://www.vatican.va/content/francesco/en/encyclicals/documents/papa-francesco_20201003_enciclica-fratelli-tutti.html.

———. *Laudato Si': On Care for Our Common Home*. Vatican City: Libreria Editrice Vaticana, 2015. https://www.vatican.va/content/francesco/en/encyclicals/documents/papa-francesco_20150524_enciclica-laudato-si.html.

Godzieba, Anthony J. *Theology of the Presence and Absence of God*. Collegeville, MN: Liturgical Academic, 2018.

Standaerd, Benoit. *Marco: Vangelo di una notte, vangelo per la vita*. Bologna: Dehoniane Bologna, 2011.

Theobald, Christoph. *Le christianisme comme style: Une manière de faire de la théologie en postmodernité*. Paris: Cerf, 2007.

U.S. Conference of Catholic Bishops. *The Challenge of Peace: God's Promise and Our Response: A Pastoral Letter on War and Peace*. Washington, DC: United States Catholic Conference, 1983.

———. *Economic Justice for All: Pastoral Letter on Catholic Social Teaching and the U.S. Economy*. Washington, DC: United States Catholic Conference, 1986.

PART FOUR

A Heart Open to the Whole World

13

Four Marks of an Ecclesiology of Migration

Idara Otu, MSP

Our response to the arrival of migrating persons can be summarized by four words: welcome, protect, promote, and integrate.

—Pope Francis, *Fratelli Tutti*, 129

Migration is constitutive of both ancient and modern societies. Every nation is a contributor to and beneficiary of human mobility. Contemporary trends and waves of migration are complicated, offering both prospects and challenges. The myriad concerns related to migration are the focus of chapter 4 of *Fratelli Tutti*. Acknowledging that the world is our common home, Pope Francis calls the faithful and people of goodwill to welcome, protect, promote, and integrate migrants through responsible migration legislation. This chapter presents a summary of the encyclical's fourth chapter and proposes theological presuppositions as a basis for an ecclesiology of migration.

Fraternity Beyond Borders

Human beings are born into fraternal relationships with other humans. Considering this existential reality, Pope Francis, in chapter 4 of *Fratelli Tutti*, affirms the universality of fraternal communion and social friendship as foundations for the care of migrants (*FT* 128). This teaching echoes his teaching in the earlier encyclical *Laudato Si'*: "Everything is related, and we human beings are united as brothers and sisters on a wonderful pilgrimage, woven together by the love God has for each of his creatures and which also unites us in fond affection with brother sun, sister moon, brother river and mother earth."[1] Pope Francis notes that "global society is not the sum total of different countries, but rather the communion that exists among them" (*FT* 149). This interdependence within humanity has gradually been eroded by regressive nationalism, a globalization of indifference, a throwaway culture, and a deficit of intrinsic human dignity at national borders (*FT* 10–12).

The universality of fraternity and social friendship moves in tandem with African anthropology, expressed in the ethos of African cultures, including songs, proverbs, and folklore. African anthropology conceives the person as a being in fraternal relationship. This is expressed among the Nguni of South Africa as *ubuntu—Umuntu ngumuntu ngabantu—*"I am human, therefore we are," or "A person is a person through other people," or "I am because we are."[2] This African anthropology has been popularized by African theologians including John Mbiti, Bénézet Bujo, and the South African Anglican bishop Desmond Tutu, whom Pope Francis describes as an inspiration of universal fraternity (*FT* 286). The quintessence of ubuntu is that the person is an interdependent being living in a fraternal community expressing openness, mutuality, dialogue, and interpersonal encounter.[3] African anthropology embodied as ubuntu calls for a rediscovery of the world as a shared fraternal home predicated on a common paternity and equal dignity as God's children.[4]

Despite the modern organization of society, every person, "whatever their origin, know(s) that they are part of the greater human family, without which they will not be able to understand themselves fully" (*FT* 149). This fraternal bond is challenged by current waves of migration precipitated by social pathologies, including war, conflicts, religious persecution, and ecological crisis. Responding to these concerns is not to be the onerous task of individuals, but a collective responsibility of humanity. For Pope Francis, "we are either all saved together, or no one is saved" (*FT* 137). The challenges of migrants are the challenges of Christians: "The joys and the hopes, the griefs and anxieties of the men of this age, especially of those who are poor or in any way afflicted, these are the joys and hopes, the griefs and

---

1. Francis, *Laudato Si'*, 92.
2. Tutu, *God Has a Dream*, 26; Otu, *Communion Ecclesiology*, 9.
3. Orobator, "Fratelli Tutti," 1.
4. Otu and Aina, "Civilization of Communion," 75.

anxieties of the followers of Christ."[5] Fraternity transcends borders, races, nations, tongues, and cultures.

Pope Francis sees the challenges of migration as being complex and without predetermined answers. A global response to migration would involve local, national, and international collaboration. Such cooperation must respect the right of nations to provide a dignified home for its citizens and ensure the dignity and rights of migrants. Within this context, the pope articulates four virtuous dynamics for a globally transformative response to migration:

> Our response to the arrival of migrating persons can be summarized by four words: welcome, protect, promote and integrate. For "it is not a case of implementing welfare programmes from the top down, but rather of undertaking a journey together, through these four actions, in order to build cities and countries that, while preserving their respective cultural and religious identity, are open to differences and know how to promote them in the spirit of human fraternity." (*FT* 129)

These four virtuous elements echo the vision expressed by Pope Francis on the 104th World Day of Migrants and Refugees.[6] In his message, the pope urges the faithful to show fraternity to migrants, "at every stage of the migratory experience—from departure through journey to arrival and return."[7] The acts of welcoming, protecting, promoting, and integrating migrants are not meant to encourage illegal movement across borders; rather, they characterize the minimum level of protection and care that migrants should expect from nations, especially with respect to their dignity and rights.

In particular, the pope proposes "indispensable steps" that governments should take in assisting refugees and migrants. These include:

> increasing and simplifying the granting of visas; adopting programmes of individual and community sponsorship; opening humanitarian corridors for the most vulnerable refugees; providing suitable and dignified housing; guaranteeing personal security and access to basic services; ensuring adequate consular assistance; . . . [a] right to retain personal identity documents; equitable access to the justice system; the possibility of opening bank accounts; . . . [a] guarantee of the minimum needed to survive; freedom of movement; . . . [the] possibility of employment; protecting minors and ensuring their regular access to education;

---

5. Second Vatican Council, *Lumen Gentium*, 1.
6. Francis, "Message."
7. Francis, "Message."

providing for programmes of temporary guardianship or shelter; guaranteeing religious freedom; promoting integration into society; supporting the reuniting of families; and preparing local communities for the process of integration. (*FT* 130)

These steps can be very demanding given the current post-pandemic challenges and the depressed economic situation facing many nations. Pope Francis advocates for short-term and long-term planning that transcends temporary responses (*FT* 130). These are geared toward integrating migrants into their host nations, while promoting development in their nations of origin (*FT* 132). Such planning would involve dialogue and cooperation among nations, especially in building a global juridical, political, and economic order that benefits both individual countries and the entire world (*FT* 137).

The present-day interplay between localization and globalization demands a balanced concern for each culture and the common good of everyone. Pope Francis disapproves of a "local narcissism" born of fear of the other that brews rejection and the closure of nations to migrants. On the one hand, the pope calls for the "need to pay attention to the global so as to avoid narrowness and banality, but on the other hand, "we also need to look to the local, which keeps our feet on the ground" (*FT* 146). There is a "joyful realization" that no one people or culture can achieve everything on its own (*FT* 150). While some nations may temporarily profit from isolation, no nation can develop and sustain itself without other nations (*FT* 150–51). Pope Francis appeals for mutual exchange between nations and healthy universal integration (*FT* 151). Fruitful exchanges between migrants and host nations are a blessing and enrichment that encourage a society to grow (*FT* 136).

In certain circumstances, when a mutual exchange is not foreseen, migrants are to be treated on the basis of "fraternal gratuitousness" (*FT* 139–41). "Gratuitousness makes it possible for us to welcome the stranger, even though this brings us no immediate tangible benefit" (*FT* 141). Modern-day approaches to migration must integrate insights from both local and global contexts in order to promote a "healthy relationship between love of one's native land and a sound sense of belonging to our larger human family" (*FT* 149).

Promoting a creative balance between the local and global entails developing "a form of global governance" for migration (*FT* 132). Such governance recognizes that migrants are not merely numbers, nor are they enemies of the state. As the African proverb goes: "Wisdom lies not in the aged but in those who venture out of their homeland."[8] Host nations should

---

8. Aihiokhai, "African Migrant Christians," 307.

consider migrants as gifts and blessings to their cultural heritage (*FT* 134). Consequently, migrants who have spent considerable time in their host nations should be considered for citizenship "based on the equality of rights and duties, under which all enjoy justice" (*FT* 131). The pope advocates for citizenship for migrants, rather than categorizing them as minorities, which engenders an inferiority complex (*FT* 131). However, Francis disapproves of those who manipulate and cheat society and live off the system (*FT* 75); thus, his words would not apply to migrants who cross borders contrary to immigration laws with a sense of entitlement to settle in another country.

In advocating for the fraternal virtues of welcoming, protecting, promoting, and integrating migrants, Pope Francis reclaims the fraternal communion that characterizes the global village. Migration provides a reciprocity of gifts and blessings among nations, continents, and the world. Current narcissistic and dehumanizing approaches applied to modern-day migrants fall short of the minimum requirements for humane and dignified treatment of the human person. Migration is integral to human society, offering the possibility of preserving and sustaining human flourishing and the mutual sharing of earthly treasures. Migrants are global citizens meriting fraternity and social friendship that supports their rights and the rights of nations.

Human Migration and the African Continent

Migration is often relegated to the affairs of governance and civil society, which seems to absolve the universal church from responding to the plight of migrants. With *Fratelli Tutti*, Pope Francis states his position that migration is a sign of the times that deserves adequate understanding and a Christian response. He has formalized the church's response through the formation of a Department for Migrants and Refugees within the Vatican's Dicastery for Promoting Integral Human Development. Pope Francis explains the rationale for the creation of this department for migration thus: "I decided that, at least for the time being, that department would be directly under the Pope, because here we have a shameful situation that can only be described by a word that came spontaneously to my lips in Lampedusa: a disgrace."[9]

Although migration can be a grace-filled encounter for peoples from diverse cultures, races, and religions, a significant population of Africans—despite human capital and natural endowments—are compelled by excruciating and inhumane existential conditions to flee their homelands for safe havens. Embarking on such a journey is a perilous decision that Africans

9. Francis, "Address."

nonetheless embrace so as to escape violence, discrimination, famine, ecological disasters, and indecent living standards.

Despite Africa being home to the world's largest refugee camp, many African nations consistently relate as good neighbors to each other. The Bidibidi camp in Uganda, which opened in August 2016, holds an estimated three hundred thousand African refugees.[10] Other large refugee camps include Dadaab and Kakuma (Kenya), Ida (South Sudan), Katumba (Tanzania), and Pugnido (Ethiopia). Africa exemplifies the globalization of fraternity and social friendship toward migrants, especially those forced out of their homelands. Contradicting such experiences, however, is the despicable treatment of African migrants *en route* to the global North, sold as slaves by some African nations.[11]

Amidst waves of increasing migration within Africa and from the global South to the global North, the church in Africa cannot remain indifferent nor complacent to the plight of millions of Africans languishing in jails in North Africa, sold as slaves in Ethiopia, and dying in the Mediterranean Sea and the Sahara Desert. Such experiences of African migrants arise from their exclusion from the larger human family and from others seeing them as usurpers who have nothing to offer (*FT* 141). How can local churches respond to the plight of African migrants? This ecclesiological question is the focus of the following exposition, understood in light of Pope Francis's teaching.

Presuppositions for an Ecclesiology of Migration

The church's mission is predicated on its self-understanding. How the church conceives of its mission to migrants underscores the theological presuppositions it needs to engage society. The Second Vatican Council's image of the church as a pilgrim people conveys the reality of migration: "The pilgrim Church in her sacraments and institutions, which pertain to this present time, has the appearance of this world which is passing and she herself dwells among creatures who groan and travail in pain until now and await the revelation of the sons of God."[12] As a pilgrim community journeying toward heaven, the church guides and accompanies humanity through earthly living.[13] Pope Francis echoes this conciliar teaching: "We must never forget that we are pilgrims journeying alongside one another.

---

10. Ilo and Otu, "Mapping a Contextual Theology," 274–75.
11. Ilo and Otu, "Mapping a Contextual Theology," 265–67.
12. Second Vatican Council, *Lumen Gentium*, 48.
13. Paul VI, *Gaudium et Spes*, 57.

This means that we must have sincere trust in our fellow pilgrims, putting aside all suspicion or mistrust, and turn our gaze to what we are all seeking: the radiant peace of God's face."[14] The pope offers a pastoral path for the mission toward migrants, rooted in fraternity and a "remarkable system of welcoming pilgrims as an exercise of the sacred duty of hospitality" (*FT* 90). Developing this "remarkable system" entails an ecclesiology of migration that is both biblical and founded on the early church's practice of fraternity: "All the believers were one in heart and mind. No one claimed that any of their possessions was their own, but they shared everything they had" (Acts 4:32, NIV). This civilization of fraternity is a mark of the early church, characterized by a sense of mutual sharing, social friendship, and fraternity (Acts 4:34–35).

An ecclesiology of migration expresses the fraternal relationship between God and the faithful, as well as between the faithful and humanity in general. Drawing from the encyclical, an ecclesiology of migration means that the church is "open to bearing witness in today's world, open to faith hope and love for the Lord and for those whom he loves with a preferential love. A home with open doors . . . because she is a mother" (*FT* 276). This is a pilgrim church that "leaves home and goes forth from its places of worship, goes forth from its sacristies" to accompany migrants, break down walls of abuse aimed at migrants, and sow seeds of reconciliation (*FT* 276). This way of being church is rooted in fraternity that fosters communion among all peoples, including migrants, who represent the neglected voice of the twenty-first century (Matt 25:35).

An ecclesiology of migration expresses the church's self-understanding as characterized by the fraternally interrelated virtues of welcoming, protecting, promoting, and integrating. The first, welcoming, requires particular churches to provide pastoral care and necessary material support to migrants. This entails that the clergy and lay faithful will assist migrants in settling in host nations. Protecting—the second virtue—pertains to ensuring the dignity and rights of migrants. Migrants deserving special protection include women, minors, the aged, and the vulnerable. Migrants deserve protection from injustice, abuse, and oppression, as well as from attitudes, structures, and policies that dehumanize. Protecting also demands preserving the cultures of the migrants, not only for their sake, but also because it enriches the host nations. The third virtue, promoting, includes advocating for equal opportunities for refugees and migrants as citizens. In some cases, this demands developing a legal path for migrants and refugees to freely choose to become citizens of their host nations. The fourth and last virtue,

---

14. Francis, *Evangelii Gaudium*, 244.

integration, does not imply an assimilation that leads to suppression of the cultural identity of migrants and refugees, but rather dictates balanced, mutual enrichment.[15]

These four proposed marks of an ecclesiology of migration raise questions for theologians. Are all migrants—legal and illegal—to be welcomed by host nations? Beyond those seeking asylum, are criminal migrants entitled to protection? How can citizens protect and promote migration in their homeland if it is hostile to migrants? How do host nations create an integration process that preserves the cultural heritage and religious traditions of migrants without promoting two-tier citizenship? These four marks strive for an openness to both migrants' respect and love for the rule of law in the host nations and their own cultural roots. Further theological development of Pope Francis's typology of responding to migration is now the task of theologians.

An ecclesiology of migration is appropriate for African Catholicism in light of the storms of conflict and division that further fragment the continent. Fraternity understood as ubuntu underlines the basis for an ecclesiology of migration—a church in Africa that fosters fraternity and friendship, in which the faithful participate in the lives and experiences of migrants and refugees. Such an ecclesiology of migration speaks of the church in Africa being animated by the fraternal communion that characterizes African anthropology. This ethos goes beyond ethnicity and clannish ties, thus embracing radical welcoming, protecting, promoting, and integrating of the other.

The domestication of this fraternal communion, according to Ikenna Okafor, is necessary for overcoming indifference, discrimination, racism, ethnocentrism, and tribalism.[16] An ecclesiology of migration seeks to break the walls of division among African nations and build instead fraternity and friendship among nations, as well as between the church and migrants. This ecclesiological conception can promote attentive listening to the stories and experiences of migrants, since their stories and experiences are part of the church in Africa.

Conclusion

Human migration poses challenges and concerns for the African continent and the church in Africa. Africa cannot rely solely on the global North to respond to these challenges and concerns. While it is within the domain of governments and civil society to address the existential conditions in their

15. Francis, "Message."
16. Okafor, *Toward an African Theology*, 166.

nations, particular churches in Africa have a Christian duty to understand and respond to the plights of migrants and refugees. Pope Francis offers a theological motif for the care of migrants that is rooted in fraternity and social friendship. These twin virtues are connatural to African anthropology, which merits rediscovery and inculturation into the theological and pastoral presuppositions of caring for migrants. In articulating a theological and pastoral basis for the care of migrants and refugees, the church in Africa's self-understanding as a family of God on a pilgrimage must be characterized by the four marks of an ecclesiology of migration: welcoming, protecting, promoting, and integrating.

Bibliography

Aihiokhai, Simon Mary Asese. "African Migrant Christians Changing the Landscape of Christianity in the West: Reading the Signs of the Times." In *The Church, Migration, and Global (In)Difference*, edited by Darren J. Dias et al., eds., 289–307. Cham, Switzerland: Palgrave Macmillan, 2021.

Dias, Darren J., et al., eds. *The Church, Migration, and Global (In)Difference*. Pathways for Ecumenical and Interreligious Dialogue. Cham, Switzerland: Palgrave Macmillan, 2021.

Francis, Pope. "Address of His Holiness Pope Francis to Participants in the 3rd World Meeting of Popular Movements." Paul VI Audience Hall, Vatican City, November 5, 2016. https://www.vatican.va/content/francesco/en/speeches/2016/november/documents/papa-francesco_20161105_movimenti-popolari.html.

———. *Evangelii Gaudium*. Vatican City: Libreria Editrice Vaticana, 2013.

———. *Fratelli Tutti: On Fraternity and Social Friendship*. Vatican City: Libreria Editrice Vaticana, 2020. https://www.vatican.va/content/francesco/en/encyclicals/documents/papa-francesco_20201003_enciclica-fratelli-tutti.html.

———. *Laudato Si': On Care for Our Common Home*. Vatican City: Libreria Editrice Vaticana, 2015. https://www.vatican.va/content/francesco/en/encyclicals/documents/papa-francesco_20150524_enciclica-laudato-si.html.

———. "Message of His Holiness Pope Francis for the 104th World Day of Migrants and Refugees 2018." Vatican City, January 14, 2018. https://www.vatican.va/content/francesco/en/messages/migration/documents/papa-francesco_20170815_world-migrants-day-2018.html.

Ilo, Stan Chu, and Idara Otu. "Mapping a Contextual Theology of African Migration." In *The Church, Migration, and Global (In)Difference*, edited by Darren J. Dias, et al., eds., 265–88. Cham, Switzerland: Palgrave Macmillan, 2021.

Okafor, Ikenna Ugochukwu. *Toward an African Theology of Fraternal Solidarity: UBE NWANNE*. Eugene, OR: Pickwick, 2014.

Orobator, Agbonkhianmeghe E. "'Fratelli Tutti' and the African Philosophical and Political Tradition of Ubuntu." *L'Osservatore Romano*, January 9, 2021.

Otu, Idara. *Communion Ecclesiology and Social Transformation: Between Vatican Council II and African Synod II*. Eugene, OR: Pickwick, 2020.

Otu, Idara, and Raymond Aina. "The Civilization of Communion: Theological Paradigms for African Migration." *Bulletin of Ecumenical Theology* 31 (2019) 61–84.

Paul VI, Pope. *Gaudium et Spes: Pastoral Constitution on the Church in the Modern World*. Vatican City: Libreria Editrice Vaticana, 1965. https://www.vatican.va/archive/hist_councils/ii_vatican_council/documents/vat-ii_const_19651207_gaudium-et-spes_en.html.

Second Vatican Council. *Lumen Gentium: Dogmatic Constitution on the Church*. Vatican City: Libreria Editrice Vaticana, 1964. https://www.vatican.va/archive/hist_councils/ii_vatican_council/documents/vat-ii_const_19641121_lumen-gentium_en.html.

Tutu, Desmond. *God Has a Dream: A Vision of Hope for Our Time*. New York: Image, 2004.

14

The Challenges of Migration in Asia

Kochurani Abraham

Migration powers economic growth, reduces inequalities, and connects diverse societies. Yet it is also a source of political tensions and human tragedies.
—Antonio Guterres[1]

In a word, it is not only the cause of migrants that is at stake; it is not just about them, but about all of us, and about the present and future of the human family. Migrants, especially those who are most vulnerable, help us to read the "signs of the times. Through them, the Lord is calling us to conversion, to be set free from exclusivity, indifference and the throw-away culture. Through them, the Lord invites us to embrace fully our Christian life and to contribute, each according to his or her proper vocation, to the building up of a world that is more and more in accord with God's plan.
—Pope Francis[2]

---

1. Quoted in United Nations ESCAP, "Plight of Migrants."
2. Francis, "Message."

As we move into the third decade of the twenty-first century, migration is no longer a new issue facing humanity. We have for some time lived in a highly globalized world where the mobility of peoples has been on the increase due to the many factors that color the contours of human landscapes. Ethnic conflicts, outrageous situations resulting from terrorism, persecution, strife, natural and human-made calamities, the adverse effects of climate change and other environmental concerns, or just the search for better prospects in life—all of these have contributed to the migration of people from one country to another or within the same country. Since migrants are not always welcomed by the people already living in the destination location, global organizations like the United Nations have consistently intervened for the purpose of lessening conflicts that result from people crossing borders.

The Catholic Church has been very attentive to the concerns of migrants over the years. In his celebrated encyclical *Rerum Novarum*, Pope Leo XIII affirmed people's right to work in order to earn a livelihood.[3] In *Pacem in Terris*, Pope Saint John XXIII stretched the scope of this right by affirming that every human being has the right to freedom of movement and the rights to immigrate to other countries and assert citizenship in the world community.[4] Catholic social teaching has time and again argued that the right to life and the conditions worthy of life—especially when threatened by poverty, injustice, religious intolerance, armed conflict, or other difficult circumstances—give rise to the right to migrate.[5] Pope Francis's latest encyclical, *Fratelli Tutti*, is yet another expression of the church's position on the migrant question. The pope reminds us that "more than ever before," migrations "will play a pivotal role in the future of our world" (*FT* 40). This observation is of crucial significance as the demographics of most of our urban societies are being significantly altered by the increasing presence of migrant communities. The phenomenon of migration is a decisive component in the evolutionary story of humans, and it is important to acknowledge that addressing it constructively is fundamental to future human growth and well-being, both individually and as communities.

In this essay we examine the challenges of migration in Asia in light of Pope Francis's call to become "A Heart Open to the Whole World" (*FT* chapter 4, 128–53). First, we shall take a look at the specifics of migration in the Asian context, reflect critically on its repercussions, and draw out

---

3. Leo XIII, *Rerum Novarum*, 44.

4. John XXIII, *Pacem in Terris*, 25.

5. US Conference of Catholic Bishops and Conferencia del Episcopado Mexicano, "Strangers No Longer," 28–29.

the theological and pastoral implications of becoming "borderless" in the particular sociocultural setting of Asia.

Asia and Migration

For Asians, migration is a phenomenon woven into the very texture of life. This fact is substantiated by the 2018 Asian Economic Integration Report, which asserts that Asia remains the world's largest continental source of international migrants.[6] One in three migrants worldwide comes from this region, and the majority of Asian migrants are semi- and low-skilled workers, such as maids, caregivers, and manual laborers, including those working on construction sites.[7]

As is true elsewhere in the world, the migration question in Asia is deeply marked by an interplay of light and shadow. In the migration stories of the millions who have moved into distant lands in search of a better future, we see their joys and hopes intricately intertwined with their fears and tears. Paying attention to this reality would help us perceive more clearly the implications of what it means to have a "heart open to the whole world" in the spirit of *Fratelli Tutti*.

A major driving force behind migration from Asia is the question of remittances, which are a vital source of income for many developing countries on the continent.[8] Migrants fill the gaps in labor markets and do work that local populations are unwilling or unable to do. In lowering production costs, they shore up entire sectors of the economies of some countries. They also contribute to the transfer of knowledge and skills and are often innovators and entrepreneurs.[9] While exposure to new and urbanized settings can be empowering for some, it can be a daunting experience for others who are unskilled or marginalized; many Asian migrants fall into this category. Because they lack legal status, many are unable to access critical public services, such as healthcare, education, and housing. In addition, they fall prey to the abuse of a range of actors like human traffickers or unscrupulous

---

6. See Asian Development Bank, *Asian Economic Integration Report 2018*, 80.

7. Édes, "Migration in Asia."

8. In 2018, the top three remittance recipients—India, the People's Republic of China, and the Philippines—accounted for 59.5 percent ($179.8 billion) of all remittances to Asia and 26.3 percent of remittances globally ($682.6 billion). Asian Development Bank, *Asian Economic Integration Report 2019/2020*, 78–82.

9. United Nations ESCAP, "Plight of Migrants."

employers who force them to work for low pay with no social protection and in abusive working and living conditions.[10]

Alongside the issue of migration from Asian countries to other continents, we need to pay attention to concerns relating to internal migration within Asia and within each country in Asia. In India alone, around four hundred million workers have migrated from the rural areas to the cities and from some of the poorer northern states to the more affluent states in the south of the country. This is true of other Asian countries as well—in some places, internal migration is an everyday occurrence. Within the pluralistic social fabric of Asia, migration accelerates the intermingling of culturally diverse groups inside national boundaries and across the borders that demarcate nations. Pluralism can create an enriching social mosaic of intercultural living, but when people with diverse religiocultural identities cohabit, the lived experience can be very distant from this idealistic picture, and even more so when some of those present in a given society are stuck on the lower rungs of the socioeconomic ladder. It is against this backdrop of Asia's religious plurality, cultural diversity, and economic disparity that we situate *Fratelli Tutti* and the challenges it issues to us on the question of migration.

Becoming "A Heart Open to the Whole World"

The "heart" is a powerful icon of love cutting across cultures and religions all over the globe, a sign that has withstood the test of time to symbolize the human capacity to love and embrace life. In the Aristotelian tradition, the "heart" was taken to be the seat of the soul,[11] and within the Christian theological framework, it became a powerful symbol of divine energies of unconditional love as manifested in the person of Jesus Christ. Pope Francis's call to become "a heart open to the whole world" reflects this Christian vision.

It is important to note that in *Fratelli Tutti*, the call to open our hearts to the world is not premised on the haze of utopian ideals but on the grounded realities of "borders and their limits" (the first subheading of chapter 4). A border—as we all would agree—is a defining reality that classifies people as insiders or outsiders, those who belong to what is accepted as "mine" or "ours" and those considered to be the dispensable "other." Borders delineate family boundaries, social groups, religious communities, and the familiar world of neighbors and friends where social friendship flows without

---

10. United Nations ESCAP and United Nations Network on Migration, "Concept Note," 2

11. O'Rourke Boyle, *Cultural Anatomies of the Heart*, xii.

inhibition. Pope Francis highlights that "complex challenges arise when our neighbour happens to be an immigrant" (*FT* 129). This complexity is dependent on the human geography and the socioreligious and cultural settings in any given societal context.

The Asian continent contains a mosaic of people belonging to various ethnic and religious identities. Even within national boundaries there are clusters of ethnic and religious groupings that are separated by cultural demarcations. This reality often leads to identity formation in "we"/"they" categories and an attendant fear of the "other." Consequently, this creates new borders in order to defend what is taken to be the exclusive rights and privileges of some people and the right to exclude others who do not belong to a particular social grouping. This sociocultural and psychological distancing is all the more acute when the "other" belongs to economically marginalized and socially disadvantaged groups of people. The majority of the migrant population belongs to these underprivileged sectors of society. All of this leads to the prevalence of xenophobic attitudes and antimigrant discourses, both in the public sphere and in domestic spaces. The exhortation to "welcome, protect, promote and integrate" migrants in an act of "undertaking a journey together" with them (*FT* 129) needs to be understood in the light of the nuances of these challenges in the specifically Asian context.

In today's global setting, in which nationalism is growing, the walls marking borders are being cemented with greater vigor by the deployment of developmental and ideological discourses that are engaged in solely for the purpose of defending vested political interests. These discourses become all the more exclusive when they are colored by religion, as is happening in India today. Religious nationalism is deeply problematic, not just at the borders marking national boundaries, but also within a nation. It affects both international and intranational migration very adversely and poses a strong challenge to the openness across borders and the notion of "full citizenship" advocated by *Fratelli Tutti* (*FT* 131).

The notion of the reciprocity of gifts in relation to migration (*FT* 133–41) apparently comes from a Eurocentric view and, thus, poses a problem from the Asian perspective. Reciprocity is generally only possible between equals; otherwise, it may fall into utilitarianism. The notions of "fruitful exchange" and "gratuitousness" discussed in this section of the encyclical acquire a different meaning depending on the direction of the migrants' journey, and specifically on whether it is from the global South to the global North or the other way around. The migrants from the global North who arrive with their country's pedigree of development are better received and their cultural baggage is generally treated as an enriching "gift" (*FT* 133). But when the migrant flow is in the reverse direction, the sociocultural and religious backpacks carried by the migrants are not generally perceived as a gift, but rather as a threat. This is all the more true when set against the backdrop of the historical yoke of colonization that most Asian countries have carried for centuries. Sociocultural, political, and economic wounds inflicted on colonized countries may not have been fully healed even after decades of postcolonial existence, a fact that may color the historical memories of those belonging to the nations that have been colonizers and those of the colonized. Hence, the question is whether a reciprocal and fruitful exchange is possible when the migrant is from the colonized global South or from poorer sections of the same country.

Pastoral Implications of *Fratelli Tutti*

On the issue of migration, *Fratelli Tutti* clearly challenges Asian churches to go beyond the comfort zones of relationality marked out by the labels "my family," "my community," "my people," and "my country." Even as Christian faith is centered on the commandment to love, it is realistic to acknowledge that members of Christian communities also carry socioreligious and cultural baggage that establishes borders and decides who is within and who stands outside the precincts they delineate. For this reason, the notion of a brotherhood/sisterhood of all as proposed by *Fratelli Tutti* poses a strong challenge to the Christian praxis of the church.

"Migrants are not seen as entitled like others to participate in the life of society," observes Pope Francis (*FT* 39). Indisputably, migrant workers continue to remain one of the most vulnerable sectors of our societies, and in many places the COVID-19 pandemic has made them "homeless" even in their own homelands. In India, when a total lockdown was declared overnight, the "stay home stay safe" slogan made sense to those who were already at home with their loved ones and could work from there. But for domestic migrant workers comprised mainly of indigenous people living and working a hand-to-mouth existence far away from their homes, this meant life came to a standstill. Overnight they became jobless. With no work and no way to feed themselves, and removed from their kinship and family support networks, they had no choice but to defy the lockdown and return to their villages. Since the lockdown had brought the public transport system to a halt, they had no other choice but to walk home. For some, this meant walking hundreds of kilometers carrying their children and meager belongings. Many collapsed and died on the highways. Though a number of civil society organizations, churches, and individuals extended a helping hand to these migrants by giving them food and shelter on their journeys, they apparently did not belong to a "home" that the nation is meant to be. Those who sustain the "invisible economies of care" found themselves excluded from the nation's "care economy."

Because homelessness is the predicament of numerous migrant workers in some of the countries of the Asian continent, actually realizing "fratelli tutti"—in the real meaning of this expression—calls for pastoral approaches that go beyond reliance on conventional charities. Welcoming the stranger is a Christian imperative and from that follows the call to protect, promote, and integrate the migrant. However, this will happen only when the living of the Christian faith moves beyond mere ritualistic and spiritual exercises and fellowship within the boundaries of the church community. It calls for widening our "tents"—the boundaries of the comfort zones of love and care—beyond family, community, tribe, and nation.

Expansion of relational boundaries happens when there is a reconfiguration of the constructed identity of individuals and communities. However, unless this reconfiguration is the result of deeper convictions of justice and equality based on deeper foundations of faith, it may remain superficial. *Fratelli Tutti* calls for anchoring the praxis of the church on the core precepts of the Christian faith. The challenge here is to embrace the vision of the "reign of God" that is borderless, inclusive, and founded on equality. The Gospels testify clearly to the kinship politics of the reign of God and its implications for Christian life.

The story of the Good Samaritan as developed in *Fratelli Tutti* (*FT* 56–86) points clearly to this kinship politics in everyday living. Revisiting this story and translating it into the realities faced by migrants in our particular contexts is the pastoral imperative before us. The divides of class, race, ethnicity, and gender and the religious nationalism that is rampant in our societies has the potential to adversely affect migrant workers. Under these circumstances, the churches can engage in a liberative mission by initiating the Christian faithful into the kinship vision of the reign of God, resulting in a countercultural praxis. This can facilitate the creation of intercultural communities, interculturality being the need of the hour.

The teaching of *Fratelli Tutti* on migration calls us to pay attention to pastoral implications that are specific to Asia. A major concern here relates to the need to strengthen "care chains."[12] Many migrant women from Asian countries move abroad to meet the need for care workers in the global North, which leads to a care deficit in their home countries.[13] This applies also to cross-border migrants within Asia and migration to the major metro

---

12. Hochschild, "Global Care."
13. Asis et al., "From Asia to the World."

areas in any country. Because many children are left in the care of grandparents, there are serious concerns relating to care for both the elderly and children, and these need to inform the pastoral plans of our local churches. In addition, in situations where only one parent migrates, there may be issues relating to the emotional needs of the spouses who remain; it is important that the church community pays attention to these.

In many places, the pandemic has led to the phenomenon of "reverse migration." Many returnees have found themselves unemployed, causing their families to fall further into debt. In such situations, finding entrepreneurial possibilities in countries of origin could be a major boost for migrants who have returned. Local church communities can be instrumental in facilitating such opportunities. Initiating "Migrant Help Desks" in every diocese and parish and using the pulpit to raise the community's consciousness of this issue could pave the way for fulfilling the "welcome, protect, promote, and integrate" call of *Fratelli Tutti*.

Conclusion

Fratelli Tutti surely poses a challenge to the "frontiers" of our hearts and to the relational boundaries conditioned by our cultural programming. We hear Pope Francis inviting us in the encyclical to prophetically and courageously stretch these frontiers and to reenvision our societies using the kinship dynamics of the reign of God initiated by Jesus Christ. This is a call to incarnate love that transcends borders. When we truly believe that life on the fringes matters, we can deconstruct the dictates of the established power structures and initiate a new social order founded on the vision of Christ. This implies building new bridges of friendship across borders so that the church becomes a "home" for migrants who are "homeless," going beyond the migrants' religious affiliations. This will enable us to translate the *text* of *Fratelli Tutti* into the *texture* of our ecclesial communities, so that the church becomes a sign of hope to migrants and a sacrament of the reign of God in this world.

Bibliography

Asian Development Bank. *Asian Economic Integration Report 2018: Toward Optimal Provision of Regional Public Goods in Asia and the Pacific*. Manila: Asian Development Bank, October 2018. https://www.adb.org/sites/default/files/publication/456491/aeir-2018.pdf.

———. *Asian Economic Integration Report 2019/2020: Demographic Change, Productivity, and the Role of Technology*. Manila: Asian Development Bank, November 2019). https://www.adb.org/publications/asian-economic-integration-report-2019-2020.

Asis, Maruja M. B., et al. "From Asia to the World: 'Regional' Contributions to Global Migration Research. *Revue Européenne des Migrations Internationales* 35:1–2 (2019) 13–37.

Édes, Bart. "Migration in Asia: Where Is Everybody Going?" *World Economic Forum*, February 12, 2019. https://www.weforum.org/agenda/2019/02/migration-in-asia-where-is-everybody-going.

Francis, Pope. *Fratelli Tutti: On Fraternity and Social Friendship*. Vatican City: Libreria Editrice Vaticana, 2020. http://www.vatican.va/content/francesco/en/encyclicals/documents/papa-francesco_20201003_enciclica-fratelli-tutti.html.

———. "Pope's Message for 2019 World Day of Migrants and Refugees: Full Text." *Vatican News*, May 27, 2019. https://www.vaticannews.va/en/pope/news/2019-05/pope-francis-message-world-day-migrants-refugees-full-text.html.

Hochschild, Arlie. "Global Care Chains and Emotional Surplus Value." In *On the Edge: Living with Global Capitalism*, edited by Will Hutton and Anthony Giddens, 130–46. London: Jonathan Cape, 2000.

John XXIII, Pope. *Pacem in Terris*. Vatican City: Libreria Editrice Vaticana, 1963. https://www.vatican.va/content/john-xxiii/en/encyclicals/documents/hf_j-xxiii_enc_11041963_pacem.html.

Leo XIII, Pope. *Rerum Novarum*. Vatican City: Libreria Editrice Vaticana, 1891. https://www.vatican.va/content/leo-xiii/en/encyclicals/documents/hf_l-xiii_enc_15051891_rerum-novarum.html.

O'Rourke Boyle, Marjorie. *Cultural Anatomies of the Heart in Aristotle, Augustine, Aquinas, Calvin, and Harvey*. Cham, Switzerland: Palgrave Macmillan, 2018.

United Nations Economic and Social Commission for Asia and the Pacific (UNESCAP). "The Plight of Migrants Under the Spotlight in COVID-19 Responses." May 6, 2020. https://www.unescap.org/blog/plight-migrants-under-spotlight-covid-19-responses.

United Nations Economic and Social Commission for Asia and the Pacific (UNESCAP) and United Nations Network on Migration. "Concept Note: Asia-Pacific Regional Review of Implementation of the Global Compact for Safe, Orderly and Regular Migration, March 2021 10–12, Bangkok." August 17, 2020. https://www.unescap.org/sites/default/files/Concept%20Note_GCM_Review_E.pdf.

United States Conference of Catholic Bishops and Conferencia del Episcopado Mexicano. "Strangers No Longer: Together on the Journey of Hope." Joint Pastoral Letter Concerning Migration, January 22, 2003. https://www.usccb.org/issues-and-action/human-life-and-dignity/immigration/strangers-no-longer-together-on-the-journey-of-hope.

15

On the Way to Pluriversal

CLEUSA CALDEIRA[1]

IN THE ENCYCLICAL *FRATELLI Tutti*, following the methodological procedure created by Joseph Cardijn's for the Young Christian Workers (YCW) called "see-judge-act" (which is currently in use in Latin America, Pope Francis's home continent), the pope begins in chapter 1 by discussing "the dark clouds over a closed world," that is, the obstacles standing in the way of an experience of universal fraternity/sorority and social friendship. This world's main characteristic is globalization, with its logic of individualism, which operates to the detriment of the communal dimension of existence (*FT* 12). The pope's diagnosis is that "radical individualism is a virus that is extremely difficult to eradicate," and that it "does not make us more free, more equal, more fraternal." He emphasizes that "the mere sum of individual interests is not capable of generating a better world for the whole human family" (*FT* 105).

So, how can we escape this individualism and rediscover our common vocation? In chapter 2, "A Stranger on the Road," Pope Francis presents the parable of the Good Samaritan as a reference. From this narrative, he offers guidance for creating social and civil society (*FT* 66). He argues that the inclusion or exclusion of the downtrodden by the wayside defines all of our economic, political, social, and religious projects. Therefore, the way out of individualism is not deciding who is close enough to be our neighbor, but rather by our becoming neighbors to all (*FT* 81–82).

1. Translated by Cristina Silva.

For the pope, there is no other solution. The title of chapter 3 emphasizes that it is necessary to "envisage and engender an open world," which is much more than relating to a small group or to those with whom we have family ties, because it is impossible to understand oneself outside of a broader relational fabric. This is where the "sacred duty of hospitality" comes into play, as a concrete way of rising to the challenge and the gift that is the encounter with all of humanity (*FT* 90).

In this apocalyptic context of accelerating the end of time, fraternity and social friendship appear to be twin siblings, together the only possibility of delaying the end of time and creating a new temporality marked by gratuity. This is precisely the challenge of learning to exist in the world in another way, a relational way, as it appears more clearly in indigenous cultures, both in the *Ubuntu* of African philosophy[2] and in the *Chacana* of Andean philosophy;[3] these were cultures that were made invisible by the logic of instrumental reason under the rhetoric of being "the other."

Toward an Open World, but with an Open Heart to the Whole World

In the fourth chapter of *Fratelli Tutti*, "A Heart Open to the Whole World," Pope Francis points out the way for universal brotherhood to become something other than a mere abstraction (*FT* 128). This path goes through social friendship (solidarity). In this chapter, Pope Francis calls us to think about our mutual interactions beyond our own ethnic and cultural borders. He challenges us to think about political processes and projects that include the traditionally excluded. If, on the one hand, the issue of migrants demands urgent and concrete actions to ensure the inalienable dignity of every human person, the cry for recognition of minorities who are already part of the social fabric, on the other, calls for an application of the concept of full citizenship (*FT* 129–31). The pope recalls that the issue of citizenship was also addressed in the "Document on Human Fraternity for World Peace and Living Together," signed in Abu Dhabi. Citizenship is intrinsically linked to the inherent and inviolable dignity of the human condition. However, he emphasizes that modern citizenship brings at its

---

2. "Ubuntu can be translated as 'that which is common to all people.' The Zulu and Xhosa maxim, *umuntu ngumuntu ngabantu* (a person is a person through other people), indicates that a human being only finds realization when he humanizes other humans." Nogueira, "Ubuntu as a Way of Existing," 148.

3. *Chacana* refers to relationality according to Abya Yala's philosophical worldview and theory of existence. It means the expression of the deepest symbolic understanding of ancestral science. See Walsh, "Interculturidad," 43.

heart the "disposal culture," as it does not include those who are different, those who are considered "others."

An authentic fraternity is marked by an encounter with what is different, with the arrival of people from a different and vital cultural context; this encounter is a gift that enriches those who welcome the others. The beauty of the world comes precisely from the presence of multiple cultures, which must all be safeguarded, while at the same time all cultures must maintain an openness to others' cultures and, through an authentic exchange of gifts enter a new reality, so they can avoid the risk of falling into "cultural sclerosis" (*FT* 134, 137). This exchange does not threaten identity, as it is carried out in the form of inculturation; that is, each culture takes on new experiences in its "own unique way" (*FT* 148). It is a relationship between cultures, which must be marked by "fraternal gratuitousness" in such a way that it does not fall into utilitarianism or "frenetic commerce" (*FT* 140). The failure of this gratuitousness is one of the characteristics of closed nationalisms (*FT* 141). Pope Francis also draws attention to a false openness to the universal practiced by some inhabitants of a country, which is, in the end, nothing other than contempt or resentment toward their own people (*FT* 145).

Therefore, the permanent local-global dialectic is essential for universal fraternity/sorority and social friendship to materialize. Faced with the extremes of individualism and exclusive nationalism, which have their origin in "ancestral fears" of the other, the different, and the unknown (*FT* 27), Pope Francis emphasizes that being well rooted in one's own culture makes it possible to open up to the universal without renouncing the "richness and possibilities" of that culture (*FT* 147). He also recalls that "all healthy culture is, by nature, open and welcoming; indeed, 'a culture without universal values is not a true culture'" (*FT* 146).

Finally, the pope emphasizes that the concept of social friendship helps us understand that openness to the universal must be based on "regional exchanges" because an "appropriate and authentic openness to the world presupposes the capacity to be open to one's neighbour within a family of nations" (*FT* 151). Therefore, "opening our hearts to the whole world" implies leaving our identity clubs without renouncing our identities, overcoming the essentialist idea of culture that leads to barrenness and, above all, abandoning the view of the other as an enemy.

Interculturality as a Path to Pluriversality

Fratelli Tutti brings to mind Latin America and its peoples. On the fringe of the "globalized world," Latin America has usually been treated as "having fallen by the wayside," and has been constantly deprived of many important things. Its peoples and, more specifically, its original peoples and Afrodiasporic peoples, seek recognition of their ancestral cultures and their multiple ways of being in the world, but instead are forced to live as if they were foreigners in their own country, without dignity and without rights to full citizenship.

A review of the history of modernity from the point of view of the global South reveals that the multiple rich cultures that make up Latin America were launched into invisibility and subordination with the advent of the modern era under the dialectic of the non-European.[4] The modern world, as well as its institutions, is founded on the denial and subordination of non-European peoples. From the fifteenth century onwards, Europe asserted itself as the center and apex of world history and relegated everything that is not European to the fringe. Therefore, modernity does not exist outside the center-outskirts binomial, that is, without its fringe counterparts, whether that is Latin America, Africa, Asia, or Oceania. Latin America was the first identity created in the modern era to legitimize European domination and, consequently, epistemicide, among other barbarities; this went along with the creation of racialized and hierarchical views of the Indian, the Black, and the white.[5]

Aware of this long process of subordination by European countries (the "whites"), the original peoples (the "non-whites" of the continent) recovered the nomenclature of *Abya Yala* to self-designate in opposition to America, with the goal of creating a feeling of resistance, unity, and belonging.[6] As a way to overcome the domain of Eurocentric modernity, Enrique Dussel defends the advent of an alternative epistemological project called "transmodernity."

> [The] strict concept of "transmodern" indicates this radical novelty that means the emergence—as if from nothing—of exteriority, alterity, of the always-distinct, of universal cultures in development. Such cultures take on the challenges of modernity and even of Euro-American postmodernity, but they respond from the other place . . . from the point of their own cultural experience, different from the Euro-American experience, and they are therefore capable of responding with completely impossible solutions for the modern culture.[7] Transmodernity is

4. For an in-depth exploration of this, see Dussel, *1492*.

5. See Quijano, "Colonialidad del poder," 96–97.

6. In the language of the Kuna people of Panama and Colombia, the phrase *Abya Yala* means "Mature Earth," "Living Earth," or "Earth in Bloom." Porto-Gonçalves, "Entre América e Abya Yala," 26.

7. Dussel, "Transmodernidade e interculturalidade," 63.

the result of authentic intercultural dialogue that, in turn, needs to be transversal, that is, dialogue that takes place between the various locations of the outskirts, a South-South dialogue. For Dussel, "transmodernity is a project for the liberation of victims of modernity and the development of their alternative potentialities, the 'other face,' which is hidden and denied."[8]

Unlike an abstract universalism, it can be said that the transmodern project proposes pluriversality or a concrete universalism, which are notions that can be grasped in Aimé Césaire's letter terminating his connection to the French Communist Party:

> Provincialism? Absolutely not. I will not confine myself to narrow particularism. But I also do not intend to lose myself in a disembodied universalism. There are two ways to get lost: through closed segregation in particularism or through dissolution into the universal. My idea of the universal is one that is rich with specifics, a profound coexistence of all specifics.[9]

If, on the one hand, abstract universalism proclaims a type of particularism that establishes itself as hegemonic and disembodied, not belonging to any geopolitical location, on the other hand, concrete universalism does not hide its place of enunciation, its bodily-political influences, and its geopolitics. Concrete universalism allows for the coexistence of particulars, without the need for each particular to hide behind an abstract or disembodied idea. If abstract universalism establishes a vertical relationship, concrete universalism, instead, presupposes a political project that proposes horizontal relationships between several peculiarities.[10]

From the Abya Yala experience, Catherine Walsh proposes the category of interculturality to think about processes and projects, both political and epistemological. Interculturality, like concrete universalism, allows us to go beyond the simple relationship between groups, cultural practices, and thoughts, that is, to incorporate the traditionally excluded into existing educational, disciplinary, and thought structures.[11] For Walsh, interculturality consists of an ideological principle of a political project that seeks to transform the current structures, institutions, and relations of society. It is about working to create alternative local powers, with respect to which land, culture, and education are no longer the center of struggles for claiming

---

8. Dussel, "Un diálogo con Gianni Vattimo," 18.
9. Grosfoguel, "Decolonizing Western Universalisms," 95.
10. Bernardino-Costa, "Decolonialidade," 125.
11. Walsh, "Interculturalidad," 39–50.

rights, but rather foster a sociopolitical perspective and struggle, in which attention is focused on intervening in the fields of marginalization and subalternation.[12]

Interculturality in this sociopolitical perspective seems to meet and illuminate the proposal of "opening our hearts to the whole world" contained in *Fratelli Tutti* as an ideological principle of Abya Yala toward pluriversality.

> Interculturality... refers to complex relationships, negotiations, and cultural exchanges on multiple paths. It seeks to develop an equitable interrelationship between culturally different peoples, people, knowledge, and practices, an interaction that stems from the inherent conflict of social, economic, political, and power asymmetries. It is not simply a matter of recognizing, discovering, or tolerating others' or one's own differences. Nor is it about making identities essential or understanding them as irremovable ethnic advertisement. Instead, it is about actively promoting exchange processes that allow the development of meeting spaces between different beings and knowledge, meanings, and practices.[13]

In this light, interculturality approaches the advent of full citizenship, as it gives directions to "fight for a world where other worlds are possible," as the Zapatista movement states, that is, to fight for a pluriversal world where silenced and subordinated voices can be heard.

In the Brazilian context, the Afro-Brazilian community, making up over 52 percent of the total population, struggle, as descendants of Africans who were forced to migrate, for the recognition of their full citizenship. With almost four hundred years of slavery behind them, up until now the cultural values of African descendants are not understood as an alterity that is capable of fertilizing other cultures and being fertilized by them. During the long period of slavery and the continuous denial and demonization of its symbolic and cultural references, the Afro-Brazilian resistance of the *quilombos*[14] managed to express a relational way of being in the world and, thus, opened the stage for re-existing.

---

12. Walsh, "Interculturalidad," 43–44.

13. Walsh, "Interculturalidad," 45.

14. *Quilombos* were Blacks who fled slavery and made up an Afro-Brazilian resistance to the ethical, political, economic, cultural, and spiritual order. Across America there was similar resistance, such as the *cimarrónes*, in countries colonized by Spain; the *palenques* in Cuba and Colombia; and the *marrons* in the Guyanas and the US. The concept goes back to the African *kilombo*, more specifically those among the Bantu-speaking peoples. See Munanga, "Origem e histórico."

The *quilombos* emerged as a force for resistance to the inhuman system of slavery and colonialism, becoming a radical protest and social experience of resistance and re-elaboration of the social and cultural values of enslaved Africans in the context of a landlord-slave society.[15] This resistance was the only way for Black women and men to regain their humanity, that is, their ability to be for themselves and to be with and for others.

One of the most subversive factors related to the *quilombos* lies in their overcoming the complex of racial hierarchization, as they were "ethnically differentiated without a hierarchical scale that would give positive (or negative) value to each ethnic connotation, classifying social agents on these differences according to their color."[16] The *quilombos* broke with the hierarchical social classification that established the inferiority of non-whites.

In this sense, Kabelengele Munanga explains the *quilombos'* cartography as a field of initiation, not only to resistance, but to the advent of an authentic multiracial democracy, one that had a pluriversal and transcultural character. Becoming a *quilombo* was open to all oppressed people in the society—Blacks, Indians, and whites—and therefore anticipated a model of multiracial democracy that is still to be established in Brazil and elsewhere. Their practices and strategies were carried out within a transcultural model that aimed at creating stable and open identities beyond the limits of their culture.[17]

The *quilombolas* cultivated an external openness in a double sense: both to give and receive cultural influences from other communities without giving up their existence as a distinct culture and without disrespecting what was common among human beings. Therefore, the *quilombolas* aimed at "forming open identities produced by incessant communication with the other, and not closed identities created by cultural barricades that exclude the other."[18]

This relational way of being in the world of the *quilombolas* is currently considered the fundamental principle of Afro-Brazilian subjectivation processes, called "Quilombism,"[19] in which the idea of re-existence is expressed as a human, ethical, and cultural affirmation, through which the Afro-Brazilian population integrates a practice of liberation and takes control of its own history.

15. See Moura, "A quilombagem," 103.
16. Moura, "A quilombagem," 116.
17. Munanga, "Origem e histórico," 63.
18. Munanga, "Origem e histórico," 63.
19. Nascimento, *O Quilombismo*, 286. Quilombism is a historical-social scientific concept that codifies and interprets the Afro-Brazilian experience.

Final Considerations

As we can see, the evangelical proposal of fraternity/sorority outlined in *Fratelli Tutti* presents itself as a critique of modern rationality in its instrumental aspect, expressed in individualism and closed nationalisms. It seems to find greatest resonance in the marginalized and invisible cultures of the global South, which struggle to rebuild their own relational identity and engender political processes and projects based on their own millenarian wisdom. Pope Francis's wise words in *Fratelli Tutti* can serve to further stimulate the political and epistemic projects already underway in the Abya Yala, showing that an authentic encounter between evangelical faith and different cultures can result in a newness of life, in a more diverse and multicolored world, and in a universal fraternal and social communion beyond ethnic and cultural borders.

Bibliography

Bernardino-Costa, Joaze. "Decolonialidade, Atlântico Negro e intelectuais negros brasileiros: em busca de um diálogo horizontal." *Revista Sociedade e Estado* 33:1 (January–April 2018) 117–35.

Dussel, Enrique. *1492: El encubrimiento del otro: hacia el origen del mito de la modernidad*. La Paz: Plural, 1994.

———. "Un diálogo con Gianni Vattimo: de la postmodernidad a la transmodernidad." *A Parte Rei: Revista de Filosofía* 54 (2007) 1–32. http://serbal.pntic.mec.es/~cmunoz11/dussel54.pdf.

———. "Transmodernidade e interculturalidade: interpretação a partir da filosofia da libertação." *Revista Sociedade e Estado* 21:1 (January–April 2016) 51–73.

Francis, Pope. *Fratelli Tutti: On Fraternity and Social Friendship*. Vatican City: Libreria Editrice Vaticana, 2020. http://www.vatican.va/content/francesco/en/encyclicals/documents/papa-francesco_20201003_enciclica-fratelli-tutti.html.

Grosfoguel, Ramón. "Decolonizing Western Universalisms: Decolonial Pluriversalism from Aimé Césaire to the Zapatistas." *Transmodernity: Journal of Peripheral Cultural Production of the Luso-Hispanic World* 1:3 (2012) 88–104.

Moura, Clóvis. "A quilombagem como expressão de protesto radical." In *Os quilombos na dinâmica social do Brasil*, edited by Clóvis Moura, 103–18. Maceió, Brazil: EDUFAL, 2001. https://movimentorevista.com.br/2019/11/a-quilombagem-como-expressao-de-protesto-radical.

Munanga, Kabengele. "Origem e histórico do quilombo na África." *Revista USP* 28 (1996) 56–63.

Nascimento, Abdias. *O Quilombismo: Documentos de uma militância Pan-Africana*. 3rd ed. Rio de Janeiro: Ipeafro, 2019.

Nogueira, Renato. "Ubuntu as a Way of Existing: General Elements for Ethics with an Afro-Perspective." *Revista da ABPN* 3:6 (2012) 147–50.

Porto-Gonçalves, Carlos Walter. "Entre América e Abya Yala—tensões de territorialidades." *Desenvolvimento e Meio Ambiente* 20 (July/December 2009) 25–30.

Quijano, Hannibal. "Colonialidad del poder y clasificación social." In *El giro decolonial: Reflexiones para una diversidad epistémica más allá del capitalismo global*, edited by Santiago Castro-Gómez and Ramón Grosfoguel, 93–126. Bogotá: Siglo del Hombre, 2007.

Walsh, Catherine. "Interculturalidad, conocimiento y decolonialidade." *Signo y Pensamiento* 46:24 (January–June 2006) 39–50.

16

Living with the Grace of Neighbors: The Promise of Universal Fraternity for Europe

STEPHAN VAN ERP

Introduction

CHAPTER 4 OF *FRATELLI Tutti* is called "A Heart Open to the Whole World," and this title indicates quite clearly the two subject matters it seeks to address: the attitude of openness to the other and the universal origin or location of that attitude. The chapter is divided into three parts. Part 1 is called "Borders and their Limits," and it mentions several issues that emerge if universal sisterhood and brotherhood are to be embodied in concrete actions, especially in dealing with migration. Part 2 is called "Reciprocal Gifts," and it describes the attitude of openness to others, which is needed when confronted with differences between cultures, for example between East and West. Part 3 is called "Local and Universal," and it addresses the tension between globalization and localization, calling for neighborliness, starting in one's own region. As in the whole document, even though it intends to address concrete problems in our current time, general concepts of unity and universality play a central role, and in fact form the heart of the document's message: a call for recognizing and performing a *universal* fraternity.

In my commentary on chapter 4, I will focus on the concepts of unity and universality that Pope Francis employs. By describing the challenges of migration in Europe, I will first show that his attention to universal concepts is a much needed one, and that, therefore, *Fratelli Tutti* is much more than an ethical call for solidarity. Then, I will argue that universal fraternity is the new catholicity, a new balance to be discovered between the local and the global, and between diversity and unity.

Europe and the Struggle for Unity

In Europe, with its multitude of nations and cultures on the one hand, and its striving for political union on the other, the tension between unity and diversity has not led to a fruitful exchange of differences, but instead has caused an ongoing political struggle. This struggle seems to intensify in the past few years, not least because of the disagreements about migration. These disagreements are entangled with a complex of problems—social, cultural, religious, economic, and ecological. The failure to politically respond to these problems in a harmonious way could be viewed as the defeat of the European vision of *in varietate concordia*, unity in diversity.[1] This vision has not resulted in a convincing consensus, or even a precarious balance supporting a functioning European political system. Rather, it has become a weakening construction, constantly threatening to collapse. One of the results has been a binary and often conflicted understanding of the dynamics of unity and diversity, a zero-sum balance determined by degree, in which one aspect is inversely proportional to the other. That balance is now a constant battle, subject to procedure rather than principle, and has become a matter of strategy rather than structure, and consequently of conflict rather than conviction.

The European struggle could be a warning for the church's quest for synodality. But that quest could also become an example for Europe. Finding unity in diversity is the rare and often temporary result of laborious negotiations instead of constituting the starting point for reflections on a common ground or actions toward a common goal, as Pope Francis proposes in *Fratelli Tutti*.

Migration Challenging the Christian Identity of Europe

Fratelli Tutti focuses on migration in our time, especially in chapter 4. We still very rarely realize just how threatening our world is to many people, and what is required first and foremost is to listen to their fears. The language of fear is often telling. Refugees come in "waves," their arrival is seen as an "invasion" or a "tsunami." Desperate people appear to us as a risk to

---

1. Cf. Zaborowski, "Heimat Europa," 83–97.

our ever-weaker social cohesion, as a threat to our prosperity, as a potential danger to our women and children. At the same time, those of us who feel they have to compete with refugees for what limited provisions we barely manage to maintain are dismissed as xenophobes and racists. Refugees do not come with glad tidings, particularly not at first sight. They show us that the world is a dangerous place in which human life is vulnerable.

Many people are insecure about the future and about all the newcomers in Europe. And the political chaos and mismanagement of the situation makes them even more apprehensive. People no longer recognize their neighborhood, where they have felt safe and at home in a world that has been an unsafe place throughout the history of mankind. There are some who are afraid of the increasing influence of Islam, which for them represents the rise of violence and repression against women and homosexuals. Others are angry about the fact that politicians do not seem to listen to their concerns while there is so much attention to the situation of the refugees. All these people think and feel that they are on the losing side, that an established and fought-for identity is breaking down. In Europe, they unmask the myth that we almost realized a society with a firm Christian identity, in which the common good was central. And their responses manifest that, for them, the current transformations entail a loss of this identity, which therefore should be protected.

Senses of fear and protection have led to political responses against migration in Europe, which were not seldomly based on a specific concept of Europe's Christian identity. Some European leaders have called attention to the apparent incompatibility between new arrivals and Europe's Christian heritage. The Hungarian government forced migrants off the train and attempted to stop refugees from moving through Hungary toward Germany, even going so far as to propose building a wall. Viktor Orbán, the Hungarian prime minister, argued that the migrants threaten the Christian identity of Europe, while Peter Erdő, the Roman Catholic archbishop of Budapest, reportedly declared that the Hungarian churches were prohibited from sheltering refugees, claiming that they would otherwise be regarded as human traffickers. Similarly, the Slovakian, Polish, Bulgarian, and Cypriot governments issued statements that they would only accept *Christian* refugees, as *Muslims* would threaten their identity. This type of rhetoric is not limited to Central or Eastern Europe but has become more common now and has been instrumental to the rise in popularity of right-wing nationalist and populist parties across Europe. The language of unity and identity is a highly contested one.

The Grace of Universal Fraternity

Instead of reformulating Europe's Christian identity into a particular one besides others, *Fratelli Tutti* accentuates the universal aspects of human fraternity that enable us to view our cultural and national identities differently. Rather than protecting these identities, they could instead be instrumental to opening them to others (*FT* 130). Hospitality, then, will not be seen as a threat to an existing identity but as a revival of what that identity actually entails. To the faithful, the willingness to help refugees is an obligation that follows directly from the gratuitousness that they believe they live by themselves. Gratitude rather than fear should be the guide for our encounter with others.

In *Fratelli Tutti*, gratuitousness is not merely an appeal to act charitably in the face of suffering and the needs of others. It is also a plea to recognize a fundamental connection between humans, a universal belonging. On the World Day of Migrants and Refugees in 2017, Pope Francis referred to the following text from the Gospel: "Whoever welcomes one of these little children in my name welcomes me; and whoever welcomes me does not welcome me but the one who sent me" (Mark 9:37, NIV; cf. Matt 18:5; Luke 9:48; John 13:20).[2] According to Pope Francis, welcoming others is the willingness to be a sign of the fact that we can see that God became human. Therefore, the faith that is evoked by the confrontation with strangers not only manifests itself in urgently needed charitable acts, but also in seeing Christ in every migrant.[3] This is also expressed in the ecumenical prayer at the end of *Fratelli Tutti*:

> Grant that we Christians may live the Gospel,
> discovering Christ in each human being,
> recognizing him crucified
> in the sufferings of the abandoned
> and forgotten of our world,
> and risen in each brother or sister
> who makes a new start.

To welcome the abandoned and forgotten is to welcome Christ, not because Christ himself was a migrant, but rather because the homelessness and the suffering of migrants violate the universal fraternity given by God. In each of these individual violations, Christ himself becomes a homeless person, and whenever He finds himself at a border or a door that stays shut, this universal givenness is ignored.

---

2. Francis, "Message."

3. Pontifical Council for the Pastoral Care of Migrants and Itinerant People, *Erga migrantes caritas Christi*, 12, 13.

Dependency as Identity

In *Fratelli Tutti*, the life of the faithful and the life of the church are defined by a call to respond to the present situation, and that response should be an expression of the desire to participate in the common good, not by ignoring, denying, or escaping the present situation, but by contributing to it through the embodiment of the promised good without any reserve, a practice of trust and risk. According to the Apostle Paul, people are each other's hope, each other's proclaimers of hope, each other's source and home, in which God's work becomes manifest in the brokenness of our dependency. This dependency is at the core of Pope Francis's view of all human life. It is a universal view that seeks to include all people of good will, who suffer and struggle, who fail and fall, who conquer and succeed when they strive for the common good. As members of a body, the community that is the church, they need each other. People are each other's hand and foot, eye and ear, heart, and head, writes Paul (1 Cor 12:14-26), so that God's glory will reveal itself in all the effort and suffering people experience on the way they walk together, with each other's help and thanks to each other's engagement.

Christian life does not cease to resurrect against suffering and injustice. It seeks to heal, not by forming an identifiable unity but instead by a call to respond to each other, by an awareness of our mutual dependency, by our laments and prayers, and our acts of mercy. For this reason, the concept of "Christian *identity*," which in the European context of migration is often used by politicians and some church leaders, is deeply problematic, because it allows for programmatic uses in which it is rather exclusively defined over against other so-called identities. Instead of living with one particular identity among others, Christians live a life incomplete, which they universally share with others, and as such their fundamental identity is not determined by a set of recognizable characteristics, but by a desire and a dependency, a common longing that lies at the basis of and manifests itself in acts of openness, mercy, and solidarity. Universal fraternity, therefore, is not merely a procedure or an ethic, but an ontology of gratuitousness (*FT* 140), a giving without cost that is deeply rooted in a receiving without cost (Matt 10:8).

Universal Fraternity as the New Catholicity

In the European situation, a new understanding of unity in diversity is needed, if it is to avoid ending up as a tool for window dressing a pragmatist handling of plurality and division. *Fratelli Tutti*, with its focus on that which universally binds us, offers a new vision of catholicity, both for the church and for Europe and the wider world. Like the idea of Europe, the catholicity of the church has often been described as *unitas in diversitas*. During the last few decades, reflections on the theology of catholicity have shown that the Catholic concept of unity is not one of sheer universality, nor of uniformity. Pope Francis articulates this when he writes that a new synthesis of cultures is needed, but that this must not be a static one, "through its ability to welcome differences" (*FT* 160). Instead, he proposes a harmonious relationship among people from diverse backgrounds. An abstract dialectic between unity and diversity has not proven to be a helpful tool for understanding the motives or goals behind the complexities of European unity and the political decision-making that should result from it. Therefore, I would like to suggest revisiting the idea of catholicity. In the one hand, it could suffer from the same tendency to lead either to a static all-embracing universality, or to an abstract, undefined unity that is supposed to be at the center of an otherwise nongovernable diversity. On the other hand, it could provide us with a dynamic concept of connectedness that could help us to perform our universal fraternity.

The term "catholic" comes from the Greek roots *kata* and *holos*, together forming *kath'holou*, which means "according to," "concerning," or "through the whole." Ancient Greek writers used the adjective *katholikos*, and the noun *katholikon*, to talk about what is universal or most general. The meaning of catholicity is a dynamic combination characterized by movement rather than a static or totalizing idea. It seems to be a quality on the move, a questing, dynamic, active quality which should engage all aspects of life.[4] Employing the term "catholicity" in a European context could lead to misunderstandings motivated by matters of identity, and especially by the concern of exclusivism. Such misunderstandings are usually caused by confusing the quantitative and qualitative understandings of the term.[5] The quantitative understanding emphasizes the geographical, historical, or sociological extension of institutional Catholicism. The qualitative understanding of catholicity focuses on ideas of fullness or holism.

The theologian Robert Schreiter has highlighted the potential of catholicity in our globalized context, reflecting on how to better integrate local and global, particular and universal. For Schreiter, it has the potential to creatively destabilize secular and religious thinking, which works with a center-periphery structure.[6] Catholicity may help develop more porous ways

---

4. For an introduction into the concept of catholicity, see McCosker, "Catholicity."

5. The distinction between quantitative and qualitative understandings of catholicity has been clearly explained by von Balthasar, "Claim to Catholicity," 65–121.

6. See Schreiter, *New Catholicity*.

of being and acting for individuals and groups in our unequal globalized context. So, catholicity provides a lens that enables us to see all of reality in the round, as interconnected and interdependent, thereby respecting the different differences. *Fratelli Tutti*'s description of the dynamic between the global and the local accentuates the inseparability of the two. The universal and the global should protect us against narrowness and nationalism, as local and social friendships could be a yeast in the dough and support enriching ways of achieving subsidiarity (*FT* 142).

The dynamic, interdependent character of catholicity entails a recognition that all members play an important and decisive role in it, and that therefore no one can be excluded or considered to be less important. So, the catholic vision of unity seeks to guarantee a form of community in which every single element assumes equal significance. In his image of the church as the Body of Christ that is made up of a plurality of distinct members, Paul also stresses a certain equality. "[T]here should be no division in the body," he cautions, "but . . . its parts should have equal concern for each other" (1 Cor 12:25, NIV). In other words, all are included, and more importantly, each distinct contribution is fully recognized. It is important to note that this unity is not so much constituted by consensus or by sheer equality, but by the active participation in the gratuitous givenness of that equality, which needs actions of openness and solidarity to become manifest and to bear fruit.

Seeing the Universal Horizon in One's Neighborhood

The title of chapter 4 of *Fratelli Tutti*, "A Heart Open to the Whole World," not only signifies what we should do in the face of suffering, by stressing the acts of openness and solidarity with our neighbors. It also presents us with a universal horizon that, despite the constructive positivity of the whole document, functions as a firm critique of the ideologies and behavior that have led to suffering and exclusion. In this particular chapter, individualist, protective, or isolationist and competitive acts are explicitly mentioned, and this concerns nations and their leaders, but also the economic systems and companies that profit from it. *Fratelli Tutti* has no tolerance for such behavior, and uses clear, judgmental language when it describes it as "local narcissism" (*FT* 146).

The document is only capable of speaking so critically about concrete situations because it relies on what it calls "a universal horizon." Migration, poverty, and the ecological crisis have redirected the focus of the church's language of salvation toward the universal. This may surprise some theologians who have especially addressed contextual and local cultural issues in the past decades, but *Fratelli Tutti* clearly points at the limits of these contextual approaches: "Life on the local level thus becomes less and less welcoming, people less open to complementarity. Its possibilities for development narrow; it grows weary and infirm" (*FT* 146). Instead, Pope Francis points at the universal promise of acts of neighborliness and fraternity, albeit only when these are based on encounter and the recognition of difference.

The word "universal" is featured fifty-two times in *Fratelli Tutti*, and the words "different" and "differences" eighty-six times. Universal, however, is used in a more positive sense, while differences can be descriptive (neutral), divisive (negative), or an opportunity for enrichment and learning (positive). The positive relation between universality and difference, according to the document, is communion and belonging to the larger human family (*FT* 149). In chapter 4, the dynamic tension between communion and difference has been made concrete, by addressing the challenges of migration and belonging to a wider family of neighbors, who are dependent on one another. That dependency calls for a politics of love, which is discussed in chapter 5 of *Fratelli Tutti*, and is envisioned as a politics that integrates and unites. It is important to note, however, that these political acts should be first and foremost based on a new discovery of our universal fraternity, as it is worded in the prayer at the end of the document:

> Come, Holy Spirit, show us your beauty,
> reflected in all the peoples of the earth,
> so that we may discover anew
> that all are important and all are necessary,
> different faces of the one humanity
> that God so loves.

Bibliography

Francis, Pope. *Fratelli Tutti: On Fraternity and Social Friendship*. Vatican City: Libreria Editrice Vaticana, 2020. http://www.vatican.va/content/francesco/en/encyclicals/documents/papa-francesco_20201003_enciclica-fratelli-tutti.html.

———. "Message for the World Day of Migrants and Refugees 2017." Vatican City, January 15, 2017. http://w2.vatican.va/content/francesco/en/messages/migration/documents/papa-francesco_20160908_world-migrants-day-2017.html.

McCosker, Philip. "Catholicity: Its Varieties and Futures." Filmed by Von Hügel Institute for Critical Catholic Inquiry, St. Edmund's College, University of Cambridge, March 1, 2019. YouTube video, 51:18. https://www.youtube.com/watch?v=pf7iDedGWho.

Pontifical Council for the Pastoral Care of Migrants and Itinerant People. *Erga migrantes caritas Christi (The Love of Christ Towards Migrants)*. Vatican City: Pontifical Counsel for the Pastoral Care of Migrants and Itinerant People, 2004. http://www.vatican.va/roman_curia/pontifical_councils/migrants/documents/rc_pc_migrants_doc_20040514_erga-migrantes-caritas-christi_en.html.

Schreiter, Robert. *The New Catholicity: Theology Between the Global and the Local*. Maryknoll, NY: Orbis, 1997.

von Balthasar, Hans Urs. "The Claim to Catholicity." In *Spirit and Institution: Explorations in Theology IV*, edited by Hans Urs von Balthasar, 65–121. San Francisco: Ignatius, 1995.

Zaborowski, Holger. "Heimat Europa—Hoffnung Europa." In *Heimat Europa?*, edited by Martin W. Ramb and Holger Zaborowski, 83–97. Göttingen, Germany: Wallstein Verlag, 2019.

PART FIVE

A Better Kind of Politics

17

Reinventing Political Arrangements: A New Starting Point

Toussaint Kafarhire Murhula, SJ

For many people today, politics is a distasteful word, often due to the mistakes, corruption and inefficiency of some politicians. There are also attempts to discredit politics, to replace it with economics or to twist it to one ideology or another. Yet can our world function without politics? Can there be an effective process of growth towards universal fraternity and social peace without a sound political life?
—Pope Francis, *Fratelli Tutti*, 176

A Case of a Neoliberal Approach to Development in Africa

The above quote portrays the current state of affairs with respect to three major aspects of the problem at issue in chapter 5 of *Fratelli Tutti*: the prevailing disdain for politics and a deliberate project to discredit politics and replace it with economics, despite the fact that politics is a necessary instrument to achieve growth, social peace, and a sound life in community. After identifying the first two aspects of the problem; namely, the mistrust in politics given the actions of political leaders and the promotion of a free market arrangement to replace the sovereign power of the state to regulate,

Pope Francis points to a third, which is an alternative view of social life based on political charity and a sound political life. I will address the first aspect by describing an example of the kind of mistrust that exists between political leaders and their communities. On a recent visit to Turkana, in the northwest region of Kenya, I experienced something that left me perplexed about the politics in Africa. Not only did I witness the disconnect between leaders and the communities they are supposed to lead, but also had a living experience of the attempts of the neoliberal market economy to outdo the state and its politics.

Kenya's Great Rift Valley region caught the interest of Western investors thanks to the discovery of oil reserves in March 2012 that may eventually amount to approximately 20 billion barrels.[1] This spurred new worries about the so-called "natural resources curse" on a country in sub-Saharan Africa that had enjoyed relative stability and peace since independence in 1963. I traveled to Turkana on an academic mission to understand the social and environmental impacts of Tullow Oil Company's extractive activities in the region. To my amazement, the Turkana people expressed satisfaction with the company's extractive activities. Although the national government signed the contract to exploit the oil as the primary beneficiary, local community leaders expounded on the benefits that trickle down from the national to the county government. The multiple benefits of Tullow Oil's involvement in the region include technology transfer, tax revenues, jobs creation, and the improvement of the road infrastructure. Local communities were feeling the difference the company was making in their lives. They even received direct benefits in land leases while the company also offered catering tenders to local women through the Turkana County Integrated Development Plan. In short, Tullow's Corporate Social Responsibility (CSR) is highly impressive as a model of neoliberal practices in providing development. As a matter of fact, the Turkana local community had felt forgotten and marginalized by Kenyan national leaders for a long time. As one elder claimed, the company has done more over a short period of less than ten years to meet local needs than the national government did in the last fifty years.

Tullow Oil Company, a foreign business, was perceived in a friendlier light by the Turkana than the Kenyan national government. How can we explain this paradox? Apparently, over the many droughts and famines that have affected the region over the years, the government response remained tepid and sluggish. The ensuing feeling of alienation brewed some unspoken grievances, encouraging these Kenyan citizens to look for relief beyond the

1. Stott, "Kenya's Paradoxical 'Resource Curse,'" 1.

competence of the national government. Indeed, both local and international NGOs as well as multinational companies have come to fill the gap in political leadership in most African nations. I was told, for instance, that the Catholic Church is often referred to as the "government of Turkana" thanks to its provision of social welfare in the form of education and healthcare services. What the local people fail to see, however, beyond the immediate provision of relief, is the fragmentation of the national community, the loss of national sovereignty, and the inability to demand accountability from elected leaders whose allegiance goes to multinational companies that bring in tax monies.

Pope Francis observes, "The twenty-first century is witnessing a weakening of the power of nation states, chiefly because the economic and financial sectors, being transnational, tend to prevail over the political" (*FT* 172). In the case of Tullow Oil, the immediate material benefits to the Turkana might obfuscate the crack in national politics but also the environmental externalities, which most local people, with low bargaining power, can discern. The loss of political sovereignty and the environmental externalities, unfortunately, will have adverse impacts in the future, leaving generations of unborn Africans to deal with climate change or pay the tab for incurred foreign debts. "Thinking of those who will come after us does not serve electoral purposes, yet it is what authentic justice demands" (*FT* 178). The slow and surreptitious death of a people's sovereignty by the subtle insinuation of economic dictates under the guise of CSR is what *Fratelli Tutti* denounces. Indeed, "welfare projects, which meet certain urgent needs, should be considered merely temporary responses" (*FT* 161).

The flag-flying of neoliberal policies tells only a partial story. For instance, in the case of Turkana, the environmental degradation is barely factored into the production cost and exchanged benefits. I discussed this with a Turkana leader, who showed awareness about the company's habit of leaving open pits where it disposed of extractive oil wastes that are in most cases toxic, even carcinogenic, but there is no scientific and policy evaluation of these dangers now and in the future. The fear that such waste may be carcinogenic is not paranoia. This has been proved worldwide, as in the case of Chevron/TEXACO, the American oil company that was adjudged liable in 2012 to pay a US$9.5 billion fine for engaging in the same violations of human, community, and natural rights in Ecuador.[2] In Turkana, the abandoned oil well called Twiga 1 is located quite close to village communities and was turned into a dump site. Although it was claimed that the site was temporary and expected to operate for at most six months as

---

2. Watts, "Nobel Laureates." See also the website, "ChevronToxico."

the law requires, it has now been there for more than five years. While the company Environmental Combustion Consulting Limited was contracted to incinerate the waste, they faced high transportation costs, not to mention the costs of cultivating political connections with powerful people in the national government. These issues caused Twiga 1 to exceed the legally allowed period of operation.

The third point I mentioned above concerns Pope Francis's advocacy of "a better kind of politics" (title of *FT*'s chapter 5). We cannot afford to settle down in the cracks left by the current neoliberal system. Instead, we need leaders and communities to implement a politics that reaches beyond the temporary social policies of the market. The pope notes that "the marketplace by itself cannot resolve every problem, however much we are asked to believe this dogma of neoliberal faith," and that "there is little appreciation of the fact that the alleged spillover does not resolve the inequality that gives rise to new forms of violence threatening the fabric of society," so therefore, "it is imperative to have a proactive economic policy directed at promoting an economics that favors productive diversity and business creativity and makes it possible for jobs to be created and not cut" (*FT* 168). The current market model produces violence, inequality, unemployment, mistrust in political institutions, financial speculation, and other social evils related to the kind of politics that has dominated our thinking up until today.

The Pope's Critique of Neoliberalism

Neoliberalism is now the dominant paradigm within which we think, feel, and act in the world. This theory contends that the welfare state model of the 1970s has become obsolete and that market arrangements are better in advancing the public welfare and private freedoms, and thus shuns social policies by the state promoting charity by the private sector. Arguably, it creates more wealth and provides the space for reinventing human freedom and welfare, contains incentives for innovation and development, and embodies the right reasons and structures for helping the poor. As a result, neoliberalism presents itself as the best path to prosperity and therefore the legitimate framework for solving all our social problems.

However, Pope Francis rejects the idea that neoliberalism embodies a panacea for all of our social ills. The problem with neoliberalism is indeed bigger than meets the eye and deeper than what it deems to be merely "collateral damage." The problem is the theory itself, for it denies the "human dimension" of our social problems and follows a "determined order," as if market forces by themselves were capable of "ensuring a bright future and providing solutions to every problem" (*FT* 167). Anyone with a different perspective, anyone who refuses to abide by the neoliberal truth, or anyone who challenges the orthodoxy of its creed is blamed and pushed to hide in shame. As the pope notes, "My critique of the technocratic paradigm involves more than simply thinking that if we control its excesses, everything will be fine" (*FT* 166).

John Rawls's contribution to the social contract debate about the theory of justice argues that "a theory, however elegant and economical, must be rejected or revised if it is untrue; likewise, laws and institutions no matter how efficient and well-arranged must be reformed or abolished if they are unjust."[3] A variant of American conservatism and libertarian political theories, neoliberalism puts an overwhelming emphasis on the right of the individual over against the community, the private over against the public and/or the common good, and personal responsibility over against historical and institutional processes. The theory also claims that individuals are "responsible and best able to provide for themselves, solve problems alone, and decide what is best for them. Individuals are responsible for their own failures and successes and should be rewarded and punished accordingly. It consists of an almost religious belief that the market . . . is the best way to promote an individual's choice [while] the state will [almost always] inhibit both the market and individual choice."[4] The conceptual framework of the theory includes beliefs, institutions, policies, and practices related to the production and distribution of social goods and services. However, these policies and practices have had negative effects on how human dignity is construed and social life structured.

Facing the failures of trickle-down neoliberal dogma and the havoc wreaked by "financial speculation" (*FT* 168), Pope Francis invites us to summon the courage to build structures that will serve the common good and human dignity. The existing global order, sadly, only pays lip service to the oneness of a globalized world, as the eruption of the COVID-19 pandemic with the different national containment policies adopted by world leaders has exposed. "The fragility of the world systems in the face of the pandemic has demonstrated that not everything can be resolved by market freedom" (*FT* 168). Pope Francis's core message is about change of attitude, conversion of heart, and "the commanded love [that is] expressed in those acts of charity that spur people to create more sound institutions, more just regulations, more supportive structures" (*FT* 186). It is indeed cynical to put a

---

3. Rawls, *Theory of Justice*, 3.
4. Hackworth, *Faith Based*, 69.

starving people on life support by providing them with only what will barely keep them from dying in order to better exploit them.

In line with the Catholic social justice tradition, Pope Francis's critique of neoliberalism, therefore, is a reminder of the core values and principles of solidarity, participation, and subsidiarity that go with this tradition (*FT* 169). Any follower of Christ, like Saint Francis of Assisi, must get ready to travel the extra mile, to give beyond what is expected, to find the courage to cross the boundaries of traditions, and to manifest the joy of trusting the Spirit at work in others, beyond the stereotypes and labels attached to their differences. Such an expression of care and love can erase the creases left by years of malpractice in our social policies, dismiss the unfounded fears and anxieties about the other, and "help make possible an integral human development that goes beyond the idea of social policies being a policy for the poor, but never with the poor and never of the poor, much less part of a project that reunites people" (*FT* 169).

Pope Francis embodies the leadership that is lacking in the international community—a leadership that can dare to think freely, to reimagine the kind of society we would like to build. Instead of relying on neoliberalism's old solutions that are mere problems instead, bringing with it a rhetoric that cultivates fear, scarcity, and the intimidation of those who think differently, *Fratelli Tutti* boldly invites us to find alternative sources of inspiration, even if these have to come from different times, locations, traditions, and cultures. The current political leadership, unfortunately, cultivates populism in the grossest and basest manner in order to establish control and dominion over the people.

A Leadership That Inspires

Chapter 5 is about "a better kind of politics," which needs a different kind of leadership to inspire a new institutional framework with love and fraternity. If new leaders begin to see the world differently, to understand life holistically, and to think of others with respect and love, this can lead to the establishment of more just and inclusive social structures. Also, what is to be distributed is not economic benefits alone but also political benefits, such as power, human worth, and dignity. This kind of leadership needs courage and generosity to reinvest faith in the multilateral agreements that will promote the truly global common good (*FT* 174). This leadership also requires understanding authority and power as services to humanity and politics as a call to promote "more effective world organizations, equipped with the power to provide for the global common good, the elimination of hunger and poverty, and the sure defense of fundamental human rights" (FT 172).

Fratelli Tutti, like the pope's earlier encyclical *Laudato Si'*, closes this leadership gap. Pope Francis's voice, reminiscent of Francis of Assisi, whose care for God's creation did not discriminate against nonhuman creatures or between Christians and non-Christian "others," is changing the tune. Unlike the realist paradigm inherited from modern thinkers like Thomas Hobbes—with his assumptions that human nature is driven by self-interest, fear of others, material scarcity, and search for status[5]—the pope is saying, like Francis of Assisi, that human beings are also naturally disposed to the social poetry of love and universal fraternity (FT 169). For instance, during the 1219 siege of Damietta, while on a Crusade expedition in Egypt, Francis of Assisi's "social love" inspired him to override all prescriptions and codes of conduct. Burning with the desire to talk of peace, he crossed all the boundaries of culture, politics, and religion and went to meet with the enemy. The influential Uruguayan writer and author of *The Open Veins of Latin America*, Eduardo Galeano, tells this story well. Francis wanted to talk of peace with Sultan Al-Kamil. He left his Catholic bastion and

> barefoot, alone, [started walking] toward the enemy bastion. The wind swept the ground and buffeted the earth-colored tunic of this skinny angel, fallen from heaven, who loved the earth as if from the earth he had sprouted. From afar they [the Muslims] saw him coming. He said he had come to speak of peace with the sultan, Al-Kamil. Francis represented no one, but the walls parted. The Christian troops were of two minds. Half thought Father Francis was crazy as a loon. The other half thought he was dumb as an ass. Everybody knew that he talked to birds, that he liked to be called "God's minstrel," that he preached and practiced laughter, and that he told his brother monks: "Try not to look sad, stern, or hypocritical."[6]

This event surely resonated with Pope Francis (FT 3). The poetry of this story is just too beautiful to leave it unfinished. Allow me to tell the rest, for this will have implications not only for our perception of otherness,

---

5. Hobbes studied and translated into English Thucydides' *Peloponnesian Wars*. The so-called Athenian thesis resonated with him; it claims "that justice is irrelevant to international politics . . . that no one with a chance to acquire something by force has ever yet been dissuaded by the argument that it is unjust to do so (1.76.2). . . . The Athenians proclaim that justice has no place in human reasoning unless the use of force is rendered ineffective by an equality of power to compel on both sides (5.89)." Ahrensdorf, "Thucydides' Realistic Critic of Realism," 236–37.

6. Galeano, *Mirrors*, 83–84.

leadership, and the need for structural change, but also for how our perception of the other might impact our construction of institutions (war and peace), social arrangements (the distribution of welfare), and political practices (acceptable policies). Galeano continues:

> People said that in [Francis's] garden in the town of Assisi the plants grew upside down, their roots pointing up. And people knew that the opinions he voiced were upside down too. He thought war, the passion and profession of kings and popes, was good for winning riches, but useless for winning souls, and that the Crusades were launched not to convert Muslims, but to subdue them. Moved by curiosity or who knows what, the sultan received him. The Christian and the Muslim crossed words, not swords. In their long dialogue, Jesus and Mohammed did not come to terms. But they listened to each other.[7]

Was it curiosity? Or, say, the fundamental human desire and longing for love, friendship, and peace? If we agree that fear, competition, and vainglory are not the fundamental characteristics of human nature, but rather the desire for self-fulfillment in love, then a better kind of politics is possible. The wars that we fight are often not of our own choosing. They are the projection of our leaders' personal anxieties and human concupiscence, which we can overcome by God's grace. In a powerful TED Talk with almost two million views, Karen Armstrong argues that religion should become a force for harmony, while reminding her audience that empathy and compassion are the surest paths toward discovering the humanity of others. Not only our shared humanity, but also the divine, starts to emerge when people suffer and cry together.

Conclusion

The central point that Pope Francis is making in this chapter, following the rich tradition of the social teaching of the church, is that we need to dare exercise the spiritual freedom to love others without fear. He preaches by example when, in each trip he undertakes, he bridges centuries of mutual suspicion, contempt, and exclusion. He has ventured beyond the confines of the imaginable; he has made friends and brothers of non-Catholic and non-Christian leaders. Ultimately, if we instill a Christian understanding of unconditional love for all, the respect for every human person, the inalienability of human dignity, and the ends to which social goods are destined, we

---

7. Galeano, *Mirrors*, 83–84.

can find the courage to reform existing distributive structures and arrangements to build up the common good. The version of the common good sold by the current neoliberal politics is biased, oriented to self-interest, and partial. But the common good that integrates into its conceptualization God's creation as a whole can lead us to happiness and fulfillment undreamed of. This is the kind of politics and leadership our world craves. It is my hope that African leaders will also pay attention and listen to the responsibility that is incumbent upon them.

Bibliography

Ahrensdorf, Peter J. "Thucydides' Realistic Critic of Realism." *Polity* 30:2 (Winter 1997) 231–65.
ChevronToxico: The Campaign for Justice in Ecuador. https://chevrontoxico.com.
Francis, Pope. *Fratelli Tutti: On Fraternity and Social Friendship*. Vatican City: Libreria Editrice Vaticana, October 3, 2020. http://www.vatican.va/content/francesco/en/encyclicals/documents/papa-francesco_20201003_enciclica-fratelli-tutti.html.
Galeano, Eduardo. *Mirrors: The Stories of Almost Everyone*. New York: Nation, 2009.
Hackworth, Jason. *Faith Based: Religious Neoliberalism and the Politics of Welfare in the United States*. Geographies of Justice and Social Transformation 11. Athens: University of Georgia Press, 2012.
Rawls, John. *A Theory of Justice*. Cambridge: Harvard University Press, 1971.
Stott, Lewis. "Kenya's Paradoxical 'Resource Curse.'" Student Paper, University of York. E-International Relations website. September 7, 2015. https://www.e-ir.info/2015/09/07/kenyas-paradoxical-resource-curse/.
Watts, Jonathan. "Nobel Laureates Condemn 'Judicial Harassment' of Environmental Lawyer." *The Guardian*, April 18, 2020. https://www.theguardian.com/world/2020/apr/18/nobel-laureates-condemn-judicial-harassment-of-environmental-lawyer.

18

Political Love: Beyond the Good Samaritan Charity

ALBERT E. ALEJO, SJ

JUST A WEEK AFTER *Fratelli Tutti* was published, Charles Cardinal Maung Bo of Yangon, the president of the Federation of Asian Bishops' Conferences, wrote a letter urging all FABC bishops to read the new encyclical in which "our Asian realities are echoed in [its] urgent message."[1] By "Asian realities" he meant the challenging cultural and political situations that Christians encounter in this part of the world.[2] Cardinal Bo would now be able to add to these challenging situations the recent violence that erupted when the Myanmar military usurped power from civilian authorities, the killings of thousands of ordinary people in the Philippines in the name of the government's war on drugs, and the many cases of corruption and conflict in the region.

1. Bo, "Fraternity Is the Foundation."
2. "As Catholics we may be but a minority in all countries except Philippines and Timor Leste, but the frank tone of Francis encourages us to speak strongly to all as brothers and sisters. The death penalty is still applied in eighteen of the countries of the Federation of Asian Bishops Conferences. The suffering of the Rohingya people is a scar on the soul of my own country, Myanmar. We feel deeply the tensions among peoples and we seek opportunities to respond to the ongoing conflicts in parts of Asia. Our hearts burn for millions who must migrate simply for their survival. We weep at the destruction of our beautiful rain forests which regenerate our sick planet and give life to our indigenous peoples" (Bo, "Fraternity Is the Foundation").

All over the world, there seems to be a growing democracy gap, as populist leaders increasingly dominate the political scene.[3] And it is in the presence of "dark clouds over a closed world" (the title of *FT*, chapter 1) that Cardinal Bo wishes to amplify Pope Francis's call for a new way of doing politics, a politics that is for the common good and practiced with love.[4] Surely, Cardinal Bo has captured the spirit and wisdom of *Fratelli Tutti*, especially of chapter 5. This chapter, the longest chapter of the document, describes in both compact and complex terms Pope Francis's vision of "a better kind of politics" (the title of chapter 5). There are a number of brief discussions of the chapter available in print and online.[5]

We may, however, approach this most talked-about chapter of the encyclical by articulating its threefold insight into the political implications of living out the Gospel message in contemporary times.

1. *Politics is essential for living out Christian charity.* The first insight is that politics is essential to the task of loving and serving people, both as individuals and as members of communities. Pope Francis deplores the fact that politics has gained a very bad reputation. "For many people today, politics is a distasteful word, often due to the mistakes, corruption and inefficiency of some politicians. . . . There are also attempts to discredit politics, to replace it with economics or to twist it to one ideology or another. . . . Yet can our world function without politics? Can there be an effective process of growth towards universal fraternity and social peace without a sound political life?" (*FT* 176).

    The pope asks whether we can we really afford to shy away from politics, maintaining that we cannot remain purely in the traditional "welfare" mode of helping individuals in need: "Welfare projects, which meet certain urgent needs, should be considered merely temporary responses" (*FT* 161). Neither can we relegate the welfare of the people to the operations of the market alone. "The marketplace, by itself, cannot resolve every problem. . . . Neoliberalism simply reproduces itself by

---

3. See Repucci and Slipowitz, *Freedom in the World*.

4. "Only a better kind of politics will create an open world with an open heart: politics for the common and universal good; politics for and with the people; politics that seeks human dignity; politics of women and men who practice political love; politics that integrates the economy and the social and cultural fabric into a consistent, life-giving human project" (Bo, "Fraternity Is the Foundation").

5. See Dini, "Cardinal Michael Fitzgerald"; Vicini, "Fratelli Tutti"; Rowlands, "Letter for Dark Times"; Gauthier, "Fratelli Tutti"; Calleja, "Philippine University"; Wejak, "How Important is 'Fratelli Tutti'?"; Fung, "Insights from Asian Indigenous Peoples."

resorting to the magic theories of 'spillover' or 'trickle'—without using the name—as the only solution to societal problems. There is little appreciation of the fact that the alleged 'spillover' does not resolve the inequality that gives rise to new forms of violence threatening the fabric of society.... The fragility of world systems in the face of the pandemic has demonstrated that not everything can be resolved by market freedom" (*FT* 168). For the pope, this means that we need politics.

Loving people demands that we transform institutions. An interesting hermeneutical innovation here is Pope Francis's powerful focus on the role of the innkeeper in his reading of the Lucan parable of the Good Samaritan. In chapter 2 of the encyclical, the personal, intimate act of caring performed by the Samaritan stranger is supplemented by the equally important institutional service of the innkeeper. Yes, the stranger stopped and approached the victim of violence on the roadside. The innkeeper, however, carried the burden of transforming the love exhibited by the initial rescue into a prolonged, institutional service, a service that is only made possible by complex social structures whose results may be less "affective" than the Samaritan's but are probably more "effective."[6] Running the inn demands managing space allocation, resource mobilization, financial security, a transportation network, medical education, and an entire legal system on which the mission of effective caring rests. Thus, charity finds expression not only in close and intimate face-to-face relationships but also in "macro relationships: social, economic and political" (*FT* 181).

The pope's interpretation has most certainly drawn from the contributions of social science and political philosophy. In particular, Paul Ricoeur's appreciation of the role of institutional and therefore impersonal—but effective—care is expressly mentioned in the encyclical.[7] "Charity," says the pope, "unites both dimensions—the abstract and the institutional—since it calls for an effective process of historical change that embraces everything: institutions, law, technology, experience, professional expertise, scientific analysis, administrative procedures, and so forth. For that matter, private life cannot exist unless it

---

6. For an incisive and mind-opening social and ecclesiological reflection on the "inn" and the "innkeeper" from an Asian perspective, see Adiprasetya, "Good Yet Missing Innkeeper."

7. See note 139 of the encyclical, which refers to Ricoeur's book, *Histoire et Verite* (published in English as *History and Truth*). Ricoeur's essay "The Socius and the Neighbor" deserves further study, especially because he generates social and ethical implications from the dialectic between the parable of the Good Samaritan and the prophecy of the Last Judgment. Ricoeur, *History and Truth*, 99.

is protected by public order. A domestic hearth has no real warmth unless it is safeguarded by law, by a state of tranquility founded on law, and enjoys a minimum of wellbeing ensured by the division of labour, commercial exchange, social justice and political citizenship" (*FT* 164).

In other words, in our desire to care for others, we must not remain on the level of individual charity, no matter how emotionally satisfying that may be. Authentic and effective love must embrace social transformation, including a proper allocation of power and the participation of the people in maintaining social institutions. We need both the ethics of the "Good Samaritan individual" and the politics of the "Good Samaritan institution."

2. *Politics needs to be practiced in love.* While the encyclical affirms the essential and constitutive role of politics in effecting love, it also asserts that the *practice* of politics must be imbued with the spirit of social fraternity and utter respect for persons, who have been blessed by the creator with dignity and utmost value. The first condition for a nobler practice of politics starts from the recognition of what it means for "persons" to be treated as a "people."

The pope asserts that "the word 'people' has a deeper meaning that cannot be set forth in purely logical terms. To be part of a people is to be part of a shared identity arising from social and cultural bonds. And that is not something automatic, but rather a slow, difficult process of advancing towards a common project" (*FT* 158). Underlining the concept of a "people" allows the pope to make a distinction between political leaders who are *popular* and those who are *populist*. Both popular and populist leaders know the character, the culture, and the guts of their people. But while the popular leader makes use of his deep understanding of the strengths and weaknesses of his people for the sake of their well-being and growth in happiness, populist leaders politically exploit the people's culture "under whatever ideological banner, for their own personal advantage or continuing grip on power," leading to the "usurpation of institutions and laws" (*FT* 159).

Bad politics thrives in and drives what Pope Francis called, in his encyclical *Laudato Si'*, the "throwaway culture." It is a culture in which "persons are no longer seen as a paramount value to be cared for and respected, especially when they are poor and disabled, 'not yet useful'—like the unborn, or 'no longer needed'—like the elderly." It is also bad political culture when we have "grown indifferent to all kinds of wastefulness, starting with the waste of food, which is deplorable in the extreme," and when "what is thrown away are not only food and dispensable objects, but often human beings themselves" (*FT* 18–19).

A little digression might help here. Chapter 5 acknowledges insights derived from bishops' conferences from Mexico to Polynesia and Brazil to Canada and Africa. *Fratelli Tutti* would have also been enriched by the much earlier pronouncement of the Federation of Asian Bishops' Conferences deploring the "misguided and selfish power politics" that has resulted in so much poverty and conflict in Asia.[8]

According to *Fratelli Tutti*, the proper virtue for the practice of better politics is "political love" (*FT* 180–82). "Recognizing that all people are our brothers and sisters, and seeking forms of social friendship that include everyone, is not merely utopian. It demands a decisive commitment to devising effective means to this end. Any effort along these lines becomes a noble exercise of charity." Pope Francis also notes that while "individuals can help others in need, when they join together in initiating social processes of fraternity and justice for all, they enter the field of charity at its most vast, namely political charity. This entails working for a social and political order whose soul is social charity" (*FT* 180).

Fratelli Tutti adds another aspect to political love. Christian charity must be "accompanied by a commitment to the truth" so that it goes beyond "personal feeling" and does "not fall prey to contingent subjective emotions and opinions." Without truth, emotion lacks relational and social content. Charity's openness to truth thus protects it from "a fideism that deprives it of its human and universal breadth" (*FT* 184). We can understand this to mean that political love makes use of all the data available in order to soundly describe and analyze a situation. Alleviation of poverty needs both stories and statistics. Stopping the pandemic requires the hard work of scientists. Attending to the immediate emotional and financial needs of the families of the victims of extrajudicial killings is virtue, but interrogating the source of the systematic pattern of the killings must not be dismissed

---

8. "Misguided and selfish power politics . . . has spawned structures and relationships in the political and economic community that are widening the scandalous gap between rich and poor, denying to the latter a fair and just access to the resources of the earth. Repression, oppression and exploitation are realities that result from the greed of vested economic interests and political power. Ethnic, cultural and linguistic conflicts which unleash violence, death and destruction are also linked with economic and political divisions. The political situation in many Asian countries has become volatile, and a sense of insecurity permeates particularly the minority groups" (Federation of Asian Bishops' Conferences, "Vocation and Mission," 25).

as irrelevant to the practice of Christian loving concern. Doing good must not suppress the search for the inconvenient truth.
3. *Being a politician is a lofty vocation.* Pope Francis appeals for "a renewed appreciation of politics as a lofty vocation and one of the highest forms of charity, inasmuch as it seeks the common good" (*FT* 180). This implies a call to a special spirituality on the part of the politician. The last portion of chapter 5 sounds like points for a spiritual retreat for those who are entrusted with leading the political community.

The first message is that it is good to be a politician. The politician is given the opportunity to render love that builds up the common good, the wider good, and the long-lasting good. The politician is tasked with and empowered to not just feed the poor, but "to organize and structure society so that one's neighbour will not find himself in poverty. It is an act of charity to assist someone suffering, but it is also an act of charity, even if we do not know that person, to work to change the social conditions that caused his or her suffering" (*FT* 186). The pope makes this social catechesis absolutely clear: "If someone helps an elderly person cross a river, that is a fine act of charity. The politician, on the other hand, builds a bridge, and that too is an act of charity. While one person can help another by providing something to eat, the politician creates a job for that other person, and thus practices a lofty form of charity that ennobles his or her political activity" (*FT* 186).

The politician is given power, and is often tempted to accumulate power, but a good politician allows herself to be moved by the weak in her community. "Amid the daily concerns of political life, the smallest, the weakest, the poorest should touch our hearts: indeed, they have a right to appeal to our heart and soul" (*FT* 194). When politicians learn how to go beyond viewing politics simply as a quest for more power, they may be sure that "none of our acts of love will be lost, nor any of our acts of sincere concern for others" (*FT* 195).

The politician must guard against being condescending to the poor. "The scandal of poverty," the pope says, "cannot be addressed by promoting strategies of containment that only tranquilize the poor and render them tame and inoffensive" (*FT* 187). Altruistic works must not hide within them a strategy to silence the poor and make them passive. Better politics offers the liberating fruits of education that leads to "greater self-expression and participation in society" (*FT* 187). The FABC vision of such participation is even more expansive. For FABC, "the entire people of God is called to engage in . . . politics, for the task of infusing the Gospel and Kingdom values of love and justice into the political, economic, cultural and social world of Asia; this is an imperative of the Gospel. Participation and involvement are duties that flow from the secular implications of the Gospel and the Reign of God."[9]

Politicians must exhibit both strength and tenderness. While politicians are expected to be firm, bold, and decisive, they are also called to express tenderness and compassion. This is the exact opposite of what happens in the "throwaway" culture that Pope Francis has been fighting against since he coined the term in *Laudato Si'*. For the pope, this teaching also includes politicians' recognition of their own humanity. They have their own families and personal relationships. They need rest. In the midst of their work, which often reduces people to anonymity, the pope reminds us that "loving the most insignificant of human beings as a brother, as if there were no one else in the world but him, cannot be considered a waste of time" (*FT* 193).

Politicians must be the first to offer sacrifice. Politicians must learn the skills and disposition that will enable them to listen to different kinds of people and hear their cries. This itself is a form of sacrifice (*FT* 190). When this happens, politicians will stop thinking so much about their ratings in the latest public surveys or about the number of votes they will have to earn in the next elections. Good politicians will be more concerned about "finding effective solutions to the phenomenon of social and economic exclusion, with its baneful consequences: human trafficking, the marketing of human organs and tissues, the sexual exploitation of boys and girls, slave labour, including prostitution, the drug and weapons trade, terrorism and international organized crime" (*FT* 188). This call for self-checks by politicians demands a corresponding internal cleansing in the internal governance of the institutional church.[10]

In sum, chapter 5 asserts that a sincere and intelligent living out of Christian charity with a special emphasis on fraternity with all must necessarily involve active engagement in politics. But this politics must be better than the usual allocation of power for selfish ends. Politics must be imbued with a spirituality that pays homage to the dignity of persons, respects people in their communities, and works for the common good. This kind of politics will have to be deeply committed to truth and the practice of tenderness, especially toward the weaker ones in society. Within this paradigm, politicians are uniquely called to live a life of nobility. Together with the people entrusted to their care, political leaders are called to find holiness precisely in their embeddedness in a career that is fraught with all kinds of dangers. All this has been and continues to be true for Christian communities in

---

9. Federation of Asian Bishops' Conferences, "Vocation and Mission," 26.
10. Cf. Bergoglio, *Way of Humility*; Alejo, *Ehemplo*, chapter 2.

Asia, whose "realities are echoed in the urgent message" of *Fratelli Tutti*, as was noted by Cardinal Bo in his letter cited above.

As this short note on chapter 5 is being written, the announcement has come that Manila now has a new pastor, Cardinal Jose F. Advincula. In his public message a few months back, then cardinal-designate Advincula stated that "human rights are key to church mission."[11] It sounds like the author of *Fratelli Tutti* has appointed a spiritual leader who shall embody the political love that informs the deeper intent of the new social encyclical: "In the face of present-day attempts to eliminate or ignore others, may we prove capable of responding with a new vision of fraternity and social friendship that will not remain at the level of words" (*FT* 6).

Many challenges remain, however. Here we mention just two. First is the need for *internal advocacy*. Pope Francis explicitly declares that the various messages of *Fratelli Tutti* should form part of the Catholic Church's social teachings. "It is important that catechesis and preaching" the pope insists, "speak more directly and clearly about the social meaning of existence, the fraternal dimension of spirituality, our conviction of the inalienable dignity of each person, and our reasons for loving and accepting all our brothers and sisters" (*FT* 86). The exhortation toward "political love" makes the "joy of the Gospel," which is the subject of Pope Francis's apostolic exhortation *Evangelii Gaudium*, not just affective but also effective. "Political love" must also go hand in hand with ecological conversion because we must listen to both "the cry of the earth and the cry of the poor."[12] The need for this internal advocacy must not be forgotten. Although Christianity may be a minority religion in Asia, our Catholic educational institutions have made a strong contribution to the formation of grassroots and political leaders in the region. "Political love" must be mainstreamed even in interreligious and intercultural dialogue, as the other chapters of *Fratelli Tutti* make clear.

The second, and more difficult, hurdle is *international diplomacy*. Pope Francis contextualizes *Fratelli Tutti* in the midst of the COVID-19 pandemic, which calls for global solidarity, a recognition that we are "all in the same boat" (*FT* 32). In Asia, at the writing of this commentary, dark

---

11. He continued: "Protecting human rights is never an option. They are at the heart of every church's mission. The dignity of the human person is the key to social problems that beset a nation. . . . The church cannot simply ignore human rights, because there is a moral dimension to them. The right to life, for example, is consistent with the church's teaching that there is dignity in the human person." He added that "poverty is one of the reasons why we have social problems" and that he sees education as "the way to develop the people so that they can earn more in order to live a more decent life" (Catholic News Service, "Philippine Cardinal-Designate").

12. Francis, *Laudato Si'*, 49.

clouds hover over the escalating maritime tension in the South China Sea.[13] The Philippines, Taiwan, Vietnam, and Malaysia are on high alert due to the aggressive claims of fishing rights and the military buildup by the Chinese government in this resource-rich region. The so-called Quad countries—the US, Australia, Japan, and India—are economically, politically, and even militarily agitated. To what extent can the call for "political love" and "social friendship" be heard in these high seas? Much more sophisticated forms of dialogue toward "a better politics" would be required to creatively extend, beyond the level of just words, the Good Samaritan "*inn*-stitution" into a global, humanitarian "*inn*-frastructure."

Bibliography

Adiprasetya, Joas. "The Good Yet Missing Innkeeper and the Possibility of Open Ecclesiology." *Ecclesiology* 14:2 (2018) 185–202.

Alejo, Albert E. *Ehemplo: Spirituality of Shared Integrity in Philippine Church and Society*. 2nd ed. Research on Spirituality Series 6. Quezon City, Philippines: Institute of Spirituality in Asia, 2016.

Bergoglio, Jorge Maria. *The Way of Humility*. San Francisco: Ignatius, 2014.

Bo, Charles Cardinal Maung. "Fraternity Is the Foundation and Pathway to Peace." *Union of Catholic Asian News*, October 13, 2020. https://www.ucanews.com/news/cardinal-bo-fraternity-is-the-foundation-and-pathway-to-peace/89864#.

Calleja, Joseph Peter. "Philippine University Dissects Pope's 'Fratelli Tutti.'" *Union of Catholic Asian News*, November 10, 2020. https://www.ucanews.com/news/philippine-university-dissects-popes-fratelli- tutti/90217#.

Catholic News Service. "Philippine Cardinal-Designate Says Human Rights Are Key to Church Mission." *Crux*, November 8, 2020. https://cruxnow.com/church-in-asia/2020/11/philippine-cardinal-designate-says-human-rights-are-key-to-church-mission/.

Dini, Elena. "Cardinal Michael Fitzgerald Comments on 'Fratelli Tutti.'" *Lay Centre*, November 12, 2020. http://www.laycentre.org/schede-580-cardinal_michael_fitzgerald_mafr_comments_fratelli_tutti.

Federation of Asian Bishops' Conferences (FABC). "The Vocation and Mission of the Laity in the Church and in the World of Asia: The Fourth Plenary Assembly of the Federation of Asian Bishops' Conferences." Tokyo, Japan, September 16–25, 1986. Hong Kong: FABC, 1986. https://fabc.org/wp-content/uploads/2022/09/FABC-Papers-47.pdf.

Francis, Pope. *Fratelli Tutti: On Fraternity and Social Friendship*. Vatican City: Libreria Editrice Vaticana, 2020. http://www.vatican.va/content/francesco/en/encyclicals/documents/papa-francesco_20201003_enciclica-fratelli-tutti.html.

———. *Laudato Si': On Care for Our Common Home*. Vatican City: Libreria Editrice Vaticana, 2020. https://www.vatican.va/content/francesco/en/encyclicals/documents/papa-francesco_20150524_enciclica-laudato-si.html.

13. Neill, "Very Real Risks."

Fung, Jojo M. "Insights from Asian Indigenous Peoples in Light of *Fratelli Tutti*." Paper Submitted for Keynote Address, Laudato Si' Research Institute's "The Politics of Land: Online Symposium." February 11, 2021. https://imcsap.org/insights-from-asian-indigenous-peoples-in-light-of-fratelli-tutti.

Gauthier, Josianne. "Fratelli Tutti: Politics as Act of Love and Courage." *Cidse* (blog post), December 4, 2020. https://www.cidse.org/2020/12/04/fratelli-tutti-politics-as-an-act-of-love-and-courage.

Neill, Alexander. "The Very Real Risks of a Dangerous Confrontation with China." *Nikkei Asia*, April 1, 2021. https://asia.nikkei.com/Opinion/The-very-real-risks-of-a-dangerous-confrontation-with-China.

Repucci, Sarah, and Amy Slipowitz. *Freedom in the World 2021: Democracy Under Siege.* https://freedomhouse.org/sites/default/files/2021-22/FIW2021_World_02252021_FINAL-web-upload.pdf.

Ricoeur, Paul. *History and Truth.* Evanston, IL: Northwestern University Press, 1965.

Rowlands, Anna. "A Letter for Dark Times: Pope Francis on the Call for a New Politics." Berkley Forum: "Fratelli Tutti and the Future of the Catholic Church." Berkley Center for Religion, Peace, and World Affairs, Georgetown University. October 26, 2020. https://berkleycenter.georgetown.edu/responses/a-letter-for-dark-times-pope-francis-on-the-call-for-a-new-politics.

Vicini, Andrea. "Fratelli Tutti: For a Better Kind of Politics." Berkley Forum: "Fratelli Tutti and the Future of the Catholic Church." Berkley Center for Religion, Peace, and World Affairs, Georgetown University. October 26, 2020. https://berkleycenter.georgetown.edu/responses/fratelli-tutti-for-a-better-kind-of-politics.

Wejak, Justin L. "How Important Is 'Fratelli Tutti' for Asia?" *Union of Catholic Asian News*, November 2, 2020. https://www.ucanews.com/news/how-important-is-fratelli-tutti-for-asia/90108.

19

Peoples on the Move: Francis's Political Utopia

Raúl Zibechi[1]

Introduction

POPULAR MOVEMENTS OCCUPY THE center of Francis's political thought as an expression of an organized people. In various speeches in which he refers to movements, he characterizes them as "social poets," as "sowers of change" who "work, propose, promote, and liberate in their own way," or also as "the future of humanity." As I will try to show in these lines, these considerations are not coincidental or capricious, but rather the consequence of lengthy reflection, extensive experience alongside society's poor, and an ethical and theological coherence.

In the section of *Fratelli Tutti* entitled "A Better Kind of Politics," Francis states that politics can be an obstacle to moving toward a different world. For this reason, he defends a politics that is capable of recovering the concept of *the people* and can thus define a common goal and identity, a collective dream that cannot be rationally explained by appealing to logical categories. I believe that the centrality of popular movements in Francis's thought and praxis comes from his choice of the people as a basic category for interpreting reality. This merits some reflection, since it is not about the preferential option for the poor established by liberation theology but rather about another proposal that, based on liberation theology, draws on other traditions.

1. Translated by Karen M. Kraft.

According to Omar Albado, the theology of the people, which centers on popular religiosity, took shape in the context of liberation theology; it was the way in which Argentine theology influenced Francis, "and he was encouraged to think about liberation from other viewpoints."[2] In the theology of the people, "people" is a historical and cultural category with its own set of goals—stated openly or barely implied—and with its own particular rationality and different ways of being and doing. It is a collective subject which, in the words of Argentine theologian Lucio Gera, can only be known and understood through love, that is, through direct participation (coexistence) in the life of the people.[3]

Besides placing popular religiosity at its center, Argentine theological reflection also transformed the people into the epistemic locus from which to know and interpret the reality of popular Christianity, involving it in the concrete history of the country's working classes. In the 1960s, several priests moved into the slums of Buenos Aires to support the people there; one in particular, in the Retiro slum, was Father Carlos Mugica. Although Mugica was assassinated by a far-right paramilitary group, his story spread and flourished among the *curas villeros* ("slum priests"), supported by the auxiliary bishop Bergoglio from the late 1990s on. It is no coincidence that the current Pope Francis, as archbishop of Buenos Aires, could be seen "supporting an effort in which the pastoral and social dimensions intersect in pursuit of the struggle for greater dignity of the people."[4]

In his defense of the working class, Francis distances himself from populism, because he believes that it can mask disdain for the weak and also because the leaders of these political currents often instrumentalize the people for personal ends or for their own power plays (*FT* 42). With the same conviction, he addresses the immediatism of certain populist governments that he considers degrading and, in a central point to which we will return, he challenges welfare assistance programs that are only temporary financial responses.

He also denounces the limits of liberalism for its individualism that tends to dissolve community ties, stating that "the marketplace, by itself, cannot resolve every problem" (*FT* 168), as the neoliberal mainstream maintains (*FT* 44). A model that limits itself to putting the economy at center stage, Francis implies, cannot place life or human dignity at center stage. This requires a "better kind of politics," which, at the risk of exaggerating, must be linked to popular movements. They can guide society toward an "integral

2. Albado, "Teología del Pueblo," 35.
3. Albado, "Teología del Pueblo," 43.
4. Albado, "Teología del Pueblo," 53.

human development," which is capable of transcending the politics of rights and social policy that is "*towards* the poor but never *with* the poor" (FT 45).

1. The Meetings of Popular Movements

In October 2014 at the Vatican and in July 2015 in Santa Cruz de la Sierra (Bolivia), Francis held respective meetings with popular movements under the slogan of the 3Ls (Land, Lodging, Labor). The first World Meeting of Popular Movements (WMPM) was convened by the Pontifical Council for Justice and Peace, the Pontifical Academy of Social Sciences, and various popular movements. More than a hundred social leaders from all continents attended to discuss challenges such as inequality, violence, and the environmental crisis. For several days the "culture of the encounter" was practiced, integrating people of different continents, generations, genders, professions, religions, and ideas, with the participation of bishops, pastoral ministers, intellectuals, and academics, who used the leadership of the poor and the popular movements as the starting point for debate.

In both meetings, despite the diversity of participants, the protagonists were the peasants, workers without rights, residents of poor neighborhoods (*favelas, villas, chabolas,* or slums, according to the various local terminology), and the emphasis was on the structural causes of poverty and exclusion. In workshops, panels, and in plenary, they articulated a diversity of views, diagnosing the circumstances in which people live, and coming to the conclusion that, when organized, the excluded, the oppressed, and the poor can address the situation the system has put them in. And I want to pause to reflect on both speeches.

2. The First Meeting: October 2014

Summarizing his position and contributions to popular movements, the speech Francis gave on October 28 in the Old Synod Hall[5] was circulated en masse after the meeting. First, he asserted that the poor do not sit back and wait for aid from the state or NGOs but that they are fighting against injustices. One of the key aspects of their struggle is the solidarity among them; they are acting in community.

Second, he harshly criticized public aid programs that have "a tendency to anaesthetize [sic] or to domesticate." In light of such state programs, he defended the need to fight "against the structural causes of poverty." He

---

5. Francis, "Address."

dedicated a good amount of time to this topic, delving deeper into it. "The scandal of poverty," he said, "cannot be addressed by promoting strategies of containment that only tranquilize the poor and render them tame and inoffensive." He said that "'[h]ypocrites' is what Jesus would say" to those who act with these objectives.[6]

Third, he defended the activism of the poor, which arises from young people on the urban peripheries, and encouraged "this breeze [to] become a cyclone of hope." On this point, Francis's experience in the slums allowed him to name as subjects of the coming changes all of the "waste collectors, recyclers, peddlers, seamstresses or tailors, artisans, fishermen, farmworkers, builders, miners, workers in previously abandoned enterprises,"[7] those excluded from labor rights, as subjects of the changes. They are the women and men who are struggling, and Pope Francis calls us to stand with them.

Fourth, he does not support any movement that is bureaucratized or subjected to the logic and manipulation of political parties or states. He is committed to "these experiences of solidarity which grow up from below, from the subsoil of the planet" and wants them to converge, coordinate, and meet. Since he knows what he is talking about, he issues a warning call: "But be careful, it is never good to confine a movement in rigid structures, so I say you should keep on meeting. Even worse is the attempt to absorb movements, direct, or dominate them."[8] In the same sense, one could add that walking together is not the same as providing ourselves with a system that imposes hegemony and uniformity.

In my view, this point is central. It has enormous implications and repercussions in terms of the kind of politics for which Francis advocates, and it raises some considerations for me. Francis knows firsthand, from the inside, the experience of the people—in particular that of the Argentine people, which is not so different from the struggles of other peoples of the world. His call to action implies a concrete reading of the history of the trade union movement, but also of church initiatives, in which the formation of enormous bureaucratic systems ends up putting leaders into power who do not dialogue with the grassroots but rather manipulate them in their own self-interest.

On the other hand, he advocates for "soft structures," such as social networks or gathering spaces, that allow for "walking together," something essential, without presenting the popular movement as if it were a unity in this day and age when diverse popular groups are deployed in multiple

6. Francis, "Address."
7. Francis, "Address."
8. Francis, "Address."

directions, to the degree that they not only fight against economic exploitation but also face the most diverse oppressions.

In this way, supporting neither systems nor forms of struggle that are violent, Francis not only commits to popular movements but also to a certain way of being, organizing, and moving through life. I want to emphasize that Francis's appeal is not inconsequential: he enters fully into the current debates in the movements, sharing Immanuel Wallerstein's ideas about decentralized, deconcentrated forms of organization. Indeed, one of the greatest analysts of antisystemic movements, Wallerstein argued for the need to concentrate on "the expansion of real social groups at community levels of every kind and variety of the community, and their grouping . . . at higher levels in a nonunified form."[9] He rejected democratic centralism and claimed that the old movements' mistakes consisted in believing that a structure was more effective the more unified it was.

2. The Second Meeting: July 2015

If Francis's position on the organization of movements is tied to the debates that occurred in the heat of the World Social Forums and his position remains relevant, the 2015 meeting implies a deepening of thought regarding collective subjects.

The Second World Meeting of Popular Movements was held July 7–9, 2015, in Santa Cruz de la Sierra, Bolivia. The fact that it took place here is not insignificant. In the first years of the Evo Morales administration, it was argued that this government was one of social movements, farmers, the indigenous, and those who lived in marginalized neighborhoods. I think it was a risky move by Francis, holding the WMPM here, but also necessary in order to place the people and the movements front and center in his political proposal.

In the speech he gave on July 9 at the Fexpocruz venue, he said that, in both meetings, he could feel "brotherhood, determination, commitment, a thirst for justice."[10] The Spanish word he used to express "determination" was *garra*, which literally means "claw." It's a term widely used in soccer and in the Río de la Plata region (between the Paraná and Uruguay rivers) in reference to the strength needed to do certain things. Francis used the term in the meeting to emphasize the need to grit one's teeth in the face of difficulties and digest the broad spectrum of them that ranges from hunger to repression by paramilitary groups and drug traffickers, while at the same time distancing

9. Wallerstein, *After Liberalism*, 109.
10. Francis, "Participation."

oneself from the violence. *Garra* and resistance are synonymous words, but the first is born of popular culture to which the pope pays tribute.

After condemning the evils of the system and the oppression suffered by the urban and rural poor, Francis asserts that "we are suffering from an excess of diagnosis,"[11] and puts the focus on the activities of the organized popular sectors. He speaks to the *cartoneros* (scrap collectors) and garbage collectors, street vendors and workers without rights, to those who live in the slums, the *villas, rancherios, favelas*. In other words, those at the bottom of society.

Several times he tells them that "they can do a lot." But he goes one step further, moving away from any paternalism, to make an uncomfortable point, both for the academy and for the political left: the poor, those who have nothing, are the protagonists of their own lives, not objects of charity or aid; they are the change makers. "I would even say that the future of humanity is, in great measure, in your own hands, through your ability to organize and carry out creative alternatives, through your daily efforts to ensure the three 'L's' [labor, lodging, land]...."[12]

Explicitly, he says that they are the change, what those without rights are doing—through small, local community action, the dignification of the popular economy, do-it-yourself home building, and the development of neighborhood infrastructures. They change the world by creating processes (Francis advocates the Bolivian notion of "process of change"), not by occupying "every available position of power."[13]

I want to return and highlight some aspects of Francis's thought that were not so clearly formulated in the first meeting. The first is the self-liberation of the poor. This may seem like a repeat of old concepts, but in reality, it is a bold bet on something new. In the hegemonic view, the people in our society who collect cardboard, paper, scraps, and garbage exist in the lowest social echelons. They have lost everything; they have no jobs, no rights, no access to quality healthcare and education. They would be the "leftovers," to use a current term, or the lumpenproletariat in the Marxist tradition. Or in the words of Eduardo Galeano, *los nadies*[14]—literally, the nobodies.

However, for Francis, the *nadies* are the protagonists of change and those who embody the hope of a new and better world. This way of seeing the world and politics runs counter to the mainstream; it has no basis

---

11. Francis, "Participation."
12. Francis, "Participation."
13. Francis, "Participation."
14. This is the title of a poem by Eduardo Galeano, published in his book, *El Libro de los Abrazos*.

in academic theses or in current political proposals. However, and this is one of the strengths of Francis's thought, it connects with some of the most beautiful traditions of the peoples of Latin America: the Canudos rebellion in northeastern Brazil,[15] the slave and indigenous rebellions over the last five centuries, and an endless number of grassroots movements that have been replicated, in his own Argentina, in the new organizations of *cartoneros* and scrap collectors.

The second is that the movements' struggle cannot entail only the demanding of rights, but rather must focus on creating alternatives based "on real needs and on the lived experience" of the marginalized and excluded. Everything they need in order to live with dignity, health, culture, sports, art, recreation, in addition to the three Ls, can come from the community work of popular movements. This is why he defines them as creators or "social poets."[16] The poet is the creator *par excellence*. The movements are creating a dignified life.

He says he doesn't have a recipe for how to do it, that he does not have a monopoly on the interpretation of social reality or the necessary solutions. He rejects even the idea that there *is* a recipe and believes that each people will find its way. As the slum priests of Argentina say, "We come to the villages to learn, not to teach." That is the approach that Francis promotes.

In Santa Cruz, Francis called for "change enriched by the collaboration of governments, popular movements and other social forces."[17] Without entering into controversy, I believe that collaboration between governments and movements is proving to be a thorny path, particularly due to the growing militarization of Latin American societies, a process that makes it difficult to foster the trust that joint work requires.

3. Walks of Life

We have seen that Francis's political thought is interwoven with his direct experience of the Argentine people, in particular with the residents of the poor neighborhoods or *villas*/slums, where around 10 percent of the population lives—more than four million people. These are families who migrated from the poor northern provinces, from Paraguay and Bolivia, people who have occupied land surrounding the streams on the urban outskirts, on flood-prone land that has no real estate market value. Francis said that

15. Translator's note: For more on the Canudos war and rebellion, see Madden, "Canudos War in History," 5–22.
16. Francis, "Participation."
17. Francis, "Participation."

he is very familiar with this situation in Santa Cruz, where different types of community organization managed "to create work where there were only crumbs of an idolatrous economy."[18]

In December 2008, in one of those neighborhoods—the Barracas (or Paraguayans') slum—I visited Father Pepe, José María di Paola. He proudly showed me the immense murals of Father Mugica and Father Daniel de la Sierra and the parish of Nuestra Señora de Caacupé, built through *minga* (community work) for the families of the neighborhood.[19] At some point, the conversation turned to the Catholic hierarchy in Buenos Aires. To my surprise, the *villero* priest told me:

> Bishop Bergoglio always comes here. The people love him very much. He will come to a meeting of four people or four hundred. He takes the *micro* (bus), gets off at the bus stop, walks to the church, and drinks mate with the locals. He doesn't come in the official archbishop's car.

I knew that Bergoglio/Francis supported the *villeros* priests but was not aware of the depth of his commitment, something that inspires this forty-six-year-old priest with long hair and casual clothes who bustles about the neighborhood and stops to spend time with those hardest hit by drugs or poverty.

Once a Paraguayan worker told Bergoglio, "The last time I left work, I took the bus and saw you sitting in the back. I told my coworkers, and they didn't believe me." Pepe smiled. "It was the only time I saw Bergoglio get emotional," he said.[20]

Bibliography

Albado, Omar César. "La Teología del Pueblo: Su Contexto Latinoamericano y su Influencia en el Papa Francisco." *Revista de Cultura Teológica* 91 (2018) 31–57. https://revistas.pucsp.br/index.php/culturateo/article/view/rct.i91.36886/pdf.

Francis, Pope. "Address of Pope Francis to the Participants in the World Meeting of Popular Movements." Speech given in the Vatican's Old Synod Hall, Rome, October 28, 2014. https://www.vatican.va/content/francesco/en/speeches/2014/

---

18. Francis, "Participation."

19. Translator's note: See Valenzuela Pérez, "Minga for the Climate": "In Latin America, *minga* is a form of collective work that is not paid with money but is done with the conviction that it is possible to get faster and better outcomes for the common good when the community works collaboratively together. The word *minga* has its roots in the Quechua language, a living Indigenous language spoken by Andean communities in Argentina, Bolivia, Chile, Colombia, Ecuador, and Peru."

20. Zibechi, *Descolonizar*, 113.

october/documents/papa-francesco_20141028_incontro-mondiale-movimenti-popolari.html.

———. *Fratelli Tutti: On Fraternity and Social Friendship*. Vatican City: Libreria Editrice Vaticana, 2020. https://www.vatican.va/content/francesco/en/encyclicals/documents/papa-francesco_20201003_enciclica-fratelli-tutti.html.

———. "Participation at the Second World Meeting of Popular Movements: Address of the Holy Father." Speech given in Santa Cruz de la Sierra, Bolivia, July 9, 2015. https://www.vatican.va/content/francesco/en/speeches/2015/july/documents/papa-francesco_20150709_bolivia-movimenti-popolari.html.

Galeano, Eduardo. *El Libro de los Abrazos*. Madrid: Siglo XXI, 1989.

Madden, Lori. "The Canudos War in History." *Luso-Brazilian Review* 30:2 (Winter 1993) 5–22.

Valenzuela Pérez, Leonardo. "A Minga for the Climate: Supporting Indigenous Climate Work at COP25." Unitarian Universalist Service Committee website, January 29, 2020. https://www.uusc.org/a-minga-for-the-climate-supporting-indigenous-climate-work-at-cop25/.

Wallerstein, Immanuel. *After Liberalism*. New York: New Press, 1995.

Zibechi, Raúl. *Descolonizar el Pensamiento Crítico y las Rebeldías*. Mexico City: Bajo Tierra, 2015.

20

Fratelli Tutti: A New Political Imagination?

ANNA ROWLANDS

A RECENT CONVERSATION WITH a ten-year-old visitor to my home stopped me briefly in my tracks. My young visitor had a keen interest in history, and we were chatting about the Cold War and its impact on the second half of the twentieth century. I had been explaining that, at the age of fourteen, I had taken part in a school history trip to East and West Berlin. Completely by chance, my history teacher had managed to time the trip to coincide with the fall of the Berlin Wall. Arriving a few weeks after the initial excitement, we were able to partake in euphoric dancing on the wall and chip off our own fragment of dusty, graffitied grey communist concrete to carry home as a memento. We stood and watched as large machines carved out the first section of the wall and a new, open space emerged between East and West. My ten-year-old friend asked me, thirty-two years later, what lasting impact that visit had on me.

The history you live through changes you. It shapes your imagination—for better and for worse. And yet, much of the shaping reality we live through remains only a partly-conscious thing to us. It becomes so much a part of us that we are barely aware of its importance, and so a question asked after thirty-two years can suddenly bring you home to yourself. In Berlin, I saw for the first time that it was possible to really change things, to overcome and to push against the walls, literal and metaphorical, that divide. I saw a whole world give way, and I came to feel that radical change, even after lengthy hopelessness, was possible. The grief and the joy I saw in Berlin left me with a deep sense of both the tragedy and the possibility of politics.

The conversation with my young visitor occurred around the same time as a Zoom call with an academic colleague and friend in New York. She shared her own reflections on the events that have shaped the political imaginations of her students. Living young years shaped by the legacy of 9/11, the financial crash of 2007, the so-called War on Terror, the culture wars of the Trump years, increased climate consciousness, Black Lives Matter, and a pandemic has had a profound impact on those she teaches. These two conversations reminded me that, while we might share a time and a space, our political defining experiences can be very different. It is not simply our political *views* that differ but our shaping political *experiences*, and these are powerful shapers of moral imagination.

This is the space—of moral and political imagination and of political experience—that chapter 5 of Pope Francis's letter *Fratelli Tutti* attempts to speak into. Francis diagnoses the social imaginations he believes lie at the heart of our current systems of power and proposes an alternative Catholic social imagination as the basis for deep societal renewal. He sees fraternal echoes of this moral imagination in other religious traditions, hence deploying the themes of social friendship, fraternity, dignity, and the common good as core teaching that forms part of a shared lexicon. The fact that this is the first social encyclical to be written out of an interfaith conversation clearly shapes the ideas in the text.

The French activist, philosopher, and mystic Simone Weil notes, in the vein of the Scriptures and the long tradition of Christian theology, that hope begins not when we sit down and imagine the blueprint of an ideal world but when we are willing to suspend mere dreaming and pay deep attention to the already present reality of the world around us.[1] Deep renewal requires us to train our attention first of all to what *is*. The problem is that our minds often recoil from this. This is exactly the methodology that *Fratelli Tutti* follows. It begins with an account of the dark clouds that hover over our times, moves on to share the parable of the Good Samaritan as a way to break open that reality to an alternative logic, and then expounds a vision of an open world, capable of dialogue, encounter, repentance, and renewal.

Beginning by paying deep attention to the world as it currently is, is not a way of limiting or shrinking our imagination to the terms of the status quo, but rather of accepting that Christian transformation comes from participation in what God is already doing in the most difficult of circumstances to redeem time. It is striking that Francis chooses the Good Samaritan

---

1. Weil, "Attention and Will," 231–37.

passage to frame this encyclical; as Francis reminds us, a Catholic vision of political renewal is a cocreative one. It takes account of, and is rooted in, the flesh and blood of our neighbors, the realities of our history, and the belief that the Spirit at work in the details of our lives now opens to us new futures. Christian hope for a better world does not, therefore, begin by taking flight but by pushing our feet down into the ground we stand on. This is the logic of incarnation, crucifixion, and resurrection. Francis roots us in the political time and space we live our lifespan in, as both gift and challenge.

In this spirit, in what follows I focus on just three elements of Francis's analysis of our political cultures, from a European perspective: his reading of populism as a manifestation of uprootedness; the shared—and interconnected—weaknesses of liberalism and populism; and finally, Francis's call for a liberationist-communitarian alternative as the grounds of a genuinely Christian social witness.

Pope Francis and Populism as a Manifestation of Uprootedness and Disorientation

A defining feature of the last decade in global politics has been the rise of new forms of populism. Populism itself is a contested term and is often used as a means of denunciation. To call something populist is to dismiss it with suspicion. For others, however, it has been adopted as a badge of honor—a counternarrative and a sign of resistance and reclamation. The very nature of our polarized times is bound up in this kind of discussion. Instead of denouncing populism per se, Francis moves beyond the polarized discussion by marking a distinction between different *kinds* of populism, open and closed, and by refocusing our attention on constructive uses of the idea of being "a people." Closed populism can be seen in leaders who manipulate the desire of persons to form community by appealing to these instincts as the basis for excluding incomers or consolidating power. Short-term advantage rather than long-term enrichment are further signs of an unhealthy populism. Francis proposes employment—dignified, meaningful, and properly remunerated work—as the "popular" thing. Drawing on Catholic social teaching on work as the way to develop the person as a dynamic, cocreative, productive, and contributive moral agent, Francis warns that welfare alone or short-term fixes are never in the interests of true political stability or the common good. Elsewhere, Francis has talked about the just distribution of, and access to, decent work, land, and housing as the three basic routes to material equality. This is a political, not merely market, matter for Francis as *Fratelli Tutti* makes clear.

Francis makes a distinction between different kinds of populism in order to retain for Christian use the idea of being "a people." A simple denunciation of populism risks throwing the baby out with the bathwater: we should not cede the idea of being "a people" to the closed populists but rather retrieve it for proper use. This proper use implies an "open-ended" populism, capable of welcoming strangers, open to external sources of renewal, and committed to the agenda of dignity noted above. Tackling inequality is core to this. Francis is deeply aware that the language of being "a people" has been part of the grammar of Christian theology and an idea used by the church to talk about its own character. As US political theologian Charles Mathewes notes, St. Augustine uses the idea of being "a people" and "a city" to talk about the pilgrim community of Christians through time.[2] The Second Vatican Council used the idea of being a people as a renewing image for the life of the church in *Lumen Gentium*. Francis is also influenced by the Argentine theology of the people, which focused on the wisdom and character of the people and of the need for the church to engage with the popular culture that marked the way communities lived their daily lives. Francis describes the notion of being "a people" as a category neither strictly logical nor mystical, but rather mythical. It speaks to a longing and a process—a longing for common bonds and shared identity and a process of forming and maintaining and revising those bonds and the common projects that give rise to them. Common action rather than simply an agreement on ideas is the basis for sustaining the life of the people. This process requires slow, patient work and is fraught with challenges and setbacks. But it is hard-wired into us. Hence, it is also so open to manipulation and abuse, especially in contexts where this desire has been frustrated, and isolation and fragmentation have been a dominant experience.

Although this teaching appears, in some ways, to be a new and fresh intervention on contemporary questions of populism, it has interesting historical antecedents. During the height of the Second World War, Pope Pius XII issued a series of radio addresses for Christmas focused on the rebuilding of the world after the war. In these, he offered a careful consideration of the possibilities of democracy and political renewal. He argued—in ways that are deeply resonant of Pope Francis's words in *Fratelli Tutti*—that any appeal to "the people" as if they were an inert mass without true individuality would destroy rather than renew politics.[3] He contrasted a logic of the masses—impersonal, homogenizing, easily manipulated—with the process

---

2. This insight was drawn out in conversation between the author and Charles Mathewes and is used here with his permission.

3. See Pius XII and Yzermans, *Major Addresses of Pius XII*.

of becoming a "people," capable of differentiated, responsible, thoughtful action toward common ends. It is this same process of becoming that Francis repeatedly lays before us in *Fratelli Tutti*.

In *Fratelli Tutti*, Francis warns of a closed populism that imagines the "people" in primarily ethnic and homogeneous identity terms, refuses the gift of the stranger, and sees itself as self-sufficient in its cultural resources. By contrast, an open populism embraces the need to form external cultural bonds, to accept and form new practices of social belonging, but practices these with an openness to those who do not yet belong—the new arrival, the next generation, and so forth. Renewal comes in an antonymous way—from who or what is not yet present. This "not yet present" can be intergenerational and intercultural. Cultures may (or may not!) be beautiful, wise, and fruitful, but they are importantly incomplete as expressions of full humanity or truth, and their possibility of human fullness lies beyond themselves, both in time and in relation to eternity. The specificity, value, yet incompleteness and fragility of cultures forms part of Francis's call for a politics of dialogue, hospitality, and gift exchange, not merely of just distribution and human rights.

Interestingly, Francis does not single out populism as the sole cause of political fragmentation. He addresses both liberalism and populism as interconnected political forces that lead to different forms of isolation and fragmentation. Just as we might view socialism as itself an offshoot of liberalism, so populism might also be viewed in a similar way. Populism might be viewed as the suppressed "other" of liberalism—the denial of communal dimensions to our identities reemerges in resurgent but distorted forms. Populism and liberalism can also be viewed, through Francis's lens, as sharing a certain set of fundamental features. Both show a degree of disdain for or disinterest in the most vulnerable and in the value of the preservation of deep cultures. For some readers, this kind of wide generalization can be deeply frustrating—seeming primarily rhetorical and too sweeping to be helpful. However, I think the genealogical mapping that such a wide-angled view offers is insightful and helps us identify that what often seem to be opposing mindsets might be fundamentally related and interconnected. Francis's account moves us beyond a narrow either/or response and into a space where we are able to identify the common traits and common unresolved problems that lie at the heart of the politics of our time. This enables both responsibility and judgment in political life, shaped by Gospel perspectives on what enables human and wider biospheric flourishing.

Francis's judgment in *Fratelli Tutti* is that both liberalism and populism tend to produce forms of uprooted politics. They uproot us from deep material and moral connection to each other, tending toward a disinterested relationship to God, earth, and neighbor. We are thus numbed to multiple forms of vulnerability and need and to the deep and complex bonds that form community over time. Interestingly, Francis examines the weaknesses of liberalism taken on its own terms. He notes that the creed of political liberalism is liberty, equality, fraternity. He suggests that liberalism has tended to leave fraternity as the poor relation of the other two aspirations and, therefore, continually fails to achieve them. Francis argues that, in fact, fraternity is the primary practice that enables equality and liberty. Interestingly, *Fratelli Tutti* does not denounce liberalism as early social teaching of the nineteenth century did. Instead, the encyclical offers a challenge to liberalism, to live up to its own values. This is not a baptism of liberalism but a dialogical engagement on the part of the church. By contrast, *Fratelli Tutti* does denounce individualism as a false creed and inimical to the building of a flourishing society. There is no constructive engagement to be had with individualism. A neoliberal era is shaped by the forces of technocracy, individualism, and consumerism. In this context, the values and aspirations to equality, liberty, and fraternity appear both unrooted and caught within a logic of uprootedness.

Francis's papacy—and this encyclical, as a summation of the social teaching of this pontificate—has been marked by a deep political concern for migration and ecology as social issues, for inequality as a primary social evil, and for a spiritual malaise that he names as indifference to the cries of our neighbors and the earth. His response to this diagnosis is to recommend a spiritual practice of social friendship, a politics of encounter and dialogue. This is the repeated, and novel, language of *Fratelli Tutti*. If indifference is the malaise, then social friendship is the antidote. What does Francis appear to mean by this phrase? In one sense, this language is a development of the idea of solidarity in Catholic social teaching. John Paul II refers to solidarity as more than a vague feeling of compassion. It is, he says, "a firm and persevering determination"[4] to act for the good of others. It is structural and not merely personal (although these responses are always personal, too). If John Paul II's task was to remind us that solidarity required structural responses that build justice and love into social worlds, then Pope Francis's task has been to remind us that we cannot really understand the way that structures already operate in our social worlds without first being willing to be proximate to the lives of those most marginal to our centers of structural power. The answer to indifference is to be willing to draw near, to be personally involved, to make what is already a deep social connection into a real social bond. This means a willingness to be moved by suffering, to be desolate in the face of awful events, to feel implicated in social issues, and to find hope

---

4. John Paul II, *Sollicitudo Rei Socialis*, 38.

in the fact that connection to others is possible. The openness to listening, to sharing, and to learning how to act with and not merely for others is critical to Francis's vision of social friendship. It is the performance of the life of Christ that he draws us into. Thus, social friendship overcomes social distance, is rooted in communities who can together perform the logic of mercy, justice, and love, and thus counters—at its root (or in its uprootedness)—the politics of indifference. This is how the logic of mercy renews our social vision and gives birth to a new social imagination. This is how the option for the poor is an entirely mainstream vision for how we shift our political systems and their flows of power.

In *Fratelli Tutti*, Pope Francis argues for a new political vision, one that is able to integrate rather than fragment and to be deeply creative of new forms of work, shelter, and stewardship of the land. This happens only when we begin by listening to those cast to the peripheries and learn to work across polarized lines. Fragmentation and polarization are key features of the European (and, indeed, global North) political landscape. Francis does not fight shy of naming this reality. He argues in this document—and further develops in his pandemic-focused book, *Let Us Dream*—that we should learn to distinguish between the conflicts that are productive and those that are deathly. Not all conflict in politics (or the church) is bad. There is a productive relationship, Francis argues, between local and universal values and realities, between goods that require ways of being reconciled into a fruitful social process. However, the conflict between good and evil is not one of tensive polarities productive in their intersection. Rather, this requires a spiritual struggle to uphold the good. The political struggle for the good can only happen when we draw near to God, and to each other, to the sites of trauma, loss, inequality, and powerlessness that mark our communities, nations, and regions, or claim our power from these locations. Pope Francis has called for every Catholic to join a social movement, to learn to act together with others to form a future worthy of the creation we are, and are called to be: *fratelli tutti*.

Bibliography

Francis, Pope. *Fratelli Tutti: On Fraternity and Social Friendship*. Vatican City: Libreria Editrice Vaticana, 2020. https://www.vatican.va/content/francesco/en/encyclicals/documents/papa-francesco_20201003_enciclica-fratelli-tutti.html.

John Paul II, Pope. *Sollicitudo Rei Socialis*. Vatican City: Libreria Editrice Vaticana, 1987. https://www.vatican.va/content/john-paul-ii/en/encyclicals/documents/hf_jp-ii_enc_30121987_sollicitudo-rei-socialis.html.

Pius XII, Pope, and Vincent Arthur Yzermans, ed. *The Major Addresses of Pius XII.* Vols. 1–2. St. Paul, MN: North Central, 1961.

Weil, Simone. "Attention and Will." In *Simone Weil: An Anthology,* edited by Sian Miles, 231–37. London: Penguin, 2005.

PART SIX

Dialogue and Friendship in Society

21

Dialogue and Encounter for Global Poverty Eradication: Global Justice Perspectives

CHARLES B. CHILUFYA, SJ

THIS CHAPTER EVALUATES POPE Francis's teaching in the sixth chapter of the encyclical *Fratelli Tutti*, which dwells on dialogue and encounter as a means of building a more just and healthier world. Pope Francis calls humanity to imagine a world that is founded on friendship, dialogue, and encounter. His proposals are akin to what Walter Brueggemann calls "prophetic imagination"—"[t]he task of prophetic ministry is to nurture, nourish, and evoke a consciousness and perception alternative to the consciousness and perception of the dominant culture around us."[1] In the spirit of prophetic imagination, the proposal of a human community founded on dialogue and encounter is not merely an intellectual or spiritual exercise. It is an engagement with the lived realities of oppression and apathy in our global community, of grief and despair, hope and energy. It is a call to imagine a different world and to see governments and faith communities like the church as centers of such imagination, kindness, and compassion.

This encounter and dialogue that Pope Francis speaks about is not only interpersonal but also international and global. It is an encounter of nations in the promotion and establishment of global justice in a borderless world. The pope speaks of the power and importance of "kindness," which is an attitude that can be adopted by nations, especially the powerful nations toward the weaker nations. It is a star "shining in the midst of darkness" and

---

1. Brueggemann, *Prophetic Imagination*, 3.

frees us from the cruelty and the anxiety that plague the contemporary era (cf. *FT*, 222–24).

In the contemporary era, nations are clearly not in dialogue; we live in a divided world split into the richer global North and the poorer global South. We live in a scandalous "global jungle," notorious for its inequality, injustice, unfairness, absurdity, and widespread poverty amid obscene wealth. With Mosse,[2] I laud Pope Francis's call for dialogue and encounter and argue for a dialogical and "relational" approach to global poverty analysis. This approach views persistent poverty as a consequence of divisive economic and political relations and as effects of a failure in dialogue and care. It is an approach that encourages an analysis of the gap between poor regions and rich regions that not only looks at the internal conditions of each country, but also draws attention to the balance of global power that influences the current global order through global institutions and rules, which determine global economic policy in favor of the interests of the more powerful nations and business elites of those nations. Authentic dialogue and encounter among nations is what will heal the current global poverty and imbalances.

Global Poverty and Inequality in a Divided World

According to the 2021 World Bank report, *Changing Wealth of Nations*, since 1995, overall global wealth grew by 91 percent, reaching US $1,152 trillion by 2018, but this growth has been attained at the expense of future prosperity and by exacerbating inequalities.[3] If divided equally, each person could have a share of nearly $40,000. Instead, 80 percent of humanity lives on less than $10 a day, nearly half on less than $5.50 a day, and 10 percent on less than $1.90 a day.[4] According to the World Bank, in 2013, 41 percent of the population of sub-Saharan Africa live on $1.90 or less per day, a principal factor in widespread poverty, which is often a cycle.[5] Globally, more than 800 million live in extreme poverty, and more than half of those are in Africa. Of the world's twenty-eight poorest countries, twenty-seven are in sub-Saharan Africa, all with a poverty rate above 40 percent. Projections by the World Bank in 2018 showed that extreme poverty was exhibiting few signs of improvement in this region, which may keep countries from ending extreme poverty by 2030.[6] While the number of poor people continues to

2. Mosse, "Relational Approach."
3. World Bank Group, *Changing Wealth of Nations*, 60–61.
4. World Bank Group, *Poverty and Shared Prosperity*, 67.
5. World Bank Group, *Poverty and Shared Prosperity*, 27.
6. World Bank Group, *Poverty and Shared Prosperity*, 2–3.

decline in South Asia and other regions, simulations indicate that there will be no comparative decline in poverty in sub-Saharan Africa. In fact, statistical forecasts show that by the last year of the Sustainable Development Goals (SDGs), 2030, by which nations had projected they would eradicate poverty in all its forms everywhere (SDG 1), the number of poor people living in sub-Saharan Africa as a share in the global total of poor people will be about 87 percent, if nothing changes in terms of economic growth over the next twelve years.[7]

The income inequality between the top and bottom tenth of the human population is a staggering 320:1. The top 25 percent of the world's billionaires together hold almost 85 percent of global income, while the remaining population squeezes into the remaining 15 percent of global income. The global bottom half holds a very small share of global income—just 8 percent—while the world's top 10 percent earns 52 percent of the total.[8] Even more disturbing and much greater than income inequality is global wealth inequality. It is estimated that 50.4 percent of global wealth is owned by the top richest of the world while the bottom half owns only 0.6 percent of global wealth. The poorest half of the world's population owns just 2 percent of the world's total net wealth, while the richest half owns 98 percent.[9]

Today's severe poverty is avoidable at a cost that is tiny compared to the incomes and fortunes of the affluent. Despite the fact that the world has experienced rapid growth in average income, billions of human beings are still condemned to lifelong severe poverty, with all its attendant evils of low life expectancy, social exclusion, ill health, illiteracy, dependency, and slavery. The challenge is that this inequality seems to be increasing unabated. According to the 2018 World Bank report, while global wealth grew significantly over the past two decades, per capita wealth declined or stagnated in more than two dozen countries in various income brackets.[10] Global wealth grew at an estimated 66 percent over this period (from $690 trillion to $1,143 trillion in 2014), but inequality was substantial, as wealth per capita in high-income Organization of Economic Cooperation and Development (OECD) countries was fifty-two times greater than in low-income countries. Similar trends have been observed since the 1980s.[11]

While some of Africa's problems are internal and arise on account of bad local decisions, many of its problems are external and beyond its

7. World Bank Group, *Poverty and Shared Prosperity*, 25.
8. Chancel et al., *World Inequality Report*, 27.
9. Chancel et al., *World Inequality Report*, 27.
10. World Bank Group, *Poverty and Shared Prosperity*, 43, 60–62.
11. World Bank Group, *Poverty and Shared Prosperity*, 44, 49–60.

control and, therefore, call for systemic reform of the current global institutional and economic order, which produces poverty. In the analysis of global poverty and inequality, the disparate fortunes of poor countries and rich countries should not be treated as separate and unrelated phenomena. As Joshi and O'Dell observe,[12] this would be in keeping with the World Bank's ideology, which generally seeks to explain and redress underdevelopment by focusing on the internal policies and institutions of poor countries. For example, explaining Africa's regression in poverty eradication between 1990 and 2015, the 2018 World Bank study almost solely attributes it to internal factors such as the region's slower rates of growth, problems caused by conflict and weak institutions, and a lack of success in channeling growth into poverty reduction; it describes global poverty as a sub-Saharan problem.[13] This narrative is incorrect.

Ethical Evaluation of the Global Institutional Order

There are reasons to agree with Thomas Pogge that the almost unilaterally designed global institutional order for which the rich northern governments bear primary responsibility has been actively causing global poverty and harming the poor.[14] Protecting and promoting the interests of corporations and rich individuals from their countries, rich nations competitively pursue their interests within a framework of rules whose adjudication may then be deformed by stronger parties to the point where the framework becomes manifestly unfair. Any institutional order must meet certain minimal conditions in terms of human rights. The existing global institutional order falls short of authentic dialogue that can enhance the possibility of meeting these conditions on account of the excessive inequalities in bargaining power and the immense poverty and economic inequality it avoidably reproduces.

The current global poverty and inequality are serious moral problems when we consider three facts. First, there is enough and plenty to go around. It would take less than 1 percent of the national incomes of the high-income countries with their one billion people to raise the approximately three billion human beings reportedly living below the World Bank's $1.90 a day poverty line above that line.[15]

---

12. Joshi and O'Dell, "Global Governance."
13. World Bank Group, *Poverty and Shared Prosperity*, 2.
14. Pogge, "Are We Violating," 22–23.
15. Pogge, *Politics as Usual*, 69–70. See also Pogge, *World Poverty*, especially endnote 122.

Second, the current international institutional arrangements are too unequal. When we measure growth, we do so in gross terms without paying attention to what accounts for the increases, which usually go to the richer people and places. When we measure gross domestic product (GDP), we value all additional dollars equally, regardless of where they go. Morally speaking, we should rather celebrate when additional income and wealth go to the poor; this would be more valuable. There exist tools and processes like national and international tax rules (and other mechanisms) that we can employ to help achieve a more equal distribution.

Third, we should look at how global institutions, systems of rules and practices, and transnational actors adversely affect the domestic life of poorer regions globally, specifically in Africa. Global institutions, rules, and practices shape the environment (for example, global markets) in which national societies in Africa exist and with respect to how they govern and tax themselves, how they organize education, healthcare, agriculture, and defense, and how they regulate foreign investment, intellectual property rights, and foreign trade. They do so through various transmission mechanisms relating to pollution and climate change, food security, global epidemics, culture and information technology, and most profoundly through market forces that condition access to capital and raw materials, export opportunities, domestic tax bases and tax rates, prices, wages, and labor standards, and enable illicit financial outflow from Africa.[16]

Why Does the Global Institutional Order Matter?

Since the development of the social sciences in the second half of the twentieth century, there has been an increased appreciation of the explanatory importance of social institutions. Institutional analysis provides another way of looking at the events of our social world. Traditionally, social phenomena have been analyzed as actions performed by individual and collective agents and the effects of those actions. But we can also see social phenomena as effects of how our social world is structured and organized in the form of laws and conventions, practices, and social institutions. In the last fifty years, social scientists, philosophers, and theologians have articulated interactional analysis that has firmly established social institutions as a distinct domain of moral assessment and have marked this domain terminologically by associating it with the term "social justice."[17] Thus, the term "justice" is now

---

16. Pogge, "Are We Violating," 22–23.
17. See, generally, Rawls, *Theory of Justice*.

applied in the moral assessment of laws, practices, social conventions, and institutions that define social rules.

Therefore, the search for global justice as it relates to poverty eradication needs a moral assessment of the way global arrangements of rules and institutions emerged or were created, often without sufficient dialogue and in highly undemocratic ways. Western international organizations have dominated the task of setting global norms and rules that tackle global issues like international trade and finance, illicit financial flows (IFFs), climate change, and others. In particular, the World Trade Organization (WTO), the Organization of Economic Cooperation and Development (OECD), the World Bank Group, and the International Monetary Fund (IMF) provide not only global norms and rules but also important research and policy advice. African countries are not well represented in such organizations. Take, for example, the OECD—it plays a leading role in tackling tax avoidance by multinational corporations, but no African country is a member of this organization. Twenty-one African countries are members of the Inclusive Framework on Base Erosion and Profit Shifting (BEPS), which discusses these issues, although it is hard to determine the extent to which this allows them to influence international efforts in this regard.

At critical moments like the coronavirus pandemic, when poorer populations need medicines, the current WTO agreement on Trade-Related Aspects of Intellectual Property Rights (TRIPS) incentivizes the production and distribution of essential medicines in richer countries, where innovators find it more profitable to sell their products. According to the *British Medical Journal*,[18] as the world faces the coronavirus pandemic in 2021, under the current TRIPS model, the world's poorest countries may wait until 2024 for mass immunization.[19] This state of affairs could cost millions of lives and push tens of millions more into poverty, and, even then, the rich nations are refusing to listen and to dialogue, and are opposed to a temporary waiver of the WTO's TRIPS agreement.

The COVID-19 crisis facing Africa is an example of why the world needs more dialogue and more extensive levels of international cooperation, coordination, compromise, and care than there are now. In *Fratelli Tutti*, Pope Francis warns against a "culture of walls" and calls on humanity to say "no" to unhealthy competition in acquiring the vaccines and to shun globalized indifference and exclusion of others. In his 2020 address to the members of the Banco Farmaceutico Foundation, the pope affirmed the need to make the new COVID-19 vaccines available and accessible to all,

18. See "Much of the World."
19. "More than Eighty-Five Countries."

stating that "if there is the possibility of treating a disease with a drug, this should be available to everyone, otherwise an injustice is created."[20]

An Opportunity for Imagining a New World

The divisions in the global community and the crises they foment offer an unprecedented opportunity for change, for a better, healthier, and more just world ruled by dialogue and listening. This calls for the conversion, dialogue, and encounter Pope Francis enunciates in *Fratelli Tutti*. At a critical time like the one we are facing, the future of human communities in Africa and the world at large cannot be guaranteed without reforms toward dialogue in the way we build the global political, economic, and financial institutions that we employ as means of helping us meet our needs. Through Pope Francis, the church offers a passionate voice, along with others, advocating for a number of alternatives for the sake of an economy of life for all. In various contexts alluded to above, the extent of gross dehumanization looks like the sin of sacrilege. There is indeed a deep need in our time for a new unity of spirituality and humanity, envisioning the abundant life for all as a convergence point.

We contend that at the root of the global economic and ecological crises is a dictatorship of the current global institutional order that disdains dialogue and listening. The global institutional order is arguably unjust and dictatorial insofar as the incidences of violence and severe poverty occurring under it are much greater than would be the case under an alternative order whose design is founded on dialogue and respect for the interests of the poor and vulnerable.

There is need for an alternative consciousness like the one the Catholic Church is evoking in the pope's message in *Fratelli Tutti*. In a world less human, deeply divided, unequal, and unjust, the vocation of the church and all other faiths is still to speak a prophetic word to help the human community to imagine a different life-giving future. As a prophetic community, the church will continue to help humanity connect the dots between the world as it is and the world as it might or should be, founded on dialogue and established as a community.

Pope Francis recognizes the power of a holy imagination to deliver us from the current hopelessness, which he describes as "dark clouds over a closed world"; his teaching opens the door to new possibilities. There is a lot to shrink our hope and constrict our vision: unemployment, illness, injustice, and poverty. These hardships can imprison us in the pain of the

20. Francis, "Address."

present moment, unable to look beyond our own current misfortunes. During such times like the current ones, we can lose our dreams, mistaking realism for reality. But we can employ the resources of our faith and our human capacity for dialogue and conversation, which can remind us that we have a destiny—a destiny to thrive. We can, therefore, look beyond our misfortunes and failures and embrace a larger vision—the power of the holy imagination, the lure of an alternative reality. This has always been the inspiration for the prophets and spiritual guides, and the church as a prophetic guide wishes to carry on that inspiration. Within what we perceive as limitations are possibilities for adventure and growth.

Pope Francis's "prophetic imagination" develops a framework of the church's prophetic role to help imagine a world beyond the coronavirus and beyond the current global divisions. The pope proposes that the work of imagining a future entails dismantling a royal, imperial, or totalitarian consciousness that promotes social and cultural domination by a few by means of the "economy of death," which promises the individualistic happiness of consumerism, self-satiation, and profiteering rather than community. Pope Francis's prophetic stance not only criticizes the prevalent reign of royal or imperial consciousness, but it also takes one step further to energize people through offering the alternative of encounter and dialogue. In a prophetic countervision of the "Economy of Francesco," which is radical, the economy of life—of dialogue, encounter, sharing, and equality—replaces the economy of death, and the economy and politics of domination are replaced by the economics and politics of justice, kindness, compassion, dialogue, and encounter.

Bibliography

Brueggemann, Walter. *The Prophetic Imagination*. Rev. ed. Philadelphia: Fortress, 1978.
Castaneda Aguilar, R. Andres, et al. *September 2020 PovcalNet Update: What's New*. Global Poverty Monitoring Technical Note 14. Washington, DC: World Bank, 2020. https://openknowledge.worldbank.org/bitstream/handle/10986/34451/September-2020-PovcalNet-Update-What-s-New.pdf?sequence=1&isAllowed=y.
Chancel, Lucas, et al. *World Inequality Report 2022*. Cambridge: Harvard University Press, 2022.
Francis, Pope. "Address to the Members of the 'Banco Farmaceutico Foundation.'" Speech given in Rome, September 19, 2020. https://www.vatican.va/content/francesco/en/speeches/2020/september/documents/papa-francesco_20200919_banco-farmaceutico.html.
———. *Fratelli Tutti: On Fraternity and Social Friendship*. Vatican City: Libreria Editrice Vaticana, 2020. http://www.vatican.va/content/francesco/en/encyclicals/documents/papa-francesco_20201003_enciclica-fratelli-tutti.html.

Joshi, Devin, and Roni Kay O'Dell. "Global Governance and Development Ideology: The United Nations and the World Bank on the Left-Right Spectrum." *Global Governance: A Review of Multilateralism and International Organizations* 19:2 (2013) 249–75.

"More than Eighty-Five Countries Will Not Have Widespread Access to Coronavirus Vaccines before 2023." *Economist Intelligence,* January 27, 2021. https://www.eiu.com/n/85-poor-countries-will-not-have-access-to-coronavirus-vaccines/.

Mosse, David. "A Relational Approach to Durable Poverty, Inequality and Power." *The Journal of Development Studies* 46:7 (2010) 1156–78.

"Much of the World May Not Have Access to a COVID-19 Vaccine Until 2022." *British Medical Journal,* December 15, 2020. https://www.bmj.com/company/newsroom/much-of-the-world-may-not-have-access-to-a-covid-19-vaccine-until-2022/.

Piketty, Thomas, and Emmanuel Saez. "Inequality in the Long Run." *Science* 344:6186 (2014) 838–43. https://eml.berkeley.edu/~saez/piketty-saezScience14.pdf.

Pogge, Thomas. "Are We Violating the Human Rights of the World's Poor?" In *Human Rights: Old Problems, New Possibilities,* edited by David Kinlet et al., 1–33. Northampton, MA: Edward Elgar, 2013.

———. *Politics as Usual: What Lies Behind the Pro-Poor Rhetoric.* Malden, MA: Polity, 2010.

———. *World Poverty and Human Rights: Cosmopolitan Responsibility and Reform.* Malden, MA: Polity, 2002.

Pogge, Thomas, and Krishen Mehta. "Introduction: The Moral Significance of Tax-Motivated Illicit Financial Outflows." In *Global Tax Fairness,* edited by Thomas Pogge and Krishen Mehta, 1–13. Oxford: Oxford University Press, 2016.

Rawls, John. *A Theory of Justice.* Cambridge: Harvard University Press, 2009.

United Nations Department of Economic and Social Affairs. "The 17 Goals." https://sdgs.un.org/goals.

World Bank Group. *The Changing Wealth of Nations 2021: Managing Assets for the Future.* Washington, DC: World Bank, 2021. https://openknowledge.worldbank.org/handle/10986/36400.

———. *Poverty and Shared Prosperity 2018: Piecing Together the Poverty Puzzle.* Washington, DC: World Bank, 2018. https://openknowledge.worldbank.org/bitstream/handle/10986/30418/9781464813306.pdf.

22

The Path of Dialogue, Solitude, and Hope: Voices from Asia

Albertus Bagus Laksana, SJ

Fratelli Tutti is a remarkable document. Using powerful language in an interdisciplinary analysis, it addresses some of the most pressing issues of our time, offering a theological ethics that touches on and unites us with respect to the fundamental truth of our existence, as well as further motivating us to work together as world citizens. My comments in this essay will focus mainly on chapter 6, "Dialogue and Friendship in Society," which I find to be quite rich. It starts with the question of social dialogue, in which citizens converse, recognizing and overcoming differences, and then are united to pursue the common good based on a deep respect for others (*FT* 199–205). In the context of his argument on social dialogue, Pope Francis is adamant about the possibility of reaching consensus on truths based on universal reason, especially with regard to the dignity of the human person. This insistence is due to the real dangers of relativism and is surely related to the larger phenomenon of post-truth (*FT* 211–14). The pope also emphasizes the necessity of creating a culture of encounter and dialogue, arguing that personal and communal encounters should evolve into a distinct culture. The language of *Fratelli Tutti* is experiential, with Pope Francis reminding us of the joy that comes when we respect others. The experience he describes should not stop there, but rather, lead to the creation of a "social covenant" in which no one is despised (*FT* 215–21). The chapter closes with some notes on kindness and the need to recover this virtue because it is fading away, especially in a consumerist culture and in times of crisis like ours. Kindness starts from simple and daily gestures of gentle love and attention to others, but it should be aimed at creating a culture that transforms relationships (*FT* 222–24).

In my view, one of the most crucial insights of this encyclical, which is particularly highlighted in chapter 6, relates to the dynamics of culture, in which the personal and the cultural go hand in hand, and in which personal experience should lead to the creation of culture and the specificities of local cultures should be combined with more universal values (*FT* 146; 148–49). Pope Francis talks about the creation of a "cultural covenant" (*FT* 219) between diverse peoples having their own distinctive cultures and encourages us to go beyond both a too-local and myopic culture and a too-universal and monolithic culture. In view of the pertinent realities in Asia, I offer three points for reflection in this essay. The first is about the quiet power of the culture of dialogue, which Pope Francis mentions but does not really elaborate. The second is about the role of solitude in building true dialogue, and the third is about the crucial role of hope.

The Quiet Power of Dialogue

One of the most striking insights of chapter 6 of the encyclical is the idea of the "quiet" power of dialogue (*FT* 198). In a world where speed and efficiency are the norms of the day, we are being reminded of the role of patience and slower movement. Throughout history, dialogue has been part of the dynamic of this patience and slower movement. The world as we know it has developed, in fact, from creative encounters between different cultures and religions that belong to diverse nations, empires, and other evolving polities. The Asian political and cultural situation was formed by these encounters over a period of millennia in a lengthy, arduous, and complex process in which fruitful and friendly dialogue often coexisted with rivalries and enmities. As this process worked out over time, true pioneers of dialogue were subject to the limited worldviews they inherited from their own cultures and religions; as a result, new social and cultural experiments were far from perfect, yet were sufficiently creative to move societies forward.

It is within this longer historical continuum and process of cultural and social dialogue that I want to situate Pope Francis's insistence on the quiet power of dialogue. Seen in this framework, patient dialogue indeed works quietly to transform the world. Oftentimes what we see on the surface, the things that make headlines, is noise and cacophony, conflicting ideas and dramatic twists and turns of history. In this context, those who work to establish dialogue often experience "dialogue fatigue" when they sense that their hard work has brought only setbacks, but no tangible fruit. More than fifty years after *Nostra Aetate,* after so many earnest initiatives toward dialogue (e.g., the interreligious prayer for peace in Assisi, the formation of the Pontifical Council for Interreligious Dialogue, and many others), and after so many years of hard work by Christian theologians and experts familiar with other religions, one might ask: What are we witnessing now? One could say that the many answers are quite depressing: bloody conflicts in the name of religion, discrimination of various kinds against minorities, distortions and caricatures of other religions, meaningless theological contentions and controversies, and so forth. We can consult the internet for information about these unfortunate realities, and we might be surprised by other things we find there; for instance, the heated debate between Christian Prince and Zakir Naik is more popular than videos on interfaith dialogue featuring Pope Francis and the Grand Imam of Al-Azhar on the occasion of the signing of the Abu Dhabi Declaration in 2019. Similarly, the politicization of religion and identity appears to become ever more rampant in Asia, including among young people, even university students.[1] In some places religious segregation and discrimination have not abated and have become even more serious during the pandemic.[2] This long pandemic has made us realize that the world at large will likely not become more united any time soon.

Against this bleak backdrop, the message of Pope Francis is particularly crucial. He admonishes us not to lose sight of the quiet power of dialogue in bringing the hearts of people together! The change of hearts indeed takes place in a quiet and simple manner, in ways that do not make the headlines, as part of a long historical process. In the city of Yogyakarta, Indonesia, where I live, a group of young people from across religious boundaries has come together weekly to deliver free meals to poor people, both before and during the pandemic. This act might be simple and does not quickly change realities, yet precisely in its simplicity, it shows how solidarity and social friendship can develop quietly in spaces created by ordinary persons.

We should also recall the quiet work of many young people who have had the audacity to cross cultural and economic boundaries to serve local communities, some in remote areas. These courageous and generous persons serve as teachers, medical doctors, community builders, and so forth. Volunteerism is still visible in many parts of the world, including in Asia. We also continue to witness the generosity of religious sisters, brothers, and

---

1. Cf. Sebastian et al., *Rising Islamic Conservatism*; and Chacko and Jayasuriya, "Asia's Conservative Moment."

2. Cf. Cholil et al., *Pembatasan Hak Beragama.*

priests who spend many good years in other countries or cultural settings. In fact, one can say that the church in Asia has been blessed by the new dynamic of an internal, Asia-to-Asia, missionary movement. Moreover, young people in Asia often come together, communicating as part of different networks (e.g., the Milk Tea Alliance and the Asian Youth Climate Network) in order to respond to the crucial challenges of our time, including climate change and various political crises. We are also witnessing the new and interesting phenomenon of "volunteer tourism" among young people in Asia, in which young people organize to volunteer their labor for noble causes. These young travelers view volunteering and working holidays as good opportunities to experience and learn about foreign countries and cultures.[3]

At the level of ideas and religious movements, there are reasons to hope for a slow and yet real transformation. In contemporary Indonesia, we have been witnessing the rise of the movement "Islam of Love" (*Islam Cinta*), which is based on the Islamic theology of love (*basmalah theology*) and the fundamental understanding of God as all-merciful and loving. This message resonates strongly with Pope Francis's message that God is merciful, a theological notion that has energized his pontificate and serves as a foundation for *Fratelli Tutti* as well.[4] In a country like Indonesia, religious transformation happens only as part of a long process and in a space opened up and sustained by a legacy of great religious leaders, as well as various religious movements that form a nexus of transformative religion. These organizations put forward Islam as the universal grace of salvation (*Islam asrahmatan lil alamiin*), cultivate a communion spirituality with God's creation (cf. *Laudato Si'*), and are ready to work for universal brotherhood.[5]

The "Dialogue" of Solitude

Along this same line of thought, I think we should talk about "dialogue" through silence or solitude. Dialogue is often too logocentric, relying on words and concepts, on discursive reasoning, to solve theological riddles. Surely this type of dialogue has its value. It needs to be engaged in not only by experts in religious knowledge and theology but also by persons with moral and spiritual integrity; otherwise, it can easily descend into banal and meaningless debates and controversies. Pope Francis reminds us of the meaning of the word "dialogue": "Approaching, speaking, listening, looking

---

3. Khoo-Lattimore and Yang, *Asian Youth Travellers*.
4. See my essay, "Naming God Together."
5. See my essay, "Signs of Hope."

at, coming to know and understand one another, and to find common ground: all these things are summed up in the one word 'dialogue.'" (*FT* 198)

We need another kind of dialogue that does not rely solely on words, concepts, or actions. In particular, we need a dialogue of and through silence or solitude, which implies a particular wisdom that various Asian religious traditions and cultures can offer. Solitude is a moment of deep opening of the heart to others and otherness, to the cosmos, to all the realities that surround us. To be truly transforming, dialogue needs to be grounded on this foundation of a deeper communion.

In this regard, many shrines, holy sites, and sacred spaces in Asia, including those in urban settings, have been serving as spots of quiet, as spaces of deep encounter with the divine where people can find peace and balance in life. The need for this quietness and balance is manifested in the popularity of yoga and other mindfulness practices in our contemporary world, which in turn need to be part of this deeper cultivation of an authentic self and its expansion into a place of solidarity. These concerns might also be related to the boom in tourism (even though temporarily disrupted by the pandemic), including religious tourism, in which people are looking for moments of refreshment enabling them to deepen their connection with family, friends, and others.

In this vein, Pope Francis talks about the phenomenon of "media noise" that pervades our contemporary lives (*FT* 201). It is "noise" because it distracts us in every moment. Sadly, religion has become part of this media noise. In a pluralistic society like Indonesia and other Asian countries, religion often enters the public sphere as noise, not as part of a constructive dialogue for the common good or through the operation of mature democratic processes. On the level of discourse, a real and robust public theology is still lacking.[6] It is ironic that in our democratic society, religious and other concerns are sometimes heard only as noise; for example, through mass rallies that do not seek consensus, but rather threaten people and sow division. Religious leaders often play a role here, fomenting division by issuing controversial statements that lead only to unhealthy commotion. The culture of noise in our digital age goes hand in hand with an identity politics that often involves religion.

This absence of silence is disturbing not only because of the noise in the public sphere involving religion, but because of the alarming phenomenon of people "fleeing from reality" (*FT* 199), turning completely to a self that is, unfortunately, empty. We know that what these people are entering into is not true solitude but harmful isolation. To give a well-known example, in

---

6. Cf. Wilfred, *Asian Public Theology*.

Asia we are witnessing the phenomenon of social withdrawal among young people. The extreme version of this in Japan is known as *hikikomori*, which amounts to total self-confinement and isolation from society. These are people who feel forced to assume a role in society but cannot find one that is fitting for them. Some are abused in school or in their families. They have lost their trust in society, in which they have not found love that is worthy of striving for. Too-strict schooling and parenting, plus economic hardship, have made many young people frustrated.[7] One *hikikomori* says he can only trust his dog—"dogs don't betray, unlike humans"—confessing that he may have given up on his life.[8]

An acute sense of loneliness can result from the fact that one is unable to find anything in one's self, which occurs when there is no deep rootedness within. Loneliness occurs when the self fails to serve as a place of dignity and hospitality, which is also one of the roots of violence. People need love and acceptance. People need to have a strong foundation of self where they can find a place of dignity. That is why *Fratelli Tutti* is so crucial and timely for us in Asia, a place where familial and communal connections are traditionally prized and kept. But these connections can be oppressive rather than supportive when they do not allow any personal space for differences and when the whole culture fails to cultivate a strong and authentic self. The spirit of *Fratelli Tutti* reminds us to pay attention to everyone's need for love, affection, and true compassion.

However, *Fratelli Tutti* is also insistent that this love, affection, and compassion need to happen on a social scale. This is crucial in view of the relationship between individual isolation and political totalitarianism and violence, as Hannah Arendt noted long ago:

> Terror can rule absolutely only over men who are isolated against each other.... Therefore, one of the primary concerns of all tyrannical government is to bring this isolation about. Isolation may be the beginning of terror; it certainly is its most fertile ground; it always is its result. This isolation is, as it were, pre-totalitarian; its hallmark is impotence insofar as power always comes from men acting together ... isolated men are powerless by definition.[9]

As we have observed, a political populism that often goes hand in hand with religious fundamentalism is gaining favor now in many parts of the world, which might be the signal of new forms of totalitarian global

---

7. For a general overview and discussion, see Tamaki, *Hikikomori*.
8. Ambrose and Koh, *Japan*, 10:08:58.
9. Arendt, *Origins of Totalitarianism*, 172.

politics. As Arendt suggested, there may be a connection between political populism and the current pandemic of existential and social loneliness. Many forms of isolation in fact occur on a social and political scale, causing communities to withdraw into themselves in different ways. This withdrawal may be the result of intense and long-term discrimination and injustice, or of the inability of states to unite their citizenry. Many ethnic groups feel isolated from the larger fabric of societies and nation-states. Among these groups, there is an overwhelming sense of being abandoned or disenfranchised through the process of minoritizing their communities. Many of these groups find themselves increasingly uneasy with the existing political frameworks that have failed to give them a fuller sense of citizenship, which includes justice and dignity. In the context of Asia, we need to listen to the many indigenous communities that feel oppressed by an increasingly powerful and unjust capitalist system.[10] Lately we have heard about an increasing number of conflicts between indigenous communities and capitalists, of which the main source is encroachment on community territories by logging and agricultural companies. Here we need to remember that "over 900 million people in the world are the poorest of the poor. At least one-third of them are indigenous peoples, and more than half of them live in Asia."[11] Against this background, we can understand why "social friendship" is such an important concept in the encyclical.

The Path of Hope

As we have observed, our contemporary world is marked by complexities and challenges. To better navigate these complexities and challenges, we need the virtue of hope, which is the art of being in touch with longer and deeper processes of change and with the bigger picture. We in fact see signs of hope on the road of building a culture of encounter and dialogue. The vision of *Fratelli Tutti* can only be sustained by the capacity to see what lies beyond and beneath the vicissitudes of history. This is what Pope Francis proposes:

> I invite everyone to renewed hope, for hope speaks to us of something deeply rooted in every human heart, independently of our circumstances and historical conditioning. Hope speaks to us of a thirst, an aspiration, a longing for a life of fulfillment, a desire to achieve great things, things that fill our heart and lift our spirit to lofty realities like truth, goodness and beauty, justice and love. Hope is bold; it can look beyond personal

10. Cf. also *FT* 220 where Pope Francis talks about the plight of indigenous peoples.
11. Perera, *Land and Cultural Survival*, introduction, 1.

convenience, the petty securities and compensations which limit our horizon, and it can open us up to grand ideals that make life more beautiful and worthwhile. Let us continue, then, to advance along the paths of hope. (*FT* 55)

In *Evangelii Gaudium*, Pope Francis talks about this same hope in terms of certainty, which is also "a sense of mystery." It involves knowing with certitude that all those who entrust themselves to God in love will bear good fruit. This fruitfulness is often invisible, elusive, and unquantifiable.[12] In Asia, this language of "mystery" may be more easily understood because it is deeply related to the space of solitude. We hope that this sense of mystery energizes us in our common journey toward the realization of universal fraternity along the winding path of our contemporary time.

Bibliography

Ambrose, Drew, and Aun Ki Koh. *Japan: The Age of Social Withdrawal*. Produced by Al Jazeera English. October 2, 2020. Video, 27:00. https://www.journeyman.tv/film/7937.

Arendt, Hannah. *The Origins of Totalitarianism*. New York: Harvest, 1976.

Chacko, Priya, and Kanishka Jayasuriya. "Asia's Conservative Moment: Understanding the Rise of the Right." *Journal of Contemporary Asia* 48:4 (2018) 529–40.

Cholil, Suhadi, et al. *Pembatasan Hak Beragama di Masa Wabah Covid-19*. Yogyakarta: Center for Religious and Cross-Cultural Studies, 2020.

Davies, William. *Happiness Industry: How the Government and Big Business Sold Us Well-Being*. New York: Verso, 2015.

Francis, Pope. *Evangelii Gaudium*. Vatican City: Libreria Editrice Vaticana, 2013. https://www.vatican.va/content/francesco/en/apost_exhortations/documents/papa-francesco_esortazione-ap_20131124_evangelii-gaudium.html.

———. *Fratelli Tutti: On Fraternity and Social Friendship*. Vatican City: Libreria Editrice Vaticana, 2020. http://www.vatican.va/content/francesco/en/encyclicals/documents/papa-francesco_20201003_enciclica-fratelli-tutti.html.

Khoo-Lattimore, Catheryn, and Elaine Chiao Ling Yang, eds. *Asian Youth Travellers: Insights and Implications*. Singapore: Springer, 2018.

Laksana, Albertus Bagus. "Naming God Together: Muslim-Christian Theology of Mercy in the Indonesian Context." *Journal of Asian Orientation in Theology* 1:1 (2019) 1–30.

———. "Signs of Hope for Christian-Muslim Relations in Indonesia." *Concilium* 4 (2020) 69–76.

Perera, Jayantha, ed., *Land and Cultural Survival: The Communal Land Rights of Indigenous Peoples in Asia*. Manila: Asian Development Bank, 2009.

Sebastian, Leonard C., et al., eds. *Rising Islamic Conservatism in Indonesia: Islamic Groups and Identity Politics*. London: Routledge, 2020.

---

12. Francis, *Evangelii Gaudium*, 278–79.

Tamaki, Saito. *Hikikomori: Adolescence without End*. Translated by James Angles. Minneapolis: University of Minnesota Press, 2013.

Van der Veer, Peter, ed. *Handbook of Religion and the Asian City: Aspiration and Urbanization in the Twenty-First Century*. Berkeley: University of California Press, 2015.

Wilfred, Felix. *Asian Public Theology: Critical Concerns in Challenging Times*. Delhi: ISPCK, 2010.

23

"Searching, We Find Ourselves"[1]: Indignation and Radical Empathy in a Suffering Mexico

CAROLINA ROBLEDO SILVESTRE[2]

Feelings that are immediate [like pain] and which may involve "damage" in the skin surface, are not simply feelings that one has but feelings that open bodies to others.[3]

—SARA AHMED, THE CULTURAL POLITICS OF EMOTION

I WRITE IN THE context of a global pandemic that prohibits us from embracing and imposes physical distance as the norm. Motivated by this book's reflection on fraternity and by the reality imposed by the pandemic, I propose a reflection on the value and physiognomy of feelings and, in particular,

---

1. This is the motto of the Red de Enlaces Nacionales (REN) or National Liaison Network in Mexico that, since 2016, has promoted the Brigada Nacional de Búsqueda de Personas Desaparecidas (National Search Brigade for the Disappeared). This network brings together community organizations, families, and individuals in the search for disappeared persons and creates spaces for peacebuilding and dialogue with authorities. Learn more about REN at https://memoriamndm.org/sobre-el-movndmx/red-de-enlaces-nacionales.

2. Translated by Karen M. Kraft.

3. Ahmed, *Cultural Politics*, 15.

through the friendship between women, its power, and its capacity to weave hope in these times.

My questions emerge from a restless feminist becoming that observes the historical progression from unusual places. This personal perspective assumes the certainty of having built oppressive, unjust, and sad bonds for other women but also the daily effort to inhabit feminine and feminist emotions differently, unlearning years of patriarchal socialization, with the conviction that feminism does not begin with what I need but what we all need.

Friendship has been a subject little explored in the feminist field, which has had a special interest in observing and transforming the loving bond and the power relations that romantic love establishes. In practice, we women grew up with the example and mandate to build love as a couple, rather than establishing diverse loving bonds, particularly with other women. Hegemonic narratives about the impossibility of friendship between us have limited the ways for us to encounter each other. Despite this, friendship between women produces hopeful forms of community and political organization, which grow through the cracks of civilization's crisis, where one imagines that only pain dwells. They flourish through indignation and empathy against the ravages of violence, state impunity, and social indifference.

In the words of Rita Segato, it's about the opposition between the historical project of bonds and the historical project of things.[4] The latter is characterized by an economic and social system that identifies with "post-emotionalism, social numbness, disconnection, and the failure of empathy,"[5] as well as the instrumentalization and capitalization of emotions and bodies.[6] In the historical project of things, what dominates is heteropatriarchal self-sufficiency and individualism that impedes our interdependence, leaving us alone and isolated. Fortunately, various experiences of defending the commons drive the desire to change this reality[7] based on ethical and loving practices and solidarity that is sensitive, contingent, and politically effective.

Particularly among the women searching for their disappeared loved ones (*desaparecidos*), emotions circulate that facilitate and nurture that bonding. In the pain and outrage that the crime leaves behind, reciprocal empathy surfaces as the driving force of their encounter. The *buscadoras*,[8]

---

4. Segato, *Guerra Contra las Mujeres*, 29.
5. Gray, "Empathy, Emotions, and Feminist Solidarities," 207.
6. See, generally, Illouz, *Cold Intimacies*.
7. See, in general, Gago, *Feminist International*.
8. Called *buscadoras* after the Spanish word *buscar*, which means "to search," they have created an identity in their efforts searching for the missing. Their search is a political commitment, a protest against the state by "victims" who are not satisfied with passivity and patience.

the women searching for their loved ones, establish diverse and flexible networks of assistance, support, and political action. Their strategies are adapted to varying regions, contexts, and common needs, and while not all of them identify as feminists, in their actions, there is a sense of friendship that can be inspiring for feminine and feminist politics.[9]

These bonding experiences can help us imagine another world, one that is possible and desirable (and so urgently needed in these uncertain times). In addition, to consider feelings and emotions is also a political issue within an arrogant academic enterprise that underestimates the emotional dimension of individuals and establishes rationality as the only vehicle of knowledge. This vision of science that has left the body, the emotions, and oral tradition on the sidelines in pursuit of the psyche, reason, and the written word is the same one that has denied citizenship to the Indian, the black, the savage, the barbarian, the woman, the child, and the madman.[10]

Feminism challenges the devaluation of the emotional life and of the body in politics and academia, which equate these dimensions with the feminine in order to water down their power.[11] From this place, we understand that emotions influence every aspect of life and that, in politics, they have the capacity to change everything[12] or maintain the status quo, because of their radical potency. This essay proposes a critique of sociopolitical structures that minimize the importance of the emotional while also reflecting on the political power of friendship between women in the context of the forced disappearance of people in Mexico.

1. Suffering and Outrage: The Seeds

A study from the University of Oxford concludes that people who dance together have a greater resistance to pain.[13] Social closeness, scientists say, facilitates the release of endorphins, which function as pain relievers and promote well-being. When I read this, a moment came to mind from our

---

9. While feminism has challenged the female essence as an imperative for women's bodies, I reclaim the principles of caregiving and the capacity to give and protect life in which we women have been socialized (though I do not consider these exclusively feminine qualities). I propose localizing those practices (disqualified and subordinate according to the patriarchal perspective) and understanding them as the foundation for a radical critique of the practice of politics.

10. González Stephan, "Economías Fundacionales," 34.

11. Ahmed, *Cultural Politics*, 23.

12. See, in general, Gago, *Feminist International*.

13. Tarr et al., "Silent Disco."

field work in northern Sinaloa with the *Rastreadoras del Fuerte*:[14] after a long and arduous day of searching unmarked graves, we met for lunch in their office, located downtown in Los Mochis. Suddenly a drum sounded in the market opposite us. A *compañera* from the Rastreadoras brought the musicians over to play songs for us . . . we danced, jumped around, and laughed. Not only is this sharing and dancing together palliative, but it also creates a powerful politics. Despite the losses, the despair, and the rage, many are the times that the women have fun and enjoy life together. At the same time, they shout in dignified rage that the search continue for their relatives; they track down and exhume unmarked graves; they visit morgues, hospitals, jails, and shelters to find their loved ones. In their communities, they have been called crazy. And their pain, expressed and mobilized through political action, is uncomfortable, inconvenient. There is no social forum for it to be heard. Sometimes it seems "toxic" and unbearable, even for their own families.

Although pain is described as a private and solitary emotion, it is a social, cultural, and political experience.[15] To think of suffering as a strictly private emotion obscures the relationships that exist between individual affliction and the structures that give rise to them,[16] and it also hinders a community's capacities to cope with the expression of suffering. Its complex relationship with language makes suffering feel untranslatable, like something that afflicts the body and mind but is impossible to communicate.[17] This inability to explain reveals the need for acknowledgement of the other in the experience of pain and, of course, the need for social relationships and communities where that pain can find a space to be articulated and expressed. Unfortunately, there are few spaces provided for this; in addition to the breakdown of language experienced in situations of extreme violence,[18] there are also conditions of cruelty and barriers to listening that are obstacles to justice and the making of reparations. Experiences of suffering

---

14. Translator's note: Fuerte is a city in Sinaloa, a state in northwestern Mexico, where this organization, Rastreadoras del Fuerte, is based. In Spanish, *rastrear* means "to track or to trace," and the *rastreadoras* are the members of this organization who tirelessly search, trying to track down their loved ones among the *desaparecidos*. As their Facebook page says, "We are a group of men and women legally incorporated and recognized as 'Las Buscadoras del Fuerte' and also as 'Las Rastreadoras'; we began on July 14, 2014, after suffering the loss of a loved one who has been found neither among the living nor the dead. Therefore, #TeBuscareHastaEncontrarte ["I Will Search for You Until I Find You"]. Our organization was founded by Mrs. Mirna Nereida Medina Quiñonez and currently consists of more than 600 people united by the same pain."

15. Ahmed, *Cultural Politics*, 47.
16. Madrid, *La Política y la Justicia*, 14.
17. Das, *Violencia, Cuerpo y Lenguaje*, 92.
18. Gatti, *El Detenido-Desaparecido*, 29.

are considered unspeakable or incomprehensible, not only because of the inability of expression but also because there is no social space in which to be heard and acknowledged.

Stories of suffering involve power relationships and radical differences between people, so that not all suffering is socially legitimate since the acknowledgment of pain is marked by social position and historical context.[19] Thus, the greater access to public resources individuals have, the better their ability to mobilize injury narratives within the public sphere.[20] Therefore, it isn't only that there are individuals more exposed to pain than others but also that the acknowledgment of their pain faces the same inequalities of articulation and empathy in the social arena.[21]

What happens to the pain? At the political level, state and humanitarian structures have been created that seek to restrict or regulate emotions that are harmful, futile, or repetitive, relegating subjectivity to statistical classification or therapeutic treatment.[22] On a daily basis, we build protective barriers against that which is unbearable to us, and looking away, we ignore or blame the victims and, in doing so, invalidate their pain.

I would like to end this section with a reflection: I do not want to call the women of whom I speak victims nor fetishize their suffering. They are much more than the wound of disappearance: they interpret the pain together, understand its causes, point to those responsible, and place their suffering in the public sphere. This pain that could be paralyzing is transformed into outrage, into a powerful emotion with political force in the face of atrocity. For Audre Lorde, pain translates into knowledge, information, and energy, and this transformation allows for inhabiting new ways of being.[23] Outrage, therefore, is a visionary, creative emotion. It invents a language, a world; it looks to the future. It is a movement that connects. Of course, outrage, and particularly that of women, is not generally well received. It is the opposite of practices of denial, neglect, and indifference. In this sense, for those whose anguish still goes unacknowledged or to whom no reparations have been made, it is cruel and inappropriate to pretend that pain is forgotten.[24]

The wound of disappearance ruptures the fabric of society and, thus, it is important to build community in the face of violence that creates

19. Madrid, *La Política y la Justicia*, 13.
20. Ahmed, *Cultural Politics*, 67.
21. Madrid, *La Política y la Justicia*, 19.
22. Aranguren-Romero, "De un Dolor a un Saber," 9.
23. See, in general, Lorde, *Cancer Journals*.
24. Ahmed, *Cultural Politics*, 67.

isolation. In shared mourning, individuals and community groups constitute a new social organism.[25] Suffering is acknowledged without being fetishized. A radical political force is created through listening and mutual acknowledgment. The established political regime and power relationships between the winners and the losers are challenged.[26] And the friendship between women who suffer is one of the most powerful communities in this politics of feelings.

2. Radical Empathy and Friendship between Women: Harvests

I imagine friendship between women as a coven, a gathering of witches who conspire, enjoy themselves, and transgress norms. This is not a haphazard image. Silvia Federici approaches the witch hunt as a historical mechanism of attack against experiences of the commons among women. In her book, *Caliban and the Witch*, the commons are linked to a community engaged in struggle and violence against the so-called "witches" in the sixteenth and seventeenth centuries, when there was a systematic effort to discipline and control women's bodies, their work, and their sexual and reproductive powers.[27]

Insanity, *disease*, and *danger* are labels that have been established to mark women who organize themselves, who transgress the norm, who possess and disseminate knowledge. As pointed out during one episode of the "Sangre Fucsia" podcast series, "[i]n *A Room of One's Own*, Virginia Woolf wonders if, in literature, women are ever presented as friends." We find a "derivative of this narrative of feminine absence"[28] in the so-called "Smurfette principle";[29] it involves integrating into works of fiction many masculine characters and a single girl who frequently responds to stereotypes of correct femininity.

What information exists about how we bond as women? Coral Herrera reviews various children's stories and finds female characters who cannot live together in harmony: stepmothers who hate their stepdaughters; sisters who compete with each other as rivals; mothers who repress or restrict their daughters' talents and condemn them to the role of "good girls."[30] And then there are witches who use their powers to harm other women. Quite the narrative effort to keep us squabbling with each other to achieve patriarchy's

25. Ahmed, *Cultural Politics*, 66.
26. Madrid, *La Política y la Justicia*, 78.
27. See, in general, Federici, *Caliban and the Witch*.
28. Sangre Fucsia, "Amistad entre Mujeres."
29. Sangre Fucsia, "Amistad entre Mujeres."
30. See, in general, Herrera, *La Construcción Social*.

prizes—a husband, a job, regulated bodies, etc.[31] In spite of this historical and patriarchal tendency to become "guardians of the gender order,"[32] we women reveal ourselves in many ways. Our friendship and the construction of the communal are part of this resistance to the role of snitch.

By sharing their wounded subjectivities, the *buscadoras* weave together a grieving and resistant communal body, along with the women that demand justice for femicides and gender violence and those that defend life and land. All of them restore the possibility of community and challenge the imperative of "every man for himself." In Mexico, there are more than eighty groups of relatives of disappeared persons. They participate in legislative debates and monitor the actions of the authorities; they document and follow cases and go to court; they learn forensic science. They support each other emotionally and financially; they march; they dance; they fall in love; they connect with themselves; they regain hope; they let themselves fall and be cared for—*apapachadas*[33]—by others. In such encounters, they realize that they are not crazy, alone, or wrong.

These groups bring together diverse women: teachers, field hands, domestic workers, cooks, shopkeepers, family breadwinners, mothers of young people associated with hitmen or drug dealing, mothers of students. Most would never have met if not for the efforts to find their missing loved ones. They confront disagreements, tensions, and falling-outs with the certainty that friendship is a challenging bond that requires constant work. Community isn't something we learn . . . rather, we arrive at it by unlearning. And that is why it's a struggle.

Friendship is an act of empathy that implies being together in the face of—and in spite of—structures of inequality and oppression. As a principle of friendship, empathy promotes ethical-political solidarity and is built on the constant effort to imagine and experience the feelings, thoughts, and circumstances of others, that is, to "put yourself in their shoes." When it's thought of and experienced that way, friendship rooted in empathy enables justice to develop, because it allows for an internalized understanding of the other person's situation. In her interest in thinking about political emotions, Martha Nussbaum invites us to cultivate empathy and see the "other" as a whole, complete being.[34] Oddly enough, the recognition of the humanity

31. See the chapter titled "Qué implica delatar" in De Hoyos and Sandoval, *Las Delatoras*, 13–15.

32. Lagarde, "La Multidimensionalidad," 8.

33. Translator's note: *Apapachar* is a word of Nahuatl origin that means in Spanish "acariciar con el elma" and can be translated in English as "to caress or embrace with the soul." See Rodríguez, "Apapachar."

34. Nussbaum, *Political Emotions*, chapter 11.

of the other is not a given. History shows that otherness—for example, the otherness of ethnic communities, migrants, those who don't conform to the hetero gender norm—has proven to be uncomfortable or unwelcome. It's no coincidence that colonial powers have instituted the idea of *savages* as beings without a soul—barbarians and strangers.[35]

The capacity for empathy produces solidarity among those who are outside the norm; it allows concern for others beyond family relationships or social belonging. Empathy is a feeling that implies a push toward justice. It's not, however, an emotion that is free from challenges. Living together means broadening our worlds and recognizing that friendship has diverse perspectives.

In their journey together, the *buscadoras* build relationships that are like family and open up spaces to make newcomers feel at home. Even the women who have found their missing loved ones maintain ties with their fellow *buscadoras*, in an act of steadfastness and commitment to the community. In more than a decade together, they have positioned themselves as a diverse and dynamic network of shared efforts and selfless exchanges. Justice not only requires that those who share a painful experience meet and come together but also that the social capacity to recognize one's own suffering and vulnerability be cultivated.[36] Therefore, it is so important that these communities of searchers grow and diversify, so that friendships among the *buscadoras* can be extended to sectors of the population that have not yet been directly affected by forced disappearance. Only in this way can empathy be radical, and only in this way can we build a more just world and honor the memory of those who have disappeared.

Bibliography

Ahmed, Sara. *The Cultural Politics of Emotion*. New York: Routledge and Taylor, 2015.

Aranguren-Romero, Juan Pablo. "De un Dolor a un Saber: Cuerpo, Sufrimiento y Memoria en los Límites de la Escritura." *Papeles del CEIC* 63:2 (September 2010) 1–27. https://identidadcolectiva.es/pdf/63.pdf.

Carmona Dávila, Doralicia. "En la Bula *Sublimis Deus*, el Papa Pablo III Declara que los Indios Tienen Derecho a su Libertad y que la Fe Debe Predicarse con Métodos Pacíficos Evitando Todo Tipo de Crueldad." Memoria Política de México website, "Efemérides," June 2021. http://www.memoriapoliticademexico.org/Efemerides/6/02061537.html.

Das, Veena. *Violencia, Cuerpo y Lenguaje*. Translated by Laura Lecuona. Mexico City: Fondo Económico de Cultura, 2016.

35. For more on this, see Carmona Dávila, "En la Bula *Sublimis Deus*." In 1537, Pope Paul III issued *Sublimis Deus,* a papal bull that affirmed the Indians' rational nature.

36. Madrid, *La Política y la Justicia,* 83.

De Hoyos, Elena, and Alma Karla Sandoval. *Las Delatoras*. Cuernavaca, Mexico: Omecihuatl, 2018.
Federici, Silvia. *Caliban and the Witch: Women, the Body, and Primitive Accumulation*. New York: Autonomedia, 2009.
Francis, Pope. *Fratelli Tutti: On Fraternity and Social Friendship*. Vatican City: Libreria Editrice Vaticana, 2020. https://www.vatican.va/content/francesco/en/encyclicals/documents/papa-francesco_20201003_enciclica-fratelli-tutti.html.
Gago, Verónica. *Feminist International: How to Change Everything*. Translated by Liz Mason-Deese. London: Verso, 2021.
Gatti, Gabriel. *El Detenido-Desaparecido: Narrativas Posibles para una Catástrofe de la Identidad*. Montevideo: Trilce, 2008.
González Stephan, Beatriz. "Economías Fundacionales: Diseño del Cuerpo Ciudadano." In *Cultura y Tercer Mundo: Nuevas Identidades y Ciudadanías*, edited by Beatriz González Stephan, 14–47. Caracas: Nueva Sociedad, 1996.
Gray, Breda. "Empathy, Emotions, and Feminist Solidarities." In *Sexed Sentiments: Interdisciplinary Perspectives on Gender and Emotion*, edited by Willemijn Ruberg and Kristine Steenbergh, 207–32. Leiden, Netherlands: Brill, 2011.
Herrera, Coral. *La Construcción Social del Amor Romántico*. Madrid: Fundamentals. 2010.
Illouz, Eva. *Cold Intimacies: The Making of Emotional Capitalism*. Madrid: Katz, 2007.
Lagarde, Marcela. "La Multidimensionalidad de la Categoría Género y del Feminismo." In *Metodología para los Estudios de Género*, edited by María Luisa González Marin, 48–71. Mexico City: Universidad Nacional Autónoma de México, 1996.
Las Rastreadoras del Fuerte. Facebook group page. https://www.facebook.com/Las-Rastreadoras-del-Fuerte-267629457048946.
Lorde, Audre. *The Cancer Journals*. San Francisco: Aunt Lute, 2006.
Lorde, Audre, and Roxane Gay, ed. *The Selected Works of Audre Lorde*. New York: Norton, 2020.
Madrid, Antonio. *La Política y la Justicia del Sufrimiento*. Madrid: Trotta, 2010.
Nussbaum, Martha. *Political Emotions: Why Love Matters for Justice*. Cambridge, MA: Belknap, 2015.
Rodríguez, Darinka. "Apapachar: El Verdadero Significado de una Palabra de Origen Náhuatl." *El País*, July 23, 2020. https://verne.elpais.com/verne/2020/07/23/mexico/1595481612_470684.html.
Sangre Fucsia. "Amistad entre Mujeres." *Pikara*, November 26, 2018. https://www.pikaramagazine.com/2018/11/amistad-entre-mujeres.
Segato, Rita. *La Guerra Contra las Mujeres*. Buenos Aires: Prometeo, 2020.
Tarr, Bronwyn, et al. "Silent Disco: Dancing in Synchrony Leads to Elevated Pain Thresholds and Social Closeness." *Evolution and Human Behavior* 37:5 (2016) 343–49. https://www.ncbi.nlm.nih.gov/pmc/articles/PMC4985033/.
Woolf, Virginia. *A Room of One's Own*. London: Penguin, 1928.

24

Why Not "Amiability and a Culture of Encounter" as the Title of Chapter 6?[1]

Neomi De Anda

Statement of the Problem

FRANKLY, I AM TIRED of Catholic encyclicals that give broad strokes of universal love and care, then within themselves—as well as at so many other levels of the church, the actions and words of the ordained leadership, theologians, ministerial practitioners, and many of the baptized—exclude and dehumanize! Such is the theology of chapter 6 of *Fratelli Tutti*, where Francis proposes an overly complex theoretization and premature solution for the path forward in society. However, not all is lost. Francis may have some answers within the Spanish and English texts of *Fratelli Tutti*. In the Spanish text, he suggests "recuperar la amabilidad" as part of the path forward.[2] The English translation of *Fratelli Tutti* should then read "recovering amiability" rather than "recovering kindness."[3] Also, *Fratelli Tutti* should have built further on the foundation of a culture of encounter rather than turning to social friendship. Therefore, "*Amabilidad* and a Culture of Encounter" would have been a better way to focus chapter 6 of *Fratelli Tutti*. However,

---

1. I would like to thank Rob Masterson, graduate assistant extraordinaire, for his close read and work on citation in this document.
2. Francis, *Fratelli Tutti: Sobre la fraternidad*, chapter 6.
3. Francis, *Fratelli Tutti: On Fraternity*, chapter 6.

a papal encyclical will not use Spanglish in a subtitle, so "Amiability and a Culture of Encounter" will suffice.

Challenges with Dialogue

In calling for a social dialogue for a new culture, Francis states, "Some people attempt to flee from reality, taking refuge in their own little world; others react to it with destructive violence. Yet 'between selfish indifference and violent protest there is always another possible option: that of dialogue. Dialogue between generations; dialogue among our people, for we are that people; readiness to give and receive, while remaining open to the truth. A country flourishes when constructive dialogue occurs between its many rich cultural components: popular culture, university culture, youth culture, artistic culture, technological culture, economic culture, family culture and media culture'" (FT 199).

In moving toward this new culture through dialogue, Francis includes building together, consensus, encounter that becomes culture, and the joy of acknowledging others. He recognizes the need for various communities and population segments to speak and listen to one another through dialogue. Further, in FT 203, "Building Together," *Fratelli Tutti* states:

> Authentic social dialogue involves the ability to respect the other's point of view and to admit that it may include legitimate convictions and concerns. Based on their identity and experience, others have a contribution to make, and it is desirable that they should articulate their positions for the sake of a more fruitful public debate. When individuals or groups are consistent in their thinking, defend their values and convictions, and develop their arguments, this surely benefits society. Yet, this can only occur to the extent that there is genuine dialogue and openness to others. Indeed, "in a true spirit of dialogue, we grow in our ability to grasp the significance of what others say and do, even if we cannot accept it as our own conviction. In this way, it becomes possible to be frank and open about our beliefs, while continuing to discuss, to seek points of contact, and above all, to work and struggle together. Public discussion, if it truly makes room for everyone and does not manipulate or conceal information, is a constant stimulus to a better grasp of the truth, or at least its more effective expression. It keeps different sectors from becoming complacent and self-centered in their outlook and their limited concerns. Let us not forget that "differences are

creative; they create tension and in the resolution of tension lies humanity's progress.'"

In this paragraph, Francis sounds extremely amenable to listening to and acknowledging differences through public discussion. In reference to *Querida Amazonia* and the film, *Pope Francis: A Man of His Word*,[4] *Fratelli Tutti* is sending the message that coming together through the good of our differences makes for the progress of humanity. However, in *FT* 208, an interesting checkpoint sentence is found: "We need to learn how to unmask the various ways that the truth is manipulated, distorted, and concealed in public and private discourse." Is this checkpoint directed internally to church teaching as well as externally to a society outside of the church? Is Francis remaining consistent with the subtitle of *Gaudium et Spes*,[5] "Church in the Modern World"? Or is Francis caught in the tension often posed by Catholic teaching that the church somehow stands counter-cultural to the world—to society? The latter seems to be the case as one keeps reading in chapter 6.

Fratelli Tutti takes a turn to a narrower perspective on dialogue in the section on "Consensus and Truth."

> In a pluralistic society, dialogue is the best way to realize what ought always to be affirmed and respected apart from any ephemeral consensus. Such dialogue needs to be enriched and illumined by clear thinking, rational arguments, a variety of perspectives and the contribution of different fields of knowledge and points of view. Nor can it exclude the conviction that it is possible to arrive at certain fundamental truths always to be upheld. (*FT* 211)

Many questions arise from this paragraph, especially in relation to *FT* 203. The tone of paragraph 211 seems quite different from that of paragraph 203. Might the author of this paragraph be different from much of the rest of the encyclical? Also, the text seems to equate fundamental truths and enduring values. However, values seem to be based more in the morality of social behavior, while truth has mostly been linked to logic and rational thought. Furthermore, the paragraph calls consensus "dynamic," while fundamental truths are not. However, many times consensus and even fundamental truths are connected to uniformity. Nevertheless, Francis has made it clear that uniformity is not the key to the path forward for society. Uniformity does not scare us. It does not make us grow. Difference and learning from

---

4. The film presents a very open, welcoming, and loving pastor in Pope Francis.
5. Second Vatican Council, *Gaudium et Spes*.

one another's differences make us grow because they scare us. They make us uncomfortable.[6]

While Francis presents dialogue as the way forward for a church for the world, dialogue as presented in *Fratelli Tutti* remains exclusive both within the document as well as when other external statements and actions of church leaders are taken into account. The pieces assumed in who is allowed to dialogue in the section "Consensus and Truth," as well as the mode of dialogue presented in *FT* 211, lean toward a segment of the global population that is very well and formally educated. When it comes to official Catholic teaching, it is men who write encyclicals. Therefore, even in the creation of official church teaching, dialogue often assumes a mutuality that does not exist. It frequently occurs in spaces where power structures have already been established. Dialogue, like any single mode of communication, centralizes some cultures and voices and, therefore, marginalizes others. Often, there's the expectation or assumption that dialogue will be followed up with a written account (such as encyclicals), which means that whoever has the final "word" in the writing possesses unique power. Unless measures are taken to account for the uneven power dynamics inherently present in dialogue, we are not fully participating in *encuentro*, which Francis sees as the mode toward cultural change, because at least one party will be guarding itself against injury and abuse.

In both paragraphs 203 and 211, *Fratelli Tutti* mentions the development of arguments. If the development of arguments is expected to enter into dialogue and to move to friendship in society, then very different assumptions and perspectives need to be taken into account. Francis does not shy away from the suffering of the poor[7] and systems of injustice, which mark some for death so that others may have economic prosperity. However, as *pastoral y teología de y en conjunto* lead us to see, daily life—*lo cotidiano*—must inform both ministry and theology. In this case, the majority of the world's population is economically poor. To be poor in this way means attending to the tiniest of details for self and others so as to sustain life, create new life, and exalt human dignity. If rational arguments are going to need to be made for the sake of theology that transforms church and society, then methodologies must be considered that include all of those who have been marked for death yet take care of the daily details in order that many others may have life.

---

6. Wenders, *Pope Francis*.

7. For a connection between options for the poor and Mary in chapter 8 of *Fratelli Tutti*, see De Anda, "Mary in *Fratelli Tutti*"; and De Anda, "Together en la Lucha."

I have formerly argued that more than one mode of communication be considered to help us build better foundations to care for and nurture the fragility of life, particularly *chisme*. In other fora beyond *Fratelli Tutti*, Francis has called *chisme* evil. What I call *chisme*—some call it gossip—is another form of communication, which is engaged by most of humanity—at least, that is my sense. I believe "we should avoid characterizing one form of communication as better than the other. We cannot simply say that communication used by people who feel disempowered is negative or sinful, and that the type of communication allowed mostly to those in power is the most positive and productive. We need to pay attention to various types of communication because people use a plurality of modes of communication to express both their suffering and their God-talk. That includes *chisme*."[8]

Proposition of Amiability

Beyond a critical approach to dialogue and an amplification of methods of communication, *Fratelli Tutti* should use the English translation of "amiability" rather than "kindness" as a foundational entree to a more mutual path forward. At the end of chapter 6, Francis suggests "recovering kindness" as a path in dialogue (*FT* 222). In the Spanish text, this section is called *Recuperar la amabilidad*. The word used in Spanish, *amabilidad*, has a very different root understanding than kindness. Kindness can be defined as "the quality of being friendly, generous, and considerate." Within this definition, one may find power imbalances such as those present in dialogue. Paragraph 222 reads,

> Consumerist individualism has led to great injustice. Other persons come to be viewed simply as obstacles to our own serene existence; we end up treating them as annoyances and we become increasingly aggressive. This is even more the case in times of crisis, catastrophe, and hardship, when we are tempted to think in terms of the old saying, "every man for himself." Yet even then, we can choose to cultivate kindness. Those who do so become stars shining in the midst of darkness.

Kindness both within the definition and as presented in this paragraph connotes one's ability to give from their surplus—generously or by choice. In general, this definition points to chosen actions from the part of someone willing to partake in these actions. The acting person is the one with agency

---

8. De Anda, "Reconsidering Chisme."

while the one who receives the acts of kindness is passive and at the will of the one acting with kindness.

The word *amabilidad* (amiability) comes from the Latin *amabilis*, which means "digno de ser amado" or worthy of being loved.[9] This understanding presents a much different perspective than the definition of kindness above. It also seems more in line with the description of kindness in FT 224:

> Kindness [*amabilidad*] frees us from the cruelty that at times infects human relationships, from the anxiety that prevents us from thinking of others, from the frantic flurry of activity that forgets that others also have a right to be happy. Often nowadays we find neither the time nor the energy to stop and be kind to others, to say "excuse me," "pardon me," "thank you." Yet every now and then, miraculously, a kind person appears and is willing to set everything else aside in order to show interest, to give the gift of a smile, to speak a word of encouragement, to listen amid general indifference. If we make a daily effort to do exactly this, we can create a healthy social atmosphere in which misunderstandings can be overcome and conflict forestalled. Kindness ought to be cultivated; it is no superficial bourgeois virtue. Precisely because it entails esteem and respect for others, once kindness becomes a culture within society, it transforms lifestyles, relationships and the ways ideas are discussed and compared. Kindness facilitates the quest for consensus; it opens new paths where hostility and conflict would burn all bridges.

As Catholics, we believe that our dignity to be loved comes from our human dignity, which is rooted in us being created in *imago dei*—the image and likeness of an ever loving, overabundant, always communal God.[10] Therefore, God always is in relationship to Godself and to creation. Creation, therefore, is in relationship to God.[11] So, each and every person deserves to be loved within their own existence due to being created in the image and likeness of God. *Encuentro* is also based in the *imago dei*, then, because to be the image and likeness of God means to be in perpetual relationship. Relationships then cannot be undone. Relationship cannot be simple gestures of friendliness and generosity.

Amiability seems to be a more fitting word for the fruit of the Holy Spirit described in paragraph 223: "an attitude that is gentle, pleasant, and

---

9. My translation.

10. Genesis 1:26–27; International Theological Commission, "Communion and Stewardship."

11. Second Vatican Council, *Gaudium et Spes*, sec. 3.

supportive, not rude or coarse. Individuals who possess this quality help make other people's lives more bearable, especially by sharing the weight of their problems, needs, and fears." This paragraph speaks of a kindness which can break power relationships, because those who are oppressed and marginalized may also act in kindness against an oppressor, which is very powerful. However, such acts may easily be abused when someone with more power forms an expectation of these acts and does not feel implicated to reciprocate in kindness.

Challenges with Friendship

Some may argue that friendship is a deeper calling than encounter. However, in a time both in church and society when the work of the Spirit is leading us to reckon with social sins of hundreds—if not thousands—of years, maybe we need to take a pause and spend more time in the phase of encounter. Maybe an end goal cannot be set yet, but rather we need to allow the path to determine the outcome.

Fratelli Tutti was promulgated in the middle of the COVID-19 global pandemic, which exposed the fault lines of all systems in the world. Care for people and the common good became imperative to sustaining life in ways that had not been seen for many years and probably had never been felt globally before this time. It was released after a summer of global protests[12] against racism. It was shared with the world when exposés on sexual abuse were being shared across the globe, including but not limited to the McCarrick Report.[13] *Fratelli Tutti* appeared when large numbers of people were deeply questioning the moral authority of the church as a global leader. There has been much criticism about the sexism inherent in the untranslated title of the encyclical and the lack of women's voices among its citations. *Fratelli Tutti* does call for equality of rights and dignity for women—especially for "those women who endure situations of exclusion, mistreatment, and violence, since they are frequently less able to defend their rights" (*FT* 23). How are we as church supposed to actually arrive at social friendship when we continue to exclude entire populations of people and topics from the conversation?

To date, many questions remain about the numbers of people who will actually return to worshiping within Catholic buildings. For example, some suggest that as many as 70 percent of Latinx Catholic youth in the US have stopped worshiping over this time of pandemic.

12. Cf. Francis, *Fratelli Tutti: On Fraternity*, 199.
13. Secretariat of State of the Holy See, *Report*.

Building on Culture of Encounter

In addition to using "amiability" rather than "kindness" in the English translation, this chapter could have had more continuity with the foundations Francis has been building since he was a young theologian, especially in connection to culture. Francis discusses friendship in society, but what he really seems to be calling for in his writings are cultural shifts toward social peace.

Paragraph 217 states, "social peace demands hard work, craftsmanship. It would be easier to keep freedoms and differences in check with cleverness and a few resources. But such a peace would be superficial and fragile, not the fruit of a culture of encounter that brings enduring stability. Integrating differences is a much more difficult and slow process, yet it is the guarantee of a genuine and lasting peace." Here, Francis directly names the culture of encounter as that to which he is pointing. Paragraph 219 seems to suggest the opposite of a culture of encounter: "When one part of society exploits all that the world has to offer, acting as if the poor did not exist, there will eventually be consequences. Sooner or later, ignoring the existence and rights of others will erupt in some form of violence, often when least expected." Yet, for some reason, he turns to "Friendship in Society" rather than continuing with the culture of encounter. Yes, the word "culture" has the same roots as "cult" and "cultivate"; therefore, these terms are all interrelated. They point to the living of life, therefore nurturing existence and creating anew. Sometimes what is forgotten about these terms is that the Latin root *colere* may also mean "to toil over." The path that chapter 6 suggests seems to be one where humanity is called to engage one another and even toil over the difficulties in building better relationships—like the classic Catholic definition of justice—being in right relationship.

Bibliography

De Anda, Neomi. "Mary in *Fratelli Tutti*." Marianist Lay Community of North America (MLC-NA) e-newsletter, August 2021. https://myemail.constantcontact.com/MLC-NA-2021-28—The-Path.html?soid=1101229960123&aid=nb2nVo-IPTo.
———. "Reconsiderando el 'chisme', construyendo un diálogo más inclusivo." Translated by Gilberto Cavazos-Gonzalez, OFM. Hispanic Theological Initiative Open Plaza, August 22, 2021. https://www.htiopenplaza.org/content/reconsiderando-el-chisme-construyendo-un-dialogo-mas-inclusivo.
———. "Reconsidering 'Chisme': Building a More Inclusive Dialogue." *Commonweal Magazine*, December 8, 2020. https://www.commonwealmagazine.org/reconsidering-chisme.

———. "Together en la Lucha: ACHTUS 2019 Presidential Address." *Journal of Hispanic/Latino Theology* 21:2 (2019) 126–32.

Francis, Pope. *Fratelli Tutti: On Fraternity and Social Friendship*. Vatican City: Libreria Editrice Vaticana, 2020. https://www.vatican.va/content/francesco/en/encyclicals/documents/papa-francesco_20201003_enciclica-fratelli-tutti.html.

———. *Fratelli Tutti: Sobre la fraternidad y la amistad social*. Vatican City: Libreria Editrice Vaticana, 2020. https://www.vatican.va/content/francesco/es/encyclicals/documents/papa-francesco_20201003_enciclica-fratelli-tutti.html.

International Theological Commission. "Communion and Stewardship: Human Persons Created in the Image of God." *Origins* 34:15 (September 23, 2004) 233–48.

Second Vatican Council. *Gaudium et Spes: Pastoral Constitution on the Church in the Modern World*. Vatican City: Libreria Editrice Vaticana, 1965. https://www.vatican.va/archive/hist_councils/ii_vatican_council/documents/vat-ii_const_19651207_gaudium-et-spes_en.html.

Secretariat of State of the Holy See. *Report on the Holy See's Institutional Knowledge and Decision-Making Related to Formal Cardinal Theodore Edgar McCarrick (1930–2017)*. Vatican City: Holy See Secretariat of State, 2020. https://www.vatican.va/resources/resources_rapporto-card-mccarrick_20201110_en.pdf.

Wenders, Wim, dir. *Pope Francis: A Man of His Word*. Universal City, CA: Focus Features, 2018.

PART SEVEN

Paths of Renewed Encounter

25

Truth, Mercy, Justice, and Peace Meet

MUMBI KIGUTHA, CPPS

Truth, in fact, is an inseparable companion of justice and mercy. All three together are essential to building peace; each, moreover, prevents the other from being altered. . . . Truth should not lead to revenge, but rather to reconciliation and forgiveness. Truth means telling families torn apart by pain what happened to their missing relatives. Truth means confessing what happened to minors recruited by cruel and violent people. Truth means recognizing the pain of women who are victims of violence and abuse. . . . Every act of violence committed against a human being is a wound in humanity's flesh; every violent death diminishes us as a people. . . . Violence leads to more violence, hatred to more hatred, death to more death. We must break this cycle which seems inescapable.
—POPE FRANCIS, *FRATELLI TUTTI*, 227

Introduction

PAIN THAT IS NOT transformed and wounds that are not healed are transferred. A glance at the African continent and indeed the entire world leads one to surmise that we are all deeply wounded and hurting terribly. How else can we explain the intractable conflicts in various regions all over the world and especially in Africa, be it in the Great Lakes region, or in the Central African Republic, or in South Sudan, Syria, Afghanistan, Myanmar? So many regions of the world are witnessing ongoing and protracted turmoil, and some of these conflicts have endured and been sustained for decades. These large conflicts are only progenitors of many other forms of violence happening at any given time in various parts of the world. The rising number of cases of femicide, police brutality, intimate partner violence, and ethnic and tribal clashes, but also the violence of increasing and sustained poverty aided and abetted by the selfish and self-serving decisions of our political leaders and heightened by the silence of religious leaders—many of whom have aligned themselves with politics or are busy cultivating the culture of silence in cases of abuse that incriminate church figures—all point to a society that is broken.

Pope Francis reminds us in chapter 7 of *Fratelli Tutti* that reconciliation and forgiveness are a cornerstone of Christian discipleship, acting as a counterwitness to the pervasiveness of injustice in our world. The two complementary actions of reconciliation and forgiveness that lead to true peace require an active and ongoing participation from us (*FT* 209). They are key to transforming our pain and healing our wounds as individuals and also collectively. I will in this commentary illustrate how a desire and commitment to reconciliation demands a forgiveness that encapsulates truth, justice, and mercy, leading to peace and thus reconciliation (healing). The invitation to practice these values begins in the Psalms, where mercy, truth, peace, and justice embrace, and we are being reminded again of the same by our Holy Father in this encyclical.

Reconciliation as the Motivation

Reconciliation is interpreted in a number of different ways depending on the context. The Hebrew scriptures do not contain the word reconciliation at all, and the word appears only fourteen times in the New Testament. As Christians, we take our impetus for this practice from God's radical act of reconciling humanity to God's very self through the unfolding of the paschal mystery. The relief, joy, gratitude, and all the other emotions that we experience as a result of God's radical love for us is the gift we desire to grant others as we actively engage in the work of reconciliation and forgiveness. Forgiveness and reconciliation in any form or shape is indeed impossible without God's grace. However, God always answers our truest prayers and thus the desire itself to reconcile and forgive is the first step in seeing our siblings in a different light, as *imago dei*, as deserving of all that we desire for ourselves.

Reconciliation fails for any number of reasons, such as demanding the mercy and peace of the victims while ignoring truth and justice, failing to honor the memory of victims with respect to the suffering they have undergone (*FT* 226), protecting the oppressor, who then goes on to cause more harm (*FT* 241), focusing on causing an equal measure of pain to the perpetrator as that which we experienced (*FT* 242), among other things. In reconciliation, God begins with the victim, and thus we should begin with the victim, honoring the memory of their experience by helping speak truth to the power of violence, and establishing justice by upending the structures or policies that grant oppressive power to some. This attempt to delegitimize oppressive power is not driven by malice, but rather by love for the perpetrator(s) who suffer harm too when they harm others.

Reconciliation is a spiritual practice because it is only in and through the work of the Holy Spirit that we are able to overcome the horrors of conflict. When listening to or reading the testimonies of various Rwandans, such as Immaculée Ilibagiza[1] or the Jesuit priest Fr. Marcel Uwineza,[2] it is their faith and belief in God that enabled them to forgive the people that murdered their families during the Rwandan genocide of 1994. Similar stories are shared by the family members of those whose lives have been lost at the hands of others and suffered horrific abuse from their parents or partners. As Fr. Marcel said when sharing with the United Nations General Assembly on the experience of encountering and then forgiving the man who killed his siblings, "There is a higher power than us. You can't measure it in a laboratory. It gives meaning to our lives, but it can't be explained. That power moved me that day."[3]

The shaky peace that has become a marker of so many agreements, treaties, and commissions is oftentimes an indicator of a process that is not centered on individuals or seeks to avoid conflict.

Forgiveness—Acknowledgment of Untruths

We grow up on our continent of Africa with subtle and overt reminders not to air our dirty linen in public but rather keep it in the family. This is how the screams of a woman suffering intimate partner violence are excused as

1. For more on Immaculée Ilibagiza, see the "About" page on the website, Immaculée.
2. For a profile of Fr. Marcel Uwineza, see Sullivan, "Healing the Wounds."
3. Sullivan, "Healing the Wounds."

being an indicator of love from her partner or as evidence of her shortcomings as a wife, and the presence of a neighbor's underage house-help is justified with statements like "at least she/he has a roof over their head and three square meals a day" or "hard labor never ruined anyone." This culture of silence for many of us is also reinforced by our religious institutions, where the avoidance of scandal becomes an all-consuming exercise with nary a thought for the victims. The little justifications we make each and every day become colossal over time, resulting in scenarios in which there are multiple versions of the truth or a complete erasure of it.

Our denial of the truth goes hand in hand with placing the blame on others in an attempt to avoid our own complicity. This is what has led to a certain form of revisionist history in our countries, resulting in a romanticization of precolonial times and upholding African values, practices, and culture as being best practices and above any reproach whatsoever. However, were precolonial times, or for that matter, any period in the history of the African continent and our world ever completely conflict-free and peaceful? Did human beings over the passage of time become violent and abusive? Lots of indicators do point to rising violence exacerbated by various factors. However, people have been and will always be just that—people—capable of incredible kindness but also extreme brutality. Acknowledging the truth, past and current, means accepting that inasmuch as we are wounded and are victims, we have also been perpetrators at times and thus are equally called to and worthy of mercy, justice, and forgiveness.

Creating spaces for truth-telling requires that we cultivate a stance of openness to what we hear from both victims and perpetrators, which may confirm or refute what we already know, or a mixture of both. It means as victims or allies of victims that we need to put our anger aside and truly listen to the other, to truly place oneself in the other's shoes, but more so to acknowledge that in different circumstances they could be me and I could be them.

Forgiveness—A Call to Justice

What is justice? We often think of justice in legalistic terms, which has led to a binary and one-dimensional understanding of it. Growing up watching American crime shows on TV, I learned the phrase, "If you do the crime, then you must do the time." We navigate justice by asking who, what, where, and how questions. Who stole from you, what did they steal, where did the stealing take place, and how did they steal? Looking to our continent and to a number of other countries, legal justice systems seem to be in place only to further oppress the poor and the most vulnerable, while the rich tend to get away with heinous crimes. In the global North, Black, Indigenous, and People of Color bear an unjust burden placed on them by the legal system as the fines and prison sentences meted out to them are extremely punitive, while white people charged with similar offenses get off relatively easy.

Justice from a Christian perspective, however, is much broader, looking not only at issues codified by law as legally wrong but more broadly at what is morally wrong. It is concerned with the "why" question. Why has our continent neglected the poor and inflicted unbearable punishment on them for acts done for their human survival? Why aren't the one percent überwealthy of the world also held responsible for exploitative business practices and hoarding of resources? Many of our countries in Africa still operate under colonial law, according to which the punishment for stealing most kinds of farm produce, no matter how little, involved harsh sentences of multiple years of incarceration. When a mother steals a chicken or a bunch of bananas for her children after spending a couple of nights without sustenance, the "why" question becomes key to unlocking not just the wrongness of her action, but also the injustice of a society that has still not guaranteed access to basic human rights for all. As Pope Francis says in *FT*, "Even perpetrators have a legitimate point of view" (*FT* 228). It unmasks our own crime of stealing by amassing and hoarding resources for ourselves while so many go without basic necessities, contrary to what God tells us—that the earth and all its fullness is for all of God's children (*FT* 229). It is impossible to build lasting peace when the society is still divided into the "haves" and the "have-nots."

True justice requires truth, truth about how we have arrived at the present moment of our existence. It requires the truth of our very selves, our authenticity, created in the image and likeness of God, living from our shared humanistic and/or Christian values, but yet so uniquely, beautifully, and wondrously different (*FT* 230). Justice is not vengeful, it is not "an eye for an eye"; rather, it seeks reparation while upholding the dignity of the perpetrator as a child of God (*FT* 266).

Forgiveness—An Act of Mercy

No one wants to be remembered by the worst action of their life. To do that is to deny that all of humanity is capable of metanoia, that deep transformation that is a gift of the Holy Spirit constantly at work in and through us. As Pope Francis reminds us, "We should never confine others to what they may have said or done, but value them for the promise that they embody" (*FT*

228). In my own work of reconciliation, I have been privileged to speak to a number of victims of horrendous crimes who have managed to forgive their perpetrators. Some of them have even befriended their onetime aggressor. What has struck me as they have shared their stories is their relating of a moment in the engagement with the perpetrator when they see themselves in the other's story.

At the Precious Blood Ministry of Reconciliation on the South Side of Chicago, a young man was once arrested after breaking into a house and stealing some valuables. The victim, who happened to be a police officer, was understandably angered by this violation and wanted the book to be thrown at the offender, but after some intervention from neutral parties, he agreed to try a restorative justice circle.[4] He first shared how the crime had impacted him and his family before the offender was given a chance to speak. The offender spoke of growing up poor and without many role models, having joined a gang as a survival tool, and how the same gang had pressured him to steal as a rite of passage. The police officer identified personally with the story as he had grown up in similar circumstances and knew how hard it was to break away from that lifestyle. The agreed reparation was that the young man stay in school and report to the police officer on a regular basis so that he could mentor him. The answer as to "why" unveiled more nuances that enabled the victim to show mercy to the perpetrator.

However, many more victims do show mercy and forgive their perpetrators without the opportunity to engage with them and hear their side of the story, reminding us all that the work of reconciliation, the path of renewed encounter, is not possible without God doing the seemingly impossible.

Reconciliation and Forgiveness as the Goal

Popular culture would have us believe that reconciliation and indeed forgiveness is a sign of weakness. Nothing could be further from the truth, as both are practices that require an intentional participation, whether it is through dredging up painful memories or seeking out the truth and demanding justice but also showing mercy. *Fratelli Tutti* supports this by noting that "it is no easy task to overcome the bitter legacy of injustices, hostility and mistrust left by conflict. It can only be done by overcoming evil with good (cf. Rom 12:21) and by cultivating those virtues which foster reconciliation, solidarity and peace" (*FT* 243).

---

4. Restorative justice circles provide a space for encounter between the victim and the offender but go beyond that to involve the community in the decision-making process.

A lot of popular clichés and sayings have emerged over the years on the subject of forgiveness, many of which I would say do not call for truth, justice, or mercy but rather an almost docile acceptance of the circumstances. One such example is that statement that "not forgiving is like drinking poison and then waiting for the other person to die." It is also important to note that, for some victims, forgiveness is an impossible task, as it is often the only thing in their lives they can leverage against a powerful perpetrator (FT 246). The overall movement of reconciliation and forgiveness is a deeply personal one and cannot be hurried along in an attempt to make others feel more comfortable.

"Forgive and forget" is another popular saying that is often bandied around. Is it truly possible to forget? First of all, it would be discounting these amazing brains that God gifted us with, which help us retain so much other information. Memory is important in helping us remember what has been, that it may strengthen our resolve to never return to that bitter time in history (FT 247). It also honors the victim(s) by showing them that this significant life event did matter, that it also moved us, as our sisters' and brothers' keepers. In recent days, members of Generation Z have reminded us, by comparing present events to history, how various policies are leading us to oppressive regimes. Those who study the criminal justice system in the US have helped us draw parallels between prison labor and slavery. Indeed, we must not forget, lest we find ourselves in the same pickle once again.

Reconciliation—An Uphill Journey

Different forms of peace exist and the means to arrive at them is different. Around the world we have UN peacekeepers stationed in various localities to maintain the peace. Their numbers and military role deter less equipped locals from engaging conflict. Beyond UN peacekeepers, governments, through close monitoring of their constituents or very punitive measures, have managed to maintain this negative peace (FT 262). However, the peace that Pope Francis speaks of in *Fratelli Tutti* is one in which the participants arrive at it through their own free will; it is engendered by seeing all humanity as equal and also as being capable of change.

The inequalities in the world both at an individual and collective level have only increased with the passage of time. Those with access to resources and power are positioned as the decision-makers and those without as their subjects. This has led to individuals, ethnic groups, and countries wanting to dominate others and hold them to a different standard than what they adhere to. Reconciliation counters this narrative by placing the victim—the underdog—first, attending to their needs by seeking truth and justice but by also believing that even the perpetrator, no matter their offence, is deserving of dignity (*FT* 269).

Reflecting on this seventh chapter of the encyclical, I draw many parallels with my understanding of reconciliation, for where Pope Francis uses the word "peace," I would use the word "reconciliation," which encompasses the values of truth, justice, mercy, and peace. In particular, I resonate deeply with the pope's stance that forgiveness is not something that we can demand of victims; rather, it is something that they have to come to all on their own. Reconciliation and forgiveness are indeed not passive stances but intentional actions, calling us all to be truthful and accountable for the times that we have been perpetrators of injustices, but also to actively work for justice, truth, and peace for our sisters and brothers. Societies and structures are the sum total of individual actions and choices, meaning that we are all responsible, that we all have a role to play in healing our world.

Bibliography

"About." Imaculée, n.d. https://www.immaculee.com/pages/about.

Francis, Pope. *Fratelli Tutti: On Fraternity and Social Friendship*. Vatican City: Libreria Editrice Vaticana, 2020. https://www.vatican.va/content/francesco/en/encyclicals/documents/papa-francesco_20201003_enciclica-fratelli-tutti.html.

Sullivan, Kathleen. "Healing the Wounds." *Boston College News*, April 2019. https://www.bc.edu/bc-web/bcnews/faith-religion/jesuit-catholic/genocide-survivor-marcel-uwineza.html.

26

Conflict, Violence, and Reconciliation

DANIEL FRANKLIN E. PILARIO, CM

ALREADY IN ITS OPENING chapter, *Fratelli Tutti* makes explicit some of the enemies of fraternity and social friendship: "War, terrorist attacks, racial or religious persecution, and many other affronts to human dignity" (*FT* 25). These forms of social violence that pervade our cultures "have become so common as to constitute a real 'third world war' fought piecemeal" (*FT* 25). Chapter 7 of the encyclical addresses the specific context of this violence. This commentary shall proceed in three steps: a description of social and political violence in Asia, a reflection on the three central points of chapter 7, and some lessons from peacebuilding efforts on the ground.

Social and Political Violence in Asia

March 17, 2021: As I was writing this article, a blogger from a Myanmar resistance group wrote: "We woke up to the news of terrorist army setting fire to a residential area in Hlaing Tharyar Township, resulting in damage of three houses including a house of well-known painter Win Pe Myint. Although the painter and his family are safe, almost half of his art pieces were destroyed. The incident reminds us of the past not long ago: no art, no culture, just fear."[1] The last private newspaper has stopped publication. The internet is regularly interrupted. And people live in fear day and night.

---

1. Anonymous, "Freedom Memoirs."

A former student, Florence, wrote me in a Facebook message: "My mind is not clear right now. My friends in Hlaing Tharyar and Shwe Pyi Thar are in danger." And where is the Catholic Church? The Bishops' Conference of Myanmar (CBCM) issued a call for reconciliation through dialogue.[2] Florence asked: "Reconciliation? We need to reconcile with the demons without them begging for forgiveness, without them paying for their crimes?" Maung John, another former student and now a director of a school of theology in Myanmar, writes to me: "It seems that all Catholics join the Civil Disobedience Movement (CDM) till the security forces began to shoot the protesters in late February."[3] But what is happening now, Maung explains, "is just a product of 67 years of violence in Myanmar producing 479,000 refugees, 810,000 stateless individuals, and 1.2 million people in need of immediate humanitarian aid."[4]

December 8, 2016: Around four years earlier, another violent event happened in the garbage dumpsite district of Payatas, Quezon City, Philippines, and I work at a parish there. Juan was shot in front of his daughter after serving his children breakfast. He begged for his life, his daughter recounted. "Please don't kill me," he pleaded, kneeling. "Imprison me if you want but please don't kill me. I have seven children and my wife is still in prison. No one is going to take care of them."[5] The armed men did not listen. Instead, they delivered four bullets to various parts of his body. While he was lying there, dead, they put a small gun on his right and illegal drugs on his left. They took a photo of the crime scene and sent it to news outlets. The next day the news report tells us that the police found .38-caliber revolvers and .45-caliber pistols. This is the government's proof that he fought back.[6] During this time of the populist Duterte regime, the police often force themselves into houses and simply shoot people who are on their list of drug users. The government acknowledged more than six thousand drug-related deaths, while human rights organizations estimated more than thirty-three thousand people killed, some minors included, connected to Duterte's "War on Drugs." The president encouraged this killing spree, saying that the program will remain "relentless and chilling";[7] and the pandemic did not stop the killing. This led to a crime against humanity

2. Bo, "Message."
3. Personal correspondence with author.
4. Personal correspondence with author.
5. Personal account given to author; see also Conde, "Our Happy Family is Gone"; and SVST QCPH, "Huwag Kang Papatay.".
6. From the original news article that reported on Juan's death. Enano, "QC Cops Kill 7."
7. Corrales, "Duterte."

filed against Duterte and his men at the International Criminal Court at The Hague in 2018.

I have related two actual events of violence on Asian soil. A research report entitled *The State of Conflict and Violence in Asia* (2017)[8] describes the present state, past roots, and future implications of violence in Asian countries using hard empirical data. It outlines five emerging trends that provide an overall view of the Asian situation. First, it states that conflict and violence affect all Asian countries, not just those often thought to be conflict-ridden. The continuing conflict in Afghanistan after the US withdrawal of its troops and the refugee tragedy of the Rohingyas are well-known. Even if violence in Indonesia and India often does not make it into the international headlines, this does not mean it does not exist. Second, Asian countries have been relatively successful at managing national crises, but often at the price of intense subnational and localized violence. National stability in Thailand, Bangladesh, or China, for example, has been achieved at the expense of the suppression of regional conflicts. Third, the politicization of ethnic and religious identities has frequently led to violence and creates major risks for the future. Hindutva ideology in India, the Islamization propaganda in Indonesia, and the Burmese hegemony in Myanmar all foster ethnic hatred and religious divisions. Fourth, lopsided development and capital-driven urbanization will likely increase rather than decrease violence in the coming decade. And finally, fifth, gender-based violence is widespread in Asia, and its impact is greater than previously understood and will be greater than is presently anticipated.

Fratelli Tutti on Social Violence and Peacebuilding

Chapter 7 of *Fratelli Tutti* should be read in Asia in the context of the conflicts and violence described above. I will comment on three areas of this chapter that are relevant to the Asian situation: capital punishment and extrajudicial killings, the immorality of war, and the work of peace and reconciliation.

Extrajudicial Killings and the Death Penalty

FT 267 observes: "Particularly serious . . . are so-called extrajudicial or extralegal executions, which are homicides deliberately committed by certain states and by their agents, often passed off as clashes with criminals or

---

8. The Asia Foundation, *State of Conflict*.

presented as the unintended consequences of the reasonable, necessary and proportionate use of force in applying the law." Though a portion of this quotation comes from the pope's address to the delegates of the International Association of Penal Law on October 23, 2014,[9] by his quoting it in *Fratelli Tutti* in 2020, one cannot help but feel that the pope is specifically referring to the Filipino situation and similar situations worldwide. Pope Francis is certainly aware of the Filipino situation. As Bishop Pablo David of the Diocese of Kalookan, one of the worst areas for extrajudicial killings in Metro Manila, relates: "When I asked Pope Francis whether or not he was aware of what is going on in the diocese of Kalookan . . . he told me he is keeping well informed."[10] "I want you to know that I know your situation. I know what you are going through. I am praying for you. Please continue," the pope told him.[11]

The pope discusses extralegal executions in the context of death penalty: "Here I would stress that it is impossible to imagine that states today have no other means than capital punishment to protect the lives of other people from the unjust aggressor" (*FT* 267). "Today we state clearly that the death penalty is inadmissible and the Church is firmly committed to calling for its abolition worldwide" (*FT* 263).

On November 17, 2020, the United Nations resoundingly voted in favor of a moratorium on capital punishment. Eleven countries out of the thirty-nine that voted against the resolution were from Asia: Afghanistan, Brunei Darussalam, China, India, Japan, Maldives, North Korea, Pakistan, Papua New Guinea, Singapore, and Tonga. Asia is the "global outlier" on the death penalty.[12] Some other Asian countries abstained—Indonesia, Vietnam, and Laos—but have executed hundreds of criminals in recent years. Even those who voted for the moratorium are not firmly committed to this position. The Duterte government, for example, is campaigning to enact it into law again. Asia's ambivalent relationship with the death penalty is founded on two things: zero tolerance for crime, even though the deterrent effect of capital punishment is statistically unproven, and knee-jerk opposition to foreign intervention on human rights issues, which is perceived as interfering with the sovereignty and autonomy of Asian leaders. *Fratelli Tutti* warns clearly of the dangers of the death penalty in authoritarian states, many of which are located in Asia: "There is at times a tendency to deliberately fabricate enemies: stereotyped figures who represent all the characteristics that

---

9. Francis, "Address."
10. Bordoni and Galgano, "Pope Backs Filipino Bishops."
11. Tenedero, "Pope Francis."
12. Strangio, "Explaining Southeast Asia's Addiction."

society perceives or interprets as threatening" (*FT* 266). The dangers of the death penalty the pope mentions, including the possibility of judicial error and using it as a means to suppress dissent and engage in religious or cultural persecution (*FT* 268), are particularly relevant to the Asian situation, which is keenly beset by the problems of racism and "othering" prevalent in contemporary populist societies. Asian societies are still far from Pope Francis's vision of a world without capital punishment (he even criticizes life imprisonment as actually constituting a "secret death penalty" (*FT* 268).

The Immorality of War

In addition to the subnational conflicts triggered by intercultural and ideological factors, there are potential international hotspots in the Asian region whose problems may escalate into war, including the territorial disputes in the South China Sea, the North Korean crisis, the Afghanistan conflict, and the tensions in the East China Sea.[13] We examine the South China Sea (also called the West Philippine Sea) situation as an example. China's economic interest in the area is obvious. Despite a ruling favorable to the Philippines in July 2016 by the UNCLOS Permanent Court of Arbitration at The Hague concerning its sovereignty over the area, China rejects the decision, and continues to reclaim the islands and create new ones, install military installations, and more recently, deploy warships.[14] This not only creates tensions with other claimant countries in the region like the Philippines, Vietnam, Taiwan, Brunei, Indonesia, and Malaysia, which can be easily bullied by China's aggressive foreign policy, but it also incites more powerful players like the US, whose economic interest in the disputed West Philippine Sea as a trade route and substantial source of natural gas is not a secret. The US has recently increased its military presence in the region. It is said that the Asian-Pacific region is now the most militarized area of the world, with the three superpowers—the US, China, and Russia—all pursuing their strategic interests. Will this and other Asian hotspots trigger the next world war?

Reading *Fratelli Tutti* from the perspective of this highly charged context reveals that it is a stinging critique of international geopolitical positioning in Asia. The encyclical makes a number of arguments to show the danger and injustice of waging war in our times, despite the humanitarian, defensive, and precautionary excuses for doing so: the danger of manipulation of information; the uncontrollable destructive power of nuclear,

---

13. Council on Foreign Relations, Center for Preventive Action, "Global Conflict Tracker."

14. Bolledo, "Over 200 Chinese Ships."

chemical, and biological warfare; persons injured and killed as "collateral damage"; the ineffective deterrent value of the threat of mutual destruction; and the risks and impacts of war weighing heavier than its supposed benefits. *Fratelli Tutti* thus rejects the long moral tradition and discourse of the "just war theory" developed from Augustine up to the present day. It even discards the "war as last resort" position set forth in the *Catechism of the Catholic Church*[15] and the *Compendium of the Social Doctrine of the Church*.[16] Against this whole tradition, *Fratelli Tutti* fosters reliance on the rule of law and the strategies of negotiation, mediation, and arbitration in the spirit of fraternity and social friendship, offering the rallying cry, "Never again war!" (*FT* 256–62).

Healing and Reconciliation in Postconflict Societies

The greater part of chapter 7 (*FT* 225–52) discusses the themes of healing and reconciliation from the perspective of so-called postconflict societies. In Asia, we can easily think of the following countries: Cambodia after the defeat of the Khmer Rouge; Timor-Leste after the withdrawal of Indonesia; Sri Lanka after the capitulation of the Liberation Tigers of Tamils Eelam (LTTE); Afghanistan after the planned withdrawal of US troops; Mindanao in the southern Philippines after the creation of the Bangsamoro Autonomous Region of Muslim Mindanao (BARMM); and many areas where peace has been negotiated. In these parts of the world, Pope Francis writes, "there is a need for paths of peace to heal open wounds. There is also a need for peacemakers, men and women prepared to work boldly and creatively to initiate processes of healing and renewed encounter" (*FT* 225).

The central themes dealt with in the encyclical are not new. They are based on decades of peacebuilding practice, which practitioners of international politics and academe have dubbed "transitional justice"—pathways toward the rehabilitation of a nation after the ravages of war, gross violations of human rights, and divided societies caused by political upheaval. The concrete processes of transitional justice in these postconflict societies are aimed at achieving healing and reconciliation, democratization and development. Allow me to summarize the themes of chapter 7. First is the role of truth and memory (*FT* 226–30, 246–52). There is a need to cultivate "penitential memory," to hear the narratives of what really happened, and even the concrete facts concerning missing relatives, recruited minors, and abused women. "Those who truly forgive do not forget" (*FT* 251). Second,

15. *Catechism of the Catholic Church*, 2307–17.
16. Pontifical Council for Justice and Peace, *Compendium*, 488–520.

there should be a viable roadmap—an architecture of peace—that includes ways of engaging in dialogue and negotiation to get "people to work together, side-by-side, in pursuing goals that benefit everyone" (*FT* 228). "Authentic reconciliation does not flee from conflict, but is achieved *in* conflict, resolving it through dialogue and open, honest and patient negotiation" (*FT* 244). This process of reconciliation involves not just high-level policymakers and well-meaning organizations but also ordinary people, especially the victims and the marginalized (*FT* 231, 235, 249). The third theme is the centrality of the human person and the common good in all political, social, and economic programs. "May this determination [to make the human person and the common good central] help us flee from the temptation for revenge and the satisfaction of short-term partisan interests" (*FT* 232). The fourth and last is the critical role of forgiveness. Even as we are called to forgive everyone, justice needs to be rendered in sociopolitical contexts. We need to confront criminals, corrupt political officials, and those who trample on people's rights and human dignity. This statement is quite helpful for deposing tyrants and dictators: "We are called to love everyone, without exception; at the same time, loving an oppressor does not mean allowing him to keep oppressing us, or letting him think that what he does is acceptable. On the contrary, true love for an oppressor means seeking ways to make him cease his oppression; it means stripping him of a power that he does not know how to use and that diminishes his own humanity and that of others" (*FT* 241).

Lessons from Peacebuilding Initiatives in Asia

We have shown the relevance of chapter 7 to the Asian continent, which is marred by violence and conflict. Many of the themes of the chapter refer directly to a number of different national and regional contexts, including the reflections on extrajudicial killings, the oppression of ethnic and cultural minorities, the death penalty, war, peacebuilding, and others. Beyond these themes, however, there are requirements for peacebuilding that relate to the specifically Asian situation which can critique *Fratelli Tutti*'s abstract discourse of healing and reconciliation. In this last part, I will enumerate three such requirements: the social conditions of such healing and reconciliation, the need for grassroots structures and the peacebuilding strategies of ordinary people, and the necessity for a concrete focus on the actual needs of Asia.

First, even as truth-telling, remembrance, dialogue, negotiation, and forgiveness are necessary for peacebuilding, there are prior social conditions necessary for these processes to happen. *Fratelli Tutti* hints at these:

"Without equal opportunities, different forms of aggression and conflict will find a fertile terrain for growth and eventually explode" (*FT* 235). People on the ground do not recognize the "post" in postconflict societies.[17] Even as independence or liberty has been achieved, violence and impunity for its perpetrators still pervade their everyday lives. In a world where armed groups dictate the everyday lives of people, there is a need to insist on the rule of law. In a world where judges and lawyers have to run for their lives, basic political institutions with credible and effective leadership and with working structures of transparency and accountability need to be created. Even though an emphasis on restorative justice is a happy development in juridical science, retributive justice needs to be summoned to curb continuing violence by uncontrolled dominant powers to prevent vigilantism, to identify criminal perpetrators, and to break the cycle of impunity.[18] In a world where people are very poor and can be easily dominated by ruthless, armed politicians, reconciliation and peace can only begin with capacity-building through education, access to employment opportunities, food and environmental sustainability, and basic physical infrastructure. In short, these concrete social and political structures are *conditio sine qua non* for peace to happen on the ground.

Second, in order to establish fraternity and social friendship, peacebuilding processes must be built from the ground up. High-profile talks among leaders and policymakers are useful and necessary, but movements for grassroots dialogue in the context of people's daily lives are necessary to counter long-held prejudices, break ideological, religious, and cultural barriers, and promote healing and social cohesion. In southern Mindanao, torn as they were by decades of violence, people unilaterally declared their villages and schools to be "peace zones" and prevented the military from carrying firearms in specified locations.[19] In Sri Lanka, dialogue between warring Sinhalese and Tamil farmers and a joint cultivation of disputed farms led to common celebrations, festive meals, and reconciliation. They posted banners saying "Peace to the Rice Fields," signaling to government forces and militants that this area is an exclusive territory of unarmed farmers in their fields on which no armed party is allowed to roam.[20] Some indigenous communities, like the Talaandig in the southern Philippines, designated women as their peacekeepers.[21] Other women employ silent protest, hu-

---

17. Shneiderman and Snellinger, "Framing the Issues."
18. Pilario, "Restorative Justice," 71–72.
19. Pilario, "Religion as Social Capital," 104.
20. Wijesinghe, "Sri Lanka," 178–80.
21. Villaluz, "Inay Malinandang, Talaandig," 179–92.

mor, and laughter to allay otherwise oppressive situations.[22] Some schools have "peace tables"—when two or three students quarrel, they have to go to the peace table at the back of the classroom to settle their differences. They are told not leave the peace table until they have reconciled. Some institutes offer a "peace curriculum," and others hold joint interreligious or intercultural retreats, among many other initiatives. These small-scale and people-led initiatives augment dialogue and consensus-making as part of cultural formation.

Third, there must be a focus on the specific needs of Asia if we are to effectively operationalize the challenges of *Fratelli Tutti* on the ground. The recommendations of the research report[23] mentioned at the outset of this chapter might prove helpful to provide some focus on these needs:

1. First is the need to target conflict hot spots with peacemaking initiatives but also to remain alert to violence happening elsewhere, in particular in post-US Afghanistan, military rule of Myanmar, China's incursion into the Philippine and Taiwanese territories, and in the populist and strongman rule of Duterte in the Philippines and in the recent return to power of the late dictator's son, Marcos. The present economic woes of Sri Lanka also generate everyday violence among the population. There is also a need to monitor the explosive areas of Cambodia, Myanmar, Thailand, Vietnam, and Laos, particularly on the borders of these countries where crime groups, human traffickers, and drug syndicates operate. The now-postconflict zones of Timor-Leste, Nepal, and Sri Lanka are also a continuing concern. In short, we need to be proactive in our work for peace.

2. The second challenge is to understand the history and politics of various conflicts. For instance, the politics of partition in South Asia, the centuries of Muslim-Christian conflict in the southern Philippines, Buddhist or Hindu hegemonies in other countries, all of which have often been exploited by local elites, will help explain the continuing irruption of violence in these areas. This knowledge is needed to make peacebuilding sustainable.

3. There is a need to focus on strengthening the rule of law. Even before peacebuilding processes, there is a need to develop effective and legitimate political and legal institutions. Their absence creates a vacuum for powerful elites, both old and new, to exercise hegemonic power.

---

22. Cruz, "Interrupting Normal Ways," 101–19.
23. The Asia Foundation, *State of Conflict*.

4. There is a need to deal with the transnational drivers of conflict and violence like drugs, guns, illicit goods, and ideologies that cross national borders. The international syndicates and their political back-ups need to be identified and dealt with in order to create preemptive strategies to uphold people's human rights.

5. We need to support local violence-monitoring systems whose processes are reflective of actual situations. Religious leaders, indigenous cultural chiefs, and other local authorities—and the dialogue among them—provide peacebuilding a crucial resource.[24] Their knowledge and strategies help us understand local and global conflict and violence.

In conclusion, I have shown the potential for *Fratelli Tutti's* dialectical reception on Asian soil with respect to the themes of violence and reconciliation. On the one hand, Asia's particular history of conflict and its present volatile situation need the pope's message of healing and reconciliation. The absence of the rule of law and viable political institutions in many places results in the resurgence of local religious and military elites, as has happened in Myanmar, Afghanistan, or in an international clash of power exemplified by the present military buildup in the West Philippine Sea. An old maxim goes: "If you only have a hammer, sooner or later most problems will look like nails." In light of the growing military arsenal in the region, the military option does not provide an effective means of settling disputes and achieving political objectives.[25] In this sense, *Fratelli Tutti* is a prophetic text for Asia. On the other hand, the continent's long history of violence ironically provides communities a laboratory for dialogue and effective peacebuilding processes. Their everyday familiarity with conflict challenges them to creatively search for healing and reconciliation. Their local knowledge and practices, born out of practical sense and doing what is necessary to survive, offer a corrective to the encyclical's theoretical—and sometimes universalist—directions.

Bibliography

Anonymous. "Freedom Memoirs—Day 45." *Mohinga Matters* (blog). https://mohingamatters.com/2021/03/17/freedom-memoirs-day-45/?fbclid=IwAR1ksD7wp1N6QVRK9TOWvovujWLNCozVAanNmDf2P3ETLWe8OBtaZ nDNkn8.

The Asia Foundation. *The State of Conflict and Violence in Asia*. Bangkok: The Asia Foundation, 2017. https://asiafoundation.org/wp-content/uploads/2017/10/The_State_of_Conflict_and_Violence_in_Asia-12.29.17.pdf.

24. Michel, "Catholic Approaches."
25. Gady, "Coming War in Asia."

Bo, Charles Cardinal Maung. "Message of Cardinal Charles Bo to the People of Myanmar and Our International Communities." Myanmar Catholic Church, February 3, 2021. http://www.catholicmyanmar.com/newview.php?id=286.

Bolledo, Jairo. "Over 200 Chinese Ships Spread Out Over West Philippine Sea Reefs." *Rappler*, March 31, 2021. https://www.rappler.com/nation/chinese-ships-remain-philippine-reefs-march-29-2021.

Bordoni, Linda, and Mario Galgano. "Pope Backs Filipino Bishop Fighting Deadly 'Drug War.'" *Vatican News*, May 30, 2019. https://www.vaticannews.va/en/church/news/2019-05/bishop-david-kaloocan-philippines-pope-drug-war.html.

The Catechism of the Catholic Church. 2nd ed. Washington, DC: United States Catholic Conference, 2000.

Cejka, Mary Ann, and Thomas Bamat, eds. *Artisans of Peace: Grassroots Peacemaking among Christian Communities*. Maryknoll, NY: Orbis, 2003.

Conde, Carlos H. "'Our Happy Family Is Gone': Impact of the 'War on Drugs' on Children in the Philippines." Human Rights Watch, May 27, 2020. https://www.hrw.org/report/2020/05/27/our-happy-family-gone/impact-war-drugs-children-philippines#_ftn49.

Corrales, Nestor. "Duterte: Drug War to Remain Relentless and Chilling." *Inquirer*, July 23, 2018. https://newsinfo.inquirer.net/1013351/duterte-drug-war-will-be-relentless-and-chilling.

Council on Foreign Relations, Center for Preventive Action. "Global Conflict Tracker." https://www.cfr.org/global-conflict-tracker/?category=us.

Cruz, Gemma Tulud. "Interrupting Normal Ways of Thinking: Resistance and Asian Women's Struggle for Peace and Liberation." In *Practicing Peace*, edited by Judette Gallares and Astrid Lobo-Gajiwala, 101–19. Feminist Theology of Liberation: Asian Perspectives. Quezon City, Philippines: Claretian, 2011.

Enano, Jhesset. "QC Cops Kill 7, Including Trash Collectors 'Wielding Guns.'" *Inquirer*, December 8, 2016. https://newsinfo.inquirer.net/851675/qc-cops-kill-7-including-trash-collectors-wielding-guns.

Francis, Pope. "Address to the Delegates of the International Association of Penal Law." Speech given in Hall of Popes, Vatican City, October 23, 2014. https://www.vatican.va/content/francesco/en/speeches/2014/october/documents/papa-francesco_20141023_associazione-internazionale-diritto-penale.html.

———. *Fratelli Tutti: On Fraternity and Social Friendship*. Vatican City: Libreria Editrice Vaticana, 2020. http://www.vatican.va/content/francesco/en/encyclicals/documents/papa-francesco_20201003_enciclica-fratelli-tutti.html.

Gady, Franz-Stefan. "The Coming War in Asia: Why It Is So Hard to Imagine the Unimaginable." *The Diplomat*, August 3, 2017. https://thediplomat.com/2017/08/the-coming-war-in-asia-why-it-is-hard-to-imagine-the-unimaginable/.

Michel, Thomas. "Catholic Approaches to Interreligious Peacebuilding: Lessons from Indonesia's 'Sad Years.'" In *Peacebuilding: Catholic Theology, Ethics and Praxis*, edited by Robert J. Schreiter et al., 240–62. Maryknoll, NY: Orbis, 2010.

Pilario, Daniel Franklin E. "Religion as Social Capital for Building Peace." In *Religion and Identity in Post-Conflict Societies*, edited by Regina Ammicht Quinn et al., 99–105. Concilium 2015/1. London: SCM, 2015.

———. "Restorative Justice Against Continuing Violence." In *Reconciliation: Empowering Grace*, edited by Jacques Haers et al., 64–73. Concilium 2013/1. London: SCM, 2013.

Pontifical Council for Justice and Peace. *The Compendium of the Social Doctrine of the Church.* Washington, DC: US Catholic Bishops' Conference, 2004.

Shneiderman, Sara, and Amanda Snellinger. "Framing the Issues: The Politics of 'Postconflict.'" *Culanth.org* (Society for Cultural Anthropology), March 24, 2014. https://culanth.org/fieldsights/framing-the-issues-the-politics-of-postconflict.

Strangio, Sebastian. "Explaining Southeast Asia's Addiction to the Death Penalty." *The Diplomat,* November 25, 2020. https://thediplomat.com/2020/11/explaining-southeast-asias-addiction-to-the-death-penalty/.

SVST QCPH. "Huwag Kang Papatay (Thou Shall Not Kill)." YouTube video, March 31, 2021. 13:53. https://www.youtube.com/watch?v=XvOloOu6e10&t=1s.

Tenedero, Erik. "Pope Francis to Bishop Critical of Duterte, I Am with You." *ABS-CBN News,* May 24, 2019. https://news.abs-cbn.com/news/05/24/19/pope-francis-to-bishop-critical-of-duterte-i-am-with-you.

Villaluz, Geraldine delos Cientos. "Inay Malinandang, Talaandig: Charting a Path Toward Peace Education." In *Theology, Conflict and Peacebuilding,* edited by Daniel F. Pilario and Robert J. Schreiter, 179–92. Quezon City, Philippines: St. Vincent School of Theology, Adamson University Press, 2019.

Wijesinghe, Shirley Lal. "Sri Lanka: Prophetic Initiatives amidst Deadly Conflict." In *Artisans of Peace: Grassroots Peacemaking among Christian Communities,* edited by Mary Ann Cejka and Tomas Bamat, 178–80. Maryknoll, NY: Orbis, 2003.

27

Paths of Re-Encounter: Forgiveness, Liberation, and Nonviolence in Times of Transitional Justice

Soledad del Villar Tagle[1]

¿Qué has hecho? La sangre de tu hermano grita desde el suelo pidiendo justicia.

—Gén 4:10, PDT

What have you done? Your brother's blood cries out to me from the ground.

—Gen 4:10, NABRE[2]

THE CENTRAL METAPHOR OF the encyclical *Fratelli Tutti* is that of brother-/sisterhood or fraternity. Promoting peace and social friendship happens, according to Francis, by recognizing each other as brothers and sisters and being invited to a love that goes beyond the borders of geography and place. Furthermore, following Francis of Assisi, the pope seeks to expand this fra-

---

1. Translated by Karen M. Kraft.
2. Translator's note: In the author's original text, the Spanish translation of the Bible she uses, *Palabra de Dios para Todos*, includes the words *pidiendo justicia* (seeking justice) in God's words to Cain. Unable to find the word "justice" among any of the English translations of this Bible verse, I opted for the NABRE translation here.

ternity to include not only humanity but all of creation (*FT* 1–2). In the face of such a noble ideal, it is at least ironic to acknowledge that, when it comes to fraternity, the biblical tradition is radically honest and recognizes that our starting point as humanity is not that of ideal fraternal relationships but of relationships broken by envy, murder, and indifference. The first "brotherly" relationship within the biblical narrative is the relationship between Cain and Abel. In fact, the word *sin* is used for the first time in the book of Genesis, not to refer to Adam and Eve but instead to speak of Cain's envy and anger toward his brother (Gen 4:7). It is precisely this paradigmatic story of the absence of fraternity that is at the root of human conflicts and from which humanity is called to rebuild its relationships.

The seventh chapter of *Fratelli Tutti* returns precisely to the harsh reality of the social and political conflict "between brothers" to propose ways of reencounter that begin with truth and memory and collectively open us to the possibility of justice, forgiveness, and reconciliation. In this, the Argentine pope is not naive. As a Jesuit priest and later archbishop of Buenos Aires, he had to deal with the tragic history of his country, marked by a long military dictatorship (1976–1983) that used torture, murder, and the disappearance of people as strategies to eliminate its enemies and exercise power. The Argentine dictatorship and its human rights violations were the local expression of broader regional conflicts linked to the world order of the Cold War and which mark the recent history of Latin America. The civil wars in Central America, the dictatorships in Chile, Uruguay, Brazil, and Argentina, and the human rights violations committed by the state in countries such as Peru, Colombia, and Mexico all bear witness to a complex history of political violence that is part of our continent's reality. For this reason, the search for truth, justice, forgiveness, and reconciliation has been at the center of Latin American politics in recent decades. Several countries have confronted their violent pasts through truth and reconciliation commissions, processes to memorialize horror, and other efforts guided by the framework of transitional justice.

Above all, it has been the victims and survivors of human rights violations who have found their voice, reclaiming their own space in the public sphere, and reshaping the way in which Latin American societies face the violence of their past and present. This political development constitutes a challenge for Christians in Latin America, where the circumstances invite them to rethink categories central to the faith, such as forgiveness and reconciliation. In chapter 7 of *Fratelli Tutti*, Pope Francis accepts this challenge and invites us to examine the Gospel call to forgiveness, taking as a starting point the victims of exclusion and violence: "If we have to begin anew, it must always be from the least of our brothers and sisters" (*FT* 235). In this,

Francis embraces the fundamental orientation of Latin American liberation theology, reconsidering central elements of the Christian tradition from the perspective of the poor and the victims of oppression and social sin.

Starting with the victims, Francis offers us a reinterpretation of forgiveness, which takes into account not only the oppressor's needs for forgiveness and mercy but above all the victims' needs for truth, justice, and liberation. The pope appears to be aware of the frequent manipulation of Christian forgiveness in the public sphere. According to Francis, the word *forgiveness* has been historically used to permit impunity for the oppressors (FT 241), to silence the victims by forgiving in their name (FT 246), to encourage oblivion (FT 246), to fuel fatalism, inertia, injustice, and even to justify intolerance and violence (FT 327). On this point, he coincides with the observation from the South African context made by theologian John De Gruchy, who states that, in the public sphere, forgiveness can become "a tool in the manipulation of power relations"[3] used by those in power to strengthen their position and weaken the victims. When the powerful demand forgiveness from the victims, they often do so to silence their voices and maintain the status quo. Consequently, we must be conscious that any political call for forgiveness or reconciliation can hide calculated strategies that are capable of corrupting the gratuitousness of the gesture.[4] For this reason, the pope's clarifications are important, as they allow for a better understanding of the place of forgiveness in societies and communities that decide to contend with a violent past, and the relationship of forgiveness with other fundamental concepts such as memory, truth, and justice, starting with the victims.

First, for Francis, the path of forgiveness requires memory. Trying to overcome the conflict and "bind wounds by decree or to cover injustices in a cloak of oblivion" (FT 246) is a false path that makes the victims invisible and hides the truth of the violence that is at the root of the constitution of the social order. Moreover, following the theologian Robert J. Schreiter, we can affirm that a constitutive part of the dynamics of violence is precisely the silencing of the narrative of the other.[5] Violence is not irrational but rather has a rationality whose objective is precisely the destruction of rationalities that are alternatives to the hegemonic. Violence, therefore, not only attacks our physical bodies but also our sense of identity and security, which are constructed via narratives.[6]

---

3. De Gruchy, *Reconciliation*, 172.
4. Derrida, *El Siglo y El Perdón*, 8.
5. Schreiter, *Reconciliation*, 30–33.
6. Schreiter, *Reconciliation*, 30–33.

In opposition to the truth of a people's own narratives, violence imposes narratives of the lie: "the purpose of torture, imprisonment, and coercion is not to end narratives—that is done most efficiently by simple execution—but to provide another narrative so that people will learn to live with and acquiesce to the will of the oppressor."[7] This narrative of the lie is key to maintaining violent control of a society. The assumption is that, sooner or later, the lie will be accepted as true in substitution of the original narratives. The truth can then be replaced or co-opted, and "[a]ny attempt on the part of a population to return to its older, favored narratives is met with violence or the threat of violence."[8]

It is precisely because the silencing of the truth is at the root of political and community cycles that perpetuate violence that the victims' memory becomes a central element in promoting human forgiveness and reconciliation. Moreover, memory becomes necessary not only to affirm the dignity of the victims and the truthfulness of their narratives but also to call to conversion those who exercise violence or face the temptation to exercise it. For this reason, Francis declares that horrors such as the Shoah, the atomic bombings of Hiroshima and Nagasaki, the persecutions, the slave trade, and the ethnic massacres that occur in different countries must be remembered time and again "and ever anew. We must never grow accustomed or inured to them" (*FT* 247–48).

Facing these horrors, the pope calls us to ask God for "the grace to be ashamed of what we men have done, to be ashamed of this massive idolatry, of having despised and destroyed our own flesh which you formed from the earth, to which you gave life with your own breath of life. Never again, Lord, never again!" (*FT* 247). Returning to the story of Cain and Abel, we can say that it is precisely the memory of Abel's blood, which cries out to humanity to jolt it out of its indifference and call it to work to guarantee the long-awaited "Never Again" that has been the banner of struggle for so many organizations of relatives of those who are victims of human rights violations in Latin America.

Second, the pope clarifies that forgiveness and mercy cannot become excuses for impunity. The call to universal love, which includes enemies and oppressors, does not imply a passive attitude toward their crimes but instead implies that we work to take away the power that allows them to oppress, while caring for and affirming the dignity of the victims:

> We are called to love everyone, without exception; at the same time, loving an oppressor does not mean allowing him to keep

---

7. Schreiter, *Reconciliation*, 35.
8. Schreiter, *Reconciliation*, 35.

oppressing us, or letting him think that what he does is acceptable. On the contrary, true love for an oppressor means seeking ways to make him cease his oppression; it means stripping him of a power that he does not know how to use, and that diminishes his own humanity and that of others. Forgiveness does not entail allowing oppressors to keep trampling on their own dignity and that of others, or letting criminals continue their wrongdoing. Those who suffer injustice have to defend strenuously their own rights and those of their family, precisely because they must preserve the dignity they have received as a loving gift from God. (*FT* 241)

Similarly, forgiveness does not oppose justice or the efforts of a society to free itself from oppressive powers but rather, it demands them (*FT* 241). In this, the pope's ideas resonate with those of theologian Jon Sobrino, who proposes a structural way of understanding forgiveness. For him, "what faith demands first is liberation from this sinful reality and the humanization of the victims and then, by derivation, the rehabilitation of the sinner and the humanization of the offender."[9] This process is what he calls "forgiving reality." If we want to forgive reality, we must commit ourselves and work to stop violence and oppression. This is done, first and foremost, to liberate the victims from their unjust sufferings. The task then involves eradicating the sin but forgiving the sinner. Liberation from oppression also means "destroying the person oppressing, in his formal capacity as oppressor."[10] Paradoxically, in doing so, the oppressor is also saved. In this way, Sobrino interprets the praxis of Jesus: "[t]hrough love of the oppressed, Jesus tells the truth plainly to the oppressors, denounces them, unmasks them, curses them, and threatens them with final dehumanization. But in this, Jesus is also paradoxically in favor of the oppressors. It is a paradoxical form of love, offering them salvation by destroying them as sinners."[11] In that sense, the process of forgiving the oppressor begins with the unmasking of his sin, with the denunciation of his narrative of the lie, and putting a stop to his ability to bring death to others. In doing so, salvation and liberation open up to the oppressor, and forgiveness is possible.

Working for a world in which there is justice is, therefore, intrinsically related to the task of forgiveness. But if we have justice, why do we still need forgiveness? What is its specific role in achieving a more fraternal society? Miroslav Volf states that we need forgiveness, because "strict restorative

9. Sobrino, *Principle of Mercy*, 60–61.
10. Sobrino, *Principle of Mercy*, 65.
11. Sobrino, *Principle of Mercy*, 65.

justice can never be satisfied."¹² Crimes cannot be undone and the consequences of them will never be repaired in full. The lives of the disappeared men and women cannot be returned to their family and friends. The minds and bodies of those who were tortured will bear the consequences for life. Nothing can compensate for the effects that sin has had on the lives of the victims. Justice shows its limits, and it is precisely in that limit that forgiveness appears as an open possibility that will prevent us from repeating the cycle of violence and oppression again and again. The paradox of forgiveness is, as Jacques Derrida says, that we can only forgive the unforgivable.¹³

In the face of the unforgivable, two alternatives remain for the pope: revenge or forgiveness. The first is a temptation, and the second, a grace from God and a free and generous decision of the victims. For Francis, forgiveness is above all the possibility that the victims have to heal their wounds and relieve the resentment and hatred that resemble "a struggle that I carry within me, a little flame deep in my heart that needs to be extinguished before it turns into a great blaze" (*FT* 243). Therefore, the key in the search for truth and justice "is not to fuel anger, which is unhealthy for our own soul and the soul of our people, or to become obsessed with taking revenge and destroying the other" (*FT* 242). As Francis says, "Those who truly forgive do not forget. Instead, they choose not to yield to the same destructive force that caused them so much suffering. They break the vicious circle; they halt the advance of the forces of destruction. They choose not to spread in society the spirit of revenge that will sooner or later return to take its toll" (*FT* 251). Consequently, forgiveness becomes a key element that allows victims to assert their own dignity and interrupt the cycle of revenge, thus opening paths for the nonviolent resolution of the conflicts that divide human societies.

As John De Gruchy makes clear, forgiveness is not something that is "earned by perpetrators."¹⁴ It is rather a gratuitous act that is in the hands of the victims. Even if the truth is revealed and the oppressor loses his ability to oppress, the decision to forgive remains in the hands of the victimized. It is not a right, nor is it the property of the former oppressor, nor does it depend on his repentance. It is, ultimately, a gift that has the potential to humanize both the aggressor and the victim in different ways. Forgiveness is thus a "'two-way process' in which both victim and perpetrator '[are] able to share a common idiom of humanity, a sense of *human* relationship

---

12. Volf, *Exclusion and Embrace*, 122.
13. Derrida, *El Siglo y el Perdón*, 8.
14. De Gruchy, *Reconciliation*, 180.

between them."'[15] The possibility of forgiveness "demonstrates that victims are no longer trapped in their 'victim-hood,' but have overcome the evil that sought to destroy their humanity and make them victims."[16] In this sense, forgiveness expresses an important change in power relations. Like revenge, forgiveness can be "a protest against being reduced to victims. It is another way of expressing power amidst powerlessness, but only now it is not an expression of destruction but of healing."[17]

The work of a more fraternal society, which Francis proposes in *Fratelli Tutti*, needs the free grace of forgiveness. This grace that ultimately comes from God is historically present in the faces of so many victims who, in their struggle for truth, justice, and reconciliation, have chosen to renounce revenge, creating space for a more humane future for all. In these men and women, it is possible to hear the cry of the earth that calls for justice for Abel and demands a new way of being brothers and sisters. In these men and women, it is also possible to see the face of the dead and risen Jesus, the one who not only gives us the gift of forgiveness but also of the ability to forgive. The victims' ability to forgive speaks of the restoration of their humanity and their willingness to love, in spite of everything. It is an affirmation that there is no sin or crime that has the power to irrevocably destroy humanity or the victims of history's capacity to love.

Bibliography

De Gruchy, John. *Reconciliation: Restoring Justice*. Minneapolis: Fortress, 2002.
Derrida, Jacques. *El Siglo y el Perdón, Seguido de Fe y Saber*. Buenos Aires: La Flor, 2003.
Francis, Pope. *Fratelli Tutti: On Fraternity and Social Friendship*. Vatican City: Libreria Editrice Vaticana, 2020. https://www.vatican.va/content/francesco/en/encyclicals/documents/papa-francesco_20201003_enciclica-fratelli-tutti.html.
Gobodo-Madikizela, Pumla. "Legacies of Violence: An In-Depth Analysis of Two Case Studies Based on Interviews with Perpetrators of a 'Necklace' Murder and with Eugene de Kock." PhD diss., University of Cape Town, 2000.
Schreiter, Robert J. *Reconciliation: Mission and Ministry in a Changing Social Order*. Maryknoll, NY: Orbis, 1992.
Sobrino, Jon. *The Principle of Mercy*. Maryknoll, NY: Orbis, 1994.
Volf, Miroslav. *Exclusion and Embrace: A Theological Exploration of Identity, Otherness, and Reconciliation*. Nashville: Abingdon, 1996.

---

15. De Gruchy, *Reconciliation*, 176. Here, De Gruchy is quoting Gobodo-Madikizela, "Legacies of Violence," 244.
16. De Gruchy, *Reconciliation*, 177.
17. De Gruchy, *Reconciliation*, 179.

28

"There Is No Life on This Side of the Fire": Conflict and Penitential Memory on the Path of Encounter

KELLY S. JOHNSON

BRYAN STEVENSON, LAWYER, AUTHOR, and anti-death penalty activist, once gave a speech in Germany after which an audience member noted that, given its history, Germany could never justify systematically executing people, and all the more so if the people being executed were disproportionately Jewish. Yet in the US, Stevenson notes, with its history of enslaving, terrorizing, and plundering African Americans and in the face of evidence of continuing racial injustice in its criminal justice system, this sensibility does not exist. We typically ask, "Do these criminals deserve to die?" Stevenson invites his listeners to ask instead, "Do we deserve to kill?"[1] This question needs to be heard, given that a recent study shows that a majority of people in the US favor continuing to use the death penalty, in spite of the fact that most people also think it does not deter crime and may result in the execution of the innocent. The data indicate that this support is rooted in moral commitments. It seems that many in the US see the willingness to kill in some cases as part of the character of a just people and see themselves as that just people.[2]

---

1. Stevenson, "We Need to Talk."
2. Pew Research Center, "Most Americans."

Memory matters. Our sense of who deserves to kill depends on the stories we remember. An author promoting Catholic support for rights to gun ownership hints at the pivotal story when he writes, "Catholics are still called to heed a chivalric code and, by Church teaching, to defend the lives of the helpless—and, these days, it might sometimes take a firearm to accomplish that."[3] The key word here is "chivalric": strong, moral people (usually imagined as masculine) protect those who are weak and passive (often imagined as feminine) from those who pose a threat (often imagined as a racial or ethnic other). Once the story is construed this way, those who identify with the noble knight can only see a call for peace as a call to abdicate justice and responsibility. It's a heavy burden, being the one with all the power, or at least with a lot of the weapons. A military budget that can put 55 billion dollars into new bombers and hundreds of billions more into updating nuclear capability[4] is justified by the belief that the good guys have a duty to pay the costs (and the right to gain the benefits) of killing the bad guys to keep the world safe. This heroic identity blots out the stories of those who have suffered violence from these good guys. The belief that our killing is chivalric closes off uncomfortable encounters.

Fratelli Tutti's opening vignette about St. Francis (*FT* 3) inverts that story. Francis goes unarmed to the court of Sultan al-Malik al-Kamil, where the encyclical tells us he "did not wage a war of words aimed at imposing doctrines; he simply spread the love of God" (*FT* 4). The saint does not rely on his innocence to ensure his right to use force. Instead, St. Francis, who in his youth dreamt of being a knight, goes to the Sultan as an unarmed Christian penitent. His faith means that instead of risking heroic confrontation with enemies, he risks encounter with a stranger in the hope that he might become a brother.

This scene illustrates much that *Fratelli Tutti* says about the qualities of Christian life in the face of violence: rather than "lording it over others" (*FT* 238), the Christian's call is to be gentle even with one's enemies (*FT* 239), to do the personal work of turning one's heart from vengeance (*FT* 251), and to build the strength that responds to injustice by doing good (*FT* 243). Without anger or fear, the Christian is to stand in the midst of conflict to promote a healing encounter that will honor the truth of our kinship[5] as God's children. But the image of unarmed St. Francis sits uneasily alongside another claim of *Fratelli Tutti*, one central to our ideas of heroic violence:

3. Fitzpatrick, "Catholic Case."
4. Burns, "In a Future Bomber Force."
5. I realize that "kinship" is not a synonym of "fraternity." It is, however, the best English approximation that is gender neutral, and its use by Fr. Greg Boyle bears a strong affinity to some aspects of *Fratelli Tutti*'s teaching. Boyle, *Barking to the Choir*.

"true love for an oppressor means . . . stripping him of a power he does not know how to use. . . . Those who suffer injustice have to defend strenuously their own rights and those of their family, precisely because they must preserve the dignity they have received as a loving gift from God" (*FT* 241). Who deserves to strip the oppressor of power? How? What stories do we need to remember as we defend human dignity?

Conflict as Encounter

The mid-twentieth century civil rights movement in the US illustrates the possibility of stripping an oppressor of unjust power without using violence, but truthful memory about it demonstrates the necessity of very clear thinking about violence, conflict, and anger. The movement's leadership strategically deployed nonviolent actions, as Martin Luther King put it, "to create such a crisis and foster such a tension that a community which has constantly refused to negotiate is forced to confront the issue."[6] Demonstrators, he wrote, "are not the creators of tension. We merely bring to the surface the hidden tension that's already alive."[7] At the time, critics blamed the movement for stirring up conflict and causing violence, even as its participants accepted insults and beatings without striking back. White Christian leaders greeted the attempt to use nonviolent pressure by blaming the organizers for actions that "incite to hatred and violence," seeing the demonstrations as only "technically peaceful."[8] For those whose very bodily presence is itself read as violence, no activity is recognized as nonviolent.

The lesson from those years should be clear: a system in which generations have been deprived of recognition as fellow human beings, terrorized and murdered for any resistance, is not only injustice. It is itself already violence. Those who disrupt it with an aim toward a more just order are not the creators of conflict; they are engaged in the work of making peace.

When Francis argues that "violent public demonstrations . . . do not help in finding solutions" because they have unclear, mixed, even counterproductive objectives and may be the result of political manipulation (*FT* 232), the pope is naming a real danger, but one that needs more careful description. The swell of heated emotion in a demonstration can make it susceptible to unjust and undisciplined action. Driven by an organized campaign of misinformation and fearmongering, people can become a mob that terrorizes those who try to stand for justice. But we need a countervailing

---

6. King, "Letter from Birmingham Jail," 89.
7. King, "Letter from Birmingham Jail," 96.
8. "Statement by Alabama Clergymen."

recognition that disruptive actions may indeed have a role in the service of justice and truth.⁹

To move toward encounter, a society mired in falsehood must go through the disruption of encountering truth, including the truth of anger. When the pope speaks of anger only as "unhealthy for our own soul and the soul of our people" (*FT* 242), he misses an opportunity to recognize kinds of anger that are "a potentially healthy, potentially healing response to oppression and exploitation"¹⁰ and a manifestation of human dignity.¹¹ Francis urges readers to listen to the voices of those who have suffered and been ignored. He knows that "if at times the poor and the dispossessed react with attitudes that appear antisocial, we should realize that in many cases those reactions are born of a history of scorn and social exclusion" (*FT* 234). Is it not possible that these "antisocial" attitudes may in fact be more just and truthful than what Augustine calls "the calmness of men of sound mind" (*FT* 265), the cool analysis of those who have not endured injustice?

Fratelli Tutti is part of a long line of Catholic teaching that treats social friction only as a danger or failing. This teaching fosters in many Catholics a suspicion of those who will not resign themselves to an unjust social order, when it needs to nourish a determination to work with them for a more truthful and just social order. Conflict, after all, is an indication that people are in contact. It can be an opportunity to deepen a relationship. Pope Francis cites John Paul II's words: "The Church is well aware that in the course of history conflicts of interest between different social groups inevitably arise, and that in the face of such conflicts Christians must often take a position, honestly and decisively" (*FT* 240). But his emphasis that "unity is greater than conflict" (*FT* 245) means that conflict is only presented as a trial to be endured or a problem to be overcome, not as an ordinary and possibly beneficial part of human life. Encounter is a contact sport. Constructive conflict must be an aspect of our repertoire for thinking about justice and peace.

The Fire of Penitential Memory

Claiming conflict as opportunity requires developing a "moral imagination" in which we can see ourselves "in a web of relationships that includes our

---

9. The work of Erica Chenoweth and Maria Stephan has highlighted the possibilities and successes of nonviolent civil resistance around the world. See Chenoweth and Stephan, *Why Civil Resistance Works*.

10. Hooks, *Killing Rage*, 12.

11. Rocha, "Gift of Blackness."

enemies."[12] The restorative justice (RJ) movement offers an example of the kind of work required. RJ refers to a diverse set of practices and theories used around the world in many contexts to address harm by prioritizing the healing of relationships. In a process called "circles," offenders offer full disclosure of their actions, victims speak of the harm they suffered and the needs arising from that harm, and offenders accept obligations to address those needs. The encounter can be both harrowing and life-giving.

A recent conference hosted by the Catholic Mobilizing Network included a session on restorative justice and "Repairing Historical Harms." Maka Akan Najin Black Elk, executive director of Truth and Healing at Red Cloud Indian School in South Dakota, and Cherylynn Branche, president of the GU272 Descendants Association, spoke of the harm their communities suffered at the hands of the Catholic Church and the Jesuit order. Both hold that as Catholics they must require the institution they love to face its sin and make costly change. They welcomed into their conversation Sr. Bridget Bearss of the Society of the Sacred Heart, an educator and social justice advocate who spoke of her realizations that her order had enslaved people and that she personally had perpetuated racial injustice, even as she had imagined herself as a champion of justice and human dignity.

> Grounded in the contradiction between what I want my life to stand for and the truth I had not let in and let touch my heart, I found myself catapulted into a despair and discouragement that left me paralyzed and immobilized. Better, I supposed, to just sit and wait until Twitter or the *New York Times* condemned us and we could slip away. Sometimes our past becomes too painful to remain in the present.[13]

She discovered, however, that she does still belong in the circle. She belongs now in the seat of the offender.

> I found a place in the circle to keep my heart open while black and brown women that I loved dearly as students told me their own experience about racism that they experienced while under my watch as their head of school, and my own blind spots that contributed to their suffering. I learned that there's a place for me to sit and listen with a cracked-open heart to what happened then and to ask for what is needed and to make it the rest of my life's work.[14]

---

12. Lederach, *Moral Imagination*, 5.
13. Catholic Mobilizing Network, "Workshop."
14. Catholic Mobilizing Network, "Workshop."

When *Fratelli Tutti* tells us that "Forgiveness is precisely what enables us to pursue justice without falling into a spiral of revenge or the injustice of forgetting" (*FT* 252), it seems to be referring to this kind of encounter, where the paralysis of shame is replaced by the hard and hopeful work of living as the offender. This is grueling work for all parties. As one participant in the conference said, "Restorative justice requires that we walk through fire. But there is no life on this side of the fire."[15]

Building a society of kinship requires that we confront the false identity of the hero so that encounter becomes possible. For those whose sense of self (as, for example, US American or Catholic, white or educated or prosperous or ordained) depends on playing the role of the hero or the victim but never the offender, the truth that our social order is founded in and continues even now in violence can be devastating. Some Catholics have taken up a defensive insistence that attention to such truths is a form of Marxist class warfare, a manipulation of long past and now irrelevant harms inimical to personal responsibility.[16] Truthful memory, however, is essential for producing a transformative "collective conscience" (*FT* 249). *Fratelli Tutti* wisely teaches that peace must "start anew from the truth" through "penitential memory" (*FT* 226). Such truth is not a weapon of the heroic savior; it is the purgatory that leads to redemption.

Fear, individualism, and a loss of shared moral vision (*FT* 25–30) are obstacles to our ability to live together as kin. But at least in my society, the greater problem, and perhaps particularly among Catholics, is that so many associate holiness with heroic triumph over evil, with chivalry, rather than courageous openness to conversion. The need to be the hero rather than a penitent sibling blocks our shared future as kin.

When Pope Francis writes, "Family disputes are always resolved afterwards" (*FT* 230), he is speaking, clearly, of an idealized family life. Actual family disputes are not always resolved and violence in the home is common.[17] Even where internal family life is loving, loyalty to one's own is a common justification of violence: in order to protect my family, I attack anyone who threatens them. Recognizing all humanity as family should not

---

15. I have not been able to find the source of this comment in my notes, although Danielle Sered offered a similar image. I extend my gratitude to this unnamed contributor.

16. Kay, "Bishop Barron."

17. In the US, about one in seven children are abused at some point during a year, and over their lifetimes, about a third of women and a quarter of men endure physical violence from a sexual partner. National Center for Injury Prevention and Control, *Preventing Child Abuse and Neglect,* 10; National Coalition Against Domestic Violence, "Statistics."

become a new heroic delusion. Family, like every natural good, is caught up in the brokenness of creation. Indeed, the family that Jesus is calling together is "always on the verge of failure."[18] The sign of the family of God in our day is not its victory over the forces of injustice, nor even its tender compassion for the wounded, but its turning with broken, humbled hearts toward mercy. The story of Christianity is dying to self and living in the hope of a kinship that humanity is only beginning to know. In that family, we may finally be able to discover who we really are.[19]

Bibliography

Boyle, Greg. *Barking to the Choir: The Power of Radical Kinship*. New York: Simon and Schuster, 2017.

Burns, Robert. "In a Future Bomber Force, Old and Ugly Beats New and Snazzy." *AP News*, July 25, 2020. https://apnews.com/article/ap-top-news-air-force-technology-mo-state-wire-politics-df0e81b91ad9a945032ba4972c754426.

Catholic Mobilizing Network. "Workshop: Repairing Historical Harms." Session hosted at the Harm, Healing, and Human Dignity: An All-Virtual Catholic Conference on Restorative Justice, October 31, 2020. Video, 1:15:19. https://catholicsmobilizing.org/conference/schedule/workshop-repairing-historical-harms.

Cavanaugh, William. "The Church among Idols." *Christian Century* 138:12 (June 16, 2021) 26–31.

Chenoweth, Erica, and Maria Stephan. *Why Civil Resistance Works: The Strategic Logic of Nonviolent Conflict*. New York: Columbia University Press, 2011.

Fitzpatrick, Sean. "A Catholic Case for the Second Amendment." *Crisis Magazine*, July 14, 2020. https://www.crisismagazine.com/2020/a-catholic-case-for-the-second-amendment.

Francis, Pope. *Fratelli Tutti: On Fraternity and Social Friendship*. Vatican City: Libreria Editrice Vaticana, 2020. https://www.vatican.va/content/francesco/en/encyclicals/documents/papa-francesco_20201003_enciclica-fratelli-tutti.html.

Hauerwas, Stanley. "Sacrificing the Sacrifices of War." In *War and the American Difference: Theological Reflections on Violence and National Identity*, 53–70. Grand Rapids, MI: Baker Academic, 2011.

Hooks, Bell. *Killing Rage: Ending Racism*. New York: Holt, 1995.

Kay, Pablo. "Bishop Barron: Why the Church Can't Stay Woke—or Stay Quiet." *Angelus News*, April 22, 2021. https://angelusnews.com/arts-culture/bishop-barron-why-the-church-cant-stay-woke-or-stay-quiet/.

King, Martin Luther, Jr. "Letter from Birmingham Jail." In *Why We Can't Wait*, 64–84. Boston: Beacon, 1986.

Lederach, John Paul. *The Moral Imagination: The Art and Soul of Building Peace*. Oxford: Oxford University Press, 2005.

---

18. Cavanaugh, "Church among Idols," 26–31.

19. My sincere thanks to Tyler Campbell, Laurie Eloe, and Katlyn Toelle for their assistance with revisions of this essay.

National Center for Injury Prevention and Control. *Preventing Child Abuse and Neglect: A Technical Package for Policy, Norm, and Programmatic Activities.* Atlanta: Centers for Disease Control, 2016.

National Coalition Against Domestic Violence. "Statistics." https://ncadv.org/STATISTICS.

Pew Research Center. "Most Americans Favor the Death Penalty Despite Concerns about Its Administration." June 2, 2021. https://www.pewresearch.org/politics/2021/06/02/most-americans-favor-the-death-penalty-despite-concerns-about-its-administration/.

Rocha, Samuel D. "The Gift of Blackness to the Church: An Interview with EWTN's Gloria Purvis." *Church Life Journal*, July 20, 2020. https://churchlifejournal.nd.edu/articles/the-gift-of-blackness/#.X5Nf_CNBPtA.twitter.

"Statement by Alabama Clergymen." The Martin Luther King, Jr. Research and Education Institute, Stanford University, April 12, 1963. https://kinginstitute.stanford.edu/sites/mlk/files/lesson-activities/clergybirmingham1963.pdf.

Stevenson, Bryan. "We Need to Talk about an Injustice." Long Beach, CA, March 2012. TED video, 23:25. https://www.ted.com/talks/bryan_stevenson_we_need_to_talk_about_an_injustice?language=en#t-482200.

PART EIGHT

Religions at the Service of Fraternity in Our World

29

An Affirmation of God's Universal Paternity and a Repudiation of Religious Persecutions

Ikenna Ugochukwu Okafor

Introduction

AFRICA'S RELIGIOUS EXPERIENCES IN modern times have been characterized by positive affectivity. In contradistinction to the West, Africans have never manifested the radical cynicism against religion that is exemplified in the Nietzschean proclamation of God's obituary or other forms of adversarial neoliberal secularism or modern atheistic rationalism. In their appreciation of especially the Christian and Islamic religions as positive forces for social transformation, Africans are open to embracing religious practices and authorities with childlike trust. Among the Igbo of southeast Nigeria, for example, many parents name their children *Ụkamaka*, which means "the church is very wonderful," in order to express their profound appreciation and joyous acceptance of the Christian religion. The radiant beauty of Christianity that many Africans celebrate is a factor in the exponential growth of the religion on the continent within a short period of missionary evangelization.[1] This beauty is intrinsically related to the social dimension of the Christian message, which fosters fraternal solidarity, social justice, peace, and egalitarianism as values of communal living. The apprehension

---

1. Africa is expected to have more adherents to World Christianity by 2050 than any other continent, with a projected number of 1,278,874,000 Christians. See Gordon-Conwell Theological Seminary, Center for the Study of Global Christianity, "Status of Global Christianity, 2019."

of this beauty speaks eloquently about the religious disposition of Africans. Elochukwu Uzukwu rightly notes that in Africa "the perception of and approach to the divine are characterized by flexibility, multiplicity, and tolerance. West African religions in particular and African religions in general, are non-imperial, non-proselytising, and non-absolutizing."[2] This explains why Christianity and Islam have been welcomed by Africans.

African writers like Chinua Achebe have blamed the "falling apart" of the dispensation of African Traditional Religion (ATR) and its sociopolitical constitution on the loss of fraternity and the marginalization of the ethics of care and compassion in church and state in Africa.[3] ATR, through some of its rigid dogmas, taboos, and caste systems, condoned or even institutionalized the marginalization and alienation that afflicted many Africans, and thus inadvertently paved the way for the evangelical advantage in the Christian mission which supplanted it. Hence, the social effects of the loss of fraternity in postcolonial discourse in Africa provide the backdrop for reading and digesting the eighth chapter of *Fratelli Tutti*.

This concluding chapter of the encyclical, which Pope Francis divides into two main topics, underscores the responsibility of religion in guaranteeing social transformation and peaceful coexistence. The first topic asks the question about the ultimate foundation of a stable society and harmonious civic coexistence, as well as the role of Christians in building on that foundation. The second delineates what should be eschewed as extrinsic and inimical to that edifice; namely, religious violence. As a continent that has suffered and is still suffering from the agonies of ethnic bigotry and religious extremisms, Africa's experiences call for honest introspection and the interrogation of its social values in the light of *Fratelli Tutti*. The havoc wrought by religious extremists repudiates the overly positive religious disposition of the inhabitants of the continent and thus challenges Africa's social ethics, theology, and pastoral praxis.

This chapter of the encyclical engages the problem with an opening statement on the goal of interreligious dialogue, which according to the Catholic bishops of India is not diplomacy or tolerance, but the establishment of friendship, peace, and harmony in a spirit of truth and fraternal love (*FT* 271). With this goal in mind, Pope Francis believes that building fraternity and defending justice in society are the principal roles of religions. How can these roles be exercised? On what ultimate foundation can this fraternity and justice be erected?

---

2. Uzukwu, "Re-Evaluating God-Talk," 58.
3. See Okafor, "Fraternal Solidarity."

In response to these questions, the pope believes that religions cannot exercise these roles without an openness to God as the father of all. Men and women cannot pretend to be religious if they do not respect every human person as a creature called to be a child of God. The divine paternity is the bedrock of fraternity and the pillar of peace and harmony in society. Where there is no peace and harmony, there will be no progress. Africa's lack of sustainable progress, therefore, apart from being the result of a faulty system, is also traceable to the practice of religion. If abundant life is to be guaranteed in Africa, the transcendent truth upon which Africans build their religious convictions must be interrogated. If one believes that God is the father of all humans and invariably that people of other faiths are his children too, how then can one justify the violation of the rights of others and their persecution for what they believe? On what basis does one lay claim to the right to kill those he or she has classified as unbelievers?

Universal fraternity is a transcendent truth that we humans cannot violate without offending God (FT 273). When we fail to acknowledge this transcendent truth, then human hubris is let loose by the destructive quest for selfish interests. From the history of how religious witness benefits cultures, Pope Francis stresses that "the effort to seek God with a sincere heart, provided it is never sullied by ideological or self-serving aims, helps us recognize one another as travelling companions, truly brothers and sisters" (FT 274). Therefore, the recognition of one another as brothers and sisters should be one of the primary precepts of all religious pedagogy.

Christian Identity as Being Part of a Family Among Families

Condemning materialistic philosophies that deify the human person and introduce worldly values in place of supreme and transcendental principles (FT 275), the pope defends the right of the church to ensure the requisite religious pedagogy and to engage issues in the public square. The church, he argues, works for the advancement of humanity and universal fraternity, offering herself as "a family among families." In imitation of Mary, the Mother of Jesus, this is a church "that serves, that leaves home and goes forth from its places of worship, in order to accompany life, to sustain hope, to be the sign of unity, to build bridges, to break down walls, to sow seeds of reconciliation" (FT 276). This self-understanding of the church helps her fulfill her mission as a religion of peace and love and to inspire other faiths similarly.

Speaking about Christian identity, therefore, the encyclical reiterates Vatican II's affirmation that the church esteems the works of God in other religions and "rejects nothing of what is true and holy in these religions. She has a high regard for their manner of life and conduct, their precepts and doctrines which ... often reflect a ray of that truth which enlightens all men and women" (FT 277, quoting *Nostra Aetate*, 2). Christian identity cannot be understood apart from interfaith social friendship and fraternity. Pope Francis conceives it as a listening to the music of the Gospel in our homes, public squares, workplaces, and political and financial lives, so that we can "hear the strains that challenge us to defend the dignity of every man and woman" (FT 277). For us Christians, the wellspring of human dignity and fraternity is in the Gospel of Jesus Christ. So, in what does the music of that Gospel consist?

This music of the Gospel resonates in my encounter with a child who, trekking a long distance with his younger sister on his back, turned down my offer of a free ride. In response to my reference to his sister as being too heavy for him to carry, he said, "She is not too heavy for me, she is my sister." It was expressed so matter-of-factly, as if to demonstrate that the principal reason why the little girl on his back is not a burden is precisely because she is his sister.[4] Indeed, no other reason could be more plausible, for it is obvious that the boy could not have been able or willing to carry any other type of load that weighs exactly as much as his sister in a similar circumstance. With his tenacity in bearing the burden, the boy demonstrated that in the consciousness of having intimate fraternal ties with one another, human beings can discover an incalculable inner strength capable of making heavy burdens seem light by virtue of a sense of responsibility that is purely motivated and nourished by love. Whenever fraternal love animates our actions, carrying one another becomes an altruistic experience. This is the music of the Gospel, whose symphony is capable of eliminating or smoothing the jangling discord of racialism, ethnicism, religious fundamentalism, and sexism. In carrying one another, we all come to partake in the merits of the cross of Christ and the redemption it brings to humankind.

Women and Fraternity in Church and State

Liberation theologies have not failed to remind us of the demands of carrying one another. Prior to the publication of the encyclical, there was dissatisfaction over the term "fraternity" because it does not adequately capture some feminists' ideas of inclusiveness or gender neutrality, ideas that have increasingly characterized postmodern discourse.[5] Pope Francis observes,

---

4. Okafor, *Toward an African Theology*, 2–4.

5. Phyllis Zagano, a senior research associate in residence at Hofstra University, penned a bitter criticism of the perceived exclusion of women in *Fratelli Tutti*. See Zagano, "'Fratelli Tutti.'"

however, that the Blessed Virgin Mary is a model and the mother of this journey of fraternity. Mary's visit to her cousin Elizabeth, her intercession at the marriage feast in Cana, and her maternal grief at the foot of the cross are manifestations of the fullness of empathy to which her life was a testimony. She is the transcript of grace that humankind receives from God. "Having received this universal motherhood at the foot of the cross (cf. John 19:26), Mary cares not only for Jesus but also for 'the rest of her children' (cf. Rev 12:17)" (*FT* 278). Accordingly, the role of women in the establishment of a fraternal and peaceful society is a cornerstone to the irenic project of which *Fratelli Tutti* is the master plan. The feminine genius, which the Blessed Virgin Mary epitomizes as the handmaid of the Lord, whose fiat was an essential key to redemption and abundant life, should shine forth in all religions, overturning the status quo of structural injustice.

In this sense, African women must take an active role in the political, economic, and religious leadership of the continent in order to midwife the birth of a new, more just, more peaceful, and more fraternal society. The recent appointment of Ngozi Okonjo Iweala as the first Black director general of the World Trade Organization is an affirmation of the African feminine genius. At a time when rogue politicians (mostly men) are mortgaging the economic future of African youths, it is important to look to women in Africa for lessons in public service and fraternal leadership. Herein lies the importance of Pope Francis's extolling of Mary's role in the economy of salvation and as the mother of the journey of fraternity. He reminds us that in the power of the risen Lord, Mary "wants to give birth to a new world, where all of us are brothers and sisters, where there is room for all those whom our societies discard, where justice and peace are resplendent" (*FT* 278). In the same vein, like the first women who encountered the risen Lord, women must not shy away from bringing Christ's message of peace and abundant life to their African brothers and sisters in all aspects of society.

African women must endeavor to cultivate a countercurrent to the culture of violence that is inimical to Africa's progress. By advocating for religious freedom, African women will contribute to safeguarding a fundamental human right, which proclaims our ability to build harmony and understanding between different cultures and religions, as well as testifies to the need to find a means of serene, ordered, and peaceful coexistence. In Africa, this freedom is increasingly becoming elusive to many. It is time to learn anew the virtue of "accepting our differences and rejoicing that, as children of the one God, we are all brothers and sisters" (*FT* 279). For Pope Francis, Christian unity is an essential desideratum for building a universal fraternity and serving humanity. Therefore, African women must educate their children and influence their husbands on the need to overcome the colonial heritage of interdenominational polemics between Catholics and Protestants. For unity among Christians is the first step to a fruitful interreligious dialogue and collaboration with Muslims and people of other faiths.

Religion and Violence

Speaking about religion and violence, Pope Francis believes that a journey of peace is possible between religions because God's love is the same for believers as for unbelievers (*FT* 281). To all people of faith, he writes that "believers are challenged to return to their sources of faith, in order to concentrate on what is essential: worship of God and love for our neighbour.... The truth is that violence has no basis in our fundamental religious convictions, but only in their distortion" (*FT* 282). One example of such distortion in Africa is an ideology proclaiming that Western education is forbidden (*haram*) by Islam. Nothing could be further from the truth than this retrograde belief, which has become the most infamous mantra of an extremist propaganda in Nigeria and in her neighboring countries for more than two decades. Sadly, the Nigerian federal government, led predominantly by fanatic Muslims, has only paid lip service to combatting terrorist cells that are inspired by that ideology. The result has been an orgy of bloodbaths, the brutish dehumanization of humans, and widespread insecurity, which all involve a flagrant repudiation of authentic religion. Authentic piety, according to Pope Francis, expresses itself in love (1 John 4:8), and for this reason, terrorism is deplorable. Religious convictions about the sacredness of human life permit us "to recognize the fundamental values of our common humanity, values in the name of which we can and must cooperate, build and dialogue, pardon and grow; this will allow different voices to unite in creating a melody of sublime nobility and beauty, instead of fanatical cries of hatred" (*FT* 283).

The Role of Power in the Establishment of Fraternity: What Is Lacking in *Fratelli Tutti*

Fratelli Tutti addresses the political and religious authorities, but it is important to note some of its shortcomings in highlighting adequately the significance and essential role of power in the establishment of fraternity and the social environment for its flourishing. A position of power is arguably indispensable for the establishment of fraternity. Such power is exercised, for instance, through forgiveness, clemency, and a renunciation of the spurious principle that "might is right." It is through the acceptance of the logic of the cross—the logic of a self-giving sacrifice for the benefit of others—that fraternity becomes established. That logic compels us to reject all temptations of revenge and abuse of power through intimidation or oppression, and thus to allow power to be animated by the spirit of love and social friendship. This understanding is exemplified in the Old Testament biblical narratives of Joseph and his brothers (Gen 37–50). Joseph's reconciliation with his brothers who sold him into slavery was the first time in biblical history where fraternity was successfully established. But what could have happened if Joseph had not risen from being a slave and the victim of fraternal betrayal to occupying a position of power in Egypt—a position which he effectively used not to get revenge for the wrong done to him, but to establish and celebrate filial affection? As Marie-Jo Thiel observes, this biblical story is "replete with hope because after all their mistakes, Joseph's brothers finally know how to renegotiate their brotherhood thanks to a new-found dialogue."[6]

The story of Joseph and his brothers, however, throws light on some important questions: Can the weak and the vulnerable establish fraternal relationships with their oppressors? Is fraternity possible as long as the powerful remains the villain? If the answers to these questions are no, then the possibility of fraternity remains anchored solely on the conversion of the hearts of the mighty, or on the transposition of power. Fraternity will then remain a utopia—a Christian religious ideal whose realization is a responsibility of the powerful, whose position of power and privilege invariably imposes on them a sacred duty to midwife a just and egalitarian society. In this sense, is it not correct to assume that fraternity can only be established when one has overpowered the oppressor and by an act of clemency realized that we are indeed brothers and sisters? The encyclical *Fratelli Tutti* did not anticipate these questions nor address how the victims of injustice who are still in a position of vulnerability and powerlessness have the capacity to establish fraternity with their oppressor(s).

Conclusion

The cross of Christ and the total forgiveness it compels are a divine reproach to the insufferable condition of the victimized and a compassionate exercise of divine power demonstrated as a model for all earthly power. At the foot of the cross, the oppressed are reminded of the power to forgive as the only power they still wield. Fraternity requires forgiveness from the oppressed and contrition from the oppressor. But as long as the

---

6. Thiel and Feix, *Le défi de la fraternité*, 28.

hearts of humans are still tainted by hubris, fraternity remains the dream of a lonely and disdained Joseph, unloved by his more powerful and senior brothers—a dream whose fulfillment is dependent on the transposition of power from the oppressor to the oppressed, whose heart is already converted by grace. The road to true fraternity is a three-way mutual interaction involving both God and humankind. It is a tetrahedron reflecting the essence of God as an undivided and indivisible community of persons united in an eternal harmony.

As if to make up for the above-mentioned shortcoming of the encyclical, Pope Francis concludes with the joint appeal he made with Ahmad Al-Tayyeb, in the name of God, of innocent human lives, of the weak and vulnerable, of all persons of goodwill, and in the name of fraternity, freedom, justice, and mercy. All of these stakeholders and values situate the building of global fraternity as a grand irenic project involving every person and every religion. It is a project that every theologian should acknowledge as the new center of theological discourse. Concluding the encyclical with an ecumenical Christian prayer and a prayer to God as creator, Pope Francis positions fraternity at the center of the spirituality of world Christianity—a Christianity that encompasses all religions and works toward achieving the shared dreams of humanity.

Bibliography

Francis, Pope. *Fratelli Tutti: On Fraternity and Social Friendship*. Vatican City: Libreria Editrice Vaticana, October 3, 2020. http://www.vatican.va/content/francesco/en/encyclicals/documents/papa-francesco_20201003_enciclica-fratelli-tutti.html.

Gordon-Conwell Theological Seminary, Center for the Study of Global Christianity. "Status of Global Christianity, 2019, in the Context of 1900–2050." https://www.gordonconwell.edu/wp-content/uploads/sites/13/2019/04/StatusofGlobalChristianity20191.pdf.

Okafor, Ikenna Ugochukwu. "Fraternal Solidarity and the Ethics of Care and Compassion in Church and State in Africa: A Theological Re-Reading of *Things Fall Apart*." In *Pastoral Renewal, Public Health and the Prophetic Mission of the Church in Africa since the Two African Synods*, edited by Stan Chu Ilo et al., 89–114. Eugene, OR: Pickwick, 2020.

———. *Toward an African Theology of Fraternal Solidarity UBE NWANNE*. African Christian Studies Series 7. Eugene, OR: Pickwick, 2014.

Thiel, Marie-Jo, and Marc Feix, eds. *Le défi de la fraternité: The Challenge of Fraternity*. Vienna: LIT Verlag, 2018.

Uzukwu, Elochukwu. "Re-Evaluating God-Talk from an African Perspective." In *Thinking the Divine in Interreligious Encounter*, edited by Norbert Hintersteiner, 55–72. Currents of Encounter: Studies on the Contact Between Christianity and Other Religions, Beliefs, and Cultures 44. Amsterdam: Rodopi, 2012.

Zagano, Phyllis. "'Fratelli Tutti' Does Not Include Women, and Neither Does 'Fraternity.'" *National Catholic Reporter*, September 21, 2020. https://www.ncronline.org/news/opinion/just-catholic/fratelli-tutti-does-not-include-women-and-neither-does-fraternity.

30

Pope Francis and Interreligious Dialogue: Reading Chapter 8 of *Fratelli Tutti*

Felix Wilfred

Whatever Pope Francis has to say about dialogue among religions should be set within the larger framework of the entire encyclical, which is centered on universal fraternity and social friendship. Consequently, we will do well to read and understand chapter 8, dedicated to interreligious dialogue, through the lens of this central concern of the encyclical; namely, how interreligious dialogue and understanding can serve as a reinvigorating source for peace, fraternity, and harmony in the world.

What the pope is trying to say flows from his own earlier experience in his country, Argentina, and his friendship with peoples of other faiths. Here is a pope who believes that friendship is the portal to interreligious dialogue and understanding. He has cultivated friendship, for example, with Rabbi Abraham Skorka, later with other leaders, and in recent times with the Grand Imam of Al-Azhar, with whom he jointly signed the historic "Document on Human Fraternity for World Peace and Living Together."[1] Pope Francis acknowledges that his friendship with the Grand Imam and their joint statement were sources of great inspiration for his recent encyclical. The Grand Imam, for his part, welcomed the encyclical with a Twitter message that read: "My brother, Pope Francis's message, *Fratelli Tutti*, is an extension of the "Document on Human Fraternity," and reveals a global reality in which the vulnerable and marginalized pay the price for unstable

---

1. Francis and Ahmad Al-Tayyeb, "Document on Human Fraternity."

positions and decisions.... It is a message that is directed to people of good will, whose consciences are alive and restores conscience to humanity."[2]

It is not only chapter 8 of *Fratelli Tutti* that speaks about interreligious dialogue—the entire document is conceived in an interreligious spirit. It is telling that a Muslim judge, Judge Abdel Salam, was one of the four panelists at the presentation of the encyclical at the Vatican; it was the first time ever a non-Christian was part of the team presenting a papal document.

Interreligious Fraternity

In my mother tongue, Tamil—one of the earliest scripted languages of humankind—the word for brother or sister (*sakōtharan/sakōthari*) means "those from the same womb." The same image is conveyed by the etymology for the Greek word for brother or sister (*adelphós/adelphé*). The bondedness originating from the same womb goes beyond religious beliefs—it is a primordial reality that is independent of one's beliefs and convictions. In his earlier encyclical, *Laudato Si'*, Pope Francis showed how we human beings form, along with all other species, the flora and fauna of but the one single family of Mother Earth. *Fratelli Tutti* expresses a deeper understanding of this bondedness among humans by focusing on the harmony and peace that should be fostered in human relationships, inspired by the spirit of fraternity and friendship. In fact, at the very beginning of chapter 8, the pope quotes from the Catholic Bishops' Conference of India saying that "the goal of dialogue is to establish friendship, peace and harmony, and to share spiritual and moral values and experiences in a spirit of truth and love" (*FT* 271).

The pope captured this Asian spirit of interreligious relationships during his apostolic visit to some of the countries on the continent. The interreligious journey of Pope Francis has taken him to visit places of worship of brothers and sisters of other faiths. He visited a Buddhist temple in Sri Lanka; he has also visited synagogues and mosques. Thus, the pope has set a sublime example that can inspire Christians to frequent the places of worship of their neighbors reverently and with a deep sense of respect for what people of other faiths hold as most sacred.

Pope Francis's visit to a Buddhist temple in Sri Lanka was not planned ahead and stage-managed, but something that happened naturally. The head of the temple, who was there to receive the pope at the airport, invited him to visit, and without further ado, the pope accepted a friend's invitation and made adjustments in his program to make the visit possible.[3] "He called

2. O'Connell, "First Muslim."
3. Cf. Kasimow and Race, *Pope Francis*, 30. One cannot help comparing this

me, so we went," is how the pope described the spontaneous nature of his visit to the temple. It is interesting to note how the pope's visit to a Marian shrine in Madhu in Sri Lanka triggered his thoughts and feelings about the Asian way of living interreligious relationships. He witnessed firsthand how Hindus, Buddhists, and Muslims went on pilgrimage to this Marian shrine. While this is quite a common sight in Asia, it was a new experience for the pope, who was very much struck and touched by this interreligious meeting of peoples of different faiths. He asked himself: If these people come to our churches to pray, why should we not go to their sacred places? He offered this question as a further reason for visiting the Buddhist temple. Francis's approach to interreligious friendship and fraternity goes beyond comparing and contrasting beliefs and doctrines. In the Buddhist and Hindu traditions, this is considered *upaya*; that is, a means of apprehending that is not the same thing as seeing the truth or walking on the path of truth, which is *prajna*, or wisdom. Excessive preoccupation with doctrine and orthodoxy can prevent the church from reaching out to other religious traditions.

The new dimension to interreligious dialogue Pope Francis brings in *Fratelli Tutti* flows from his ecclesiology or image of the church. It is not a church *incurvata in se*—bent in on itself. From the beginning of his pontificate, Pope Francis has contemplated a centrifugal church that would be present in the midst of the world and reach out to address the conditions of society and people's aspirations and dreams. The kind of interreligious dialogue he promotes echoes his ecclesiological orientation toward the world and its pastoral needs, very much in line with the teaching of *Gaudium et Spes*. In his words and deeds, Pope Francis blends interreligious dialogue with a pastoral practice that is oriented to the world, beautifully bridging *Nostra Aetate* and *Gaudium et Spes*. From a theological point of view, what he does is indeed a public theology. The realization of his vision of universal fraternity entails that religious resources be brought to bear upon our present-day world and its conflictual situations for the promotion of peace and harmony.

---

approach of Pope Francis with what Cardinal Joseph Ratzinger (later Pope Benedict XVI) voiced about Buddhism from the perspective of a hard-edged doctrinal system: "If Buddhism is attractive, it is because it appears as a possibility of touching the infinite and obtaining happiness without having any concrete religious obligations. A spiritual auto-eroticism [un autoerotism spirituel] of some sort." Quoted in Lefebure, "Cardinal Ratzinger's Comments on Buddhism," 221. If such was his doctrinal posture vis-à-vis Buddhism, I wonder what he would make of interreligious dialogue!

Focus on Common Issues

There was a time when approaching religious diversity meant looking for doctrinal commonalities. The attempt was to discover what we all believe in common, regardless of our particular belief systems. For example, it was thought that theocentrism; that is, a belief in God in general without naming any deity in particular, would bring together all believers. Such an approach may not have successfully facilitated interreligious dialogue, as history and experience amply attest. Pope Francis, instead, draws our attention to the common issues and questions that humanity is grappling with today. This, for him, should be the focal point on which religious beliefs, convictions, and engagements need to converge. The pope names some of these common issues and questions; for example, "religious convictions about the sacred meaning of human life permit us to recognize the fundamental values of our common humanity, values in the name of which we can and must cooperate, build and dialogue, pardon and grow" (FT 283).

In the encyclical, there is a deep acknowledgement of diversity, which fosters mutual respect and goes beyond the search for commonalities. The real challenge we need to face in order to foster a new world of fraternity and solidarity is mutually recognizing and respecting our differences. This logic is true as much for interpersonal as for intergroup relationships. To represent unity in diversity, the pope uses the image of the polyhedron, in which the whole is more than the sum total of its parts, and in which each part remains unique and singular.

Theological and Anthropological Roots of Pope Francis's Teaching on Friendship and Fraternity

According to Christian belief—which is shared by many other religious traditions, including the indigenous ones—human beings have the same origin: all of them are created in God's image, and they are brothers and sisters, friends, and partners who have embarked on a journey with a common destination. This basic theological principle laid down in *Nostra Aetate*[4] is deepened further in *Fratelli Tutti* by setting forth the consequences of this belief for the life of humankind. Because we are friends and brothers and sisters, there needs to prevail in human societies equality in dignity and equity in sharing the common resources of Mother Earth. The conviction that we are primordially bonded is the dynamic force for cooperation to create a world of justice and peace in harmony with nature.

---

4. Vatican Council II, *Nostra Aetate*, 1.

We cannot but be struck by the convergence of Christianity with Islam in the belief of a common origin of the entirety of humankind when we read in the Quran:

> O humanity! Indeed, We created you from a male and a female and made you into peoples and tribes so that you may get to know one another. Surely the most noble of you in the sight of Allah is the most righteous among you. Allah is truly All-Knowing, All-Aware. (Quran 49:13)

Friendship and fraternity are noble human realities that go beyond any utilitarian calculus and the spirit of consumerism. They take root when we consider other persons to be valuable in themselves and when our friendship and fraternity are based on the truth, goodness, and beauty that others embody. We enjoy such a genuine friendship and fraternity for what it is and not because the other might benefit us somehow. Pope Francis seems to apply this principle to interreligious relationships. We need to look at other religions for what they are in themselves, not what they are in contrast or comparison to one's own religion so that one can feel a sense of superiority. This way of looking at other religions is what Pope Francis calls "gratuitousness." He describes it as follows: "There is always the factor of 'gratuitousness': the ability to do some things simply because they are good in themselves, without concern for personal gain or recompense. Gratuitousness makes it possible for us to welcome the stranger, even though this brings us no immediate tangible benefit. . . . Life without fraternal gratuitousness becomes a form of frenetic commerce, in which we constantly weigh up what we give and what we get back in return" (*FT* 139–40).

In the Hindu tradition, this is known as *nishkâma karma* (selfless actions without attachment to their fruits), which is clearly described in the sacred book *Bhagavad Gita*. The spirit of gratuitousness should animate cooperation among believers of different religions for the common good and for the welfare of the society, of the entire world, and of all creation. Gratuitousness brings a new quality to interreligious cooperation and must not to be likened to "cooperation" as seen from a modern organizational perspective. Nor should interreligious friendship and dialogue be analogized to modern-day networking and social media. The pope distinguishes such forms of communication from a dialogue based on genuine friendship and appreciation of the other in their otherness. "Dialogue is often confused with something quite different: the feverish exchange of opinions on social networks, frequently based on media information that is not always reliable. These exchanges are merely parallel monologues" (*FT* 200).

Religious Freedom—The Cornerstone of Interreligious Understanding

Religious freedom is an important component in this eighth chapter relating to interreligious relationships. Pope Francis views religious freedom in a much wider perspective than the liberal one, in which it is a matter of individual conscience. It is also more than a matter of the autonomy of a religious group to profess its faith and engage in worship. For him, religious freedom is essential for a community to contribute to the common good of society. This is of great relevance in Asia—in many Asian countries, Christians are allowed to profess their faith and carry on their worship; however, like other minority groups, they are not allowed to fully participate in shaping policies and orientations meant for the whole community of the nation. In the view of the pope, religious freedom needs to be integral and comprehensive: "With this religious freedom has also come the possibility for every person to offer, according to their own religious convictions, a positive contribution; firstly, to the moral reconstruction of the country and then, subsequently, to the economic reconstruction."[5] The pope's concern is not only about the Christian community but also about other religious communities. As a matter of fact, in Asia, the question of religious freedom is bound up with the situation of minorities in general and religious minorities in particular, whose freedom is being increasingly curtailed by centralized and authoritarian regimes. Because of this, the pope's words in this chapter on religious freedom have direct relevance for Asia. During his recent visit to Iraq, he pleaded that Christians be given the same kind of religious freedom that Muslims enjoy in the West.

The Solidarity of All Religions against Terrorism and Violence

The pope is keen that the world's rich and abundant religious resources are not lost but are harnessed for the common good. Religions need to step in as voices for the common good and not shy away from a public role. "It is wrong when the only voices to be heard in public debate are those of the powerful and 'experts.' Room needs to be made for reflections born of religious traditions that are the repository of centuries of experience and wisdom" (*FT* 275).

The contribution of the world's religions to peace is one of the chief concerns of *Fratelli Tutti*, especially in chapter 8. After treating peace and its relationship to justice and truth in chapter 7, the pope in the next chapter

---

5. Francis, "Address."

reflects on how religions today can contribute to peace. He knows the ambiguous relationship of religion to peace—both in history and in present times, religion has been misused and interpreted to justify acts of violence and terror. However, religion possesses plentiful resources for the promotion of peace, and the pope underlines the importance of believers of all religions joining together to do so. He previously stated clearly in *Evangelii Gaudium* how interreligious dialogue could contribute to the promotion of peace. In the present encyclical, the pope cites from the joint statement with the Grand Imam: "Religions must never incite war, hateful attitudes, hostility and extremism, nor must they incite violence or the shedding of blood" (*FT* 285).

Building peace is no easy task. The pope speaks about the importance of cultivating the "art" of peace, which is more than an institutional "architecture of peace." Genuine religiosity and worship of God will shun all forms of violence. For "sincere and humble worship of God bears fruit not in discrimination, hatred and violence, but in respect for the sacredness of life, respect for the dignity and freedom of others, and loving commitment to the welfare of all" (*FT* 283). One very important way of promoting peace is building trust; trust is the glue for reconciliation and peace. In many instances, religious leaders are more trusted than politicians in facilitating and advancing the cause of peace.

We can see a new theology of public life at work in this encyclical. "Although I have written it from the Christian convictions that inspire and sustain me, I have sought to make this reflection an invitation to dialogue among all people of good will" (*FT* 6). Here is an example of how the encyclical could trigger the pursuit of public theology, a theology that prompts us to address, together with other people of goodwill, all of those issues affecting human life and fraternity.[6] In Pope Francis's vision, there should be an "overlapping consensus" of religions on the need to cooperate for peace, justice, and the transformation of societies. As part of this process, each of the religions will draw inspiration from what they have been given. Francis notes that "others drink from other sources. For us the wellspring of human dignity and fraternity is in the Gospel of Jesus Christ" (*FT* 277).

Dialogue with Islam as a Model?

Dialogue with Muslims seems to be a priority in Francis's pontificate, though the words "Muslim" and "Islam" never figure in *Fratelli Tutti*. The encyclical expands on the meeting between Pope Francis and the Grand

---

6. Cf. Wilfred, *Religious Identities*, 273–99. See also Wilfred, "Fratelli Tutti."

Imam of Al-Azhar. The pope mentions four times how it was influenced by the Grand Imam (*FT* 29, 136, 192, 285). Further, the encyclical's title is drawn from Saint Francis of Assisi, whose efforts to dialogue with the sultan of Egypt when Christianity was at war with Islam during the period of the Crusades is well-known. The example of St. Francis is recalled in the encyclical. The pope also recalls Charles de Foucauld, whose presence in the Islamic regions of North Africa had great significance for interreligious understanding.[7] The experience of Catholicism's dialogue with Islam also seems to animate the spirit of the encyclical's chapter on interreligious dialogue. Both for historical reasons and the geographical proximity of Europe to the Middle East and North Africa, where Islam is the dominant religion, this emphasis is understandable.

However, there are unique aspects of Hinduism, Buddhism, Sikhism, Shintoism, Daoism, and other religious traditions that would not fit well into a framework of interreligious understanding that arose from dialogue between Catholicism and Islam. I think the experiences of Asian local churches in South, Southeast, and East Asia could help the Vatican better understand the specific circumstances one needs to attend to in interreligious dialogue with Asian religions other than Islam. These religious traditions are addressed in generalities in the encyclical, whereas Islam is addressed directly. This reminds us of the origin of Vatican II's declaration *Nostra Aetate*, which began by reaching out to Jews in dialogue, was expanded to the other Semitic religion, Islam, and finally as if in an afterthought, to other Asian religious traditions.[8]

Conclusion

The emphasis on interreligious dialogue in *Fratelli Tutti* has been received by Asians as a great message of encouragement and support. The call to work together with peoples of other religious traditions for the transformation of societies and the world cannot but find a very warm welcome in Asia, as it confirms the decades-old Asian pursuit of interreligious understanding and harmony, primarily through the many initiatives of the Federation of Asian Bishops' Conferences (FABC). Interreligious dialogue that takes place

---

7. The pope also refers to non-Catholic thinkers and saints—Martin Luther King, Desmond Tutu, and Mahatma Gandhi (*FT* 286).

8. The ambiguity toward Buddhism could be seen in John Paul II's comments on Buddhism as an atheistic system in his 1994 *Crossing the Threshold of Hope* (John Paul II, *Crossing the Threshold of Hope*, 49), for which Buddhist monks in Sri Lanka called for an apology from the pope. These comments marred his early 1995 visit to that island nation. See Dahlburg, "ASIA."

in friendship and fraternity values dialogue in itself and does not view it as a means for evangelization. This is a point that Asian bishops and theologians have sought to highlight for several decades amidst stiff opposition. *Fratelli Tutti* is a validation of these Asian efforts. As far back as 1987, Asian bishops and theologians made this point very clear when they said,

> We affirm that dialogue and mission have their own integrity and freedom. They are distinct but not unrelated. Dialogue is not a tool or instrument for mission and evangelization, but it does influence the way the Church perceives and practices mission in a pluralist world . . . Dialogue offers opportunities for Christian witness."[9]

Further, Pope Francis's interreligious orientation is significant against the background of certain theological impositions on Asians, including suspicion and even harassment of several Asian theologians working on the theology of various religions and on interreligious dialogue. One can recall here the contributions of Fr. Michael Amaladoss and Fr. Jacques Dupuis. They have been teaching in India for several decades in dialogue with peoples of other religions, the experiences of which they have tried to crystallize and articulate in their theologies of religion and dialogue. It is most unfortunate that the Congregation for the Doctrine of the Faith under the then Cardinal Joseph Ratzinger went so far as to excommunicate an Asian theologian, Tissa Balasuriya, at the far end of the twentieth century, for alleged doctrinal errors hardly anyone took note of at the time, and probably no one remembers today! I have recalled these facts to underline the exceptional significance of *Fratelli Tutti*, which has the potential to take Asian Christians to new frontiers of encounter with peoples of other faiths, encouraging them to further their joint work with "brothers and sisters of other faiths"[10] for the purpose of creating a peaceful and harmonious world.

---

9. FABC et al., "Living and Working Together," 104–5.

10. It is remarkable that as early as 1987, FABC was referring to peoples of other religions as "brothers and sisters of other faiths" (from the title of the joint conference of the CCA and FABC in Singapore). Pope Francis's words validate this: "The first attitude is that of regarding every man and woman, even those of different religious traditions, not as rivals, less still enemies, but rather as brothers and sisters." Kosimow and Race, *Pope Francis*, 37.

Bibliography

Dahlburg, John-Thor. "ASIA: Pope's Remarks on Buddhism May Mar His Sri Lanka Visit." *Los Angeles Times*, January 13, 1995. https://www.latimes.com/archives/la-xpm-1995-01-13-mn-19567-story.html.

Federation of Asian Bishops' Conferences (FABC) et al. "Living and Working Together with Brothers and Sisters of Other Faiths in Asia: An Ecumenical Consultation." Singapore, July 5–10, 1987. Hong Kong: Christian Conference of Asia/Federation Asian Bishops' Conferences, 1989.

Francis, Pope. "Address at the Meeting with the Leaders of Other Religions and Other Christian Denominations." Speech given at the Our Lady of Good Counsel Catholic University, Tirana, Albania, September 21, 2014. https://www.vatican.va/content/francesco/en/speeches/2014/september/documents/papa-francesco_20140921_albania-leaders-altre-religioni.html.

———. *Fratelli Tutti: On Fraternity and Social Friendship*. Vatican City: Libreria Editrice Vaticana, 2020. https://www.vatican.va/content/francesco/en/encyclicals/documents/papa-francesco_20201003_enciclica-fratelli-tutti.html.

Francis, Pope, and Grand Imam Ahmad Al-Tayyeb. "A Document on Human Fraternity for World Peace and Living Together." Summary of Bulletin, Holy See Press Office, February 4, 2019. https://press.vatican.va/content/salastampa/en/bollettino/pubblico/2019/02/04/190204f.html.

John Paul II, Pope. *Crossing the Threshold of Hope*. New York: Alfred A. Knopf, 1994.

Kasimow, Harold, and Alan Race, eds. *Pope Francis and Interreligious Dialogue: Religious Thinkers Engage with Recent Initiatives*. Cham, Switzerland: Palgrave Macmillan, 2018.

Lefebure, Leo D. "Cardinal Ratzinger's Comments on Buddhism." *Buddhist-Christian Studies* 18 (1998) 221–23.

O'Connell, Gerald. "First Muslim to Ever Present a Papal Encyclical Praises 'Fratelli Tutti.'" *America*, October 5, 2020. https://www.americamagazine.org/faith/2020/10/05/first-muslim-ever-present-papal-encyclical-praises-fratelli-tutti.

Vatican Council II. *Nostra Aetate: Declaration of the Relation of the Church to Non-Christian Religions*. Vatican City: Libreria Editrice Vaticana, October 28, 1965. http://www.vatican.va/archive/hist_councils/ii_vatican_council/documents/vat-ii_decl_19651028_nostra-aetate_en.html.

Wilfred, Felix. "Fratelli Tutti as an Exercise in Public Theology." *Vidyajyoti Journal of Theological Reflection*, forthcoming.

———. *Religious Identities and the Global South: Porous Borders and Novel Paths*. Cham, Switzerland: Palgrave Macmillan, 2021.

31

To the Whole Inhabited Earth

Carmenmargarita Sánchez de León[1]

1. Who Inhabits that Earth?

THOUSANDS OF GREEN BANDANNAS on necks, arms, and heads form a great tide that is summoned not by the moon, nor the sun, nor the universe's forces of gravity but rather by the power of a right denied to women for a very long time—the right to decide about their own bodies. The women in green bandannas organize themselves without hierarchy, without elite leadership, and they take over the streets, the squares, the spaces colonized by states, by churches. In those colonized spaces, we are told what we should think, how we should think, and when we should think. However, despite the colonization of hundreds of years, more and more forces are emerging that organize themselves in other ways, and they propose *Tesis*[2] (in English, "theses") that are uncomfortable: "the rapist is you." And who is this physical and symbolic rapist? It is the judicial institutions, the state, the legislatures, the religious hierarchies, the militarized forces; each of these is

---

1. Translated by Karen M. Kraft.

2. Las Tesis is a group of Chilean female performers who, in the face of gender violence, worked on a theatrical piece to address the situation, and from that project comes the song, "Un Violador en Tu Camino" (A Rapist in Your Path). It was performed by thousands of women on the planet, its impact taking the creators by surprise. They reflected: "We did not think of it as a protest song; it was part of our performance piece.... But the truth is that the performance got out of hand, and the beauty of it is that it was appropriated by others." See Pais, "Las Tesis."

directly responsible for ensuring the immutable structures that gave birth to the patriarchy. Of course, there *are* changes such as, for example, greater participation of women in various spheres of public life, the process of decriminalizing some sexual orientations, or the slow process of recognizing the diversity of families. However, these changes sometimes seem like reforms that never strike at the colonizing core of the institutions in power.

In recent women's marches around the world, some participants have painted graffiti, altering the face of national monuments or the walls of institutions. Those monuments and walls tell a single story, and they forget the unofficial ones because they are inconvenient. In her reflection on the danger of a single story, Nigerian writer Chimamanda Ngozi Adichie recalls that starting from a single narrative will always be a danger that leaves us without perspectives of diversity,[3] the unique narratives that start from places of power are efforts to make invisible not only some sectors of humanity, but they are also an effort to make the narratives of resilience and resistance disappear from the stage. Those unofficial stories are proclaimed by subaltern female bodies[4] that travel in and out of the hegemonic peace that is managed and administered from above. That "above"—constituted by the political, economic, and social centers of power—administers *paces*,[5] ensuring that the structures of oppression are not radically transformed but rather that they adapt to some demands and needs of the subaltern—that is, they are concessions within a patriarchal, capitalist, and racist matrix.[6]

2. The Emerging Paradigm beyond Hegemonic Structures

I propose taking a fresh look at *Ekklesia* (εκκλησία) as the coming together of an assembly which must urgently repair structural evils—an experiment in new social possibilities where, for a moment, people go out of their way to ensure that their claims for peace/*pazes* and justice are understood. This

---

3. Adichie, "Danger of a Single Story."

4. The concept of the subaltern developed by Antonio Gramsci is "rescued" by the Subaltern Studies Group of India. For Gayatri Chakraverty Spivak, the subaltern should not be understood as monolithic beings who assume an identity with a unitary consciousness: "the colonized subaltern subject is irretrievably heterogeneous." See Spivak, "Can the Subaltern Speak?," 79.

5. In this chapter, I will use the following plurals for the word *peace*: *paces*, to refer to the proposals from hegemonic powers, and *pazes*, for actions from anti-systemic movements.

6. See Lorde, "Master's Tools," 110–11. "What does it mean when the tools of a racist patriarchy are used to examine the fruits of that same patriarchy? It means that only the most narrow perimeters of change are possible and allowable."

form of *Ekklesia* does not always result in a specific plan of how to live in society; rather, it more likely takes on different shapes in the particular national contexts where it arises. These *Ekklesiae* (εκκλησίες) sprout up in various places, even within the very walls of institutional churches, and others are assembled beyond those walls. The latter are free movements that arise from the needs of the people themselves. On the one hand, *Ekklesiae* within institutional churches are the pockets of resistance that have existed since the movement created by Jesus's followers became an institution of the empire. In recent times, these pockets of internal resistance have found a voice in the grassroots base ecclesial communities, in feminist thinkers within institutional churches, in anti-racist movements,[7] and in the movements that support the rights of the LGBTIQ+ communities. They are the prophets who often cry out in the desert and fight for radical changes within religious institutions.

The *Ekklesiae* on the "outside," beyond the institutional walls, are the new *quilombos*,[8] the new *palenques*[9]—a *marronage*[10] that is breaking down the walls of the hegemonic powers. Colonized and built by the slave system, *quilombos* and *palenques* existed throughout the entire *Abya Yala*.[11] Seeking freedom, these settlements of black communities helped in part to dismantle black slavery on the continent; they represented resistance and a new social project.[12] The encyclical *Fratelli Tutti* does not call forth the *Ekklesia*

---

7. In his 1963 "Letter from Birmingham Jail," Martin Luther King, Jr. develops a strong but sincere claim against the churches of the southern United States, including some African American churches. He criticizes them for their inaction and silence in the face of racial segregation. For different reasons, black as well as white ecclesiastical structures found the struggles of the anti-racist movements problematic. See King, "Letter from Birmingham Jail."

8. Translator's note: For an explanation of the origin of *quilombos*, see Reis and Dos Santos Gomes, "Quilombo."

9. Translator's note: For an explanation of the origin of *palenques*, see Fletcher, "Colombia Dispatch 4."

10. Translator's note: For a general discussion of *marronage*, see Kars, "Maroons and Marronage."

11. Translator's note: See Cleusa Caldeira's discussion of *Abya Yala*—a term some indigenous communities use for the continents of North and South America—in chapter 15 of this book.

12. From the start of black slavery in Abya Yala, slaves resisted in various ways. As early as 1521 at Diego Colón's sugar mill in Santo Domingo, Dominican Republic, there was a major revolt to bring down the slave system; see Stevens-Acevedo, *Santo Domingo Slave Revolt of 1521*. Slaves who managed to flee were called *maroons*, and *marronage* is the term for the traditional resistance and resilience of black communities. One of the largest liberated communities was Palmares in Brazil, which had a population estimated at anywhere from 11,000 to more than 30,000 people; see Reis and Dos Santos Gomes, "Quilombo." In the so-called Kingdom of New Spain (Veracruz, Mexico),

that resist the inner core of religious institutions—the *aquilomba*[13] Ekklesia, the maroon Ekklesia—however, they are in themselves alternatives to the exclusionary summons of the ecclesiastical hierarchies.

3. Rethinking the Ekumene from the Perspective of Negated Bodies

The word "ecumenism" has a Greek root—*ekumene*—that means belonging to the entire inhabited earth. So, we have to ask ourselves who the entire inhabited earth is. This is complicated, because the entire inhabited earth is made up of a great diversity of life, including human life and beyond (biodiversity). We are *invited* to welcome this diversity, not only "horizontally but in the multiple directions in which it is constituted."[14] With respect to human life, this summoning of the entire inhabited earth creates a problem or a crossroads. The question posed by the philosopher Judith Butler—why are there lives that don't count?[15]—is a probing scalpel for examining the concept of ecumenism, because admittedly, in our political, economic, and religious systems, not all lives count, and there are some that these systems sacrifice.

Indigenous and Afro-descendant communities have been great defenders of life beyond human life; dating back to their ancestral wisdom, they have privileged and embraced a relationship of respect, not a utilitarian or predatory one. However, this wisdom and these spiritualities of African matrices and native peoples are not typically taken into consideration at the time of convening official ecumenical events; they have instead, for some time, been criminalized and persecuted, particularly by conservative movements in Christian churches.

Gaspar Yanga founded a settlement of free slaves, which in 1618 agreed to a treaty with Spain and formed its own peaceful government; see Carillo, "Mexico's First Liberated City." It is important to note the black women who also played an important role in this marronage; some were *quilombo* leaders and warriors such as the following: Tereza de Benguela (see Aguiar, "Tereza de Benguela"); Dandara (see Travae, "Dandara"); and Aqualtune Ezgondidu Mahamud da Silva Santos (see "In 1665, Kongo Princess Aqualtune Ezgondidu Mahamud").

13. Faced with the serious situations that Brazil is experiencing today, the Metropolitan Community Churches of Brazil have coined a new verb in Portuguese to speak of their resistance: *aquilombar*.

14. Gebara, *Ensayo de Antropología Filosófica*, 28.

15. See, generally, Butler, *Frames of War*, especially the introduction and chapter 1.

4. The Logic of Peace of the Hegemonic Sectors

Peace is a very diffuse and privatized concept.[16] It has long been articulated from the centers of power with little or no participation from the people directly affected by armed conflicts. Some studies indicate that, beginning with the postwar process, an epistemic hegemony of peace studies was consolidated with an understanding of war and conflicts from the global North's perspective. The countries involved managed to "impose a theoretical-political agenda, through protocol measures that consisted of a set of norms, procedures, and regulations based on the commercial, private, and corporate dynamics of establishing a pacification scenario based on the conception of a modern/liberal-capitalist democracy."[17]

Religions, in general, articulate peace from non-spaces, from positions they claim as neutral, and they assume the same as an ideal that transcends the tangible and exists outside the earthly world—that is, a neutral and universal peace. This idyllic neutrality, either intentionally or unintentionally, is very useful for hegemonic peace projects and requires critical reflection. States, mega government organizations, NGOs, and academic studies of peace and religion must problematize their epistemic presuppositions with regards to peace.

At different times in history, institutional churches have participated in the construction of and have collaborated with exclusionary systems. Patriarchy, racism, colonialism, and capitalism developed in the very bowels of ecclesial power. These structures have had a direct relationship with political systems such as Roman imperialism, medieval kingdoms and city-states, nation-states, monarchies, constitutional democracies, fascist national security states, and the colonial empires of nation-states. Economically, the church has been associated with and part of systems such as the Roman slave economy, feudalism with a serf economy, mercantilism, the transatlantic slave trade, early and advanced capitalism, various forms of socialism and communism, and multinational corporations.[18] In this sense, the church does not have an innocent relationship with each of these systems, from which narratives have been constructed, that have excluded, *among others*, entire peoples, women, and persons of gender diversity.

The organization Association for Women's Rights in Development (AWID) has noted that these policies of harassment on the part of churches

---

16. Sandoval-Forero and Capera Figueroa, "Una Mirada Antihegemónica y Descolonizadora," 19–50.

17. Sandoval-Forero and Capera Figueroa, "Una Mirada Antihegemónica y Descolonizadora," 21.

18. Cf. Ruether, *Christianity and Social Systems*.

against the rights of women, among other populations, have not only had the effect of increasing violence toward these segments of the population but have also resulted in a decrease in the security of advocates for the rights of women and diverse sex/gender populations.[19]

Through their preaching and exclusionary practices, the hierarchies of many churches have been directly responsible for the lack of well-being of many sectors of the population. It cannot be denied that ecclesiastical hierarchies have contributed to the non-peace suffered by these groups and have been the architects of systemic violence. In this sense, the church is not a home for everyone, a house with open doors, as the encyclical claims. In a beautiful text, Archbishop Desmond Tutu states:

> The church of Jesus Christ, far from being inclusive and welcoming of all, has over and over again pushed many to the periphery; instead of being hospitable to all, it has made many of God's children outcasts and pariahs on the basis of something which, like race or gender, they could do nothing about: their sexual orientation. The church has joined the world in committing what I consider to be the ultimate blasphemy: making the children of God doubt that they are children of God.[20]

5. The *Pazes/Transpazes* that Arise from Antisystemic Movements

On one of the walls of a small wooden house, painted white with a thatched roof, is a large multicolored flower and, in large letters, the following expression: "resistance is not just enduring but building something new." This phrase makes it clear that resistance is not about leaving things as they are but rather taking different steps to build something innovative. It is an attempt to heal the earth and *ourselves*, to transform the pain of centuries and turn it into fresh and useful compost from which we hope the biodiversity that is needed will emerge again so that the earth blesses us with its fruits.

Among the women of the anti-racist movement with whom I have had the opportunity to dialogue, there is a certain awareness about the struggle they have been bearing for many years. They know that they have been invisible to the racists and the patriarchies; however, in the same way, they know that their resistance efforts have been forming new ways of understanding society, deconstructing and carefully laying the foundation of

---

19. Balchin, *Toward a Future Without Fundamentalisms*, 43–46.
20. Cf. Germond and Gruchy, *Aliens in the Household of God*.

new structures. This building process has taken place in the midst of anger and mourning. Both are necessary: "if we forget that we are in mourning, we become mere recipients of anger; if we forget to turn our anger into a demand for justice"[21] and for *pazes*, we become pure destruction.

There is contempt on the part of hegemonic structures for the work that is done on a small scale, in direct communication with the communities that nobody reaches. The recent phenomena of widespread demonstrations against racism and sexism are the fruit of much of this work in the shadows.

The new *pazes* are transgressive; they cross the line imposed on them and achieve alliances beyond political or social borders. To a great extent, they are builders of bridges or tunnels that seek to reach the other side. The other side is a child of uncertainty;[22] it is the magic wand of *transpazes*, because there will never be a single way to construct the bridges or tunnels, nor do they follow linear processes. Rather, they move in a spiral pattern, where there is no up or down. As some of the anti-racist feminist activists say, "today we are fine; tomorrow maybe not, but we always resist." *Pazes* are "trans," because they move between possibilities; the focus is not on the final solution but rather the journey. They spread in a wild and uncontrolled way as they emanate from the very daily life of those affected.

Bibliography

Adichie, Chimamanda Ngozi. "The Danger of a Single Story." Transcript of TED talk given in Oxford, England, July 2009. https://www.ted.com/talks/chimamanda_ngozi_adichie_the_danger_of_a_single_story/transcript.

Aguiar, Marli. "Tereza de Benguela: Hail to Black Women's Struggle and Resistance." Translated by Rosana Felício dos Santos. *Capire: Feminist Voices to Change the World*, September 7, 2021. https://capiremov.org/en/experience/tereza-de-benguela-hail-to-black-womens-struggle-and-resistance/.

Aguirre Rojas, Carlos Antonio. *Movimientos Antisistémicos: Pensar lo Antisistémico en los Inicios del Siglo XXI*. Rosario, Argentina: Prohistoria, 2010.

Balchin, Cassandra. *Toward a Future Without Fundamentalisms: Analyzing Religious Fundamentalist Strategies and Feminist Responses*. Toronto: AWID, 2011. https://issuu.com/awid/docs/towards_a_future__eng_1_/1?e=2350791/7939553.

Boff, Leonardo. *Saint Francis: A Model for Human Liberation*. New York: Crossroad, 1989.

Butler, Judith. *Frames of War: When Is Life Grievable?* London: Verso, 2016.

———. "Vulnerabilidad y Resistencia Revisitadas." Paper presented at "Mesas de Diálogo: Subjetivación Sur-Norte" event, Universidad Nacional Autónoma

---

21. Butler, "Vulnerabilidad y Resistencia Revisitadas."

22. Ivone Gebara raises uncertainty as a new space for theological reflection; see, in general, Gebara, *Ensayo de Antropología Filosófica*.

de México, Mexico City, March 23, 2015. https://www.youtube.com/watch?v=6taXkozajec.

Carillo, Karen Juanita. "Mexico's First Liberated City Commemorates Its Founding." *JSTOR Daily*, October 20, 2021. https://daily.jstor.org/mexicos-yanga-commenorates-founding/.

Cavarero, Adriana. *Inclinations: A Critique of Rectitude*. Stanford: Stanford University Press, 2016.

Cone, James H. *The Spirituals and the Blues: An Interpretation*. Maryknoll, NY: Orbis, 2000.

Cruz, Juan Daniel. "Paces Dominantes y Paces Subalternas: El Caso de los Refugiados Colombianos." In *Epistemologías Decoloniales para la Paz en el Sur Global: Homenaje al Filósofo del Pensamiento Antihegemónico, Álvaro Ballardo Márquez-Fernández*, 119–47. Mérida, Venezuela: Fondo de Publicaciones del Laboratorio de Investigaciones Semióticas y Literarias (LISYL), Red de Pensamiento Decolonial, Red CoPaLa, Revista FAIA Argentina, and Fondo Editorial "Mario Briceño-Iragorry," 2020. https://dialektika.org/wp-content/uploads/2020/11/EPISTEMOLOGIAS-DECOLONIALES-LIBRO-28-AGOSTO-2020.pdf.

Delgado Wise, Raúl and Humberto Márquez Covarrubias. *El Laberinto de la Cultura Neoliberal*. Mexico City: Miguel Ángel Porrúa, 2013.

Fletcher, Kenneth. "Colombia Dispatch 4: Palenque: An Afro-Colombian Community." *Smithsonian Magazine*, October 28, 2008. https://www.smithsonianmag.com/travel/colombia-dispatch-4-palenque-an-afro-colombian-community-87781979/.

Francis, Pope. *Fratelli Tutti: On Fraternity and Social Friendship*. Vatican City: Libreria Editrice Vaticana, 2020. https://www.vatican.va/content/francesco/en/encyclicals/documents/papa-francesco_20201003_enciclica-fratelli-tutti.html.

Fontan, Victoria C. *Decolonizing Peace*. Lake Oswego, OR: Dignity, 2012.

Foucault, Michel. *The History of Sexuality: The Will to Knowledge*. Translated by Robert Hurley. London: Penguin, 1998.

Gebara, Ivone. *Ensayo de Antropología Filosófica: El Arte de Mezclar Conceptos y Plantar Desconceptos*. Translated by Graciela Pujol. Navarra, Spain: Verbo Divino, 2020.

Germond, Paul, and Steve Gruchy, eds. *Aliens in the Household of God: Homosexuality and Christian Faith in South Africa*. Cape Town: David Philip, 1997.

"In 1665, Kongo Princess Aqualtune Ezgondidu Mahamud Led 10,000 Men to Battle Before She Was Shipped to Brazil as a Slave." *Urban Woman Magazine*, November 7, 2018. https://urbanwomanmag.com/princess-aqualtune-ezgondidu-mahamud-da-silva-santos-10000-men-battle-shipped-brazil-slave/.

Jaime-Salas, Julio Roberto. "Descolonizar los Estudios de Paz: Un Desafío Vigente en el Marco de la Neoliberalización Epistémica Contemporánea." *Revista de Paz y Conflictos* 12:1 (2019) 133–57.

Kars, Marjoleine. "Maroons and Marronage." Oxford Bibliographies Online, August 27, 2018. https://www.oxfordbibliographies.com/view/document/obo-9780199730414/obo-9780199730414-229.xml.

King, Martin Luther, Jr. "Letter from Birmingham Jail, April 16, 1963." Stanford University, The Martin Luther King, Jr. Research and Education Institute, Stanford, CA. https://kinginstitute.stanford.edu/sites/mlk/files/letterfrombirmingham_wwcw_0.pdf.

Lorde, Audre. "The Master's Tools Will Never Dismantle the Master's House." In *Sister Outsider: Essays and Speeches*, edited by Audre Lorde, 110–13. New York: Random House, 2007.
Pais, Ana. "Las Tesis sobre 'Un Violador en Tu Camino.'" *BBC News Mundo*, December 6, 2019. https://www.bbc.com/mundo/noticias-america-latina-50690475.
Reis, João José, and Flávio dos Santos Gomes. "Quilombo: Brazilian Maroons during Slavery." *Cultural Survival Quarterly* 25:4 (December 2001). https://www.culturalsurvival.org/publications/cultural-survival-quarterly/quilombo-brazilian-maroons-during-slavery#:~:text=Palmares%20was%20a%20federation%20of,20%2C000%2C%20and%20even%2030%2C000%20people.
Ruether, Rosemary Radford. *Christianity and Social Systems: Historical Constructions and Ethical Challenges*. Lanham, MD: Rowman and Littlefield, 2009.
Sandoval Forero, Eduardo Andrés, and José Javier Capera Figueroa. "Una Mirada Antihegemónica y Descolonizadora de los Estudios de Paz en Nuestra América." In *Epistemologías Decoloniales para la Paz en el Sur Global: Homenaje al Filósofo del Pensamiento Antihegemónico, Álvaro Ballardo Márquez-Fernández*, 19–50. Mérida, Venezuela: Fondo de Publicaciones del Laboratorio de Investigaciones Semióticas y Literarias (LISYL), Red de Pensamiento Decolonial, Red CoPaLa, Revista FAIA Argentina, and Fondo Editorial "Mario Briceño-Iragorry," 2020. https://dialektika.org/wp-content/uploads/2020/11/EPISTEMOLOGIAS-DECOLONIALES-LIBRO-28-AGOSTO-2020.pdf.
Spivak, Gayatri Chakravorty. "Can the Subaltern Speak?" In *Marxism and the Interpretation of Culture*, edited by Cary Nelson and Lawrence Grossberg, 271–313. London: Macmillan, 1988.
Stevens-Acevedo, Anthony. *The Santo Domingo Slave Revolt of 1521 and the Slave Laws of 1522: Black Slavery and Black Resistance in the Early Colonial Americas*. New York: CUNY Dominican Studies Institute, 2019. http://www.dominicanlandmarks.com/Slave-Revolt-1521-Slave-Laws-1522-Monograph.pdf.
Travae, Marques. "Dandara, the Wife of Zumbi, Brazil's Greatest Black Leader, Was a Revolutionary Warrior in Her Own Right." *Black Brazil Today*, November 20, 2014. https://blackbraziltoday.com/dandara-the-wife-of-zumbi-brazils-greatest-black/.
Zizek, Slavoj. *Violence: Six Sideways Reflections*. London: Profile, 2008.

32

Religions Serving Fraternity: Roots, Trunk, Fruits

DANIEL IZUZQUIZA, SJ

AT THE END OF the encyclical *Fratelli Tutti*, Pope Francis refers to various figures recognized for their contribution to universal fraternity (St. Francis of Assisi, Martin Luther King, Desmond Tutu, Mahatma Gandhi) and, specifically, he stresses Charles de Foucauld, whose canonization was announced in May 2021. His life continues to inspire many Christians in their solidarity with the poorest, in their interreligious dialogue and in their nonviolent struggle for justice.

Three aspects of his life itinerary and of his spiritual dynamics will help us to present this contribution on chapter 8 of *Fratelli Tutti*. First, Brother Charles was a radical man, in the sense that he located his roots on this ultimate foundation: as the Pope points out, "Blessed Charles directed his ideal of total surrender to God towards an identification with the poor, abandoned in the depths of the African desert" (*FT* 287). Second, Charles de Foucauld managed to embody transparently the most authentic of Christian identity, the radical identification with Christ and with the poor: "only by identifying with the least did he come at last to be the brother of all" (*FT* 287). Thirdly, the martyrdom of this apostle to the Tuaregs bore fruit of universal fraternity and of an encounter between believers of different religions, although apparently it ended in the most absolute failure, in the midst of violence. I will develop this threefold division following a tree metaphor: roots, trunk, fruits.

Roots: The Ultimate Foundation

In 1961, shortly after becoming a widower, French philosopher Jacques Maritain began to live with a fraternity of the Little Brothers of Jesus, of the spiritual family of Charles de Foucauld, which he formally joined in 1970. Maritain is known for his active role in helping to draft the United Nations Universal Declaration of Human Rights in 1948. He always defended the idea that human rights had their philosophical foundation in natural law and, finally, their ultimate root in divine paternity. At the same time, he argued that the Universal Declaration should have a culturally open and rationally argued formulation, without making explicit its philosophical or religious foundations.[1]

A similar question reappears in this eighth chapter of *Fratelli Tutti*, which raises the question about the foundations of fraternity. Quoting St. John Paul II, in what he regards as a "memorable statement," Pope Francis states:

> If there is no transcendent truth, in obedience to which man achieves his full identity, then there is no sure principle for guaranteeing just relations between people. . . . The root of modern totalitarianism is to be found in the denial of the transcendent dignity of the human person who, as the visible image of the invisible God, is therefore by his very nature the subject of rights that no one may violate—not individual, group, class, nation, or state. (*FT* 273)

This quote is taken from the 1991 encyclical, *Centesimus Annus*, written in the context of the fall of the Berlin Wall and the collapse of Soviet totalitarianism. From a more theoretical philosophical-theological point of view, this conviction lies at the core of Benedict XVI's main social encyclical, *Caritas in Veritate*, of 2009, cited twelve times by Francis throughout *Fratelli Tutti*.

Without fatherhood, there is no brotherhood or sisterhood. If the Father disappears, we become orphans. "We are certain that only with this awareness that we are not orphans, but children, can we live in peace with one another" (*FT* 272). Already in the 1960s, German physician and psychoanalyst Alexander Mitscherlich described our cultural context as a "society without the Father," pointing out at the same time that this feature creates a "detachment effect" and a "sibling fear of ties."[2] This does not imply, of course, a deterministic description of reality, as if we were doomed to failure. Also in contemporary society we can live a true fraternity and recreate the bonds of

---

1. Maritain, *Man and the State*.
2. Mitscherlich, *Society*.

social friendship. The pope insists on this, while inviting all citizens, and all believers as well, to make their contribution along these lines.

Defending the public role of the church is not always evident in contemporary societies, which are usually complex and diverse. This is a particularly delicate issue in Europe and North America. It is a basic truth of Catholic social teaching, though, that "the Church, while respecting the autonomy of political life, does not restrict her mission to the private sphere" (*FT* 276). Moreover, the Christian community "has a public role over and above her charitable and educational activities. She works for the advancement of humanity and of universal fraternity," always aiming "to build bridges, to break down walls, to sow seeds of reconciliation" (*FT* 276). At times, it seems that public discourse is dominated by aseptic language, coming from certain rationalist or individualistic elites. "It is wrong when the only voices to be heard in public debate are those of the powerful and 'experts.' Room needs to be made for reflections born of religious traditions that are the repository of centuries of experience and wisdom" (*FT* 275).

In fact, the majority of the population of the globe is made up of religious believers. "Yet often they are viewed with disdain" (*FT* 275). In saying this, the Argentinian pope, the first one who has come from the global South, seems to be criticizing certain elites of the North who forget or reject this ultimate and religious foundation shared by the great majority of the planet—unjustly impoverished and strongly religious majorities. It is significant that Francis speaks not only "from our faith experience and from the wisdom accumulated over centuries but also from lessons learned from our many weaknesses and failures" (*FT* 274). Therefore, the ultimate root underlying the Christian contribution to universal fraternity is found in the madness of the cross, in the wisdom of weakness (cf. 1 Cor 1:18–31). Here we find the *what*—freely given service in favor of universal fraternity—and the *how*—genuine humility. Thus, "we, the believers of the different religions, know that our witness to God benefits our societies" (*FT* 274).

Trunk: Christian Identity

Having described the "roots," I will now comment upon the "trunk" of this chapter. *Fratelli Tutti* clearly states that Christian identity springs up at the foot of the cross (*FT* 278), next to the tree of life. This image of the tree planted by the streams of water is common in biblical writings as a way to refer to the fruitfulness of the believing and honest life (cf. Ps 1). Sustained and supported by Christ's tree, we can live universal fraternity. As branches united to this trunk (cf. John 15:1–8), we can bear abundant fruit. Jesus himself, in the parable of the mustard seed (Mark 4:30–32), suggested that this tree represents the community, "where there is room for all those whom our societies discard, where justice and peace are resplendent" (FT 278).

The encyclical recognizes that there is a plurality of worldviews, ethical criteria, and foundations for values. "Others drink from other sources. For us the wellspring of human dignity and fraternity is in the Gospel of Jesus Christ" (FT 277). The pope refers to the "music of the Gospel" that should not only resonate in our inner selves but also "in our homes, our public squares, our workplaces, our political and financial life" so that we can "defend the dignity of every man and woman" (FT 277). Thus, this Gospel music becomes the lifeblood that nourishes and enlivens Christian identity. Therefore, the trunk ceases to be a rigid straightjacket; it becomes a true channel of grace for all.

In the context of contemporary debates around identities, the image of the trunk can be useful, but it can also be misleading. Let me clarify, then, how I imagine it: Not like the linear trunk of a sequoia or any other rectilinear stem. I am thinking, rather, of the olive tree or the South American ceiba. In these cases, the trunk is branched and has an asymmetrical shape, which gives it both beauty and stability. With this image in mind, we can better understand Pope Francis's way of proposing Christian identity in our world. I will focus on three areas.

First of all, let me say a word about Christian identity in relation to the world around it. The debate around identities has marked much of the public discussion in the field of political philosophy and theology, but it is far from over.[3] In this context, the pope is committed to a Christian identity that is open, welcoming, inclusive, and, especially, respectful of the threatened cultures of the poor. On the one hand, he says, "I can welcome others who are different and value the unique contribution they have to make, only if I am firmly rooted in my own people and culture" (FT 143). On the other hand, he underlines that his proposal "has nothing to do with watering down or concealing our deepest convictions when we encounter others who think differently than ourselves. . . . For the deeper, stronger, and richer our own identity is, the more we will be capable of enriching others with our own proper contribution" (FT 282). All of this is obviously connected with respect for freedom of conscience and the right to religious freedom, which the pope once again emphasizes in FT 279.

A second aspect mentioned in this chapter refers to the Christian identity of the churches as a whole, that is, the challenge of ecumenism. It is

---

3. See, among other references: Fukuyama, *Identity*; Appiah, *Lies*; Volpe, *Rethinking*; Budde, *Borders*.

evident that we Christians are called to be agents of communion, witnesses of social friendship, and servants of universal fraternity. But it is also clear that we can only be so, in a credible way, to the extent that we live it within the same Body of Christ, still sadly and dramatically divided today. For this reason, the pope says: "It is also urgent to continue to bear witness to the journey of encounter between the different Christian confessions," adding that "we recognize with sorrow that the process of globalization still lacks the prophetic and spiritual contribution of unity among Christians" (*FT* 280).

Finally, Pope Francis offers some clues about our identity within the Catholic Church itself. "Called to take root in every place, the Church has been present for centuries throughout the world, for that is what it means to be 'Catholic'" (*FT* 278). Universal love is always embodied in local examples, socially rooted and culturally varied. It is not surprising, then, that the pope once again resorts to a metaphor he had already used in his programmatic apostolic exhortation *Evangelii Gaudium* and which applies both to civil society and to the church. "I have frequently called for the growth of a culture of encounter capable of transcending our differences and divisions. This means working to create a many-faceted polyhedron whose different sides form a variegated unity, in which 'the whole is greater than the part' [*Evangelii Gaudium*, n. 237]. The image of a polyhedron can represent a society where differences coexist, complementing, enriching, and reciprocally illuminating one another, even amid disagreements and reservations" (*FT* 215).

Fruits: Religion and Peace

Religions play an active and significant role in building universal fraternity, thus contributing to peace in the world. They already do it, they can do it more, and they must do it even better, for internal coherence and responsibility for the common good. Of course, our world also suffers from the heartbreaking interactions between religions and violence.[4] Pope Francis is well aware of this, to the point of dedicating the last section of this chapter to the issue of "religion and violence." But he also prefers to start by focusing on a somewhat more positive outlook, stating: "A journey of peace is possible between religions. Its point of departure must be God's way of seeing things" (*FT* 281).

As Jesus of Nazareth said, "a healthy tree bears good fruit, a sick tree bears bad fruit. A healthy tree cannot bear bad fruit, nor can a diseased

---

4. An original and relevant theological clarification of this topic can be seen in Cavanaugh, *Myth*. See also Silvestri and Mayall, *Role of Religion*.

tree bear good fruit" (Matt 7:17–18). The fruit of religions is peace, while "violence has no basis in our fundamental religious convictions but only in their distortion" (*FT* 282). On various occasions, the pope has insisted on this idea, not only saying that "violence promoted and carried out in the name of religion can only discredit religion itself," but also describing those actions and justifications as "idolatrous caricatures of God" and locating them "among the greatest blasphemies."[5] Violent conflict "is not due to religion, even when terrorists instrumentalize it. It is due, rather, to an accumulation of incorrect interpretations of religious texts and to policies linked to hunger, poverty, injustice, oppression, and pride" (*FT* 284).

Although the issue cuts across all religious confessions and even some secularist movements, in this twenty-first century it appears, frequently, associated with Islam and with relations between Christians and Muslims. Jihadist terrorism is a global phenomenon present not only in the Middle East, but also in Asia and Africa, in Europe, and in North America. For this reason, it is particularly relevant that Pope Francis explicitly acknowledges that he has "felt particularly encouraged by the Grand Imam Ahmad Al-Tayyeb" and that *Fratelli Tutti* "takes up and develops some of the great themes raised in the Document that we both signed" in Abu Dhabi (*FT* 5). At the end of the encyclical, he returns to this brotherly encounter and turns it into an urgent appeal: "religions must never incite war, hateful attitudes, hostility, and extremism, nor must they incite violence or the shedding of blood" (*FT* 285).

An example of this spirit can be found in Brother Charles de Foucauld, who felt a special vocation to share his search with Islam. He lived among Muslims for a good number of years, established true friendly relations with them and, dramatically, died assassinated in the Algerian desert at the beginning of the twentieth century. Today, his spiritual influence continues to encourage firm commitments of radical insertion among the poor, of true inculturation, of the struggle for a peace based on justice and of daily initiatives of interreligious dialogue, also in the most abandoned areas of North America and Europe. Here, specifically, this spirituality is embodied in contexts marked by immigration, where many Muslims struggle to get ahead, with and alongside of their Christian neighbors.

Migration has become one of the sources that increases religious diversity and that facilitates new possibilities for interreligious dialogue. Take, for example, Sadiq Khan, London's first Muslim mayor, from a Pakistani immigrant family or also the case of Muslims Ugur Sahin and Öezlem Türeci, the Turkish-German couple who founded BioNTech, one of the companies

---

5. Francis, "Address to Participants."

that has achieved a vaccine against COVID-19. Very often, Pope Francis has called attention to the unjust suffering of migrants and challenged the conscience of humanity to respond adequately to this sign of the times (see, for example, chapter 4 of *Fratelli Tutti*). Attention to migrants constitutes a concrete field in which religions clearly contribute to peace and human fraternity, "by uniting and not dividing, by extinguishing hatred and not holding on to it, by opening paths of dialogue and not by constructing new walls" (*FT* 284).

It is important to remember, in this context, the fourfold level of interreligious dialogue.[6] First, the dialogue of life, through friendship in an open and neighborly spirit. Second, the dialogue of action, that is, a shared commitment toward peace, justice, and the liberation of people. Third, the dialogue of religious experience, where people, rooted in their own religious traditions, share their spiritual riches. Finally, the dialogue of theological exchange, usually led by academic specialists. All these are different and complementary ways through which religions can and must contribute to world peace, human understanding, and universal fraternity.

Conclusion

I want to end these reflections going back to the title of *Fratelli Tutti*'s eighth chapter, "Religions at the Service of Fraternity in Our World." And I want to emphasize the attitude of service. Religions contribute to world peace not by imposing their views or through their power or influence. Rather, religions can help fraternity in our world simply by serving. This is basic to our Christian worldview (cf. John 13:1–15). In chapter 3 of *Fratelli Tutti*, Pope Francis talks about the virtue of solidarity as a way to promote the common good, focusing on those who are most vulnerable: "Service always looks to their faces, touches their flesh, senses their closeness and even, in some cases, 'suffers' that closeness and tries to help them. Service is never ideological, for we do not serve ideas, we serve people" (*FT* 115). This is the way religions support universal fraternity. This is what Charles de Foucauld embodied. And this is our own challenge.

Bibliography

Appiah, Kwame A. *The Lies That Bind: Rethinking Identity*. New York: Liveright, 2018.
Budde, Michael L. *The Borders of Baptism: Identities, Allegiances, and the Church*. Eugene, OR: Cascade, 2011.

6. Pontifical Council for Interreligious Dialogue, *Dialogue and Proclamation*, 42.

Cavanaugh, William T. *The Myth of Religious Violence: Secular Ideology and the Roots of Modern Conflict*. New York: Oxford University Press, 2009.

Francis, Pope. "Address to Participants in the Conference on Violence Committed in the Name of Religion." Speech given in Rome, February 2, 2018. https://www.vatican.va/content/francesco/en/speeches/2018/february/documents/papa-francesco_20180202_conferenza-tacklingviolence.html.

———. *Fratelli Tutti: On Fraternity and Social Friendship*. Vatican City: Libreria Editrice Vaticana, 2020. https://www.vatican.va/content/francesco/en/encyclicals/documents/papa-francesco_20201003_enciclica-fratelli-tutti.html.

Fukuyama, Francis. *Identity: The Demand for Dignity and the Politics of Resentment*. New York: Farrar, Straus, and Giroux, 2018.

Maritain, Jacques. *Man and the State*. Chicago: University of Chicago Press, 1951.

Mitscherlich, Alexander. *Society without the Father: A Contribution to Social Psychology*. Translated by Eric Mosbaher. London: Tavistock, 1969.

Pontifical Council for Interreligious Dialogue. *Dialogue and Proclamation: Reflection and Orientations on Interreligious Dialogue and the Proclamation of the Gospel of Jesus Christ*. Rome, May 19, 1991. https://www.vatican.va/roman_curia/pontifical_councils/interelg/documents/rc_pc_interelg_doc_19051991_dialogue-and-proclamatio_en.html.

Silvestri, Sara, and James Mayall. *The Role of Religion in Conflict and Peacebuilding*. London: The British Academy, 2015.

Volpe, Medi A. *Rethinking Christian Identity: Doctrine and Discipleship*. Oxford, UK: Willey-Blackwell, 2013.

Index

abstraction, 30, 48, 62, 116, 141, 144, 154, 172, 251
Abu Dhabi, 102, 141, 308
Abu Dhabi Declaration. *See* Vatican documents
abundant life, 205, 277, 279
Abya Yala, 141n3, 143–45, 143n6, 147, 296, 296n11–12
Adichie, Chimamanda Ngozi, 295
Advincula, Jose F., Cardinal, 177
Afghanistan, 238, 247–50, 253–54
Africa
   anthropology (*see* anthropology)
   children (*see* children)
   church in, 50, 126, 128–29
   continent, 9, 125, 128, 237–38, 240
   desert, 303
   divides in, 9–16
   Great Lakes region, 238
   interdependence, 11
   migration, 125–26
   North, 126, 291
   openness to the other in, 83–90
   Sahara Desert, 126
   spirituality, 89, 297
   sub-Saharan, 162, 200–202
   Traditional Religion (ATR), 276
   Xhosa people, 141n2
   West, 275–76
   women, 279–80
   Zulu people, 141n2
Afro-descendance, 297
agency
   collective, 203, 307
   international, 52–53, 94
   national, 247
   pastoral, 54, 87
   personal, 53, 191, 203, 230–31
   social, 146
aggression, 84, 242, 248, 252, 262
   nationalist, 28, 106, 178, 249
   social, 19, 30, 230
agriculture, 104, 183–84, 203, 214, 241, 252
Aguilar, Mario, 84
Ahmed, Sara, 217
Al-Kamil, Sultan, 102, 167, 265
Al-Tayyeb, Ahmad, Grand Imam of Al-Azhar, 17–18, 58, 102, 113, 282, 284–85, 290–91, 308
   Abu Dhabi Declaration and, 22, 141, 210, 284
Albado, Omar, 181
Algeria, 308
alienation, 18, 31, 37, 58, 69, 105, 162, 276
   inalienability, 84, 98, 102, 141, 168, 177
alterity, 113, 143, 145
Amaladoss, Michael, Father, 292
Amazonia, 104, 106, 228
amiability, 226–27, 230–33
ancestors, 74, 104–6, 105n10, 141n3, 142–43, 297
anger, 151, 240, 258, 262, 265–67, 300
anthropocentrism, 2, 96
anthropology, 36, 287–88
   African, 122, 128–29
antisystemic movements, 184, 299–300

312 INDEX

apapachadas, 223, 223n33
aquilomba, 296–97, 297n13
Aquinas, Saint Thomas, 37–38
Arendt, Hannah, 213–14
Argentina, 106, 181, 183, 186, 187n19, 192, 258, 284, 305
  Barracas, 187
  Buenos Aires, 181, 187, 258
    Catholic hierarchy, 187
  dictatorship, military, 258
  Nuestra Señora de Caacupé, parish, 187
  Retiro slum, 181
Aristotle, 134
Armstrong, Karen, 168
Asia, 23, 60–62, 131–37, 170, 170n2, 172n6, 174–78, 208–15, 285–86
  (Asian) Economic Integration Report, 133
  Asians, 60, 133, 291–92
  continent, 1–2, 135, 137, 143, 251, 308
  countries, 20, 134, 136–37, 174n8, 212, 247–48, 289
  East, 291
  Foundation
    State of Conflict and Violence in Asia, The, 247
  migration and, 131–37
  Milk Tea Alliance, 211
  Philippines and (*see* Philippines)
  religion and, 289, 291–92
  South, 21, 200–201, 253, 291
  Southeast, 21, 291
  violence in, 245–54
  Youth Climate Network, 211
Association for Women's Rights in Development (AWID), 298
asylum, 93–97, 97n21, 128
atheism, 275, 291n8
Athenians, 167n5
Augustine, Saint, 38, 192, 250, 267
  City of God, 38
Australia, 18n4, 178
authoritarianism, 1, 21, 205, 248, 251, 253, 258, 289

authority, 15, 38, 50, 111, 113, 166, 232

Banco Farmaceutico Foundation, 204
Bangladesh, 20, 93, 247
Bantu, 145n14
baptism, 107, 194, 226
Bartholomew, Ecumenical Patriarch, 58, 113
Base Erosion and Profit Shifting (BEPS), Inclusive Framework on, 204
Bearss, Bridget, Sister, 268
believer, 39, 41–43, 74, 101, 127, 280, 287
  of different religions, 288, 290, 303, 305
  unbeliever, 39, 41–43, 277, 280
Benedict, Saint, 109, 117
Benedict XVI, Pope, 17, 113, 285n3, 304
  Ratzinger, Joseph, cardinal, 285n3, 292
benevolentia, 116
Bergoglio, Jorge Mario, bishop (Pope Francis), 181, 187
Bible, 2–3, 88, 102, 112, 117, 127, 257–58, 281, 305
  Abraham and Sarah, 2, 109, 117
  Adam and Eve, 258
  Cain and Abel, 68, 257n2, 258, 260, 263
  Cana, marriage feast, 279
  Chaldeans, 2
  Deuteronomy, 3
  Exodus, 3
  Genesis, 258
  Good Samaritan (*see* Good Samaritan)
  Gospels, 52, 112, 117–18, 137, 152, 175–77, 193, 258, 278
    flavor of, 27–28
    John, 58
    Luke, 56–59, 73, 75, 77, 111
    Mark, 57, 111–12
    Matthew, 37, 57, 68
    message, 74, 171
    music of, 278, 306
    of Jesus, 4, 71, 278, 290, 306
    interpretation of, 56–61

Joseph (Genesis), 281–82
Last Judgment, 3
model of love, 73–79
Nazareth, 4
New Testament, 3, 57, 70, 73, 112, 238
Old Testament, 3, 73, 281
Psalms, 238
Samaritan woman, parable of the, 58, 63, 99
Tobit and Sarah, 41
Torah, 57
Ur, 2
Visitation (Mary and Elizabeth), 279
YHWH, 3, 111–12, 117
binaries, 47, 63, 98, 150, 240
biodiversity, 297, 299
biology, 2, 34, 250
BioNTech, 308–9
biopolitics, 93–96
biopower, 92, 95
Black Elk, Maka Akan Najin 268, 275
blasphemy, 41, 85, 299, 308
blindness, 48, 69, 96, 99, 268
Bo, Charles Maung, Cardinal, 170–71, 177
Bolivia, 105, 182, 184–86, 187n19
  Aymara language, 105n10
  Fexpocruz, 184
  Santa Cruz de la Sierra, 182, 184, 186–87
Borda, Orlando Fals, 106
Boyle, Greg, Father, 265n5
Branche, Cherylynn, 268
Brazil, 145–46, 174, 186, 258, 296n12–13, 297
  Afro-Brazilians, 145–46, 145n14, 146n19
  Candudos rebellion (*see* war)
  Metropolitan Community Churches, 297n13
  Palmares, 296n13
  Rio de Janeiro, 50
British Medical Journal, 204
brokenness, 40, 42, 47–48, 54, 89, 153, 238, 258, 270
brotherhood, 3, 68, 112, 141, 184, 211, 281
-sisterhood, 2, 4, 101–2, 107–9, 136, 149, 257, 304
Brueggemann, Walter, 199
Brunei Darussalam, 248–49
Buddhism, 253, 285–86, 285n3, 291, 291n8
Bujo, Bénézet, 122
Bulgaria, 151
bureaucracy, 4, 183
buscadoras, 218–19, 218n8, 220, 223–24
business, 22, 32, 164, 200, 204, 241
  corporations, 93, 162, 202, 220n14, 298
  multinational, 163, 204, 298
Butler, Judith, 297

Caldeira, Cleusa, 296n11
Cambodia, 23, 250, 253
  Khmer Rouge, 250
Cameroon, 85
Canada, 40, 78, 174
capital punishment, 247–49
capitalism, 34, 161–62, 203, 214, 218, 247, 298
  liberalism and, 20, 32, 54, 95, 298
  patriarchy and, 2, 295, 298
carcinogens, 163
Cardijn, Joseph, 140
  see-judge-act, 140
castes, 276
catechesis, 34, 175, 177, 250
Catholic Mobilizing Network, 268
Catholic social teaching, 17, 132, 166, 168, 191, 194, 248, 305
  of Francis, Pope, 27, 32, 177, 194
catholicity, 38, 150, 153–55, 155n4–5
CCA (Christian Conference of Asia), 292n10
ceiba, 306
Central African Republic, 238
Central America, 2, 258
centralization, 12, 70, 184, 229, 289
century
  first, 74
  fifteenth, 143
  nineteenth, 194
  twentieth, 189, 203, 266, 292, 308
  twenty-first, 127, 132, 163, 308

Césaire, Aimé, 144
Chenoweth, Erica, 267n9
childbirth, 85
children, 50, 52, 107, 136, 222, 246,
   269n17, 275, 278
 African, 53, 85, 89
 care of, 15, 21, 138
 of God, 49, 108, 122, 152, 265, 277,
   279, 299, 304
 perpetrators as, 241
 women and, 95, 98, 151, 219, 241,
   279
Chile, 187n19, 258, 294n2
China, 2, 22, 133n8, 178, 247–49, 253
 Wuhan, 22
chisme, 230
chivalry, 265, 269
Christ, body of, 50, 155, 307
Christmas, 37, 192
cimarrónes, 145n14
citizenship, 57, 92–95, 97–98, 115,
   123–28, 162, 173, 214,
   219, 305
 full, 135, 141, 143, 145
 global, 125, 132, 208
 modern, 141–42
civil society, 115, 125, 128, 136, 140, 307
civilization, 5, 20, 31, 33, 127, 218
Cleveland Clinic, 37
climate change, 1, 51, 132, 163, 187, 190,
   203–5, 211
 global warming, 2
 greenhouse gases, 2
coexistence, 85, 87, 107–8, 144, 181,
   209, 276, 279, 307
Colombia, 106, 143n6, 145n14, 187n19,
   258, 296
 Kuna people, 143n6
Colón, Diego, 296n12
colonialism, 4, 40, 88, 103–7, 136,
   145n14, 224, 294–95,
   295n4, 298
 cultural, 18, 29, 36, 103
 heritage, 2, 280
 law, 241
 neo-, 40, 103–5, 107, 110
 post-, 61, 136, 276
 pre-, 240

Roman, 61
slavery and, 146, 296
commerce, 142, 173, 288, 298
common good, 3, 15, 62, 90, 187n19
 biopolitics of, 93–96
 global, 166–67
 interest in, 75–76, 124, 151, 212, 232,
   251, 307
 promotion of, 73, 75–76, 79, 171,
   171n4, 190, 309
 pursuit of, 29, 32, 60, 153, 165, 169,
   175–76, 208
 religion and, 288–89
 subordination of, 10, 32, 165, 191
common home, 14, 51–52, 66, 96, 103–
   4, 106–8, 121
communion, 9, 86–87, 121–22, 125,
   127–28, 147, 156, 211–
   12, 307
 fraternity and, 121–22, 128
communism, 144, 189, 298
complaint, 36–43, 71
confession, 37, 39, 112, 307–8
conscience, 25, 31, 53, 269, 285, 289,
   306, 309
consensus, 150, 155, 208, 212, 227–29,
   231, 253, 290
conservatism, 21, 49, 165, 297
Constantinople, 113
consumerism, 18, 30, 115, 194, 206, 209,
   230, 288
cooperation, 5, 89, 280, 288, 290
 international, 24, 94, 99, 105–6, 123–
   24, 201, 204, 287
corazonar, 106, 106n13
Corporate Social Responsibility (CSR),
   162–63
corruption, 4, 78, 83, 87, 161, 170–71,
   251, 259
cosmos, 53, 101–10, 212
coup, 21, 95
covenant, 112, 117, 208–9
COVID-19 pandemic
 lockdown, 22–23, 93, 136
 personal protective equipment (PPE),
   88, 93
 post-pandemic, 21–24, 124
 social distancing, 23, 88, 93

vaccines, 94, 98, 204–5, 308–9
　Pfizer, 94
virus (coronavirus, SARS-CoV-2), 19, 22–23, 51, 69, 92–93, 95–96, 105, 204, 206
crime, 39–40, 60, 62, 77, 93, 218, 240–43, 246–48, 295, 297
　hate, 60
　justice, 240, 243, 246–48, 251–52, 260–64
　migrants, 128
　organized, 18, 176, 253
cross (crucifixion), 50, 69–70, 152, 191, 278–79, 281, 305
Crusades, 102, 167–68, 291
Cuba, 24, 145n14
curas villeros, 181
cynicism, 165–66, 275
Cyprus, 151

Daoism, 291
dark clouds, 10, 14, 25, 28, 31, 36, 41, 43, 190
　over a closed world, 9, 28, 37, 40, 42, 56, 140, 171, 205
David, Pablo, Bishop, 248
deconstruction, 47, 67, 99, 103–4, 138, 299
dehumanization, 41, 49, 79, 84, 125, 127, 205, 226, 261, 280
democracy, 12, 14, 184, 192, 212, 298
　Africa and, 14
　Asia and, 21, 95, 212, 250
　Brazil and, 146
　erosion of, 1, 14, 21, 24, 31, 95, 171, 204
demons, 112, 118, 246
demonstrators, 266, 295, 300
deportation, 92–97
Derrida, Jacques, 262
desaparecideos, 217n1, 218, 220n14
Descartes, René, 117
determinism, 304
dialectics, 65, 102, 142–43, 154, 172n7, 254
dialogue
　authentic, 18, 28, 144, 200, 202, 227, 251

culture of, 193, 208–9, 214, 227, 229, 253
intercultural, 14, 143–44, 177, 209, 212, 227, 229
religion and, 3, 209, 212, 252, 254, 308
intergenerational, 104, 182, 193, 227, 243
dictatorship, 205, 251, 253, 258
diplomacy, 177, 276
disabled people, 32, 85, 88, 115, 173
discernment, 27, 88, 106, 163
discipleship, 52, 87, 112, 117, 238
discrimination, 18, 85–86, 98, 109, 126, 128, 167, 210, 214, 290
disease, 22, 69, 93–95, 205, 222, 307
disenfranchisement, 83, 85, 96, 98, 214
Dominican Republic
　Santo Domingo 296n12
dreams, 28–29, 54, 101–10, 106n14, 169, 180, 190, 206, 265, 282
　aspirations and, 286
　Latin American, 4, 106–7, 106n14
　Let Us Dream (book), 195
　shattered, 10, 28, 33, 36
　universal, 2
drugs, 21, 71, 94, 170, 187, 205, 246
　trafficking, 30, 176, 184, 223, 253–54
Dupuis, Jacques, Father, 292
Dussel, Enrique, 143–44
Duterte, Rodrigo, 21, 246–48, 253

East China Sea. *See* West Philippine Sea
ecclesiology, 54, 114, 121, 126–29, 172n6, 286
ecology, 108, 115, 122, 126, 150, 155, 177, 194, 205
ecosystem, 104
Ecuador, 105–6, 163, 187n19
　Quechua language, 105n10
ecumenism, 58, 113, 152, 282, 297, 306–7
ego, 30, 113
Egypt, 17–18, 57, 102, 167, 281, 291
　Damietta, 102, 167
Ekklesia, 295–97
Eklund, Rebekah, 40, 42

elderly people, 32, 36–37, 88, 124, 127, 138, 162, 173, 175
elites, 12–13, 24, 31, 116, 200, 253–54, 294, 305
empathy, 93, 168, 217–18, 221–24, 279
employment, 57, 88, 123, 138, 162, 164, 175, 191, 205, 252
  employers, 134
  unemployment and, 22, 69, 136, 164, 205
  workers, 93–96, 133–34, 136–37, 140, 182–83, 185, 187, 223
encounter, culture of, 102, 194, 208, 214, 226–27, 233, 307
encuentro, 229, 231
encyclicals. *See* Vatican documents
endorphins, 219
Enlightenment, the, 96
entitlement, 13, 125, 128, 136
environment (nature), 32–33, 104, 132, 162–64, 182, 252
epistemology, 105, 109, 143–44, 147, 181, 298
equality, 18, 96–97, 103, 114, 125, 164, 172, 191, 194, 287
  Christian, 137, 155
  egalitarianism, 275, 281
  equitable distribution, 29, 105, 287
  equity, social, 14, 47, 51–52, 79, 86–87, 89–90, 93, 123, 145
  freedom and, 85
  in- (*see* inequality)
  inequity, 47, 93
  justice and, 76, 137
  power and, 167n5
  rights and, 93, 97, 125, 232
  solidarity and, 93
  women and, 18, 232
eschatology, 52, 114
eternity, 73, 114, 193, 282
Ethiopia, 126
  Pugnido camp, 126
ethnicity, 12, 50, 74, 128, 141, 145, 193, 214, 224
  conflicts, 2, 12, 60, 84, 132, 137, 174n8, 238, 247
  differences, 2, 146, 243, 260
  loyalties, 12, 84
  minorities, 94, 251

politics, 12, 238
  religion and, 5, 97, 135, 137, 247, 276, 278
ethnocentrism, 12–13, 128
ethos, 92–93, 96, 117–18, 122, 128
Eucharist, 117
Eurocentrism, 135, 143
Europe, 88, 143, 149–54, 191, 195, 291
  Central, 151
  Christian identity of (*see* Christian identity)
  Eastern, 151
  North America and, 2, 18n4, 20, 143, 305, 308
evangelization, 112, 147, 275–76, 292
exorcism, 111
experts, 53, 172, 210–11, 289, 305
exploitation, 2, 14, 104, 162, 174n8, 184, 241, 253
  of humans, 30–31, 36, 83, 166, 173, 267
  sexual, 39, 176
  of natural resources, 20, 104, 162, 233
extraction, 104, 162–63
extrajudicial killing, 174, 247–49, 251

family of God, 13, 51, 129, 270
fanaticism, 39, 280
father, 37, 103
  fatherhood, 304
  God the, 9, 49, 277, 304
  Holy, 238
  St. Francis as, 167
Federation of Asian Bishops' Conferences (FABC), 170, 170n2, 174–76, 291, 292n10
Federici, Silvia, 222
  Caliban and the Witch, 222
femininity, 63, 218–19, 219n9, 222, 265, 279
feminism, 218–19, 219n9, 278, 296, 300
feudalism, 298
  serf economy, 298
finance, 163–65, 172, 174, 181, 190, 203–5, 223, 278, 306
  sector, 33, 36
  speculation, 164–65
fishing, 104, 178, 183

INDEX   317

Floyd, George, 76
food banks, 54
foreigner, 29, 57, 86, 89, 98, 101–10,
    115, 117, 143
forgiveness, 4, 237–44, 246, 250–51,
    257–63, 269, 280–81
Foucauld, Charles de, 62, 291, 303–4,
    308–9
    martyrdom, 303
Foucault, Michel, 92, 95
fragmentation, 4, 33, 49, 86–87, 128,
    163, 189, 192–93, 195
France, 2, 96, 144, 190, 304
    Communist Party, 144
    French Revolution, 2, 96
Francis of Assisi, Saint, 56, 102, 107,
    109, 166–68, 257–58,
    265, 291, 303
French, 57
fundamentalism, 104, 213, 278

Galeano, Eduardo, 167–68, 185, 185n14
Gandhi, Mahatma, 62, 291n7, 303
gangs, 242
Generation Z, 243
genocide, 50, 95
    Rwandan, 83–84, 239
geography, 2, 87, 135, 154, 257, 291
geopolitics, 144, 249
Georgetown University, 78
    GU272 Descendants Association,
    78, 268
Germany, 57, 151, 264, 304, 308
    Berlin, 189–90, 304
    East and West, 189
    Wall, 189
Ghana, 15
    Kasena people, 15
gift, 1, 53, 149, 191, 193, 231, 262–63
    of God, 49, 103, 109, 238, 241, 243,
    261, 266
    of guest, 117, 141, 193
    of hospitality, 97
    of migration, 125, 135–36, 142
global North, 18, 104, 106, 128, 135,
    137, 195, 241, 298, 305
    global South and, 18n4, 20, 126, 135–
    36, 143–44, 147, 200, 305

global South, 18n4, 20, 126, 135–36,
    143–44, 147, 200, 305
global village, 20, 20n6, 125
globalization, 24, 33, 39, 61, 88, 96, 126,
    140, 307
    context of, 154–55
    localization and, 124, 149
    of indifference, 18, 29, 31–32, 53–54,
    70, 122, 204
    of solidarity, 54
    progress and, 11, 29, 33
    unevenness of, 19–21
    world, 20, 25, 70, 132, 142, 165
Gobodo-Madikizela, Pumla, 263n15
González, Albarrán, 106n13
Good Samaritan, parable of the, 3–4,
    47–79, 85, 96, 99, 111,
    114, 170–78, 190–91
    fraternal solidarity and, 47–54, 140
    innkeeper, 62, 74, 79, 172, 172n6, 178
    kinship politics and, 137
    Last Judgment and, 3, 172n7
    priest and Levite, 39, 50, 67, 69–70,
    74–75, 78
    robbers, 54, 60–61, 67, 75, 77–78
    wounded man, 48, 53, 67, 75
grace, 4, 39, 41, 168, 238, 260, 262–63,
    279, 282, 306
    of neighbors, 149
    of salvation, 211
    of universal fraternity, 152
Gramsci, Antonio, 295n4
grassroots, 177, 183, 186, 251–52, 296
gratuitousness, 66–68, 103, 124, 135,
    141–42, 152–53, 155,
    259, 262, 288
    fraternity and, 288
    mysticism of, 109
Greek language, 154, 285, 297
gross domestic product (GDP), 203
gross national product, 95
Guerrero, Patricio, 106
guests, 117
Guterres, Antonio, 131
Gutiérrez, Gustavo, 70
Guyanas, 145n14

318   INDEX

health, 101, 124, 142, 186, 231, 307
   care, 12, 14–15, 22, 29, 71, 133, 163, 185, 203–4
   lack of (unhealthiness), 50, 76, 191, 201, 204, 212, 262, 267
      society, 27–34, 68
   public, 23
   sexual, 95
   world, 51–52, 124, 205
hegemony, 2–4, 104, 144, 183, 185, 218, 247, 253, 259, 298
   power, 103, 253, 296
   sectors, 298–99
   structures, 295–97, 295n5, 300
hermeneutic, 3, 172
Herrera, Coral, 222
heterogeneity, 295n4
heterosexuality, 95
   heteronormativity, 95, 98
   heteropatriarchy, 218
hierarchy, 294
   religious, 187, 294, 297, 299
   racial, 143, 146
   social, 47, 95, 146
Hillel, Rabbi, 58
Hinduism, 247, 253, 286, 288, 291
   Bhagavad Gita, 288
Hobbes, Thomas, 167, 167n5
Hofstra University, 278n5
holism, 154, 166
Holy Spirit, 49, 103, 112, 156, 166, 191, 232, 239, 241
homeland, 89, 124–26, 128, 136
homelessness, 71, 136–38, 152
homosexuality, 95
   homophobia, 96
Horton, Richard, 34
hospital, 22, 47–48, 54, 59, 220
   field hospital, 47–48, 54
hospitality, 96–97, 108–9, 113, 116–17, 127, 141, 152, 193, 213
human
   development, integral, 17, 97, 125, 166, 181–82
   family, 29, 31–32, 88, 99, 105, 107–8, 122, 131, 140, 156
      failings of, 38, 126
   flourishing, 11, 20, 25, 53, 105, 125, 193–94, 218, 227, 280

mobility, 23, 121, 132
   rights, 19, 32, 93–97, 167, 177, 193, 241, 248, 254, 304
      protection of, 97, 177n11
      Universal Declaration of Human Rights (*see* United Nations)
      violation of, 21, 24, 29, 61, 177n11, 202, 246, 250, 258, 260
   trafficking, 18, 30, 133, 151, 176, 184, 253
humanitarianism, 33, 52, 123, 178, 221, 246, 249
humility, 67, 109, 270, 290, 305
Hungary, 151
   Budapest, 151
   Erdő, Peter, Cardinal, 151
   Orbán, Viktor, 151
hunger, 11, 16, 51, 68, 89, 167, 184, 308
   famine, 126, 162

identity, 135, 137, 147, 180, 192–93, 218, 227, 259, 295n4
   Christian, 277–78, 303–7
   European, 150–54
   cultural, 36, 105, 107, 123, 128, 142, 173
   documents, 123
   heroic, 265, 269
   national, 152
   politics, 212
   religious, 54, 60, 102, 108, 123, 210, 212, 247
   spiritual, 29
   transnational, 51, 143
idolatry, 39, 187, 260, 308
Ilibagiza, Immaculée, 239, 239n1
Illich, Ivan, 3–4
illicit financial flows (IFFs), 203–4
illiteracy, 14, 86, 201
imagination, 18n4, 30, 33, 103, 168, 218, 222–23, 248, 265, 306
   church and, 199
   holy, 205
   moral, 14–16, 190, 267–68
   of the future, 19, 25, 199, 205–6, 219
   political, 189–95
   prophetic, 199, 206
   reimagination, 166

social, 190, 195
imago dei, 231, 239
immanence, 117
impunity, 218, 252, 259–60
inclusion, 20, 23, 58, 61, 98, 137, 140, 204, 278
　church and, 299, 306
　community and, 115
　cooperation and, 24
　encompassing, 109
　hospitality and, 107
　humanity and, 108
　society and, 115, 166
　solidarity and, 21
　welcoming and, 299, 306
　world, 10, 25
inculturation, 129, 142, 308
Independent Commission on International Development Issues ("Brandt Commission"), 18n4
India, 21, 134–36, 224, 276, 285, 292, 295n4
　Catholic Bishops' Conference, 276, 285
　Hindutva ideology, 247
　other countries and, 20, 23, 133n8, 178, 247–48
indigenous
　culture, 141, 254
　peoples, 2, 4, 40, 109, 136, 170n2, 184, 186–87, 241, 297
　　Amerindians, 40, 104–7, 105n10, 109, 141, 143, 146, 219, 224n35, 268
　　buen vivir, buen convivir, 4, 105, 105n10, 106n13, 109
　　Indian Schools of Canada, 40
　　language, 187n19, 296n11
　Asian, 214, 214n10, 252
　spirituality, 103, 109, 287
indignation, 48, 59, 217–18
individualism, 10, 15, 22, 97, 106, 181, 192, 218, 269, 305
　consumerism and, 194, 206, 230
　nationalism and, 11, 142, 147, 155
　radical, 32, 108–9, 140

selfishness and, 32
technocracy and, 194
xenophobia and, 18
Indonesia, 20, 23, 93, 210–12, 247–25
　Islamization propaganda, 247
　Yogyakarta, 210
inequality, 1, 32, 103, 164, 172, 182, 192, 194–95
　gap, 1, 13, 83, 86, 133, 174n8, 200
　global, 18, 34, 200–202
　social, 18, 34, 86, 95
　structures of, 18, 69, 93, 223
infrastructure, 15, 162, 185, 252
innovation, 10–11, 14, 133, 164, 172, 204, 299
interconnection, 20, 30, 33–34, 73, 79, 107, 109, 155, 191, 193
intercultural aspects, 104, 134, 137, 141–42, 144–45, 177, 193, 249, 253
　dialogue, 108, 144, 177
interdependence, 11, 19, 22, 99, 109, 122, 218
International Association of Penal Law, 248
International Criminal Court, 247
international law, 92, 92, 96–97, 97n21
International Monetary Fund (IMF), 204
internet, 24, 210, 245
interreligous
　dialogue, 58, 177, 276, 280, 284–92, 285n3, 303, 308–9
　"ecology of knowledges," 108
　prayer, 210
　retreats, 253
Iraq, 289
irenic project, 279, 282
Islam, 2, 113, 151, 211, 247, 275–76, 280, 288, 290–91, 308
　Allah, 288
　jihad, 308
　of love, 211
　Muslims, 84, 92, 151, 167–68, 250, 253, 280, 285–86, 289–90, 308
　Qu'ran, 288
　Sunni, 113

isolation, 18, 22, 30, 69, 86, 192–93, 212–14, 218, 222
  comfortable, 48, 59
  national, 106, 124, 155
Israel, 57, 74, 112
  Jerusalem, 39, 57
  Judea, 60
Italy
  Assisi, 210
  Lampedusa, 125
  Rome, 37, 61, 298
Iweala, Ngozi Okonjo, 279

Japan, 178, 213, 248
  hikikomori, 213
  Hiroshima, 260
  Nagasaki, 99, 260
    Atomic Bomb Hypocenter Park, 99
Jesuits, 78–79, 239, 258, 268
  Jesuit Conference of Canada and the United States, 78
  Slavery, History, Memory, and Reconciliation (SHMR) Project, 78–79
John XXIII, Pope Saint, 132
John Paul II, Pope Saint, 13n4, 194, 267, 291n8, 304
  Crossing the Threshold of Hope, 291n8
Joshi, Devin, 202
Judaism, 2, 58–60, 74, 264, 291
judge (role), 252, 285
justice
  global, 199, 204
  restorative (RJ), 38, 61, 76, 79, 242, 242n4, 252, 262–63, 268–69
  transitional, 250, 257–58

Kairos, 4–5, 86
Katongole, Emmanuel, 12–14
Kelsey, David, 85
Kenya, 126, 162–64
  Dadaab and Kakuma camps, 126
  Great Rift Valley, 162
  Nairobi, 50
  Turkana, 162–64
    Turkana County Integrated Development Plan, 162
    Twiga 1 oil well, 163–64

Khan, Sadiq, 308
kilombo, 145n14
kindness, 199, 206, 208–9, 226, 230–33, 240
King, Martin Luther, 62, 266, 291n7, 296n7, 303
  "Letter from Birmingham Jail," 296n7
kinship, 12, 63, 136–38, 265, 269–70

La Civiltà Cattolica, 47
labor, 20, 78, 93, 95, 133, 183, 203, 211, 240, 243
  lodging, land, and (three Ls), 182, 185
lamentation, 37, 40–43, 86, 153
Laos, 248, 253
Las Tesis, 294n2
Latin America, 1, 3–4, 104, 106n13, 140, 142–43, 167, 186, 187n19, 258–60
  Afrodiasporic peoples, 143
  theological perspective, 65–72, 68, 71
Latin language, 231, 233
Latinx, 232
law, rule of, 21, 97, 128, 250, 252–54
lawyer, 57, 73–74, 252, 264
Lent, 97
Leo XIII, Pope, 132
Levine, Amy-Jill, 58, 61
LGBT*, 62–63, 71, 85, 98, 296
liberalism, 30, 32–33, 115, 169, 171, 181, 275, 289
  capitalism and (*see* capitalism)
  neoliberalism, 4, 32–33, 54, 95, 161–66, 169, 171–72, 181, 194, 275
  populism (*see* populism)
liberation theology, 3, 70–71, 180–81, 278
liberationist interpretation, 58–59
libertarianism, 165
liberty, 93, 96, 114, 194, 252
Little Brothers of Jesus, 303
localization, 124, 149, 219n9, 247
logging, 104, 170n2, 214
loneliness, 22, 29, 213–14, 282
Lorde, Audre, 221
love, universal, 19, 24, 52, 86, 92, 96–99, 226, 260, 307
  of God, 38, 52

INDEX   321

majorities, 42, 90, 98, 114, 133, 135, 229, 264, 305
Malaysia, 23, 92–99, 178, 249
  Catholic Bishops' Conference of, 96
  High Court, 92, 97
  Movement Control Order, 93
Maldives, 248
manipulation, 10, 12–14, 31, 63, 125, 191–92, 227–28, 249, 259, 269
  political, 13, 183, 192, 266
Marcos, Bongbong, 253
marginalization, 65, 145, 186, 194, 232, 251, 276
  Christianity and, 49, 52, 63, 102
  global, 20, 22–23, 25, 104, 147, 284–85
  group factors, 63, 77, 86, 104, 135, 162, 184, 229
  margins, the, 18, 52, 65, 116
  of migrants, 19, 21, 94, 133
Maritain, Jacques, 304
marketing, 20, 24, 31–34, 133, 162, 164–65, 171–72, 181, 191, 203
  freedom, 32–33, 161–62, 165, 172
  human organs and tissues, 176
  real estate, 186
  techniques, 29
marrons, 145n14, 296–97, 296n10, 296n12
martyrs, 104
Marxism, 185, 269
  lumpenproletariat, 185
Mary, Blessed Virgin, 63, 229n7, 277, 279, 286, 297
masculinism, 98
masculinity, 98, 222, 265
materialism, 277
Maung John, 246
Mayans, 103, 107
Mbiti, John Samuel, 13, 15n8, 122
media noise, 212
medicine, 14, 22, 29, 93, 172, 204, 210
Medina, Mirna Nereida, 220n14
Mediterranean Sea, 126

men and women, 4, 13, 47, 62–63, 68, 75, 220n14, 250, 262–63, 277–78
  women and men, 103, 107, 146, 171n4
Mesoamerica, 106n14, 107
metanoia, 241
Mexico, 18n4, 174, 217, 219–20, 223, 258, 296–97
  Red de Enlaces Nacionales (REN, National Liaison Network), 217n1
  Brigada Nacional de Búsqueda de Personas Desaparecidas (National Search Brigade for the Disappeared), 217n1
  Nahuatl people, 223n33
  Sinaloa, 220, 220n14
    Fuerte, 219–22
    Los Mochis, 220
  Veracruz, 296n12
  Zapatista movement, 145
Middle East, 2, 291
migrants, 24, 30, 32, 36, 39, 83, 131–38, 141, 224, 308–9
  crisis, 11
  ecclesiology of, 121–29
  immigrants, 89, 94, 135
  marginalization of, 19, 21, 94, 133
  refugees, 53, 89, 92–97, 123, 125–29, 150–52, 246–47
  remittances, 133, 133n8
  undocumented, 94
migration, 1, 11, 20, 93, 96, 121–38, 149–56, 194, 308
  emigration, 11
  immigration, 125, 132, 308
military, 2, 23, 178, 181, 243, 249, 252–54, 258, 265, 294
militarization, 186
Myanmar, 21, 95, 170, 253
  para-, 184–85
minga, 187, 187n19
mining, 85, 104
minorities, 83, 90, 94, 98, 125, 141, 174n8, 210, 214, 251
  religious, 170n2, 177, 289

mission, 51–53, 78, 97, 126–27, 172, 174, 276
  of church, 9, 28, 38, 48, 52–53, 126, 137, 277, 292, 305
    human rights and, 177, 177n11
  praxis, 52, 137
missionaries, 78, 211, 275
Mitscherlich, Alexander, 304–5
modernity, 40, 74–75, 79, 113, 141, 143–44, 275, 288, 298, 304
  criticism of, 3, 75, 147
  migration, 125–25
  post-, 3, 143, 278
  rationality, 147, 275
  society, 121–22
  states, 2, 92, 95
  thought, 2, 167
  trans-, 143–44
  world, 17–19, 24, 40, 87, 143, 228
Modi, Shri Narendra, 21
Mohammed, 168
monarchy, 298
Mongolia, 23
monk, 109, 167, 291n8
monoculturalism, 104
Morales, Evo, 184
Mosse, David, 200
mother, 103, 107, 117, 127, 222–23, 241, 277, 279
  Earth, 103, 122, 287
  Earth-Water, 107
  motherhood, 279
  tongue, 285
  Water, 103
Mugica, Carlos, Father, 181, 187
Munanga, Kabelengele, 146
murder, 76, 88, 239, 258, 266
Myanmar, 21, 92–96, 170n2, 238, 245–47, 253–54
  Bishops' Conference of Myanmar (CBCM), 246
  Burmese hegemony, 247
  Chin and Kachin people, 94
  Civil Disobedience Movement (CDM), 246
  Hlaing Tharyar Township, 245–46
  NLD government, 95
  Shwe Pyi Thar, 246
  Yangon, 97, 170
mystery, 68, 103, 215, 238
mysticism, 109, 190, 192
myth, 83, 151, 192

Naik, Zakir, 210
narcissism, 124–25, 155
narrative criticism, 58, 58n4
nationalism, 2, 11, 21, 36, 77, 102, 122, 135, 155
  aggression and (*see* aggression)
  closed, 142, 147
  individualism and (*see* individualism)
  populism and (*see* nationalism)
  religious, 135, 137
  United States and (*see* United States)
natural gas, 249
natural law, 304
Nepal, 93, 253
nepotism, 83
Netherlands, 57
  Hague, The, 247, 249
New York Times, 278
New Zealand, 18n4
NGO (non-governmental organization), 52–53, 163, 182, 298
Nietzsche, Friedrich, 275
Nigeria, 50, 84, 275, 280, 295
  Igbo people, 275
  Lagos, 50
nihilism, 113
nonrefoulement, 92, 97
nonviolence, 257, 262, 266, 267n9, 303
North America, 1–2, 18n4, 20, 296n11, 305, 308
North Korea, 248–49
Nussbaum, Martha, 223

Oceania, 143
O'Dell, Roni Kay, 202
oil, 104, 162–63, 249
  Chevron/TEXACO, 163
  Environmental Combustion Consulting Limited, 164
  Tullow Oil, 162–63
    Corporate Social Responsibility (CSR), 162

Okafor, Ikenna, 128
olive tree, 306
ontology, 85, 117, 153
option for the poor, 180, 195, 229n7
Organization of Economic Cooperation and Development (OECD), 201, 204
outsider, 12, 54, 71, 75, 93, 108–9, 134, 136, 224, 296
Oxford, University of, 219

paces, 295, 295n5
painful gap, 40–42
Pakistan, 248, 308
palanques, 145n14, 296n9
palenques, 145, 296n9
Panama, 143n6
 Kuna people, 143n6
Paola, José María di (Father Pepe), 187
Papua New Guinea, 248
paradox, 29, 39, 162, 261–62
Paraguay, 186–87
paralysis, 221, 268–69
Paraná River, 184
paradigm, 75, 107, 117, 164–65, 167, 176, 258, 295–97
parents, 15, 21, 86, 138, 213, 239, 275
parish, 13, 54, 138, 187, 246
parochialism, 12–13, 16
particularism, 144
partisan interests, 103, 251
pastorality, 2, 27, 50, 54, 127, 129, 181–82, 228n4, 229
 agents of, 87
 implications, 132–33, 136–38
 practice, 276, 286
paternalism, 185
paternity, divine, 122, 275, 277, 304
path forward, 226, 228, 230
patriarchy, 2, 4, 18, 110, 218–19, 219n9, 222–23, 294–95, 295n6, 298–99
 heteropatriarchy, 218
Paul, Saint, 153, 155
Paul III, Pope, 24n35
Paul VI, Pope Saint, 17
pazes, 295, 295n5, 299–300

peacebuilding, 25, 217n1, 245, 247, 250–54
penitence, 37, 39–40, 42, 250, 264–65, 267, 269
peripheries, 20, 52, 86, 102, 108, 116, 154, 183, 195, 299
perpetrators, 77–79, 239–44, 252, 261–62, 268–69
persecution, 11, 29–30, 97–98, 102, 132, 249, 260, 277
 religious, 122, 245, 249, 275, 297
Peru, 187n19, 258
Philippines, 20–21, 23, 170n2, 170n2, 177–78, 248–50, 252–54
 Asia and, 20, 23, 56, 58, 61, 63, 133n8
 Bangsamoro Autonomous Region of Muslim Mindanao (BARMM), 250
 Manila, 177, 248
  Kalookan, diocese of, 248
 Mindanao, 250
 Payatas, Quezon City, 246
 Talaandig people, 252
philosophy, 106, 141, 172, 190, 203, 277, 297, 304, 306
physiognomy, 217
Pius XII, Pope, 192–93
pluralism, 3, 134, 212, 228, 292
pluriversality, 140, 142–46
Pogge, Thomas, 202
Poland, 151
polarization, 10, 12, 29, 36, 191, 195
police, 21, 23, 76, 238, 242, 246
policy, 54, 163–64, 166, 182, 200, 204, 249, 251–52
political love, 24–25, 170–71, 171n4, 174, 177–78
politicians, 12–13, 105, 151, 153, 161, 171, 175–76, 252, 290
 men and women, 63, 279
polychromy, 104
polyhedron, 113, 287, 307
Polynesia, 174
polyphony, 116
poor countries, 2, 11, 20, 30, 105–6, 134, 136, 200–204
popular culture, 40, 185, 192, 227, 242
popular movements, 2, 180–84, 186

324 INDEX

popular religion, 181, 186
populism, 21, 30, 61, 166, 171, 181, 213–14, 246, 253
    closed, 191–93
    liberalism and, 191, 193–94
    nationalism and, 2, 10, 151
    open, 191–93
    popularity and, 173
    racism and, 249
    uprootedness and disorientation, and, 191–95
Portuguese, 57, 297n13
postconflict societies, 250, 252–53
poverty, global, 53, 199–206
    eradication of, 199, 201–2, 204
prejudice, 51, 75, 252
pride, 308
Prince, Christian, 210
prison, 68, 114, 205, 241, 243, 246, 249, 260
    incarceration, 241
    jail 126, 220, 296n7
privilege, 15, 52, 69, 84, 95, 111, 135, 281, 297
profit, 31, 36, 95, 107, 155, 204, 206
progress, 10–11, 14, 19–20, 29, 33, 37, 49, 228, 277, 279
propaganda, 30, 247, 280
property, 33, 89, 98, 115, 203–4, 262
prosperity, 15, 52, 104, 151, 164, 200, 229, 269
    of countries, 11, 18n4, 31, 36
Protestants, 280
protesters, 76, 85, 97, 146, 218n8, 227, 232, 252, 263, 294n2
    attacks on, 21, 95, 246
proverb, 122, 124
provincialism, 144

Quad countries, 178
quilombos, 145–46, 145n14, 146n19, 296–97, 296n8, 296n12–13
    Quilombism, 146, 146n19

races
    Black Lives Matter, 190
    black people, 32, 50, 54, 71, 76, 145–46, 219, 241, 279, 297
        white, and, 143, 296 (*see also* white people)
    racialization, 95, 143
    racism, 12, 49–50, 54, 95–96, 128, 249, 268
        anti-, 54, 232, 296, 296n7, 299–300
        assumption, 60
        conflicts, 19
        patriarchy and, 295, 295n6, 298–99
        sexism and, 399
        xenophobia and, 151
    white people, 76, 93, 98, 146, 241, 266, 269, 299
rape, 294–95, 294n2
Rastreadoras del Fuerte, 220, 220n1
Rawls, John, 165
reciprocity, 1, 103, 109, 125, 135–36, 149, 218, 232, 307
reconciliation, 42, 127, 195, 238–39, 242–47, 250–54, 277, 281, 305
    conflict and, 245–54
    forgiveness and, 4, 237–39, 242–44, 258–60
    healing and, 79, 104–5, 238, 250–51, 254
    justice and, 258, 263
    love and, 76
    memory and, 78
    peace and, 242, 247, 252, 290
    race and, 78
    reparation and, 78
    restoration and, 76
    slavery and, 78
    Slavery, History, Memory, and Reconciliation (SHMR) Project, 78–79
    solidarity and, 242
    truth and, 4, 79, 258, 263
    understanding and, 79
    violence and, 245–54
refugees. *See* migrants
regulation, 23, 75, 95–96, 161, 165, 203, 221, 223, 298

relationality, 96, 106, 136–38, 141,
            141n3, 145–47, 174, 200
  fraternity and, 121–22, 127, 258
  human, 9, 13, 92, 109
relativism, 208
religion
  diversity, 3, 5, 102, 104, 117, 125, 134,
            209, 285n3, 287, 308
  freedom, 25, 124, 279, 289, 306
  peace and, 25, 253, 277, 280, 289–90,
            298, 307–9
  Semitic, 291
  violence and, 247, 276, 280, 289–90,
            307–8
religiosity, 50, 70, 181, 290
resentment, 142, 262
revenge, 237, 241, 251, 262–63, 265,
            269, 281
rhetoric, 21, 141, 151, 166, 193
Rico, Santiago Alba, 34
Ricoeur, Paul, 172, 172n7
Rindge, Matthew S., 60
Rohingya, 60, 93–94, 170n2, 247
Roma, Francisco de, 105
rural areas, 12–13, 50, 53, 134, 185
Russia, 249
Rwanda, 83–84, 239
  Hutu people, 84
  Tutsi people, 84

Sabbath, 114
sacraments, 9n1, 126, 138
Sahin, Ugur, 308–9
Saint Louis African-American History
            and Genealogy Society,
            78
Saint Louis University, 78
Salam, Abdel, Judge, 285
salvation, 4, 28, 155, 211, 261, 279
Samaria, 58, 74
Sangre Fuscia podcast, 222
Sankara, Thomas, 14
Santos, Boaventura de Sousa, 108
scandal, 174–75, 183, 200, 240
scapegoat, 93
scholarship, 1, 56, 111
schools, 40, 189, 213, 242, 246, 252–53,
            268

science, 2, 14, 31, 53, 141, 163, 172, 219
  ancestral, 141n3
  forensic, 223
  judicial, 252
  scientist, 105, 174, 219
  social, 3, 146n19, 172, 182, 203
  technology and, 10, 29, 87
Scripture, 73, 190
  Hebrew, 238
secularism, 42, 93, 97, 112–13, 154, 176,
            275, 308
security, 19, 33, 52, 115, 172, 215, 299
  food, 52, 203
  forces, 23, 246
  insecurity, 29, 151, 174n8, 280
  national, 23, 298
  personal, 123, 151, 259
  social, 88
Segato, Rita, 218
selfishness, 30, 32, 36, 89, 174, 174n8,
            176, 227, 238, 277
sentipensar, 106, 106n13, 109
sequoia, 306
Sered, Danielle, 269n15
sexism, 95, 232, 278, 300
  heterosexism, 95
sexual abuse, 39, 50, 98, 176, 232, 238,
            269n17
sexual orientation, 77, 295, 299
Shintoism, 291
Shoah, 39, 260
  Yad Vashem memorial, 39–40
shrines, 97, 212, 286
Sierra, Daniel de la, Father, 187
signs of the times, 17, 27–28, 87, 125,
            131, 309
Sikhism, 291
Singapore, 23, 248, 292n10
Singer, Merrill, 34
Skorka, Abraham, Rabbi, 284
slavery, 18, 29, 98, 145–46, 186, 201,
            243, 260, 264, 281
  African, 126, 145–46, 145n14, 296–
            98, 296n12
  church and, 41, 50, 63, 268
  Jesuits and, 78–79
  Israelites (biblical), 57, 281
  trafficking and, 18, 176

Slovakia, 151
slums, 50, 86, 181–83, 185–87
　chabolas, 182
　favelas, 50, 182, 185
　rancheríos, 185
　villas, 182, 185–86
Smurfette principle, 222
social
　dialogue, 24, 208–9, 227
　justice, 50, 54, 166, 173, 203, 268, 275
　media, 18–19, 93, 97, 288
　　Facebook, 37, 220, 246
　　Twitter, 268, 284
　network, 183, 288
　peace, 15n8, 161, 171, 233
　poetry, 4, 167, 180, 186
　transformation, 20, 70, 87, 144, 172–73, 229, 231, 275–76, 290–91
socialism, 98, 193, 298
Society of the Sacred Heart, 268
sociocultural aspects, 17, 133, 135–36
sociopolitical aspects, 3, 13, 105, 145, 219, 251, 276
solidarity, 51–54, 58, 89, 97, 104–5, 108, 115, 153, 166, 182–83
　Catholic social teaching, in, 194
　empathy and, 223–24
　equality and, 93
　ethical, 3, 47, 99, 150, 218, 223
　fraternity and, 3, 47–54, 85, 93, 275, 287
　generosity and, 42
　global, 51, 53–54, 99, 177, 212
　healing and, 1
　human, 9–10, 24
　inclusive, 21
　openness and, 155
　pseudo-, 16
　reconciliation and, 242
　religions and, 289–90, 303
　serving and, 309
　social friendship and, 9, 17, 24, 51, 141, 210
　unity and, 10
solitude, 208–9, 211–12, 215
sorority and fraternity, 1, 140, 142, 147

South Africa, 83, 122, 259
　apartheid, 83
　Nguni people, 122
South America, 296n11, 306
　Andes, 141, 187n19
　　Chacana, philosophy and, 141, 141n3
　　Quechua language, 187n19
South China Sea, 178, 249
South Korea, 23
South Sudan, 84–85, 126, 238
　Ida camp, 126
sovereignty, 86, 92, 97, 161, 163, 248–49
Soviet Union, 304
Spain, 145, 296n12
　New Spain, Kingdom of, 296n12
Spanglish, 227
Spanish, 57, 105–6, 184, 218, 220, 223, 226, 230, 257
spillover (economic), 32, 162, 165, 172
Spivak, Gayatri Chakraverty, 295n4
Sri Lanka, 250, 252–53, 285–86, 291n8
　Liberation Tigers of Tamils Eelam (LTTE), 250
　Madhu, 286
　Sinhalese people, 252
　Tamil people, 252
　　Tamilone language, 285
status quo, 87, 89, 114, 190, 219, 259, 279
Stephan, Maria, 267n9
Stevenson, Bryan, 264
stranger, 57–58, 61, 65–76, 92–93, 105, 109, 152, 172, 224, 265
　in need, 74–75
　on the road, 45, 56–57, 73, 76, 140
　welcoming the, 124, 137, 192–93, 288
subaltern, 145, 295, 295n4
subordination, 32–33, 143, 145, 219n9
subsidiarity, 76, 86, 155, 166
subversion, 98, 118, 146
suspicion, 77, 127, 168, 191, 267, 292
sustainability, 66, 96, 201, 252–53, 277
synodality, 101, 104, 107–8, 110, 116, 150
Syria, 238

taboos, 75, 276
Taiwan, 178, 249, 253

Tanzania, 126
  Katumba camp, 126
taxation, 88, 162–63, 203–4
technology, 14, 19, 24, 30–31, 70, 96,
      162, 172, 203, 227
  science and (*see* science and
      technology)
  technocracy, 165, 194
temptation, 31, 39, 104, 175, 230, 251,
      260, 262, 281
tent, 102, 107–8, 117, 137
territory, 97n21, 98, 109, 114–15, 214,
      249, 252–53
terror, 213, 290
  terrorism, 29, 132, 176, 190, 245, 264,
      266, 280, 289–90, 308
  War on Terror, 190
tetrahedron, 282
Thailand, 20, 247, 253
theocentrism, 287
theologian, 112, 122, 128, 155, 203, 210,
      226, 233, 282, 292
  African, 122
  American, 192
  Argentine, 181, 192
  Asian, 292
  Balasuriya, Tissa, 292
  Christian, 210
  Francis, Pope, 233
  French, 2
  Gera, Lucio, 181
  Gruchy, John De, 259, 262–63
  Mathewes, Charles, 192, 192n2
  Scannone, Juan Carlos, 106
  Schreiter, Robert J., 154–55, 259
  Sobrino, Jon, 70, 261
  South African, 259
  Thiel, Marie-Jo, 2, 281
theory, 20, 53, 87, 141n3, 164–65, 226,
      254, 268, 298, 304
  just war, 250
  spillover (*see* spillover)
throw-away culture, 2, 36, 122, 131,
      173, 176
Thucydides, 167n5
Timor-Leste, 170n2, 250, 253
Tonga, 248
torture, 97, 97n21, 258, 260, 262
totalitarianism, 104, 206, 213–14, 304

transcendence, 24–25, 63, 102, 113–15,
      123–24, 182, 277, 298,
      304, 307
  immanence and, 117
  of borders, 48–50, 75, 85, 123, 138
  of prejudice, 51, 75
  self-, 84–85, 88
transgression, 49, 112, 222, 300
transnational entities, 20, 29, 31, 51,
      163, 203, 254
tribalism, 2, 84, 88–89, 128, 238
trickle-down (economics) (*see* spillover)
Trump, Donald, 21, 190
Tuareg people, 303
Türeci, Özlem, 308–9
Turkey, 308
Tutu, Desmond, 62, 122, 291n7, 299,
      303

Ubuntu, 4, 9, 15–16, 122, 128, 141,
      141n2
Uganda, 83, 85, 126
  Bidibidi camp, 126
Ujama, 9
uncleanliness, 75, 93, 111
uniformity, 118, 154, 183, 228
union, trade, 183
United Kingdom
  London, 50, 308
United Nations (UN), 18, 86, 95, 97,
      132, 243, 248
  Convention against Torture and
      Other Cruel, Inhuman,
      or Degrading Treatment
      or Punishment, 97n21
  Declaration on Territorial Asylum,
      97n21
  gender equality, 18
  General Assembly, 239
  Refugee Convention, 94, 97
  Refugee Protocol, 94, 97
  Sustainable Development Goals
      (SDGs), 96–97, 201
  UNCLOS (United Nations
      Convention on the Law
      of the Sea), 249
      Permanent Court of Arbitration,
      249

United Nations (UN) (*cont.*)
  UNHCR (United Nations High Commissioner for Refugees), 94–95
  Universal Declaration of Human Rights, 18, 97, 97n21, 304
United States, 77–78, 145n14, 178, 192, 232, 253, 266, 269, 269n17, 296n7
  African Americans, 78, 264, 296n7
  Chicago, 242
    Precious Blood Ministry of Reconciliation, 242
  civil rights movement, 266
  Conference of Catholic Bishops (USCCB), 116, 116n4
  "Challenge of Peace," 116n4
  "Economic Justice for All," 116n4
  culture, 240
  military, 2, 178, 247, 249–50
  nationalism, 2, 21
  New York, 190
  social advocacy, 76, 243, 264, 266
  South Dakota, 268
    Red Cloud Indian School, 268
universality, 24, 96–98, 107, 121–22, 144, 149, 154, 156, 254
  abstract, 144
  concrete, 144
urban areas, 12–13, 48, 132–33, 183, 185–86, 212, 247
Uruguay, 167, 258
  River, 184
utilitarianism, 135, 142, 288, 297
utopia, 2, 19, 29, 98, 106, 134, 174, 180–87, 281
Uwineza, Marcel, Father, 239, 239n2
Uzukwu, Elochukwu, 276

Vatican, 125, 182, 285
  Dicastery for Promoting Integral Human Development, 125
  Department for Migrants and Refugee, 125
  documents
    Abu Dhabi Declaration (Document on Human Fraternity for World Peace and Living Together), 22, 141, 210, 284
apostolic exhortations, papal
  Ecclesia in Africa, 13, 13n4
  Evangelii Gaudium, 3, 70, 113, 177, 215, 290, 307
  Querida Amazonia, 228
bulls, papal
  Sublimis Deus, 224n35
Catechism of the Catholic Church, 250
Compendium of the Social Doctrine of the Church, 250
Congregation for the Doctrine of the Faith, 292
encyclicals, papal
  Caritas in Veritate, 304
  Centesimus Annus, 304
  Fratelli Tutti (chapters)
    Without Borders, 1, 49, 56, 96
    1. Dark clouds over a closed world, 9–43, 56, 60, 66, 140, 171, 205, 245
    2. A stranger on the road, 39, 47–80, 140, 172
    3. Envisaging and engendering an open world, 24, 83–118, 141, 309
    4. A heart open to the whole world, 24, 121–57, 309
    5. A better kind of politics, 22, 24, 39, 75, 156, 161–96
    6. Dialogue and friendship in society, 40, 199–234
    7. Paths of renewed encounter, 237–71, 289
    8. Religions at the service of fraternity in our world, 229n7, 275–310
  Laudato Si', 58, 96, 113, 115, 122, 167, 173, 176, 211, 285
  Pacem in Terris, 132
  Rerum Novarum, 132

McCarrick Report, 232
Second Vatican Council
  Gaudium et Spes, 27, 228, 286
  Lumen Gentium, 9, 9n1, 192
  Nostra Aetate, 210, 278, 286–87, 291
Old Synod Hall, 182
Pontifical Academy of Social Sciences, 3, 182
Pontifical Biblical Commission, 58
  Interpretation of the Bible in the Church, 58
Pontifical Council for Interreligious Dialogue, 210
Pontifical Council for Justice and Peace, 182
Second Vatican Council, 9n1, 27, 87, 126, 192, 277, 291
  documents of (*see* Vatican documents)

Vietnam, 23, 178, 248–49, 253
violence, gender-based, 63, 98–99, 223, 247, 294n2, 298–99
vocation, 3–4, 84–86, 89, 131, 140, 175, 205, 308
Volf, Miroslav, 261–62

Wallerstein, Immanuel, 20, 184
Walsh, Catherine, 144
war, 10–11, 29–30, 89, 122, 132, 167n5, 245, 250–52, 265, 269
  Canudos, 186, 186n15
  civil, 85, 258
  Cold, 189, 258
  culture, 190
  immorality of, 247, 249–50
  on drugs, 21, 170, 246
  on Terror, 190
  peace and, 4, 168, 247, 250–51, 298
  religion and, 290–91, 308
  Second World, 33, 36, 99, 192
wealth, 2, 32, 50, 85, 164, 200–201, 203, 241

weapons
  biological, 250
  chemical, 250
  guns, 246, 254, 265
  nuclear, 99, 249, 265
Weil, Simone, 190
welfare, 15, 29, 123, 163–64, 168, 171, 181, 191, 288, 290
Wenders, Wim, 112
  Pope Francis: A Man of His Word, 112, 228
West, the, 11, 13, 60, 96, 106, 109, 204, 275, 289
  East and, 62, 149, 189
  education in, 84, 280
  world of, 14, 116
West Philippine Sea, 249, 254
Win Pe Myint, 245
witches, 222
Woolf, Virginia, 222
World Bank, 200–202, 204
  Changing Wealth of Nations, 200
World Day of Migrants and Refugees, 123, 152
World Meeting of Popular Movements (WMPM), 182–85
World Social Forums
World Trade Organization (WTO), 202, 204, 279
  Trade-Related Aspects of Intellectual Property Rights (TRIPS), 204
world without borders, 1, 49, 56, 96

xenophobia, 11, 18, 30, 36, 83, 135, 151

Yanga, Gaspar, 297n12
yoga, 212
Young Christian Workers (YCW), 140
youth, 211, 227, 232, 265, 279

Zagano, Phyllis, 278n5

www.ingramcontent.com/pod-product-compliance
Lightning Source LLC
Chambersburg PA
CBHW032013300426
44117CB00008B/1010